Tourism, Hospitality & Event Management

This book series covers all topics relevant in the tourism, hospitality and event industries. It includes destination management and related aspects of the travel and mobility industries as well as effects from developments in the information and communication technologies. "Tourism, Hospitality & Event Management" embraces books both for professionals and scholars, and explicitly includes undergraduate and advanced texts for students. In this setting the book series reflects the close connection between research, teaching and practice in tourism research and tourism management and the related fields.

More information about this series at http://www.springer.com/series/15444

Rui Pedro Marques • Ana I. Melo •
Maria Manuela Natário • Ricardo Biscaia

Editors

The Impact of Tourist Activities on Low-Density Territories

Evaluation Frameworks, Lessons, and Policy Recommendations

 Springer

Editors
Rui Pedro Marques 🆔
Higher Institute of Accounting and
Administration (ISCA-UA)
University of Aveiro
Aveiro, Portugal

Ana I. Melo 🆔
School of Technology and Management
(ESTGA)
University of Aveiro
Águeda, Portugal

Centre for Research in Higher Education
Policies (CIPES)
Matosinhos, Portugal

Maria Manuela Natário 🆔
Higher School of Technology and
Management
Polytechnic of Guarda, Research Unit
for Inland Development (UDI-IPG)
Guarda, Portugal

Ricardo Biscaia 🆔
School of Technology and Management
(ESTGA)
University of Aveiro
Águeda, Portugal

Centre for Research in Higher Education
Policies (CIPES)
Matosinhos, Portugal

ISSN 2510-4993   ISSN 2510-5000   (electronic)
Tourism, Hospitality & Event Management
ISBN 978-3-030-65523-5   ISBN 978-3-030-65524-2   (eBook)
https://doi.org/10.1007/978-3-030-65524-2

Preface

There is no consensus in the literature—or at least a unified approach—on the scientific term used for territories characterized by an increasing depopulation, stagnation, delay, and levels of economic and social imbalances that are difficult to reverse, associated with low levels of development. Some of the terms used are "sparsely populated areas", "rural territories", "peripheral areas", "deprived communities", or "low-density territories".

In spite of the term used, these territories present important economic and social challenges which have to be addressed. Often left with an ageing population unable to pursue economic and social development, tourism emerges as an excellent opportunity to promote innovative dynamics, to lure investment, and to attract people to these territories. This opportunity arises mainly due to the specific touristic resources of these territories, which add value to the touristic experience, making it attractive for visitors and tourists alike. In fact, the natural resources, the traditional knowledge, the artisanal production, and the historical and cultural heritage of these areas present themselves as relevant factors to attract people.

However, it is important to promote sustainable tourism, meaning that it is important not only to foster economic development but also to preserve the environment and the quality of life of communities. These are, in fact, the three main axes of sustainable development: economic, social, and environmental. As such, sustainability in tourism will only be attained if tourism policies cater for these topics.

But how to promote sustainable development on these low-density territories based on tourist activities? And how to measure the impact of tourist activities on these territories? As the editors found out while researching on the topic, the measurement of the impact of sustainable tourism strategies in low-density territories is a difficult issue to tackle. In fact, some conventional approaches at the micro level are designed mainly for urban tourism—for instance, problems of traffic or business congestion, or even the contribution of the destination to the national GDP—and are certainly not suitable for a low-density reality, where the specificities of the territory add relatively more to the value of the tourist than certain services that are expected to be present in urban areas. Furthermore, the measurement of sustainable tourism implies addressing not only indicators from an economic perspective but also from social and environmental perspectives.

Hence the need for this book, which gathers 10 chapters from 32 authors. Its aim is to provide a set of contributions related to the promotion of sustainable tourism in low-density territories and was edited with the purpose of enriching namely researchers and decision-makers' knowledge regarding this topic. In terms of structure, the book firstly provides methodologies for the definition of low-density territories, for developing performance indicators to measure the impact of tourist activities on these territories and to collect the data needed to measure that impact. Secondly, it presents a number of possible solutions towards the resolution of many of the problems faced by low-density territories, through the lens of sustainable tourism. Examples of Greece, Italy, Portugal, Serbia, and Spain are provided, enriching the book enormously.

A logical first step is the identification of what should be considered a "low-density territory" for the purpose of tourism policy. That is the contribution of Ricardo Bento, Alexandre Guedes, and Luís Ramos, with the chapter "A New Methodology for Low-Density Definition and its Effect on Tourism Development Analysis—the Case of Portugal". In this chapter, the authors discuss a new methodology on how to delimit territories according to their rurality, introducing some objectivity to the concept of "rural" or "low-density" territory, not based only on population variables. The methodology is then tested in Portugal.

Then, in order to discuss how to measure the impact of tourist activities on a given territory, the book proceeds with the chapter "Assessing the Impact of Tourist Activities on Low-Density Territories: The Case of the Historical Villages of Portugal", from Ricardo Biscaia and colleagues. This chapter provides a theoretical framework on what and how to measure the touristic impact on these territories. It also provides a set of indicators to be used, as well as recommendations in terms of periodicity of measurement.

In order for the impact of tourism in low-density territories to be measured, data needs to be collected in a consistent and less expensive manner. The chapter "Information Systems and Technologies as Promoters of the Low-Density Territories Sustainability", from Rui Marques and colleagues, discusses how technology can serve the interests of tourism impact measurement on low-density territories, aiding the theoretical frameworks on the subject. Technology can aid in data collection procedures, by allowing the collection of real-time data; in tourist engagement, by providing a platform in which the tourist enhances his or her experience; and by organizing the resulting database, which can inform decision-makers.

After these three chapters, several possible solutions to overcome many of the problems faced by low-density territories are presented, through the lens of sustainable tourism.

An important competitive advantage for some low-density territories is their cultural heritage and resources. Following this line of thought, the chapter "Releasing Cultural Tourism Potential of Less-privileged Island Communities in the Mediterranean: An ICT-enabled, Strategic and Integrated Participatory Planning Approach", written by Dionisia Koutsi and Anastasia Stratigea, explores how such heritage and resources can be used towards the sustainable development of those territories. It provides an integrated framework on how to conduct strategic planning in a low-density territory, bearing in mind the integration of information and communications technologies, the participation of citizens, and the respect for the existing cultural heritage in the destination.

Focusing on the social axis of sustainable development, the contribution of Rita Salvatore, Emilio Cocco, and Anna Mines, entitled "Sustainable Tourism, Young Entrepreneurship and Social Innovation in Peripheral Rural Areas: Case studies from Southern Italy", provides a detailed theoretical contribution on how rural tourism can revitalize the economic and social activity in peripheral rural areas through the framework of social innovation. This chapter identifies the main actors of tourism development in several destinations in Southern Italy and focuses on the character-istics that these actors possess which lead them to have a social innovation role.

A very relevant question for low-density territories is whether there is enough housing available for tourists when they are attempting to visit a given place. The chapter "Transformation to Seasonal Villages: Second-home Tourism as Initiator of Rural Diversification", from Aleksandra Terzić and Biljana Petrevska, provides a solid theoretical contribution on the specific challenges of peripheral rural areas and the role of tourism in such areas. The chapter evaluates the role of tourism, and more specifically, the role of the reconversion of second homes to tourism establishments. This case study is fueled by the existing decline of population and agricultural activity in South-East Serbia.

An interesting case study on how low-density territories can be revitalized through tourism and migration is the contribution of Anabela Dinis, entitled "Tour-ism, Immigrants and Lifestyle Entrepreneurship: The (In)coming of People as a Key Factor for Sustainability of Low-density Territories—a Case Study in Portugal". This chapter tells the story of the ageing village of Penamacor, which has been recently receiving new and permanent residents from England.

A discussion around the effect of transportation in tourism in low-density terri-tories is addressed in the chapter "High-speed rail and tourism in Spanish low-density areas: not always a solution", written by Daniel Albalate del Sol, Javier Campos Méndez, and Juan-Luis Jiménez. The authors discuss whether the existence of an additional mode of transportation in Spanish low-density territories has a positive impact on tourism. They use a panel data approach and seek to evaluate whether building intermediary stations in such low-density territories will be helpful or not.

For tourism strategies to be successful, a contribution from different types of stakeholders is necessary, normally including residents, business owners, and decision-makers. The contribution of Hélder Lopes and colleagues, entitled "The Role of Residents and their Perceptions of the Tourism Industry in Low-density Areas: The case of Boticas, in the North-East of Portugal", is a case study on how residents in a low-density territory perceive their touristic capacity and the tourism strategies the territory needs to follow. The chapter sheds light on the role that is expected from residents in such strategies and in incorporating tourism in the local economy.

Finally, the chapter "Decision Support Indicators for Municipal Investment in Low-Density Territories: A Case Study in the Portuguese Historical Villages", written by Antónia Martins and colleagues, focuses on the role of local policymakers towards the design of tourism strategies for the network of the historical villages of Portugal. The chapter aims at understanding whether a framework of indicators built by the authors can be successful in evaluating and shaping local policymakers' decisions regarding tourism.

It is believed that this book will be a helpful resource, full of rich material, on how to promote sustainable tourism in low-density territories and on how to measure the impact of tourist activities in these territories. The chapters presented will be helpful mainly for researchers interested in this topic, for students of tourism, and for decision-makers, who have to devise and implement tourism-related policies in low-density territories.

Finally, we acknowledge and thank all the authors for their insightful contributions and for showing the commitment and continuous cooperation needed to finalize this book. We would also like to thank Springer for giving us a unique opportunity to publish this volume in such a professional manner.

Aveiro, Portugal   Rui Pedro Marques
Águeda, Portugal   Ana I. Melo
Matosinhos, Portugal
Guarda, Portugal   Maria Manuela Natário
Águeda, Portugal   Ricardo Biscaia
Matosinhos, Portugal

Contents

A New Methodology for Low-density Definition and Its Effect on Tourism Development Analysis: The Case of Portugal

Ricardo Bento, Alexandre Guedes, and Luís Ramos

1 Introduction

The rise of an urban-industrial society since the eighteenth century triggered the loss of economic, social, and symbolic centrality of the rural world (Ferrão 2000). This transformation established a diachronic understanding of rural areas as archaic environments, contrasting to a progressive setting developed within urban-industrial agglomerations (Ferrão 2000). Urban areas have increasingly developed into places of economic growth and service provision, leading to power asymmetries between rural and urban environments. Both spaces have manifested conflicting territorial dynamics based on disparities, namely in population, economic activity, quality of life, access to public goods and services, technological infrastructure, and political control synthesized by dual interactions between high and low-density areas (Carvalho 2018).

This work is supported by national funds, through the FCT—Portuguese Foundation for Science and Technology under the project UIDB/04011/2020.

R. Bento
Department of Engineering, Centre for Transdisciplinary Development Studies (CETRAD), University of Trás-os-Montes and Alto Douro, Vila Real, Portugal
e-mail: rbento@utad.pt

A. Guedes (✉)
Department of Economics, Sociology and Management (DESG), Centre for Transdisciplinary Development Studies (CETRAD), University of Trás-os-Montes and Alto Douro, Vila Real, Portugal
e-mail: aguedes@utad.pt

L. Ramos
Department of Engineering, University of Trás-os-Montes e Alto Douro, Vila Real, Portugal
e-mail: lramos@utad.pt

© Springer Nature Switzerland AG 2021
R. P. Marques et al. (eds.), *The Impact of Tourist Activities on Low-Density Territories*, Tourism, Hospitality & Event Management,
https://doi.org/10.1007/978-3-030-65524-2_1

Overall, the underlying territorial imbalance is an outcome of low-density economies' dependence on the extraction and 'first stage processing of local natural resources' that are then exported elsewhere (OECD 2016, p. 141), often to urban areas. The challenge arising from such asymmetry is how to preclude a trend of territorial polarization (Salvatore et al. 2018) to allow the future existence of society as a whole (Ribeiro and Marques 2002). As a result, rural tourism has been approached as an economic alternative for rural restructuring and described as a "potential development vehicle," particularly since 1987 when the OECD's 24 members began discussing this issue (Lane and Kastenholz 2015, p. 1134).

Addressing the Portuguese case, after its accession to the European Community, the Structural Funds have constituted the central assistance mechanism for regional development. An important part of this financial aid has been directed to the tourism sector by supporting investments in low-density regions through rural tourism (Costa 2012). The evaluation of these funds' impact on rural area's development is measured and compared under a scalar rationale, namely at the NUTS3 level, a territorial scale introduced by EUROSTAT in 1970, which presently includes a minimum population of 150,000 and a maximum population of 800,000 people. Consequently, regional economic changes have been assessed under a rationale of geographical continuity which has implications on the classification of low-density regions as well as on the evaluation of the European Union's funds contribution toward regional development.

Though it may seem intuitive to define low-density areas as rural territories with low human occupation, the current degree of urbanization that allows distinguishing between urban and rural areas (European Commission 2014) relies mostly on population density, inhibiting a full interpretation of low-density's multidimensionality. This is particularly relevant considering that the current funding instruments in Portugal which originate from the National Program for Territorial Cohesion (*Programa Nacional para a Coesão Territorial*) aim to endorse tourism development in interior regions[1] and support economic, social, and territorial cohesion.

Despite identifying the spatial scope of interest, as well as defining a set of holistic intervention programs,[2] the National Program for Territorial Cohesion fails to define "interior territories," acknowledging that an inclusive and clear idea of what can be described as the «*Interior of Portugal*» is missing. So, given the undefined and somewhat fluid conceptual and methodological scope of low-density territories, as well as its implications concerning the effective use of structural funds meant to promote territorial cohesion, what are the implications in terms of tourism development analysis? This is critical if the definition of low-density extends its scope to a wider set of dimensions beyond population density which the National Program for Territorial Cohesion requires.

---

[1]Linha de Apoio à Valorização Turística do Interior.

[2]Aging with quality; Innovation of the Economic Base; Territorial Capital; Cross-border cooperation; Rural-Urban relationship; Digital accessibility; Territorial attractiveness; Approaches, networks, and participation.

   Therefore, this chapter first proposes a new methodology that allows classifying low-density territories by including physical, demographic, and socioeconomic characteristics but also considers other factors according to a multi-dimensional approach. The methodology that will be presented and discussed here produces a composite index (low-density indicator) that can be deployed and used regardless of the territorial scope and scale of approach. The identification of low-density territories is based on an index that results from the combination and weighting of the individual indicators organized in sub-indexes (profiles) related to the lowest administrative unit (civil parishes) in mainland Portugal. These are subject to an algorithm that computes partial indexes (profiles) corresponding to an intermediate step toward the construction of a global index that is further computed at the municipality and NUTS3 level. Next, this study applies bivariate linear regression models at the municipality and NUTS3 level to determine the low-density indicator's (LDI) impact on the analysis of tourism development, using as response and proxy variables a set of quantitative tourism non-financial and financial tourism lodging variables published by Statistics Portugal (INE). To operationalize this investigation, this study looks at mainland Portugal.

   The purpose of this chapter is twofold. First, to discuss a new methodology that defines the spatial outline of low-density areas at different contexts and territorial scales (parish, municipality, and NUTS3), which expands on the traditional population density dimension. Second, to assess the implications of the proposed methodology, which captures a new low-density outline and spatial context, on the analysis of tourism development.

2   Literature Review

The following section is divided into two parts. The first part reviews and discusses the issue of the low-density spatial outline, considering its conceptual ambiguity and dependence on population density, lacking a more comprehensive approach that incorporates other factors (e.g. settlement and accessibility). The second part analyses tourism in peripheral and low-density rural areas, and particularly on how it has affected agricultural land use transition toward a multifunctional economy. This section further debates the problem of peripherality as a geographical matter imbued of social, political, and economic implications. The literature review concludes by discussing the fragmented benefits sought of rural tourism, resonating the ongoing transformation and transition of peripheral rural areas.

2.1   Low-density Spatial Outline

As Hopkins and Copus (2018, pp. 1-2) have observed, "Unlike sectoral (agricultural) rural development policy—which targets beneficiaries on the basis that they are farmers, or other primary producers, in a «spatially-blind» way—place-based approaches seek to address the needs of specific rural areas holistically, with beneficiaries identified according to their location. Thus, a key precondition for place-based rural policies is a definition of the rural area, and some understanding of rural diversity, perhaps captured by some kind of typology." This constitutes the same perspective that we address in this chapter when referring to the typological definition of low-density territories in the context of this work.

Studies covering low-density delimitation are, as a general rule, part of a broader issue that includes the conceptual definition and mapping of territorial typologies. This covers a wide spectrum, ranging from operational territorial typologies determined mainly to ensure coherence within data collections for statistical purposes (Eurostat 2019) to the classical urban-rural dichotomy (Stewart 1958) which has become increasingly blurred (Hugo 2004; Cloke 2006; Woods 2009), with new concepts like "rurban," "peri-urban" or "exurban" emerging to somewhat remedy this fuzziness (Antrop 2000; Theobald 2001; Meeus and Gulinck 2008; Qviström 2013).

The definition of low-density territories might come across as straightforward and intuitive, referring to a rural territory with a population density below a previously fixed threshold. In practice, however, its application gives rise to numerous questions and difficulties: from the fixing of the quantity to be attributed to the referred threshold to the set of other components and problems that go far beyond demographic and population characteristics that should be included. This challenge raises the recurring criticism of the lack of objectivity or scientific foundation of the adopted values, given the distinct realities and specificities that mark the territories.

Particularly in Europe, several studies incorporating multiple dimensions have been developed in the last decades and applied in different national and international contexts and under different perspectives, to classify geographical areas of distinct sizes, giving rise to a great diversity and heterogeneity of typologies, mostly associated with rural spaces, that may be assumed as low-density. Most of the identified typologies in previous works attend to specific purposes, ranging from the characterization, diagnosis, and delimitation of relatively homogeneous areas to the identification of areas with common and specific problems and for targeting sectoral or territorial interventions and policies. The latter is of particular importance and, to some extent, an indispensable requirement in the current context of policy design within the framework of the European Union aimed at rural areas. In this study, we compiled and analyzed several of the recognized classifications (Table 1) to allow the definition of a new standard framework for the categorization of low-density territories in Portugal that can support place-based policies.

Low-density is a notion associated with the most disadvantaged rural space, and it is defined, at first, through the demographic component. This notion has negative connotations and is approached as a problem: low-density is synonymous with agricultural abandonment and rural depopulation, social and economic dependence, "decline," "emptiness," and "desert" (Simard 2005). Low-density territories are characterized by a broader set of negative attributes, classified as such in the light of urban norms: scarcity/absence of population, especially young people, services,

Table 1 Synthesis of studies regarding low-density or rural typologies definition

Study	Low-density corresponding typology	Main classification criteria
EC Regulation 1257/1999	Less-favored areas	Topography, altitude, and land-use
Baptista et al. (2003)	Rural fragile with fragile agriculture	Population density, demography, agricultural economy, and socioeconomic dynamics
Nordregio-Nordic Centre for Spatial Development (2004)	Mountain areas	Topography, altitude, and temperature
Resolução do Conselho de Ministros n.° 11/2004	Less-favored municipalities	Purchasing power per capita index
Bengs et al. (2004)	Low urban influence, low human intervention	Population density and accessibility to populated centers
Marques (2004)	Classes with references to "low-density context"	Population density, demography, socio-economic performance, agricultural population, land use, and accessibility to populated centers
EUROSTAT (2005)	Thinly populated areas	Population density
MADRP (2006)	Significantly rural areas	Population density and agricultural population
MiPAAF (2007)	Rural areas with comprehensive development problems	Population density, elevation, and agricultural economy
Dijkstra and Poelman (2008)	Predominantly rural remote	Population density and accessibility to populated centers
Martín et al. (2008)	Dominantly rural	Population size, settlement structure, population density, demography, socioeconomic performance, and accessibility to public services
MAGRAMA (2009)	Rural area to be revitalized	Population density, agricultural population, income levels and accessibility to populated centers
Öğdül (2010)	Dominantly rural	Employment structure, population density, population size, rate of urbanization, settlement structure, educational level, accessibility to main transport infrastructures, budget income per capita, and the number of branch banks.
OECD (2011)	Predominantly rural	Population density and size of the urban centers
IGE (2011)	Sparsely populated areas	Population density
Barthe and Milian (2011)	Low-density and desertified	Population density
Brezzi et al. (2011)	Predominantly rural remote	Population density, size of the urban centers, and accessibility to populated centers

(continued)

Table 1 (continued)

Study	Low-density corresponding typology	Main classification criteria
Copus (2011)	Predominantly rural remote, agrarian and in depletion	The EDORA Cube multi-dimensional analysis framework comprises three typologies: Dijkstra/Poelman, economic restructuring, and socioeconomic performance
Hilal et al. (2011)	Aged rural at very low density	Population density, demography, socio-economic performance, and accessibility to populated centers
Bibby and Brindley (2013).	Rural village and dispersed in a sparse setting	Settlement structure
INE (2014)	Predominant rural areas	Population density and land use
INSEE (2015)	Very low-density communes	Population density
Quintá and Arce (2018)	Very rural	Population density and evolution, demography, settlement structure, agricultural population, accessibility to populated centers

and activities. Territories that appear in this context, as residual spaces, have been labeled as "deep rural," "fragile rural" (Azevedo 2013), or "space of crisis and abandonment" (Figueiredo 2018).

There are very different typologies at the territorial level (European, national, regional, and local) and with distinct scales (regional and local), giving rise to a huge diversity of approaches used to define different categories of territories. The conceptual framework itself varies between a theoretical nature and a relatively rational application. However, most cases are based on empirical references, more precisely on indicators. All of this, considering the typologies presented, leads to the establishment of different guiding dimensions, namely: 1) the territorial dimension that refers to the region or location and its geomorphological characteristics and/or economic, social, and political performances; 2) the temporal dimension that refers not only to the time frame of the analyzed dynamics but also to the historical evolution of technical options, economic and/or behavioral nature; 3) the development dimension, namely rural development, understood as a multi-sectoral concept that encompasses multiple aspects of different nature and which underlies the majority of the presented typologies; and 4) the important issue related with the scope of application since it implies the consideration of multiple factors, namely in cases where their elaboration is aimed at implementing place-based policies.

The typologies and classifications presented are diverse according to the stated objectives. The definitions are so varied that a common standard is elusive: they change based on the purpose of the study and the institutions and actions demanding them. These approaches present relevant aspects of the delimitation of rural spaces. However, they tend to be defined by operational objectives or integrated into sectoral logic (agricultural sector) limiting, in most cases, differentiation of rural spaces by the diverse components that characterize them. Most studies suggest that there could be differentiated low-density territorial outlines according to each sectoral viewpoint.

Furthermore, recent studies have been referring that multiple factor approaches are more suitable to classify low-density areas in the context of policy-making, although the thresholds in each variable differ both in time and in space, adjusting to the context and objective of the respective research. In most of the examined investigations, the perspectives adopted favor the population density indicator serving, simultaneously, as the main criterion for defining geographic units. These perspectives assume the establishment of a threshold below which it is pertinent to speak of low-density territories, which is based on the observation of the distribution of the population, varying according to the author, country, or geographical scope. From our point of view, this approach reveals some shortcomings and limitations, namely in terms of its struggle to accurately establish a value for the threshold to be widely adopted. Furthermore, it reveals a challenge related to the heterogeneity of the territorial units (municipalities, parishes, NUTS3), which necessarily alters the results. In this sense, the population density threshold to be adopted should be understood as an order of magnitude and not a strict criterion.

Besides population density, we have identified five other main dimensions as essential components for the identification of low-density territories: a) physical-geographic; b) demographic; c) settlement; d) socioeconomic; and e) accessibility. Based on these factors we have developed profile indexes and a global composite index computed at the smallest possible administrative unit (parishes) level, depending on the available statistical data (Table 2). Each profile integrates variables that correspond to the defined conceptual delimitation. The physical-geographic characteristics integrate the components of altitude, climate, and artificial land use. As altitude and thermal amplitude increase, a strong rural landscape is usually associated with the dominance of agricultural, forestry, or natural associated land uses. The demographic profile classifies parishes by their recent population growth, but also by their long-term sustainability, integrating the share of youth and elderly population. The settlement profile considers the weight of the population living in settlements classified by their population size. This allows us to differentiate urban and denser areas from low-density territories and to distinguish, among the latter, those that have a more nucleated, dispersed, or isolated settlement pattern. The socioeconomic profile intends to characterize each parish in terms of the available active population, income level, social dependence of the State, and economic dependence on agriculture. The accessibility profile considers the access, measured in terms of travel time by car from each parish to its subsequent hierarchical metropolitan hubs and reference points (municipal major city or town, the district capital and regional capital) as described in the Central Place Theory (Christaller 1933) as a measure of social inclusion and effectiveness of public policies in ensuring the quality of life and the reduction of territorial inequalities in access to public services.

Table 2 Variables and data sources used in each profile

Profile	Variables	Sources
Population density (P_d)	Population density (persons per sq. km)	Population census 2011 (INE)
Physical-geographic (P_1)	Elevation (m) Temperature annual range (°C) Share of artificial land (%)	ASTER GDEM v2 (METI and NASA) BIO7—Global Climate Data (Hijmans et al. 2005) COS 2007 (DGT)
Demographic (P_2)	Population growth rate (%)	Population census 2001 and 2011 (INE)
	Share of the elderly population (%)	Population census 2011 (INE)
	Share of young population (%)	Population census 2011 (INE)
Settlement (P_3)	Share population living in large urban settlements ($\geq$ 2000 inhabitants) (%)	Population census 2011 (INE)
	Share of population living in small urban settlements ($\leq$ 100 inhabitants) (%)	Population census 2011 (INE)
Socioeconomic (P_4)	The average monthly wage of employees (€)	Earnings and working hours survey 2009 (GEP/MTSSS)
	Share of agricultural family population in total population (%)	Agricultural census 2009 (INE)
	Share of population with lower secondary education 3rd. cycle completed or higher (%)	Population census 2011 (INE)
Accessibility (P_5)	Travel time by car to third-tier/municipal urban center (min.) Travel time by car to second-tier/district capital (min.) Travel time by car to first-tier/regional capital (min.)	Google Maps batch routing

2.2 Tourism in Peripheral and Low-density Rural Areas

Tourism is an asymmetric phenomenon that polarizes flows, facilities, and services (Salvatore et al. 2018), developing imbalanced and binary relationships that have been widely interpreted under the postindustrial dependency theory (Britton 1981; Chaperon and Bramwell 2013) as hierarchical core-periphery relations. Among these, the structural biased relationship between urban and rural areas is one of the most conspicuous due to the control of "urban cores" (Smith and Still 2009, p. 52) over rural resource-based communities, which enacted mainly production and supply roles, rather than places to be consumed. The inherent deterministic resource extraction paradigm between urban (the core) and rural (the periphery) areas has amplified asymmetry. And so, peripherality is not only a geographical issue but is also imbued of social, political, and economic implications, frequently meaning "economic disadvantage, lack of technological infrastructure, and political weakness" (Salvatore et al. 2018, p. 42).

Due to changes in food production (Salvatore et al. 2018) at the beginning of the 1970s in parts of Europe, agriculture started to decline (Lane and Kastenholz 2015). The arising crisis affecting rural areas, and rural land base traditional production functions—mainly agriculture—progressively modified rural's economy towards a multifunctional model (Gerowitt et al. 2003; Marsden and Sonnino 2008). In this context, tourism was perceived as an easily accessible tool to deal with the economic decline (Lane and Kastenholz 2015), by providing employment and a means to promote rural economic diversification (Ribeiro and Marques 2002; Williams and Shaw 1998). These changes gave rise to a post-productivist paradigm whereby rural areas came to be regarded "as consumption spaces to be exploited not only by industrial capital but by the growing urban and exurban populations" (Marsden and Sonnino 2008, p. 423). Rural areas have since begun to be targeted as consumption subjects "based on establishing new commodities or in reimaging and rediscovering places for recreation and tourism" (Hall and Page 1999, p. 180).

The first approach to diversify agricultural land use through tourism was based on the notion of agritourism, or farm tourism. The word agritourism was first used to designate what later became known as rural tourism which acquired a holistic and sectoral meaning by framing a variety of activities. In various countries, tourism in rural areas was first developed by adapting "rooms in village houses or in converted, often historic buildings" (Lane and Kastenholz 2015, p. 1136). This was the case in Portugal, with the introduction in 1978 of what was then named "*Turismo de Habitação*" (Programa do IV Governo Constitucional 1978), through the renewal of manor houses in four pilot areas[3] (Silva 2007). In 1986, rural tourism was formally introduced and since then subject until recently (2017) to numerous legislation changes that have included further forms of accommodation and activities.

Since joining the European Economic Community (EEC), in 1986, Portugal has been benefiting from European funding programs to support the development of rural tourism under the assumption that rural area's economic diversification can mitigate regional asymmetries (*Programa do X Governo Constitucional*). The amount of political and financial engagement to develop rural tourism has therefore resulted in many positive outcomes, particularly in terms of infrastructural and amenity supply. However, it seems to have been less capable to address social and demographic constraints. The fact that only a small number of rural tourism businesses remain in a family when the owner retires (Lane and Kastenholz 2015), frequently due to rural exodus factors, is a clear illustration of these challenges. Hence, the strategy that has been pursued in Portugal, and other European countries, has been more successful in addressing tangible factors rather than intangible and more fluid issues.

The Portuguese case indicates that the government's strategy, at least at an early stage, mirrored in the published legislation, was more concerned with tourism rather than with rural area's economic regeneration and development (Ribeiro and Marques

---

[3]Ponte de Lima, Vouzela, Castelo de Vide and Vila Viçosa.

2002). This strategy favored mainly affluent families rather than ordinary farmers due to the high level of requirements that were imposed to authorize new accommodation units (Ribeiro and Marques 2002). Despite this issue and the unevenly geographic distribution of rural tourism accommodation units, mostly concentrated in northern Portugal, the regional development agenda established an important framework toward rural regeneration and conservation of existing properties and heritage resources. By allowing the recovery of built heritage, rural tourism has contributed to the maintenance of a landscape full of symbolic value (Silva 2007). The downside of rural tourism's development policy though has to do with its inability to justify the infrastructural investment effort, namely through job creation and local trade and services development, and so failing to reduce population decline and low density in rural areas (Silva 2007).

Along with the discussed transformations affecting the economic fabric of rural areas resulting from the reconfiguration of regional development policies, there has also been a profound change in the tourism consumption paradigm, which was addressed by Poon (1989) as a "Post-Fordist" trend, defined as a shift from an "old tourism" to a "new tourism" and described by individual consumption patterns with greater volatility in preferences as well as tailored and adaptable in both time and space (Poon 1989, p. 181). Demand for rural areas is also believed to attract a post-modern market pursuing exclusive experiences (Kastenholz et al. 2012). Hummelbrunner and Miglbauer (1994) referred to a new "new rural tourism" (p. 41), based on the tourist's re-orienting choices namely toward an "increasing environmental awareness" (p. 42), escaping from polluted areas and searching for an undamaged environment. Also, rural areas are deemed to represent a nostalgic return to the past and the origins, as well as authenticity (Chen and Kerstetter 1999; Kastenholz et al. 2012). So, the commonly labeled "rural tourists" are far from being a homogenous market (Kastenholz et al. 2012; Silva 2007) and several authors have shown its fragmented structure (Frochot 2005; Kastenholz et al. 1999). Rural tourism is a complex activity and rurality has many manifestations (Lane 1994) suggesting "that consumers can consume this world in many ways" (Frochot 2005, p. 336).

Given the fragmented benefits sought of rural tourism and the fact that "the multiplier effect is often more impacting in rural areas" (Kastenholz et al. 1999, p. 353), it highlights the significance of planning and managing the ongoing process of "tourism transition" (Salvatore et al. 2018). The sustainability of rural areas is dependent on tackling fluid issues, namely demographic, social, and economic factors, along with tangible and physical concerns. These are vital in guaranteeing local genuine products to respond to a new consumer trend which is more sensitive to local qualities and "sense of place" (Jepson and Sharpley 2015, p.1).

Thus, the literature review echoes an ongoing transformation and transition of peripheral rural areas, suggesting a development tendency that looks at the same characteristics and qualities that were formerly deemed to be detrimental as new opportunities (Brown and Hall 2000; Salvatore et al. 2018). Moreover, the literature indicates the importance of tourism as a tool for regional local development to manage the decline of peripheral rural areas and tackle problems related to low-density resulting from demographic decline as well as physical, social, and economic disruptions.

3   Methodology

3.1   Research Setting

To fulfill this study's goals, a new methodology that calculates a low-density index (LDI) and defines the spatial outline of low-density areas in mainland Portugal at different territorial scales (parish, municipality, and NUTS3) is presented. Additionally, to evaluate the implications of the proposed index on tourism development analysis, bivariate regression models were applied to estimate the explanatory significance of the LDI on 10 demand and supply tourism lodging statistical indicators in 2018, as proxy variables, as well as on each variable's percentage change for the period of 2013 to 2018 at both the municipality and NUTS3 levels.

3.2   Research Data and Methods

3.2.1   LDI and Spatial Outline

The statistical variables were obtained from the most currently available statistical datasets at the lowest level administrative division in mainland Portugal (civil parishes) from the population and agricultural censuses. Elevation values were extracted, for each civil parish main urban central point coordinates, from the Advanced Spaceborne Thermal Emission and Reflection Radiometer Digital Elevation Model (ASTER GDEM v2) at 30m resolution. Temperature data was extracted from the Annual Thermal Amplitude (BIO7) data provided by WorldClim – Global Climate Data, which is based on the annual averages between 1950 and 2000. The share of the artificial area was estimated from COS land cover maps produced by the Portuguese General Directorate for the Territory. These are land cover maps at the 1:25.000 scale, with a minimal cartographic unit of 1ha, based on orthophoto maps with four spectral bands (blue, green, red, and near infra-red). These datasets were photo-interpreted with an average interpretative accuracy of 95%. Land cover was divided into hierarchical levels, from level one containing five primary types (artificial areas, agricultural areas, and agroforestry, forests and natural and semi-natural areas, wetlands, and water bodies) to level five containing up to 190 classes (Abrantes et al. 2016). In this study, the first level was used to adequately estimate the total artificial area. Access times were estimated using Google Maps routing capabilities, where the circulation time in each road section considers both the characteristics of the road network such as hierarchy, crossings, intersections, and

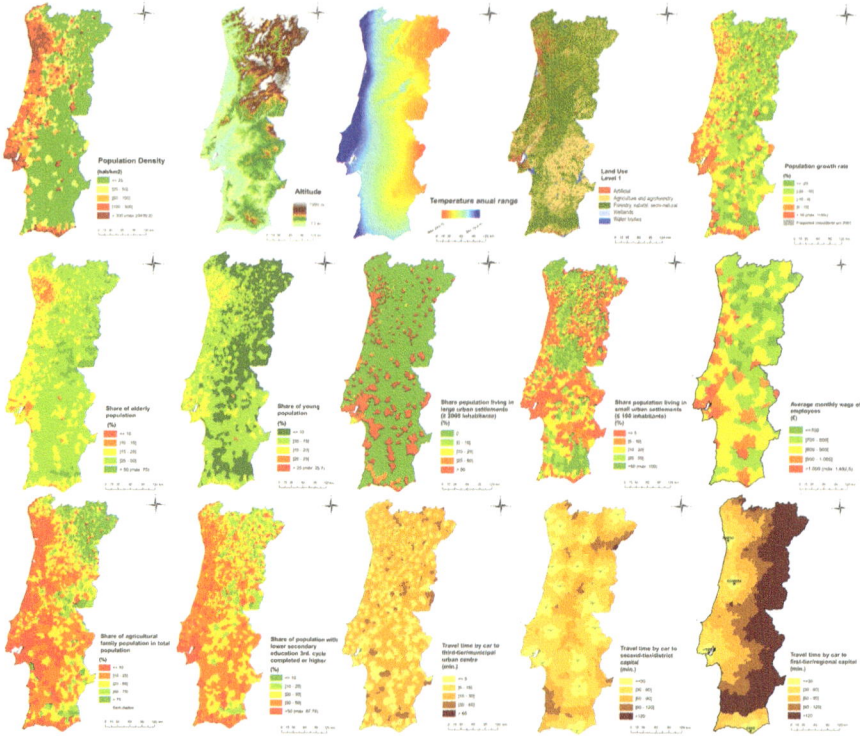

Fig. 1 Maps for continental Portugal of each of the variables used in each profile

the average speed of driving a light vehicle. Table 2 and Fig. 1 present all the variables used in the low-density index calculation.

Individual profile indexes were based on standardized (Z-scores) variables by applying Eq. 1:

$$X' = \frac{X - \mu}{\sigma} \tag{1}$$

where X' is the standardized data value, μ is the mean of the data set, and σ is the standard deviation of the data set.

Statistical standardization ensures the removal of issues related to the unit of measurement and scale, generating indicators with zero mean and unitary standard deviation. Zero averages avoid bias in the aggregation resulting from mean differences. Dividing the means by the standard deviations allows the variables to be rescaled but does not prevent indicators with extreme values to have a greater impact on each profile index since the range of effective variation of these indicators will be greater. This approach has a positive effect, given that the objective of the global composite indicator is exactly to highlight the differences between statistical units and to identify the specific subset of low-density civil parishes. In the second phase, a normalization procedure was carried out by applying a min-max rescaling to eliminate the analytical inconveniences resulting from the inevitable negative performances in the z-score method and to ensure the incorporation of dispersion between extreme values present in the resulting indexes. This process was performed using Eq. 2:

$$X' = \frac{X - \min(x)}{\max(x) - \min(x)} \tag{2}$$

where X' is the normalized data value and X is the input data value.

Each profile index was transformed by division with the respective mainland Portugal's average, thus obtaining relative values referenced to the national average, allowing a measure of the distance of each parish concerning the national reference value. Where no such average existed, it was estimated through the parishes' average weighted by its population. After the application of the standardization and normalization procedures, the value of each profile index was drawn from the average value of the corresponding individual variables. The global index was calculated from the weighted average of the population density (with a weight of 50%) and each of the profile indexes (with a weighting equal to 10% each, meaning, therefore, that the results reflect a view where the same importance of the various profiles is assumed in the identification of low-density territories), as expressed in Eq. 3.

$$LDI = P_d * 0,5 + \sum_{1}^{n} 0,1 * P_n \tag{3}$$

where LDI is the low-density index value, P_d is the population density index, and P_n represents each one of the other profile indexes.

More recent estimates regarding some of the demographic variables do exist but only at the municipal level. So, in this study, the most recent data available at the civil parishes level was used. It is expected that the economic crisis that occurred in the past decade may have altered the population structure and distribution which could eventually increase the number of parishes being classified as low-density territories. We cannot effectively determine its current impacts, so LDI calculation should be periodically revised (preferably every decade, with every new Census) and the resulting maps changed accordingly.

3.2.2 Bivariate Regression Models

In total, 20 bivariate regression models were built to provide a precise analysis of the relationship between the LDI, the regressor, each tourism lodging demand and supply indicator in 2018, and the respective percentage change for the period of 2013 to 2018, as dependent variables (Table 3).

Table 3 Bivariate linear regression model's predictor and dependent variables

Predictor variable	Dependent variables (Y)	
Low-density index (LDI)	Tourism indicators (TI):	Overnight stays – total (OS)
		Overnight stays – Portuguese residents (OSP)
		Overnight stays – foreign residents (OSF)
		Lodging revenue (euro) (LR)
		Lodging capacity (units) – total (LC)
		Lodging capacity (units) – hotels (LCH)
		Lodging capacity (units) – local accommodation (LCLA)
		Lodging capacity (units) – rural tourism (LCRT)
		Bed occupancy rate (%) (BR)
		Length of stay (nights) (LS)
		OS percentage change: 2013–2018
		OSP percentage change: 2013–-2018
		OSF percentage change: 2013–2018
		LR percentage change: 2013–2018
		LC percentage change: 2013–2018
		LCH percentage change: 2013–2018
		LCLA percentage change: 2013–2018
		LCRT percentage change: 2013–2018
		BR percentage change: 2013–2018
		LS percentage change: 2013–2018

Bivariate regression models allow for the assessment of individual regression coefficient signs and the measurement of the proportion of the variation (R-squared) in each dependent tourism indicator that is expected to be affected by the *LDI*. Each bivariate linear regression model was specified as follows:

$$TI = \beta_0 + \beta_1 LDI + \varepsilon \tag{4}$$

where *TI* represents the predicted value for a given tourism indicator (dependent variable), *LDI* is the Low-density index value (independent variable or regressor), β_0 and β_1 are constants describing the functional relationship between *LDI* and each considered criterion (the y-intercept and the slope respectively), and ε is the error term (residuals).

4   Results and Discussion

4.1   *LDI Index and Spatial Outline*

The main objective for the delimitation of low-density territories is to allow the development of specific place-based public policies to tackle the vulnerabilities caused by the vicious cycle of depopulation/aging/socioeconomic decline normally associated with these areas, aiming at fostering territorial cohesion and economic development. The resulting geographical distribution of the LDI indicates that this reality is not exclusively associated with the most inland regions of mainland Portugal (Fig. 2).

The LDI adjusts very well to the national urban system, with both metropolitan areas presenting the higher LDI values, followed by second-tier cities outside metropolitan regions like Aveiro, Braga, Coimbra, and Faro. Most of the civil parishes with lower LDI values are located in the north and central regions, mainly in the interior areas, where only major municipal urban centers present somewhat higher LDI values. Exceptions occur, namely in coastal regions such as *Alto Minho* located in the northwest and *Alentejo Litoral* situated in the southwest of Portugal, which exhibits significant areas with low LDI values that be explained by the presence of relevant natural protected areas.

The operationalization of place-based policies raises the question of how the results obtained should be used to define a low-density map. Parishes are an adequate territorial scale for some specific programs like the LEADER community program, but bearing in mind the principles of coherence, functionality, and effectiveness of public policies, other administrative levels, namely the municipalities and NUTS3, need to be taken into account. For these levels, LDI was determined by the average of the total corresponding lower administrative units (Fig. 3).

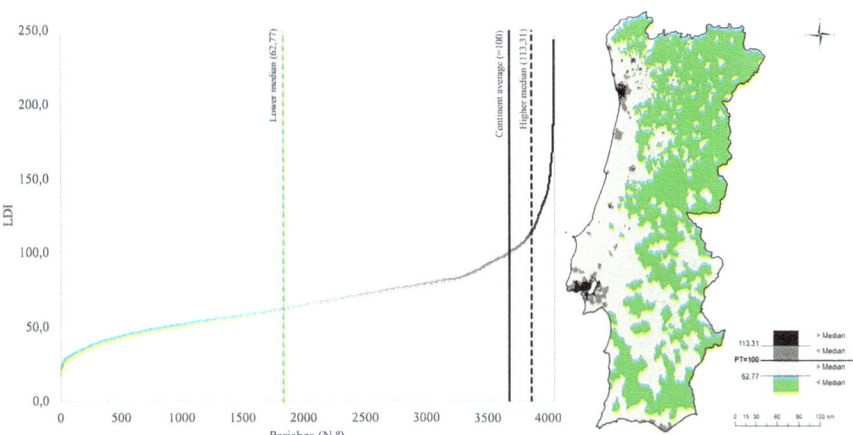

Fig. 2 LDI of continental Portugal parishes (lowest LID values correspond to low-density areas)

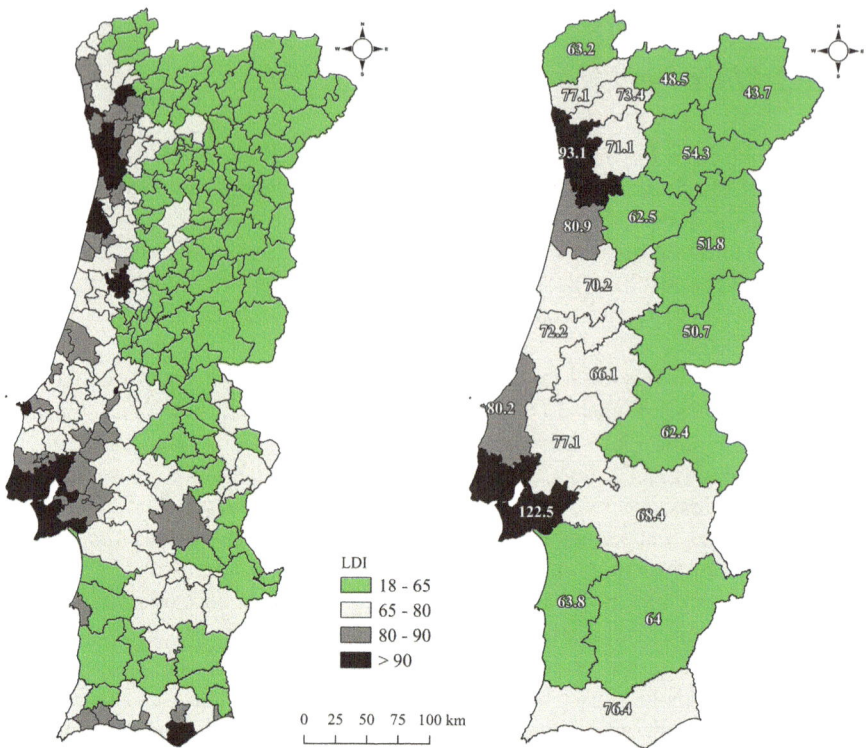

Fig. 3 LDI average values at municipal (left) and NUTS3 (right) administrative levels

The LDI mapping (Fig. 3) provides an overview of the effect that occurs following a process of aggregation of multiple constructs when shifting from the municipal to the NUTS3 level, helping to circumstantiate local policy measures within a sub-regional context (NUTS3). This is particularly important when sectoral policy and supra-municipal action are required to articulate the territory comprehensively. One of the most evident effects of tourism is its contribution to regional development (Fazenda et al. 2008), and so anchoring tourism planning action at a meso level, i.e., the NUTS3, is particularly appropriate.

4.2 Level of Influence of the LDI on Each Tourism Indicator in 2018 and the Respective Percentage Change for the Period of 2013 to 2018

The bivariate linear regression models were first applied at the municipality level, exhibiting either a non-significant effect of the predictor variable (LDI) on most response variables (tourism indicators and corresponding percentage change for the period of 2013 to 2018) or either heteroskedasticity issues. Once heteroskedasticity was corrected, the bivariate linear regression models provided insufficient significant results for analysis and a negligible explanation toward response, i.e., a low coefficient of determination (R^2). The overall effect of the LDI at the municipality level does not provide substantial and robust information toward the implications that low-density has on tourism.

Yet, when applied at the NUTS3 level, the individual simple linear regression models exhibit a statistically significant predictor variable (LDI) and important results in terms of the coefficient of determination in all tourism indicators for 2018 (Table 4). Furthermore, the results also exhibit an overall non-significant effect of the LDI on the percentage change of each tourism lodging indicator for the period of 2013 to 2018, except for the "local accommodation capacity" and "rural tourism capacity" percentage change (Table 4).

This study's findings also suggest that the LDI tends to explain a similar level of the proportion of the variation (R^2) of the response data around each mean, i.e. >34%, on every aggregate demand and supply tourism indicator (e.g., overnight stays, lodging revenue, lodging capacity). Aggregate indicators provide flat results that include both urban and rural contexts and thus tend to primarily reflect the influence of the demand and supply beyond the low-density outline. This is particularly striking due to the positive coefficient on all models apart from those which have "lodging capacity (units): rural tourism" and "LCRT percentage change: 2013–2018" as dependent variables. A positive coefficient means that an increase in the LDI, i.e., convergence toward a higher density context, determines a rise in both demand and supply tourism indicators in 2018. The contrary, a negative coefficient, which was only observed when regressing either "lodging capacity (units): rural tourism" or "LCRT percentage change: 2013–2018" on the LDI, indicates that an increase in the LDI, i.e., a divergence from peripheral and lower density areas, determines a decrease in lodging typologies that are specific to rural and outlying areas of around 1.7%,[4] as well as a positive percentage change of rural tourism lodging capacity between 2013 and 2018. This shows that the investment in specific accommodation typologies is being accomplished according to the territorial profile, which is condensed in the LDI.

Additional implications can be observed from the application of bivariate linear regression models which are associated with the relevant effect of the LDI on either the "lodging capacity (units): local accommodation" and "bed occupancy rate" response variables, explaining a significant proportion of the variation (R^2) around each indicator's mean of, respectively, 63% and 72%. Due to the positive sign of both coefficients, these results are again determined by the pull effect of urban and denser areas. In the case of the "lodging capacity (units): local accommodation," it is a result of a governmental legal change in 2008 which purged several lodging

---

[4]By converting the "Lodging capacity (units)—Rural tourism" variable to the log scale, the beta coefficient for "LDI" provides the percentage change in "Lodging capacity (units)—Rural tourism" for every unit increase in "LDI".

Table 4 Bivariate regression models' results (NUTS3)

Predictors	Coefficient	R^2	Adjusted R^2
Overnight stays—Total (OS) (2018)	200939** (55609.2)	0.38	0.35
OS percentage change: 2013–2018	***	–	–
Overnight stays—Portuguese residents (OSP) (2018)	42982.7** (12231.6)	0.37	0.34
OSP percentage change: 2013–2018	***	–	–
Overnight stays—foreign residents (OSF) (2018)	157956** (43560.7)	0.39	0.36
OSF percentage change: 2013–2018	***	–	–
Lodging revenue (euro) (LR) (2018)	2245.39** (677.337)	0.34	0.31
LR percentage change: 2013–2018	***	–	–
Lodging capacity (units)—total (LC) (2018)	9.18081** (2.10396)	0.48	0.45
LC percentage change: 2013–2018	***	–	–
Lodging capacity (units)—hotels (LCH) (2018)	3.67148** (1.01204)	0.39	0.36
LCH percentage change: 2013–2018	***	–	–
Lodging capacity (units)—local accommodation (LCLA) (2018)	6.25182** (1.04218)	0.63	0.61
LCLA percentage change: 2013–2018	0.002525* (0.001192)	0.18	0.14
Lodging capacity (units)—rural tourism (LCRT) (2018)	−0.742492** (0.372602)	0.16	0.12
LCRT percentage change: 2013–2018	−0.003571** (0.001363)	0.25	0.21
Bed occupancy rate (%) (BR)	0.488908** (0.06577)	0.72	0.71
BR percentage change: 2013–2018	***	–	–
Length of stay (nights) (LS)	***	–	–
LS percentage change: 2013–2018	***	–	–

Dependent variable: Average (based on municipality) LDI–NUTS3
*, ** indicates significance at 95% and 99%, respectively
*** Coefficients estimates are not significantly different from zero ($p > 0.05$)
Standard errors are reported in parentheses

classifications highly embedded in urban areas. This process led to the conversion of a vast number of lodging units to the newly legalized form of accommodation, i.e., the "local accommodation." Moreover, this result can also be explained by the enormous increase in the investment in new "local accommodation" units, particularly in urban areas. Lisbon is a clear illustration of what has been occurring in the last few years. Just in 2016, the Metropolitan Area of Lisbon has had an increase of 95% in the number of new "local accommodation" units, which resulted in a 75% increase in its accommodation capacity compared to 2015 (AHRESP 2017). The bivariate regression results show that a rise in 1 point in the LDI (convergence towards higher-density areas) corresponds to an increase of around six "local accommodation" units.

Finally, the "bed occupancy rate" indicator's prominent proportion of response variation, i.e., 72%, provides an insight into the sustainability capability level of tourism businesses determined by the low-density indicator. Again, results suggest that lodging units that diverge from low-density areas tend to increase their bed occupancy rate significantly: i.e., a 2-point increase in the LDI means a 1 percentage point growth in the bed occupancy rate. Given the lowest NUTS3 occupancy rate in 2018, i.e., 17%, it exposes the extreme impact and imbalance of sustainable opportunities in terms of tourism development determined by geographic conditions.

5   Conclusion

By looking at mainland Portugal as an example, this study proposes and operationalizes a new methodology that can be replicated to construct a composite measure/index which allows classifying low-density areas, regardless of the territorial scale of analysis (parish, municipality or NUTS3). This index is based on a set of factors that improve on the conventional limits of demographic indicators, by integrating territorial, settlement structure, socioeconomic, and accessibility profiles. This study also contributes to theory by providing evidence about the relationship between low-density areas and tourism development through the regression of the LDI on tourism logging indicators, applied in this study as proxy variables, due to the lack of disaggregation of tourism indicators.

Moreover, this investigation demonstrates a clear polarizing influence of denser areas in terms of demand and supply by exposing their pull effect, either through positive regression coefficients or a higher proportion of response variation to the LDI. It also provides strong evidence of how territorial imbalances, condensed in the LDI, compromise sustainable tourism development.

Further empirical evidence confirms that there is a negative association between rural tourism lodging and the LDI. This can have significant managerial implications by providing a preliminary geographical reading that links spatial dissonances and tourism development trends, particularly in low-density areas. Given this evidence, this research has also policy implications by encouraging a critical interpretation of a territory's functional differences, and so offering guidance on land-use planning and development policies consistent with a complex territorial outline.

References

Abrantes P, Fontes I, Gomes E, Rocha J (2016) Compliance of land cover changes with municipal land use planning: evidence from the Lisbon metropolitan region (1990-2007). Land Use Policy 51:120–134. https://doi.org/10.1016/j.landusepol.2015.10.023

AHRESP (2017) O impacto económico do Alojamento Local na Área Metropolitana de Lisboa 2016–2020. AHRESP, Lisboa

Antrop M (2000) Changing patterns in the urbanized countryside of Western Europe. Landsc Ecol 15(3):257–270. https://doi.org/10.1023/A:1008151109252

Azevedo NMF (2013) Tempos de mudança nos territórios de baixa densidade: as dinâmicas em Trás-os-Montes e Alto Douro. Fundação Calouste Gulbenkian, Lisboa

Baptista F, Rosa M, Rolo C (2003) Portugal rural: Territórios e Dinâmicas. MADRP/GPPAA, Lisboa

Barthe L, Milian J (2011) Les espaces de la faible densité - état des lieux et problématiques. In DATAR, Des systèmes spatiaux en perspective. In: Revue d'études et de prospective, 3, coll. Territoires 2040. La documentation française, Paris, pp 141–160

Bengs C, Schmidt-Thomé K, Ristisuo H (2004) Urban-rural relations in Europe. ESPON 1.1.2. Final Report. Luxembourg/Helsinki: ESPON/Helsinki University of Technology. Retrieved from https://www.espon.eu/sites/default/files/attachments/presentation_1.1.2.pdf

Bibby P, Brindley P (2013) Urban and rural area definitions for policy purposes in England and Wales: methodology (v1.0). Department for Environment, Food and Rural Affairs

Brezzi M, Dijkstra L, Ruiz V (2011) OECD extended regional typology: the economic performance of remote rural regions, OECD Regional Development Working Papers n.° 2011/06, OECD Publishing, Paris. Retrieved from https://doi.org/10.1787/5kg6z83tw7f4-en

Britton S (1981) Tourism, dependency and development: a mode of analysis. In: Development Studies Centre Occasional Paper 23. The Australian National University, Canberra

Brown F, Hall D (eds) (2000) Tourism in peripheral areas: case studies. Channel View, Clevedon

Carvalho, P. (2018). Dynamics of rural low-density spaces in Portugal. Méditerranée [Online], 130, Retrieved from http://journals.openedition.org/mediterranee/10516

Chaperon S, Bramwell B (2013) Dependency and agency in peripheral tourism development. Ann Tour Res 40:132–154

Chen JS, Kerstetter DL (1999) International students' image of rural Pennsylvania as a travel destination. J Travel Res 37(3):256–266

Christaller W (1933) Die Zentralen Orte in Süddeutschland. Wissenschaftlische Buchgesellschaft, Darmstadt. English edition (1966). The Central Places in Southern Germany. Englewood Cliffs, NJ: Prentice- Hall

Cloke P (2006) Conceptualizing rurality. In: Cloke P, Marsden T, Mooney PH (eds) Handbook of rural studies. Sage, London, pp 18–28. https://doi.org/10.4135/9781848608016.n2

Copus, A. (2011). Macro scale patterns of differentiation (spatial generalizations), In Copus, A. and Hörnström, L. (Eds.), The new rural Europe: towards rural cohesion policy. Stockholm: Nordregio Report 2011:1. ISBN: 978-91-89332-77-5. Retrieved from http://urn.kb.se/resolve?urn=urn:nbn:se:norden:org:diva-131

Costa, R. (2012). Dinâmicas territoriais geradas pelo investimento privado no turismo. Doctoral dissertation, University of Aveiro. Retrieved from http://hdl.handle.net/10773/10272

Dijkstra, L. and H. Poelman (2008). Remote rural regions: how the proximity to a city influences the performances of rural regions". Regional Focus, n.° 1. Retrieved from https://ec.europa.eu/regional_policy/sources/docgener/focus/2008_01_rural.pdf

EC [European Comission]. EC Regulation 1257/1999, Luxemburg.

European Commission (2014). A harmonized definition of cities and rural areas: the new degree of urbanization [Online]. Retrieved from https://ec.europa.eu/regional_policy/sources/docgener/work/2014_01_new_urban.pdf

EUROSTAT (2005) Statistics for rural areas. EUROSTAT, Luxembourg

Eurostat (2019) Methodological manual on territorial typologies — 2018 edition. European Commission. https://doi.org/10.2785/930137

Fazenda, N., Silva, F. and Costa, C. (2008). Política e planeamento turístico à escala regional o caso da agenda regional de turismo para o norte de Portugal. *Revista Portuguesa de Estudos Regionais,* 18, 2.° quadrimestre, 77-100

Ferrão J (2000) Relações entre mundo rural e mundo urbano: evolução histórica, situação actual e pistas para o futuro. Sociologia, Problemas e Práticas 33:45–54. Retrieved from http://www.scielo.mec.pt/scielo.php?script=sci_arttextandpid=S0873-65292000000200003andlng=ptandtlng=pt

Figueiredo E (2018) Entre o Abandono e o Idílio – Representações sociais dos territórios rurais em Portugal. Cultivar – Cadernos de Análise e Prospetiva 11:39–48. Retrieved from https://www.gpp.pt/images/GPP/O_que_disponibilizamos/Publicacoes/CULTIVAR_11/SeccaoIArtigoElisabeteFigueiredo.pdf

Frochot I (2005) A benefit segmentation of tourists in rural areas: a Scottish perspective. Tour Manag 26:335–346

Gerowitt B, Bertke E, Hespelt SK, Tute C (2003) Towards multifunctional agriculture – weeds as ecological goods? Weed Res 43:227–223

Hall M, Page J (1999) The geography of tourism and recreation: environment, place and space. Routledge, New York

Hijmans RJ, Cameron SE, Parra JL, Jones PG, Jarvis A (2005) Very high resolution interpolated climate surfaces for global land areas. Int J Climatol 25:1965–1978. https://doi.org/10.1002/joc.1276

Hilal, M., Barczak, A., Tourneux, F-P, Schaeffer Y., Houdart and Cremer-Schulte, D. (2011). *Typologie des campagnes françaises et des espaces à enjeux spécifiques (littoral, montagne et DOM).* 2011. hal-00911232

Hopkins J, Copus A (2018) Definitions, Measurement Approaches and Typologies of Rural Areas and Small Towns: A Review. James Hutton Institute, Aberdeen. Retrieved from www.sruc.ac.uk/downloads/file/3810/342_definitions_measurement_approaches_and_typologies_of_rural_areas_and_small_towns_a_review

Hugo G (2004) New forms of urbanization: beyond the urban-rural dichotomy. Routledge, London. https://doi.org/10.4324/9781315248073

Hummelbrunner R, Miglbauer E (1994) Tourism promotion and potential in peripheral areas: the Austrian case. J Sustain Tour 2(1–2):41–50

IGE (2011) Clasificación do grao de urbanización das parroquias e dos concellos galegos. Instituto Galego de Estatística, Santiago de Compostela

INE (2014) Tipologia de Áreas Urbanas. Instituto Nacional de Estatística, Lisboa

INSEE (2015). Une nouvelle approche sur les espaces à faible et forte densité. In *Les zonages d'étude de l'Insee: Une histoire des zonages supracommunaux définis à des fins statistiques.* Insee Méthodes n.° 129

Jepson D, Sharpley R (2015) More than sense of place? Exploring the emotional dimension of rural tourism experiences. J Sustain Tour:1–22

Kastenholz E, Davis D, Paul G (1999) Segmenting tourism in rural areas: the case of north and central Portugal. J Travel Res 37:353–363

Kastenholz E, Carneiro M, Marques C, Lima J (2012) Understanding and managing the rural tourism experience — The case of a historical village in Portugal. Tour Manag Perspect 4:207–214

Lane B (1994) What is rural tourism. J Sustain Tour 2(1 and 2):7–21

Lane B, Kastenholz E (2015) Rural tourism: the evolution of practice and research approaches – towards a new generation concept? J Sustain Tour 23:8–9

MADRP (2006) Plano Estratégico Nacional. Desenvolvimento Rural 2007-2013. Ministério da Agricultura, Desenvolvimento Rural e Pescas, Lisboa

MAGRAMA (2009) Programa de Desarrollo Rural Sostenible (PDRS) 2010-2014. Ministerio de Medio Ambiente y Medio Rural y Marino, Madrid

Marques T (2004) Portugal na transição do século: retratos e dinâmicas territoriais. Edições Afrontamento, Porto

Marsden T, Sonnino R (2008) Rural development and the regional state: denying multifunctional agriculture in the UK. J Rural Stud 24:422–431

Martín, J., Martín, V., Lopes, H., Guerrero, E. and Oliveira, A. (2008). Modelo de dados socio-económico e físico-ambiental do OTALEX: metodologias, análise e resultados à escala regional. In OTALEX. Observatorio Territorial Alentejo Extremadura: Resultado Final Projecto. DGUOT (coord.). Retrieved from http://www.ideotalex.eu/OtalexC/Publicaciones/OTALEX/LIBRO%20OTALEX_web.pdf

Meeus SJ, Gulinck H (2008) Semi-urban areas in landscape research: a review. Living Rev Landscape Res 2(3):1–45. https://doi.org/10.12942/lrlr-2008-3

MIPAAF (2007) National Strategy Plan for Rural Development 2007-2013. Ministero delle Politiche Agricole Alimentari e Forestali, Rome

Nordregio-Nordic Centre for Spatial Development (2004) Mountain areas in Europe: analysis of mountain areas in Eu member states, acceding and other European countries. Nordregio-Nordic Centre for Spatial Development, Stockholm

OECD (2011) OECD regional typology. OCDE, Paris

OECD (2016) OECD regional outlook 2016: productive regions for inclusive societies. OECD Publishing, Paris. https://doi.org/10.1787/9789264260245-en

Öğdül H (2010) Urban and rural definitions in regional context: a case study on Turkey. Eur Plan Stud 18(9):1519–1541. https://doi.org/10.1080/09654313.2010.492589

Poon A (1989) Tourism, technology and competitive strategies. CAB International, Wallingford

Programa do IV Governo Constitucional (1978). Retrieved from https://www.historico.portugal.gov.pt/pt/o-governo/arquivo-historico/governos-constitucionais/gc04/programa-do-governo/programa-do-iv-governo-constitucional.aspx

Quintá F, Arce X (2018) Reflexiones acerca de la delimitación y definición del medio rural. Diseño de un índice de ruralidad para Galicia. [Reflections on the delimitation and definition of rural areas. Design of a rurality index for Galicia]. Finisterra 52(106). https://doi.org/10.18055/Finis9955

Qviström M (2013) Searching for an open future: planning history as a means of peri-urban landscape analysis. J Environ Plan Manag 56(10):1549–1569. https://doi.org/10.1080/09640568.2012.734251

Resolução do Conselho de Ministros n.° 11 da Presidência do Conselho de Ministros (2004). Diário da República, 1.ª série - N.° 40. Retrieved from https://dre.pt/application/conteudo/570534

Ribeiro M, Marques C (2002) Rural tourism and the development of less favoured areas – between rhetoric and practice. Int J Tour Res 4:211–220

Salvatore R, Chiodo E, Fantini A (2018) Tourism transition in peripheral rural areas: theories, issues and strategies. Ann Tour Res 68:41–51

Silva L (2007) A procura do turismo em espaço rural. Etnográfica 11(1):141–163

Simard M (2005) Les espaces à faible densité: un défi au développement des milieux ruraux québécois. Can J Reg Sci XXVIII:111–136

Smith C, Still B (2009) Core-periphery relationships of resource-based communities. J Commun Dev Soc 26(1):52–70

Stewart CT (1958) The urban-rural dichotomy: concepts and uses. Am J Sociol 64(2):152–158. https://doi.org/10.1086/222422

Theobald DM (2001) Land-use dynamics beyond the American urban fringe. Geogr Rev 91 (3):544–564. https://doi.org/10.2307/3594740

Williams AM, Shaw G (1998) Introduction: tourism and uneven economic development. In: Williams AM, Shaw G (eds) Tourism and economic development. European experiences. Wiley, Chichester, pp 1–16

Woods M (2009) Rural geography: blurring boundaries and making connections. Prog Hum Geogr 33(6):849–858. https://doi.org/10.1177/0309132508105001

Assessing the Impact of Tourist Activities on Low-Density Territories: The Case of the Historical Villages of Portugal

Ricardo Biscaia, Ana I. Melo, Maria Manuela Natário, Augusta Ferreira, Carlos Santos, Dalila Dias, Gonçalo Gomes, Graça Azevedo, Rui Pedro Marques, Paula Rocha, and Rúben Duarte

1 Introduction

The historical villages of Portugal network (nHVP) integrates 12 historical villages, inserted in three NUTS III: Beiras and Serra da Estrela, Beira Baixa, and Coimbra Region.

R. Biscaia (✉) · A. I. Melo
School of Technology and Management (ESTGA), University of Aveiro, Águeda, Portugal

Centre for Research in Higher Education Policies (CIPES), Matosinhos, Portugal
e-mail: ricardob@ua.pt; ana.melo@ua.pt

M. M. Natário
Higher School of Technology and Management, Polytechnic of Guarda, Research Unit for Inland Development (UDI-IPG), Guarda, Portugal
e-mail: m.natario@ipg.pt

A. Ferreira · C. Santos · G. Azevedo · P. Rocha · R. Duarte
ISCA, University of Aveiro, Aveiro, Portugal
e-mail: augusta.ferreira@ua.pt; carlos.santos@ua.pt; graca.azevedo@ua.pt; paula.rocha@ua.pt; rubenduarte@ua.pt

D. Dias
Historical Villages of Portugal, Belmonte, Portugal
e-mail: dalila.dias@aldeiashistoricasdeportugal.com

G. Gomes
Turismo Centro de Portugal, Aveiro, Portugal
e-mail: goncalo.gomes@turismodocentro.pt

R. P. Marques
Higher Institute of Accounting and Administration (ISCA-UA), University of Aveiro, Aveiro, Portugal
e-mail: ruimarques@ua.pt

© Springer Nature Switzerland AG 2021
R. P. Marques et al. (eds.), *The Impact of Tourist Activities on Low-Density Territories*, Tourism, Hospitality & Event Management,
https://doi.org/10.1007/978-3-030-65524-2_2

The territory associated to the historical villages of Portugal (HVP) is characterized by low population density, with very concentrated but distant building clusters,
increasing the feeling of isolation. In this sense, the great challenges of this territory
are: (1) to attract population; (2) to create employment; and (3) to provide more and a
greater diversity of services. In this limbo, tourism emerges as an opportunity to
develop the territory, by promoting innovative dynamics, luring investment, and
attracting people. However, it is important to promote a sustainable tourism, meaning that it is important not only to foster economic development, but also to preserve
the environment and the quality of life of communities.

Given the importance of tourism to these territories and the absence of studies in
this knowledge area, which take into account the specific characteristics of
low-density territories, such as HVP, it is crucial to analyze the impact of tourism
in this region. As such, a set of sustainable and viable indicators, aggregated in a
framework of analysis, sufficiently broad to cover all the types of impacts of tourism,
will be presented in this chapter. This will help to mitigate the negative impacts of
tourism and highlight its strengths, thus promoting sustainability and contributing to
the strategic planning of tourist activities in this type of territories.

This chapter is structured as follows: after the introduction, the literature review
on the measurement of the impact of tourist activities is presented in Sect. 2. In Sect.
3, a framework to analyze the impact of tourism on low-density territories is
proposed. In Sect. 4, the indicators devised to monitor the impacts of tourism are
presented. Finally, in Sect. 5, the final considerations are drawn.

2 Low-Density Territories, Sustainable Tourism, and Indicators

2.1 Low-Density Territories and Sustainable Tourism

The historical villages of Portugal (HVP)—Almeida, Belmonte, Castelo Mendo,
Castelo Novo, Castelo Rodrigo, Idanha-a-Velha, Linhares da Beira, Marialva,
Monsanto, Piódão, Sortelha e Trancoso—have a set of characteristics that enable
the creation of a common identity: history, culture, and heritage. Despite these
valuable elements, these territories are strongly affected by the effects of human
desertification, enhanced by interiority and the migratory movement of populations
to coastal areas.

These villages are inserted in the so-called "low-density territories," characterized
by increasing depopulation (Santos & Ferreira 2010), stagnation and delay (Azevedo
2011; Johansson and Rauhut 2002), and levels of social and economic maladjust-
ment that are difficult to reverse, associated with lower levels of development
(Domingos 2009). Nevertheless, these territories offer potentialities and opportunities that must be identified and exploited. Territorial capital, associated with productive capacity and natural resources, traditional knowledge, artisanal production,

or historical and cultural heritage, are relevant factors of attraction and mobilization of people (Ferrão 2015).

The development and promotion of innovation processes and dynamics in low-density areas, coupled with greater efficiency in the use of resources, is fundamental to improving competitiveness, boosting job creation and sustainability. The sustainability of these territories requires a strategy based on endogenous resources and in line with the objectives of the Europe 2020 strategy for smart growth. In this context, it is important to know how regions and their actors can generate endogenous wealth creation mechanisms based on their specific resources (Alves 2007).

In this context, tourism is regarded by many as a great opportunity to develop these territories. In fact, this activity is recognized as one of the key sectors for a country's development and an important source of income, employment, and wealth creation with social, economic, and environmental impacts. Given these impacts, governments from various countries and the European Commission (EC) have shown growing concerns about the sustainability of the tourist activity. As a result, the EC has developed the European Tourism Indicators System (ETIS) for sustainable destination management (European Commission 2013).

The European Commission considers that competitiveness and sustainability are intrinsic, as the quality of tourist destinations is affected by the natural and cultural environments, and by the integration of local communities (European Commission 2013; European Commission 2016). Thus, in the long run, there should be a balance between economic, social, cultural, and environmental sustainability. That means that sustainability depends on the interaction between economic changes and social, cultural, and ecologic transformations (Laimer and Weiß 2016; Obst 2016). A sustainable economy means that economic development should not neglect environmental conservation.

The concern with sustainable tourism and its integration in strategic planning is fundamentally due to the fact that tourist activities have caused several environmental and socioeconomic problems (Tanguay et al. 2013), particularly overloads, pressures, and saturation of the territories. The first step to a sustainable tourism is the existence of a monitoring system, which allows for the continuous reintegration of feedback from these processes, in an attitude of reproducibility. The tourism planning models, namely, the 'Third Way for Tourism Planning' (Burns 2004), show the need for constant evaluation in the various moments of the process, so that it is feasible to correct deviations in a timely manner (Brito 2011).

Indeed, all forms of tourism, in all types of destinations, including mass tourism and the various tourism segments or niches, can apply sustainable tourism development guidelines and management practices. An appropriate balance must be struck between the three dimensions—environmental, economic, and socio-cultural aspects—to ensure their long-term sustainability, taking into account the sustainability principles referred to by Obst (2016) for the development of tourism. The sustainable development of tourism also requires the participation of all stakeholders, as well as strong political leadership, to ensure broad participation and consensus building. Achieving sustainable tourism is an ongoing process and requires constant monitoring of impacts, with preventive and /or corrective measures whenever necessary. It is therefore important to maintain a high level of tourist satisfaction to ensure tourist awareness of sustainability issues and to promote sustainable tourism practices (Obst 2016).

2.2 Indicators to Monitor the Impact of Tourist Activities

The theme on how to monitor the impacts of tourism has been analyzed by several researchers (Burns 2004; Blackstock et al. 2008; Tanguay et al. 2013; Obst 2016), with the objective of developing models of analysis to find indicators that are based on the development and competitiveness of sustainable tourism and that contribute to the quality of life of the inhabitants of the territories. In fact, in the last 20 years, numerous theories have emerged in the academy on how to monitor the impact of tourism in territories, in order to minimize its negative impacts and maximize its gains.

The World Tourism Organization (UNWTO 2017) has sought to develop a statistical framework to measure sustainable tourism. To do so, it also considers the three pillars, namely, economic, social, and environmental impacts, highlighting the need to include the five P's: People, Planet, Peace, Prosperity, and Partnership. In the same sense, Laimer and Weiß (2016) consider that sustainability is anchored in three types of sustainability: ecological, social, and economic.

However, more important than continually alerting to the needs to be met is the continuous operationalization and monitoring of these indicators, especially adapted to the territories under study. It is clear the need to define a framework adapted to low-density territories, with the notion that a theoretical framework of characterization and analysis of territories for mass tourism cannot be applied to territories such as HVP.

In light of the sustainability of tourism expected for tourist destinations, and for this type of territory in particular, the World Tourism Organization (UNWTO) referred to Laimer and Weiß (2016) to indicate four large dimensions of indicators that should be considered:

1. Economic, tourism demand and supply (including employment and number of visitors).
2. Environmental, resources used by tourism industries (e.g. water, energy) and waste generated by tourism industries and tourists (e.g. greenhouse gas emissions, solid waste).
3. Ecosystem, about the condition and changes in their condition, within the selected area. Data can be broadened to include the measurement of ecosystem services through service flows obtained in dimensions (1) and (2).
4. Cultural and social, related to the tourist activity (e.g., cultural site numbers, visit rates).

Although it is recognized that each region should have its own indicators, which are legitimized by the uniqueness of each territory, this approach can, according to

Table 1 Problems associated to sustainable tourism

Categories			
1. Ecosystem	6. Landscapes and nuisances	11. Public participation	16. Economic vitality
2. Water	7. Resilience and risk	12. Culture	17. Employment
3. Atmosphere	8. Security and safety	13. Accessibility	18. Marketing
4. Energy	9. Health	14. Investments	19. Reputation
5. Waste management	10. Satisfaction	15. Promotion of ecotourism	20. Traffic

Source: Tanguay et al. (2013, p. 868)

Table 2 Issues to monitor sustainable tourism

Issues	
Volume and spread of tourism	Affordable housing
Visitor satisfaction	Sustainability of land use in terms of tourism
Tourism enterprise performance and satisfaction	Social benefits and environmental justice
Community reaction	Visitor behavior
Environmental impact	Population stability
Awareness of sustainable tourism by visitors and locals	Communities of "interests" as well as spatial

Source: Blackstock et al. (2008)

Tanguay et al. (2013), ignore the basic principles of sustainable tourism for political purposes. In the field of tourism, where issues of attractiveness and competitiveness are important, it is desirable to have a minimum level of consistency in assessing sustainable tourism by using basic indicators to avoid manipulating the concept for marketing purposes, reduce the risk of losing an important dimension of sustainable development in order to meet specific policy objectives and encourage greater compatibility in the development of sustainable tourism strategies proposed by the various levels of the government (Tanguay et al. 2013).

Highlighting the diversity and high number of indicators available, namely, related to development of sustainable tourism, Tanguay et al. (2013) considered 20 main categories (Table 1).

Blackstock et al. (2008) added the dimension of social responsibility (Table 2). These authors believe the following issues should be considered in order to monitor sustainable tourism.

Having looked at the theoretical frameworks most related to the reality studied here—low-density territories—as well as at the various possibilities of measuring the local and regional impact of tourism, we devised a framework and indicators that would better monitor this impact. The proposed framework and indicators were adjusted to the needs and specificities of a low-density territory, such as HVP.

3   A Framework to Analyze the Impact of Tourism on Low-Density Territories

3.1   Methodology

The framework development process started with an exhaustive review of the literature on indicators to measure the impact of tourist activity on the territory and on ways of aggregating these indicators. In addition, the indicators collected by UNWTO, OECD, INE, Biosphere and the Central Region Strategic Plans were looked at. This first analysis allowed us to note that the existing indicators were too macro, not reflecting the specific characteristics of low-density territories. This "mismatch" was reinforced after a first visit to the nHVP territory, aimed at understanding the concerns and needs in loco. The idea was to visit the HVP and speak with tourism technicians, allocated to the tourist offices and/or with functions related to tourism. During these visits, the research team also sought to get a sense of the lifestyle of each village and gather opinions about the tourist activity among residents and some economic agents.

According to Burgos and Mertens (2016), the members of the community are fundamental agents for intervention and to influence the development of the tourist activity. In this way, involving them in the process of knowledge of the reality of this territory allows them to integrate a participatory and collaborative network, fostering multiple effects, such as the strengthening of social organization, its development, and the implementation of sustainable tourism.

This exploratory study made it possible to observe that both the indicators and the aggregation dimensions to be defined should cover the three main needs of low-density areas—to combat depopulation and lack of investment; improve competitiveness; and to stimulate job creation. It made the research team aware that the sustainability of these territories depends greatly on the focus on strategies based on endogenous resources and factors and on the promotion of innovation dynamics associated with greater efficiency in the use of resources.

Thus, based on a group of topics relevant to tourism, the three pillars of sustainable development and the study of Tanguay et al. (2013), the research team made a theoretical adaptation to the reality of nHVP, considering the following characterization dimensions: economic, social, and environmental—and its subsequent subdivision—habitability, viability, equity, and sustainability. It was also considered pertinent to include themes to ensure the organization and planning of the indicators to be built, inspired by the problems advanced by Tanguay et al. (2013)—called "aggregation dimensions." Eight dimensions of aggregation were considered— "ecosystem," "well-being," "satisfaction," "employment," "economic vitality," "employment," "marketing," "mobility and accessibility." It should also be noted that the aggregation dimensions were thought considering the tourism intended for a low-density territory, even if they do not yet fully reflect the reality of the nHVP, as is the case with some issues related to mobility.

After reaching the first version of the framework (which integrates characterization and aggregation dimensions), it was considered important to validate it with stakeholders (economic agents—owners of accommodation, travel agencies, etc.—mayors and councilors; tourism technicians; academics and other specialists). For this purpose, focus groups were organized. This method was chosen because it allows greater proximity to the participants, placing them in an informal context and enabling them to discuss about the territory where they work in with their peers. It also allows participants to reflect on problems and needs of the territory, considering the monitoring of the tourist activity perspective. In addition, the focus group can capture non-verbal communication and increase the discourse of trust to develop a sincere discussion about what will be the main concerns and priorities (Tecau and Tescasiu, 2015).

Two sessions were held, one in Aveiro (in ISCA-UA) and another in Sortelha (one of the HVP). The sessions were guided by project investigators, who started by presenting the proposed framework, composed of characterization and aggregation dimensions. The participants' opinion on the framework was questioned. The framework was unanimously considered broad enough to address all the vertices of the impact of tourism in the territory.

3.2 The Framework

Performance indicators (PIs) can be separated by the type of impact they want to measure. The creation of dimensions related to this type of information is certainly controversial and dimensions are not mutually exclusive. The controversy relates to the hybrid nature of the PI, which implies that it is not unanimous the decision of appointing such PI to a given dimension; and the non-exclusivity relates to the fact that a given PI, say, the number of beds available in an historical village, is definitely an economic indicator, but can be also considered a social one.

3.2.1 Characterization Dimensions

In the literature, there are some proposals of classification of indicators according to the type of impact these are measuring. Lozano-Oyola et al. (2012), with the goal of measuring sustainable tourism and building a composite index, divide the indicators in three dimensions: economic, social, and environmental. Tanguay et al. (2013) analyzed a system with 507 PIs, which they distributed according to the three dimensions mentioned above, plus a combination of them, resembling a Venn Diagram: "liveable" (social and environmental); "viable" (economic and environmental); and "equitable" (social and economic), with "sustainable" comprising indicators that satisfy all classic dimensions of sustainable tourism. Respecting the hybrid nature of a PI, we have adopted the division proposed by Tanguay et al. (2013) for our analysis (see Fig. 1).

Fig. 1 Characterization
dimensions for a sustainable
tourism (Tanguay et al.
2010, p. 408)

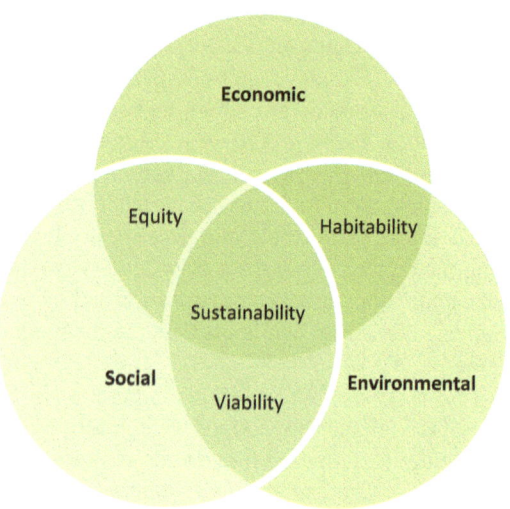

(a) Economic dimension

The analysis of the economic impact follows the flow of the expenses related with the tourist activity in a given region in order to identify a set of changes in revenues, sales, rents, and employment levels.

According to the World Travel and Tourism Council (WTTC) (WTTC 2017), travelling and tourism (T&T), being an important economic activity to the majority of countries in the world, has a direct economic impact and, consequently, an indirect economic impact for other industries. According to this division, direct impacts relate to the industries linked to the hospitality provided (the catering sector, transportation, cultural, sportive, and recreation services), and the sources of expenditure (T&T expenses from residents and government; domestic goods; and business traveling).

The indirect contribution of T&T relates to three key-indicators: investment expenses in T&T, government public expenditure in T&T, and impact of purchases from suppliers (Jucan and Jucan 2013).

(b) Social dimension

This dimension is associated with the protection of the natural and cultural resources on an area, that is, to the quality of life (Deery et al. 2012). The perception of locals regarding the impact of tourism can be analyzed according to a set of specific impacts: economic benefits, employment opportunities, opportunity costs, maintenance of infrastructures, interesting things to do, local pride, environment, and regional specificities (Enemuo & Oyinkansola 2012). Each of these effects may or may not operate toward the development of tourism. This impact is considered as a consequence of the development of the tourism industry and the presence of tourists in their destination, and has a significant effect in the life of the receiving communities.

(c) Environmental dimension

The environmental impact relates to questions such as the significant change in the natural habitat of the species, the increase in the usage of resources, pollution, climate change, and waste. Therefore, PIs such as energetic consumption and atmospheric pollution are relevant. The main concern is to maintain the quality of the hydric, land and air ecosystems, the diversity of fauna and flora, and the environmental management and policy. According to the European Union (European Commission 2013), the environmental impacts of tourism are associated with two fundamental political questions: the air pollution related to touristic transportation and the direct impacts on the territory. Such problems are analyzed through the contribution of tourism on the production of CO_2 and in the energetic consumption of transports; and in the touristic density, respectively (WTO 2004).

According to Sunlu (2003), the development of tourism can put some pressure over natural resources and increase their consumption in areas where they are already scarce. Therefore, the author raises the flag over the degradation of local natural resources, land degradation, pollution, and physical impacts of the development of tourist activities.

Given the direct relation of tourism to the environment, it is important to reflect on the reverse relationship, that is, how environmental impacts affect tourism. Natural disasters, such as forest fires like those experimented in Portugal in 2017, have a significant effect over visitors, domestic tourism, and local touristic industries. Climate change influences the tourism itself depending on how its severity affects a given touristic region, namely, the presence of storms and extreme temperature that can reduce the attractiveness of the region. This point is even more important if the touristic destination is attractive due to its weather, which is the case of HVP.

The habitability, viability, and equity dimensions characterize indicators that relate simultaneously and significantly with two of the aforementioned dimensions. In fact, given the "not mutually exclusive" characteristic of the dimensions, it is the natural that some of the indicators may be related with more than one of those "pure" dimensions. If the indicator relates strongly with the three dimensions, it is labelled "sustainable."

3.2.2 Aggregation Dimensions

In order to aggregate the indicators that are able to measure the social, economic, and environmental impact of the HVP touristic activity in the low-density territories in which the destination is inserted, eight dimensions were developed. These dimensions relate to the areas that are deemed relevant to measure that impact, namely: "Ecosystem," "Welfare," "Satisfaction," "Culture," "Economic Vitality," "Employment," "Marketing," and "Mobility and Accessibility." These dimensions were built based on the proposed division of Tanguay (Tanguay et al. 2013) and were adapted in order to provide a deep focus on the problems that are associated with low-density territories.

The "Ecosystem" dimension consists of the aggregation of indicators of environmental character. This dimension includes the energy and water consumption, the distribution of equipment in the destination that promotes nature conservation, transportation, "green" equipment, and the commercial establishments that have an environmental certificate. These indicators are intended to monitor environmental health (Rogers and Greenaway 2005; Salamon 2002), namely, the ecological footprint generated by tourism (Manning 1999). The "Welfare" dimension refers to the satisfaction of those that reside in the HVP territory relatively to the impact of tourism. It relates to healthcare, education and skills of the population, the quality of the job routine, security, and the satisfaction with life itself (OECD 2011).

The "Satisfaction" dimension refers to the satisfaction of the visitors relatively to the destination, namely, their global experience: existing attractions, amenities, and the supply of tourist services. Dupeyras and MacCallum (2013) underline that the satisfaction of the visitors is a proxy for the attractiveness of the destination based on its actual and future competitiveness. "Culture" refers to the cultural supply of the destination, both in terms of the existing cultural infrastructures, and in terms of the cultural activities that the destination provides—continuously or sporadically. According to Craik (1995), there are three ways of analyzing tourism from a cultural perspective: tourist products; the perceptions of tourists regarding cultural experiences; and the cultural consequences of the development of tourism in local communities.

"Economic Vitality" is related to the influence of tourism over housing, catering, and other services directly related to the tourist sector, both from the point of view of monetary flow and the evolution of supply. Nocca (2017) considers that the number of licenses of activities related to tourism, the promotion of tourist projects, the investment in new tourist units, the percentage of hotels that contribute to the increase of tourism revenues, the average lifetime of tourist firms, as well as the investment in cultural activities characterize all that should be considered in such dimension. "Employment" includes the jobs that are generated due to the tourist sector and the characterization of employment conditions of the employees (Roberts and Tribe 2008).

"Marketing" incorporates the characterization of the external promotion of the tourist destination: budget and allocated expenses; involved economic agents; satisfaction of the agents relatively to the promotion activities; and brand perception of the tourist destination. Summing it up, it provides some understanding regarding the promotion activities and their effectiveness (White 2010). The "Mobility and Accessibility" dimension integrates indicators that allow for the understanding of the visiting conditions for tourists with reduced mobility, as well as indicators that track the flow of visitors, that is, the routes these have taken to reach the destination and the time spent in those routes. It also provides an understanding of the impact of mobility on the destination and how it might change during different tourist seasons (Scuttari et al. 2013). It is believed that these dimensions are useful to guarantee that every topic that leads to the sustainability of the territory is covered by the set of proposed indicators.

4 Indicators for a Sustainable Tourism

4.1 Methodology

Literature review has shown that low-density territories are a well-known reality shared by many countries. Nevertheless, in order to overcome the problems of these territories, a micro-level analysis is required, since they have a lot of specificities. Thus, a strategy of proximity to its few, and therefore, relevant stakeholders is of upmost importance. As such, this was the approach chosen by this research team for the definition of performance indicators for the territory of HVP.

After the literature review, we have identified 544 relevant indicators that would fit into the dimensions discussed in the previous sections. These indicators came not only from the review undertaken by Tanguay et al. (2013), but from other non-academic entities, such as the United Nations World Tourism Organization (UNWTO), the Organization for the Economic Cooperation and Development (OECD), the Biosphere Project, the Portuguese National Statistics Office (INE), and from strategic documents from the Portuguese "Centro" Regional Office. The analysis conducted led to more than 544 indicators altogether, but there was a first removal of duplicates and similar indicators, as well as a first refinement of those that seemed irrelevant from the start. We also removed indicators that we knew were difficult to calculate, given the lack of information at a micro-level.

After organizing those indicators according to our dimensions of analysis, we have conducted some fieldwork, with two main objectives: firstly, we wanted to get to know the territory to acknowledge the existing problems and see whether the indicators would really represent the territorial challenges and whether the information to build them could be easily and repeatedly collected; secondly, we wanted to present our project to the local stakeholders to ease the data collection process. The fieldwork was extremely relevant, as some important practical information was obtained that allowed the shortening of the list of indicators to 90. To provide some examples: some of the indicators we had were unclear regarding the different type of accommodation establishments; some of the indicators would only make sense at the macro-level, not being relevant for the territory itself.

The next step consisted in the validation of both the framework and the corresponding list of indicators. With that in mind, the project team organized two focus groups. One in Sortelha, one of the HVP, with the goal of gathering the opinion of local stakeholders, namely, residents, economic agents and politicians; and the other at the University of Aveiro, with the goal of gathering the opinion of academics and regional tourist officers. One of the main advantages of focus groups is that they allow participants to engage with project members in an informal manner, allowing for a sincere opinion regarding the framework and corresponding indicators (Tecau and Tescasiu 2015). In both focus groups, the framework—with an emphasis on the characterization and aggregation dimensions—was presented, and later the indicators were discussed, not only regarding their relevance, but also regarding the feasibility of data collection. The framework was unanimously considered broad enough to address all the vertices of the impact of tourism on the territory.

Regarding the indicators—and as expected—a considerable amount of feedback was received and contributed to the improvement of the final list of indicators. The discussion flowed on a number of topics, for example, on providing a better specification on how to collect information for each indicator; on taking advantage of existing authorities to obtain information instead of duplicating efforts; on the need to give something back to the community, by presenting the results to them; on the awareness that some indicators might be distorted because of sectorial differences in businesses; on the adaptation of the health indicators to the reality of low-density territories; and by suggesting the need to the account for the satisfaction of the residents with the way the territory is being managed.

4.2   The Indicators

After the focus groups, the final framework (presented already in the previous section) was stabilized as well as a final list of 88 indicators. These were distributed among our dimensions of characterization and aggregation according to Table 3. In the annex we provide some detail regarding the indicators divided by the aggregation dimensions.

Naturally, some aggregation topics relate more with some of the dimensions of sustainable development than others. For instance, the Ecosystem indicators are highly associated with the environmental dimension of sustainable development; and Economic Vitality indicators are mostly related with the economic dimension. Globally, we can see that out of the 88 indicators, 25 relate to the environmental dimension; 62 with the economic dimension; and 63 with the social dimension. Therefore, we believe that every aspect related with the impact of tourism is covered within this set of indicators.

Regarding the operationality of the framework and of the set of indicators, we have also determined how often data for each indicator is supposed to be collected within each village, based on the importance of the information and on the ease of collection; the method of collection, namely whether the information comes from questionnaires conducted within the village, by the municipality, from tourist offices' questionnaires to tourists, or whether it comes from the online platform we have created (ILDA) for economic agents to report their own information; and the targets for each indicator, namely, whether the information is required from visitors, economic agents or residents. See Table 4 and the annex for more detail on the indicators.

Table 3 Distribution of the indicators between the dimensions of the framework

Aggregation	Characterization			Habitability	Viability	Equity	Sustainability
	Economic	Social	Environmental				
Ecosystem			2	2	4		
Welfare		3		1		3	5
Satisfaction		8		2		7	4
Culture		1		2			
Economic Vitality	17					2	1
Employment		3				8	
Marketing	2	3					3
Mobility and ACCESSIBILITY		1				5	1
Total	19	19	2	5	4	25	14

Table 4 Distribution of the indicators by operationalization category

Periodicity	Real-time	Monthly	Yearly	
Number of indicators	27	29	32	
Method of collection	Paper	Online	Paper + online	INE
Number of indicators	27	21	39	1
Respondents	Businesses	Town hall	Residents and visitors	INE
Number of indicators	35	21	31	1

Therefore, we can see that among the different indicators, these are evenly spread between different periodicities, methods of collection, and types of respondents. At this stage, the project is testing the collection of data to see whether there is enough information (note that given the fact that we are studying low-density territories, we might not have enough visitors during some months of the year, therefore not giving enough significance to the data, especially for real-time and monthly updates of the indicators).

5   Final Considerations

Given the emerging need to know more about the impact of tourism on low-density territories, taking into consideration the specificities of these territories, a set of performance indicators, organized within an analytical framework, is proposed. Inspired by the formula advanced by Tanguay et al. (2013), duly adapted to the territory, seven dimensions were devised in order to characterize the indicators developed to assess the impact of tourist activities (denominated "characterization dimensions"): economic, social, environmental, feasibility, habitability, equity, and sustainability. Additionally, eight aggregation dimensions for indicators were also devised, incorporating the areas considered fundamental for measuring the impact of tourism in the territories under study: Ecosystem, Welfare, Satisfaction, Culture, Economic Vitality, Employment, Marketing, Mobility, and Accessibility.

The proposed framework was unanimously validated by all stakeholders who participated in two focus groups promoted by the research team, one in Aveiro and the other in Sortelha, one of the HVP. It is thus regarded as an important tool for monitoring tourism in the HVP and for strategic planning regarding the tourist sector. We are confident that its use can be extended to other low-density territories, due to the characteristics that are shared between them.

Annexes

Table A.1 Ecosystem indicators

Indicator	Characterization	Periodicity	Collection	Respondents
Number of charging stations for electric vehicles in the territory, per number of visitors	Environmental	Annual	Online	Town Hall
% of tourist economic agents in the territory that have at least one employee with environmental training	Habitability	Annual	Paper + online	Businesses
% of tourist economic agents in the territory that have formal environmental certification beyond the mandatory minimum	Environmental	Annual	Paper + online	Businesses
% of tourist economic agents that were subjected to a formal inspection by the authorities	Habitability	Annual	Paper + online	Businesses
Ratio of water consumption of businesses compared with the consumption of water in the territory	Viability	Monthly	Paper + online	Businesses
Ratio of electricity consumption of businesses compared with the consumption of electricity in the territory	Viability	Monthly	Paper + Online	Businesses
Number of garbage collection visits in the territory, per month and per visitor	Viability	Monthly	Online	Municipality
Number of recycled garbage collection visits in the territory, per month and per visitor	Viability	Monthly	Online	Municipality

Table A.2 Welfare indicators

Indicator	Characterization	Periodicity	Collection	Respondents
Level of satisfaction of residents, in the territory, with the impact of tourism in the community	Equity	Annual	Paper + online	Residents
Level of satisfaction of residents, in the territory, with the tourist brand associated to the territory	Equity	Annual	Paper + online	Residents
Number of abandoned buildings in the territory per acre	Equity	Annual	Online	Municipality
Number of formal complaints of residents regarding tourism, per resident	Social	Monthly	Online	Municipality
% of residents proud of belonging to the local community and culture	Social	Annual	Paper + online	Residents
% of residents that participate actively in tourist activities	Social	Annual	Paper + online	Residents

Table A.3 Satisfaction indicators

Indicator	Characterization	Periodicity	Collection	Respondents
Level of satisfaction of visitors with their global experience in the territory	Sustainability	Real-rime	Paper	Visitors
Level of satisfaction of reduced mobility visitors with their global experience in the territory	Equity	Real-time	Paper	Visitors
Level of satisfaction of visitors with the security of the territory	Social	Real-time	Paper	Visitors
Level of satisfaction of visitors regarding restaurants	Social	Real-time	Paper	Visitors
Level of satisfaction of visitors regarding beverage establishments and similar	Social	Real-time	Paper	Visitors
Level of satisfaction of visitors regarding accommodation estab-lishments and similar	Social	Real-time	Paper	Visitors
Level of satisfaction of visitors regarding sports facilities and activities	Social	Real-time	Paper	Visitors
Level of satisfaction of visitors regarding cultural activities	Social	Real-time	Paper	Visitors
Level of satisfaction of visitors regarding the cleanness and hygiene of public spaces	Habitability	Real-time	Paper	Visitors
Level of satisfaction of visitors regarding the information made available on the territory	Equity	Real-time	Paper	Visitors
Level of satisfaction of visitors regarding local or traditional commerce	Equity	Real-time	Paper	Visitors
Level of satisfaction of visitors regarding tourist sites	Equity	Real-time	Paper	Visitors
Level of satisfaction of visitors regarding access	Equity	Real-time	Paper	Visitors
Level of satisfaction of visitors regarding public transportation	Equity	Real-time	Paper	Visitors
Level of satisfaction of visitors regarding pedestrian routes	Sustainability	Real-time	Paper	Visitors
Level of satisfaction of visitors regarding network communications	Social	Real-time	Paper	Visitors
Level of satisfaction of visitors regarding the existing health units in the territory	Social	Real-time	Paper	Visitors
% of visitors that would recom-mend the territory	Sustainability	Real-time	Paper	Visitors
% of visitors that intends to repeat the visit	Sustainability	Real-time	Paper	Visitors
% of visitors whose experience corresponds to expectations	Sustainability	Real-time	Paper	Visitors

Table A.4 Cultural indicators

Indicator	Characterization	Periodicity	Collection	Respondents
Total capacity of existing show-rooms and auditoriums, in closed venues, per visitor	Social	Annual	Online	Municipality
% of events related with culture and immaterial patrimonium	Sustainability	Monthly	Online	Municipality
% of events related with sports and natural patrimonium	Sustainability	Monthly	Online	Municipality
% of events related with the food industry	Sustainability	Monthly	Online	Municipality
% of tickets sold for cultural spaces of the territory for visitors	Sustainability	Monthly	Online	Municipality
Number of infrastructures of permanent animation per acre of the territory	Habitability	Annual	Online	Municipality
Number of points of interest of the territory per acre of the territory	Habitability	Annual	Online	Municipality

Table A.5 Economic vitality indicators

Indicator	Characterization	Periodicity	Collection	Respondents
Average budget for the trip, per visitor	Economic	Real-time	Paper	Visitors
Number of overnight stays, by type of tourist	Economic	Monthly	Paper + online	Businesses
Number of overnight stays, by type of accommodation establishment	Economic	Monthly	Paper + online	Businesses
Average overnight stays, by type of accommodation establishment	Economic	Monthly	Paper + online	Businesses
Overall volume of expenses with staff of tourism businesses	Economic	Monthly	Paper + online	Businesses
Overall volume of expenses (except with staff) of tourist businesses	Economic	Monthly	Paper + online	Businesses
Average number of visited villages across the network	Equity	Real-time	Paper	Visitors
Average price of a meal in the territory	Economic	Monthly	Paper + online	Businesses
Average price of an overnight stay in the territory	Economic	Monthly	Paper + online	Businesses
% of purchases from local suppliers	Economic	Monthly	Paper + online	Businesses
Survival rate of firms created in the last two years	Economic	Annual	Paper + online	Businesses
Revenues stemming from licenses, concessions, and taxes on tourist activities	Economic	Annual	Online	Municipality

(continued)

Table A.5 (continued)

Indicator	Characterization	Periodicity	Collection	Respondents
Monthly occupation rate by type of accommodation establishment	Economic	Monthly	Paper + online	Businesses
Accommodation capacity of collective housing establishments in the territory	Economic	Annual	Paper + online	Businesses
Restaurants' capacity by type of establishment	Economic	Annual	Paper + online	Businesses
Capacity of other tourist establishments, by type of establishment	Economic	Annual	Paper + online	Businesses
% of tourist establishments owned by residents in the territory	Equity	Annual	Paper + online	Businesses
% of public investment allocated to each village	Sustainability	Annual	Online	Municipality
Volume of support to entrepreneurship in the territory	Economic	Annual	Online	Municipality
% of accommodation establishments that serve meals	Economic	Annual	Paper + online	Businesses

Table A.6 Employment indicators

Indicator	Characterization	Periodicity	Collection	Respondents
Number of employees, by type of accommodation establishment	Equity	Monthly	Paper + online	Businesses
Number of employees, by type of food or beverage establishment	Equity	Monthly	Paper + online	Businesses
Number of employees, by type of "other tourist economic activity"	Equity	Monthly	Paper + online	Businesses
% of workers in the tourist sector with knowledge of foreign languages, in the territory	Social	Monthly	Paper + online	Businesses
% of direct employment in the tourist sector, in the territory	Equity	Monthly	INE	INE
% of workers in the tourist sector residing in the territory	Equity	Monthly	Paper + online	Businesses
Number of workers in the tourist sector, in the territory, broken down by education level, age, and gender	Equity	Monthly	Paper + online	Businesses
% of workers in the tourist sector that are permanent (have a position throughout the year)	Equity	Monthly	Paper + online	Businesses
Average monthly salary of workers in the tourist sector, in the territory	Equity	Monthly	Paper + online	Businesses
% of workers in the tourist sector with higher or professional education in the area of tourism, in the territory	Social	Monthly	Paper + online	Businesses
% of workers in the tourist sector that have had training in tourism, in the territory	Social	Monthly	Paper + online	Businesses

Table A.7 Marketing indicators

Indicator	Characterization	Periodicity	Collection	Respondents
Total expenditure in marketing for the territory, broken down by stakeholder	Economic	Annual	Online	Municipality
Number of promotion actions in the territory (fairs, expositions, etc.)	Economic	Annual	Online	Municipality
% of businesses that carry the brand of the destination	Sustainability	Annual	Paper + online	Businesses
Number of visitors broken down by the way they received information on the territory	Social	Real-time	Paper	Visitors
Number of awards received in the field of tourism	Sustainability	Annual	Paper + online	Businesses
Level of satisfaction of local businesses with the promotion of their business	Social	Annual	Paper + online	Businesses
Level of satisfaction of local businesses with the information made available for tourists on the territory	Social	Annual	Paper + online	Businesses
% of visitants attracted to the territory, broken down by their motivations	Sustainability	Real-time	Paper	Visitors

Table A.8 Mobility and accessibility indicators

Indicator	Characterization	Periodicity	Collection	Respondents
% of tourist attractions with accessibilities for reduced mobility visitors	Equity	Annual	Online	Municipality
% of accessible accommodation for visitors with reduced mobility	Equity	Annual	Paper + online	Businesses
% of visitors that use public transportation to reach the territory	Sustainability	Real-Time	Paper	Visitors
% of visitors with reduced mobility	Social	Real-Time	Paper	Visitors
% of tourist attractions with infoaccessibility	Equity	Annual	Online	Municipality
Ratio between the number of infrastructures of soft mobility (people) and total infrastructures of mobility	Equity	Annual	Online	Municipality
Ratio between the number of infrastructures of soft mobility (cycling) and total infrastructures of mobility	Equity	Annual	Online	Municipality

References

Alves P (2007) Planeamento estratégico e marketing de cidades [Strategic planning and cities' marketing]. Confederação do Comércio e Serviços de Portugal, Lisboa

Azevedo N (2011) Tempos de mudança nos territórios de baixa densidade: as dinâmicas em Trás-os-Montes e Alto Douro. Fundação Calouste Gulbenkian, Lisboa

Blackstock KL, White V, Mccrum G, Scott A, Hunter C (2008) Measuring responsibility: an appraisal of a Scottish National Park's sustainable tourism indicators. J Sustain Tour 16 (3):276–297

Brito M (2011) Monitorização dos impactos turísticos: uma proposta de modelo aplicável a territórios em mudança. Cadernos de Geografia 30/31:249–256

Burgos A, Mertens F (2016) As redes de colaboração no turismo de base comunitária: implicações para a gestão participativa. Tour Manag Stud 12(3):18–27

Burns PM (2004) Tourism planning: a third way? Ann Tour Res 31(1):24–43

Craik J (1995) Are there cultural limits to tourism? J Sustain Tour 3(2):87–98

Deery M, Jago L, Fredline L (2012) Rethinking social impacts of tourism research: a new research agenda. Tour Manag 33:64–73

Domingos E (2009) Interacção, aprendizagem colectiva e criatividade em Regiões de Baixa Densidade. Estudo de caso sobre a Região do Alentejo. In Livro Atas do XV Congresso APDR: Redes e Desenvolvimento Regional, 1073–1101

Dupeyras A, Maccallum N (2013) Indicators for measuring competitiveness in tourism – a guidance document. OECD Tourism Papers, 2

Enemuo OB, Oyinkansola O (2012) Social impact of tourism development on host communities of Osun Oshogbo sacred grove. J Humanit Soc Sci 2(6):30–35

European Commission (2013) The European tourism indicator system – tourism – EU bookshop. Publications Office of the European Union, Luxembourg

European Commission (2016) The European tourism indicator system – ETIS toolkit for sustainable destination management. Publications Office of the European Union, Luxembourg

Ferrão J (2015). Relatório do Grupo de Trabalho Temático "Territórios Vulneráveis". Governação Integrada: A Experiência Internacional e Desafios para Portugal, Conference Proceedings

Johansson M, Rauhut D (eds) (2002) ESPON project 1.1.4 – the spatial effects of demographic trends and migration, final report. ESPON Monitoring Committee, Luxembourg

Jucan CN, Jucan MS (2013) Travel and tourism as a driver of economic recovery. Procedia Econo Finan 6:81–88

Laimer P, Weiß M (2016) Pilot study "measuring sustainable tourism" (MST) Austria. Statistics Austria, Vienna, pp 37–39

Lozano-Oyola M, Blancas F, González M, Caballero R (2012) Sustainable tourism indicators as planning tools in cultural destinations. Ecol Indic 18:659–675

Manning T (1999) Indicators of tourism sustainability. Tour Manag 20:179–181

Nocca F (2017) The role of cultural heritage in sustainable development: multidimensional indicators as decision-making tool. Sustain For 9(10):1882

Obst C (2016) UNWTO statistics and tourism satellite account programme measuring sustainable tourism: developing a statistical framework for sustainable tourism

OECD (2011) Compendium of OECD well-being indicators. OECD, Paris

Roberts S, Tribe J (2008) Sustainability indicators for small tourism enterprises – an exploratory perspective. J Sustain Tour 16(5):575–594

Rogers SI, Greenaway B (2005) A UK perspective on the development of marine ecosystem indicators. Mar Pollut Bull 50(1):9–19

Salamon L (2002) The tools of government – a guide to the new governance. Oxford University Press, Oxford

Santos C, Ferreira A (2010) Governação pública em rede: Resposta à desertificação do território. In V Congresso Nacional da Administração Pública, Lisboa

Scuttari A, Della Lucia M, Martini U (2013) Integrated planning for sustainable tourism and mobility. A tourism traffic analysis in Italy's South Tyrol region. J Sustain Tour 21(4):614–637

Sunlu U (2003) Environmental impacts of tourism local resources and global trades: environments and agriculture in the Mediterranean region Bari: CIHEAM options Méditerranéennes: Série a environmental impacts of tourism. Séminaires Méditerranéens 57:263–270

Tanguay GA, Rajaonson J, Lefebvre JF, Lanoie P (2010) Measuring the sustainability of cities: an analysis of the use of local indicators. Ecol Indic 10(2):407–418

Tanguay G, Rajaonson J, Therrien M (2013) Sustainable tourism indicators: selection criteria for policy implementation and scientific recognition. J Sustain Tour 21(6):862–879. https://doi.org/10.1080/09669582.2012.742531

Tecau A, Tescasiu B (2015) Nonverbal communication in the focus-group. Bull Transilvania Univ Brasov Econ Sci Series V 8(2):119–124

UNWTO (2017) Measuring sustainable tourism: a call for action report of the 6th international conference on tourism statistics, 21–23. Manila, Philippines

White S (2010) Measuring tourism locally, guidance note four: tourism benchmarking and performance indicators. Measuring tourism locally, 1–18

WTO (2004) Indicators of sustainable development for tourism destinations: a guidebook. WTO, Madrid

WTTC (2017) Travel & tourism – global economic impact and issues 2017. WTO, Madrid

Information Systems and Technologies as Promoters of the Low-Density Territories Sustainability

Rui Pedro Marques, Carlos Santos, Rúben Duarte, Ana I. Melo, Augusta Ferreira, Dalila Dias, Gonçalo Gomes, Graça Azevedo, Maria Manuela Natário, Paula Rocha, and Ricardo Biscaia

1 Introduction

The sustainability of low-density territories, where the historical villages of Portugal (AHP) network is inserted, requires the development and implementation of strategies based on endogenous factors and resources. In fact, in these territories, mainly characterized by increasing depopulation, stagnation and backwardness, it is essential to promote innovative dynamics, associated with greater efficiency in the use of resources, to improve competitiveness and boost job creation.

The economic and social impact of low-density territories, in general, and of the AHP network, in particular, is not sufficiently studied, and there is a lack of

R. P. Marques (✉)
Higher Institute of Accounting and Administration (ISCA-UA), University of Aveiro, Aveiro, Portugal
e-mail: ruimarques@ua.pt

C. Santos · R. Duarte · A. Ferreira · G. Azevedo · P. Rocha
ISCA, University of Aveiro, Aveiro, Portugal

A. I. Melo · R. Biscaia
School of Technology and Management (ESTGA), University of Aveiro, Águeda, Portugal

Centre for Research in Higher Education Policies (CIPES), Matosinhos, Portugal

D. Dias
Aldeias Históricas de Portugal, Belmonte, Portugal

G. Gomes
Turismo Centro de Portugal, Aveiro, Portugal

M. M. Natário
Higher School of Technology and Management, Polytechnic of Guarda, Research Unit for Inland Development (UDI-IPG), Guarda, Portugal

© Springer Nature Switzerland AG 2021
R. P. Marques et al. (eds.), *The Impact of Tourist Activities on Low-Density Territories*, Tourism, Hospitality & Event Management,
https://doi.org/10.1007/978-3-030-65524-2_3

indicators to support studies on this topic. In this context, the development and implementation of a framework of indicators that allows assessing the impact, namely, economic and social, of the activities that generate wealth, in particular tourism, associated with the AHP network, is of utmost importance.

Thus, project PLowDeR (Framework for Analysis of the Economic and Social Impact of Tourist Activities in Low Density Territories: the Case of Historical Villages of Portugal) (Natário et al. 2019; Santos et al. 2020a), in which this work is included was developed, having as a case study the AHP network. Its main objective is to develop and implement a framework of indicators that can support economic agents and policy makers in making decisions about investments and related public policies, not only within the AHP network, but also in other low-density territories.

In addition, by assessing the economic and social impact of tourist activities within the AHP network, PLowDeR will provide economic agents, decision makers and politicians with the necessary information so that they can plan their development strategy. It also aims to enhance the attraction of tourists, new investors and inhabitants to the destinations that integrate the AHP, thus contributing to their sustainability and to the development of the low-density territories where they are inserted.

The role of technology has been having a significant impact on the tourism industry through the integration of intelligent equipment (Ivanovic et al. 2016). Based on this principle, PLowDeR aims to develop and integrate a digital platform that will support the assessment of the impact of the tourist activity within the AHP network.

This platform includes: a mobile application (App) to collect data from visitors; a web application to collect data from the AHP network's stakeholders (economic agents, municipalities and residents); a front-office for making the indicators available (the data for the indicators will be collected through the App and the web application); a database for managing the collected data.

Thus, this platform is an innovative and essential element that enables and digitally transforms the purposes of PLowDeR. This chapter focuses on the conceptual presentation of this digital platform, and the interoperability between its components.

In addition to this introduction, this chapter is structured as follows: in Sect. 2 the literature review is presented, subdivided into three subsections (impact of technology on tourism, mobile applications and digital platforms); Sect. 3 presents the conceptualization and prototyping of the digital platform developed within the scope of PLowDeR; and in Sect. 4 conclusions are presented.

2 Literature Review

The AHP network integrates 12 tourist destinations which have different elements that allow creating a common identity (e.g. history, culture and heritage). The primary objective of this network is to provide villages in the interior of the central region of Portugal with a development and enhancement strategy centred on their distinctive elements.

The short-, medium- and long-term sustainability of these territories requires a strategy based on endogenous factors and resources which will promote a smart, sustainable and inclusive growth. It is focused on results and seeks to maximize the impact of investments and, at the same time, promote development through innovative dynamics associated with greater efficiency in the use of endogenous resources. This strategy is essential to improve competitiveness and boost job creation in these territories, thus promoting their sustainability (European Commission 2010).

For this process to be feasible, it is necessary to acquire knowledge on the impact of historic villages as entities endowed with innovative capacity and capable of finding new ways to intensify their own dynamics of innovation and competitiveness, based on the comprehensive and inclusive innovation paradigm. It is from this knowledge that a methodological framework, capable of being extended to other low-density territories, can be operationalized to implement the "Europe 2020 Strategy" (Madureira et al. 2013).

The lack of indicators on tourist flows and economic transactions motivated the need to develop and implement a framework of indicators which allows the assessment of the impact of the AHP network as a reference that generates innovative processes and tourism products, capable of stimulating the development of these territories and promoting their self-sustainability (Natário et al. 2019; Santos et al. 2020a, 2020b).

The innovative and relevant characteristics of this project are essentially based on the design of adequate and complete indicators, which will enable data collection that can be used to foster the strategy of promoting the smart, sustainable and inclusive growth of these territories, a vision of European social economy for the twenty-first century.

2.1   Technological Impact on Tourism

The Fourth Industrial Revolution (4IR) created new opportunities for business, government and individuals by redefining the way we work, live and interact with each other (Schwab 2018). Considering the importance of 4IR in economies and for policy-makers and other stakeholders, in 2018, the World Economic Forum introduced the Global Competitiveness Index 4.0. Its aim is to foster growth, inclusion and sustainability (Schwab 2019). Industry 4.0, also known as the fourth industrial revolution, describes the implementation of new production concepts, originated in Germany, having been used publicly for the first time at the Hannover Fair in 2011 (Lee et al. 2017).

Also, in the tourism industry, the effect of the technological development has been felt. Hence, it is also common to associate the Industry 4.0 concept with this activity. In fact, this new concept of technology integration is of great importance in creating value in the tourism industry, supporting the development of new innovative products using the most diverse technological resources available. According to Ivanovic et al. (2016), the role of Industry 4.0 in tourism is directly related to the increase that has been verified in its competitiveness through the use of intelligent equipment, which makes use of information related to some characteristics of the client, to some resources, to energy efficiency and urban trends, as well as smart destinations/smart cities.

Some issues related to the tourism industry (e.g. competitiveness and innovation) are part of the forecast of what the tourism industry may become in the context of the fundamental role of science, information and communication technologies (ICT) and innovative ideas as decisive factors for the development and innovation of that industry (Alexieva 2014). However, the sustainable development of tourism cannot be thought of without considering investments in scientific advancement, in creative ideas and in the emerging technological transformations that use the power of online communication in a dynamic and effective way (Alexieva 2014).

Digital technologies have been playing a pivotal role as a factor that enhances creative expression associated with cultural and natural heritage, science, technology and several other operations that take advantage of digital plasticity (e.g. Industry 4.0). These potentialities, associated with ICT and its expansion, led to the emergence of the digital economy that has been promoting the integration of economic activities with social activities, enabling the successful use of technological platforms such as the internet, mobile and sensory systems (Roblek et al. 2016). According to Korže (2019), due to the important share of tourism in the global economy and its continuous growth for the last few decades, the effects of the 4IR on tourism (demand and supply side) need closer attention. Nevertheless, there are not many tangible examples of the implications of Industry 4.0 in the tourism sector. There is a subtle transition to Tourism 4, in which the Internet of Services is one of the few examples (Yıldız and Davutoğlu 2019). However, the transition from Industry 4.0 to Tourism 4.0 is happening (Yıldız and Davutoğlu 2019).

2.2   Mobile Applications

The form of content production to feed the tourism industry has been changing in order to respond to the needs posed by the information society, knowledge and social interactions (Santos et al. 2017). The use of mobile applications in tourism is very common nowadays, with the massive use of this type of devices. The tourism mobile applications currently can be argued to be one of the most useful applications that can facilitate the movement of travellers (Hashim and Isse 2019).

Recent trends in the development of mobile applications in tourism refer to visualized technology (e.g. augmented reality and gamification), which increases the attractiveness of certain places. GPS, location-based tracking and applications are useful for providers to get some information and for travellers, by making their lives easier (Dorcic et al. 2019).

Silva (2014) developed a prototype with the objective of identifying some of the limitations and advantages of gamification and technologies in encouraging people to visit and discover new sights. This study concludes that an application that provides information on tourist sites, using gamification techniques, can please most tourists and influence their choice regarding the next place to visit. In fact, games have been used in the tourism industry with the aim of making the experience of tourists or visitors to a given destination more remarkable (Souza et al. 2017).

The development of mobile applications in the field of tourism motivated Kennedy-Eden and Gretzel (2012) to propose a taxonomy for these applications from two perspectives: a taxonomy on what travel-related services provide to the user and a taxonomy based on the level of personalization that the user establishes with the mobile application.

Borges (2017) analyzed the advantages, from the tourist perspective, associated with the development of mobile applications based on geo-location: being able to view and have information regarding the reasons of interest; have information about the points of interest that can be visited at the destination they intend to visit; have information about the tourist points that can be inserted in the geographic information systems: videos, photos, product brochures, etc.; being able to plan routes and have different information (accommodation, cultural events, special attractions, etc.); and being able to access iterative maps.

Also, according to Borges (2017), the geographic information needed to support a mobile application with this type of functionality can be collected through the georeferenced open data platform – Geodados4, belonging to the Lisbon City Council.

Pereira (2016) created a mobile application to allow the narration of stories located in specific places of a certain destination. The narration of these stories can be done by using various types of media (text, images and audio), which can be read as a game, meaning that the user must go through a certain route and reach specific places to be able to access its content.

Pereira (2013) developed a mobile application for the Android operating system. This application allows any visitor to the Botanical Garden of Coimbra, with access to the mobile application, to enjoy a richer and more pleasant experience. A web application was also developed for statistical treatment of the various data collected by the mobile application and sent to a server. The use of applications using augmented reality (AR) can maximize the tourist experience of tourists and visitors, enriching their experience and also their knowledge about different tourist destinations (Martins et al. 2015).

Pina (2016) analyzed whether the usability of the website of a tourist destination management organization (DMO) can influence its demand, and whether there are different levels of digital satisfaction. It concluded that the digital satisfaction index of the tourist destination makes it possible to use benchmarking and improve the usability of websites.

Another recent study (Chen and Tsai 2019) showed that tourism information based on location-based services is very convenient to use, being the main motive for the adoption of mobile applications. In fact, an easy-to-use system design allows users to master the system quickly, increasing its acceptance. Information quality and perceived usefulness also positively influence the intention to use. In sum, the quality of the information and the ability of the system to help users positively affect users' willingness to use it.

The impact of mobile technologies on tourism has motivated several scientific studies with the aim of enriching the tourist experience. One of the directions that have been explored aims to explore the digital footprint of tourists to automatically generate and update their profile, which is safely maintained on the user's side (Efraimidis et al. 2016).

Given the aforementioned, it seems clear that mobile technologies are experiencing an enormous growth in the tourism industry, thus being pertinent to think not only about their use, but also about the negative aspects that such use may have. In this sense, Rodrigues (2016) analyzed the use of technology in the scope of the tourism industry, questioning its real use. The author concluded that technology is not used equally in all phases of the trip and that tourists experience failures related to the technology and that there are negative consequences caused by its use (e.g. hardware, software, infrastructure and operators, usage and services).

According to Gonçalves et al. (2020), new technology based on Bluetooth Low Energy the beacons can be configured and implemented near each point of interest. Given the hyper-local and contextual capabilities of beacons, they are of immense value to both travellers as well as players in the tourism industry.

2.3   Digital Platforms

The notion of digital platform clearly points to a constellation of digital arrangements (data and algorithms) that serve to organize social and economic activity (Kenney and Zysman 2016). In this sense, according to the authors, digital platforms are, together with automatic learning and big data, some of the technological characteristics that define the current era consisting of intelligent tools (Industry 4.0). The concept of cloud computing and mobile computing that can be viewed in an integrated way, generating the concept of mobile computing in the cloud, offers an unprecedented potential for computing power, allowing for the creation of infrastructures that are a fertile ground for the development and implementation of digital platforms (Gustavsson 2017).

Tiwana et al. (2010) studied and defined the architecture associated with the development of digital platforms as a conceptual model. These authors describe this model as a partitioned ecosystem, constituting a relatively stable platform and a set of complementary modules that are encouraged to vary and to establish rules of connection between them.

According to Rong et al. (2013), the concept of digital platform, in the ecosystem associated with the business world, includes three main functions: interaction interface, value creation and network formulation. Interaction interface means that members of the ecosystem should have the skills to leverage the interface as a type of tool to build their own products. Value creation means that the platform should allow ecosystem partners to work together to create value. Network formulation means that if the platform provides conditions for partners to work together to create value together, they will be able to formulate specific network standards themselves to compete with their competitors' ecosystems.

A central question that arises is whether intelligent tools, including digital platforms, inevitably lead to the displacement of work, increasing human capacities and creating a new era of equitable growth, in line with the expectations expressed by the Industry 4.0 concept (Zysman and Kenney 2017a).

Digital platforms and cloud computing are fundamental characteristics of the current phase of the digital revolution. These technological paradigms are integrated with what we call intensive computing. At the origin of this concept is a huge capacity of computing power that enables the generation and analysis of data on a scale never imagined before, allowing for the reorganization/transformation of different types of services (Zysman and Kenney 2017b).

As we can see, from the above, digital platforms use various digital infrastructures such as cloud computing and data analysis (Jarvenpaa and Markus 2018). The authors consider that the study of ecosystems (Hein et al. 2019), in which digital platforms are located, is important because these systems can lead to new markets, new industries or, in the case of science, new domains of knowledge or even new specialties. Thus, digital platforms can be conceptualized as data repositories (Vassilakopoulou et al. 2016).

Digital platforms are the basis on which an increasing number of activities based on the link of other diverse activities (e.g. market, social and political) have been organized. If the industrial revolution happened around the factory, today's changes are organized around digital platforms and processing processes (e.g. algorithms) that support huge data repositories using cloud computing. The relevance of these digital platforms suggests that we are in the midst of a reorganization of our economy (Lewandowski 2013).

The availability of Internet access, within the AHP network, to which several interactive digital platforms and instruments can be associated, enables the collection of data, making the information available to the various stakeholders of the AHP network. This will foster the implementation of relationships between all the actors, thus enhancing their loyalty towards the AHP network (Liberato et al. 2016, 2018). The "Historical Villages of Portugal—Smart Lands" project provided a Wi-Fi network in the villages of the AHP network.

3 Methodology

The design science methodology was chosen for the development of the digital platform, because this methodology is fundamentally associated with the problem-solving paradigm through the conceptualization, development and evaluation of technological artefacts to solve a problem or identified need (Hevner 2007; Hevner and Chatterjee 2010).

This methodology includes several steps (Peffers et al. 2006): problem identification and motivation; definition of the solution objectives; conceptualization and development; application; evaluation; and disclosure.

Instantiating the methodology in this work, we can refer that the problem identification and motivation (step 1) are closely linked to the main purpose of the PLowDeR project, in which this work is inserted, that is, to digitally support the set of indicators, namely regarding the collection and management of data, the calculus of the of indicators and the dissemination of that information. In this step, in addition to the literature review, an ethnographic method was used to improve our understanding of human thought and action through interpretation of human action in context (Myers 1997). In fact, researchers interacted with local actors (residents, economic agents and policy makers) in order to undertake active learning, through civic participation, within the scope of the reality lived in the target territories of this study, of the existing practices and processes.

The definition of the solution objectives (step 2) and some aspects of conceptualization and development (step 3) are presented in the next section of this chapter. In this step, literature review was carried out, namely regarding the impact of intelligent ICT (Industry 4.0) on the tourism industry. This review was conducted bearing in mind that the intent of the authors was to develop and implement a digital platform that provided support for the collection, storage and processing of data related to the indicators aimed to assess the impact of tourist activity in low-density territories, particularly within the AHP network.

The application (step 4) implied testing the digital platform in the real environment. Tests were conducted in nine villages which integrate the AHP network.

The evaluation (step 5) was carried out at the end of the conceptualization in two Focus Groups that included different stakeholders. In these Focus Groups, the practices and processes found in the literature and in the ethnographic method were discussed and analyzed, translated into the selection of a set of indicators. Moreover, the role that Industry 4.0 might play in the collection, storage and processing of data to support the set of indicators was also discussed.

Finally, the disclosure of the digital platform (step 6) was made: in organised workshops with the main stakeholders of the AHP network; through marketing strategies for how visitors could use the mobile application; through conference communications and scientific journal publications, which can be read by the scientific community; in a final event aimed at publicizing the results of the PLowDeR project to the community.

4   Conceptualization, Prototyping and Deployment of the Digital Platform

4.1   Architecture and Requirements

The literature review, carried out within the scope of the PLowDeR project, the active interaction of researchers with local actors and the organisation of the Focus Groups referred to in the previous section, confirmed the interest in the development of a digital platform to support the set of indicators, the main objective of the project. Figure 1 shows an overview of its architecture.

From Fig. 1, we can see the following core components: Project Database, Mobile App, Project User-Interface, Back-Office and Project Web Application.

The Project Database is the database that interacts directly and indirectly with all the other components, as it stores and manages all the data in the set of indicators, as well as the data supporting the functionality of other components of the architecture, namely the mobile application (Mobile App).

The Mobile App is a mobile application to be used by the AHP network's visitors, being its main objective to collect data on the visits (e.g. level of satisfaction of the visitors). These data are sent to the database to feed the production of the indicators. In order to attract users, this application includes a set of useful information regarding the visit, which can function as a tourist guide, and some gamification functions to promote the user's loyalty. The useful information contained in this application can be inserted by users in the back-office (Back-Office User) interested in the tourism industry of their territories (e.g. economic agents).

Project User-Interface is an interface for access and consultation of the indicators by those interested in the outputs of PLowDeR (End User).

The Back-Office is an interface for certain users (Back-Office User), whose function is to enter data into the database, either for the production of indicators (mainly data that does not come from visitors and that has to be inserted in an application web, for example, data referring to economic agents, municipalities and residents), or to feed the mobile application. It is also an interface for accessing platform administration features.

The Project Web Application is a web application that provides the functionalities to the interfaces and manages the data flow between them and the database.

4.2   Users

For the use of the platform (Back-Office and Project User-Interface), different types of user were defined (Unregistered User, Registered User, Researcher, Supervisor and Administrator), each with a specific set of privileges.

The Unregistered User can consult some generic information about some of the available indicators. This user does not have a profile on the platform and, as such,

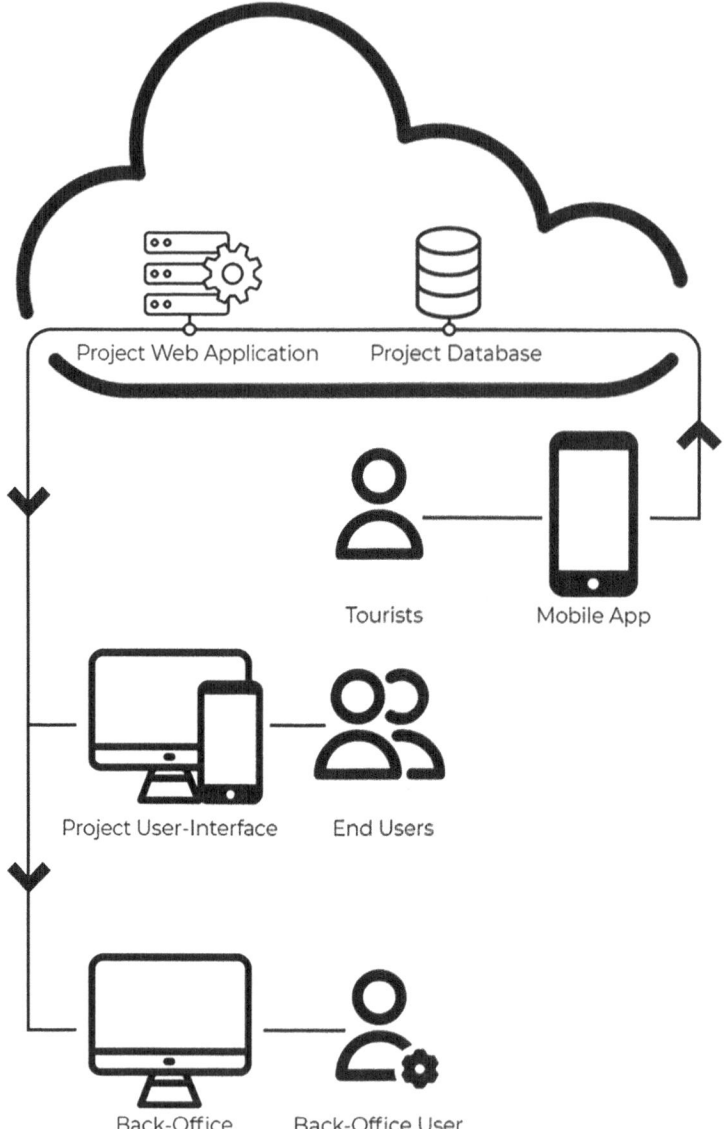

Fig. 1 Functional architecture of the solution proposal (Marques et al. 2018)

has no relationship with the AHP network. It is also part of the End User class of users and interacts only with the Project User-Interface.

The Registered User can check which surveys are missing, view and edit previous surveys and still have an overview of the indicators. This user can assume several roles on the platform and have relationships with several villages (e.g. the user can be resident in one of the villages in the network and be an economic agent in another). In this case, the user has the possibility to respond to inquiries directed to each of the roles he/she plays. This user is part of the Back-Office User class, when responding to questionnaires in the Back-Office, and of the End User class when interacting with the Project User Interface for the generic consultation of the indicators.

The user with a Researcher profile can access and filter the different indicators in different ways. This user also has the possibility to access the data that are the source of the indicator values. It is also part of the End User class of users and interacts only with the Project User-Interface.

The Supervisor profile is responsible for the validation of various components of the platform, namely the validation of users and their relationships with the AHP network, the possibility of listing the unanswered questionnaires and corresponding users, validation of new entities, among others. Like the researcher, the Supervisor can access the data behind the indicator values. This user is part of the Back-Office User class and interacts mostly with the platform's Back-Office.

The Administrator has the possibility to change the usage profiles (e.g. convert a Registered User into a Researcher). In addition, this type of user can list and delete registered users. This user can also analyze suspicious manipulation inquiries and, in case of confirmation, eliminate the respective response. It is also part of the Back-Office User class, and mainly interacts with the platform's Back-Office.

4.3   Database

Regarding the database, it is possible to divide it into two main parts: one for the insertion and management of information useful to tourists, to be included later in the mobile application; another for managing the data collected to produce the indicators.

For the management of information useful to tourists, tables and relationships were created according to the logical view presented in Fig. 2.

This figure highlights the existence of the *villages*, *pois*, *events* and *categories*. These entities represent, respectively, the villages that integrate the AHP network, points of interest in the territory, events and categories.

The *villages* table stores information related to each of the villages, such as name, geographical location, description, among others. The *pois* table (of Point of Interest), in turn, stores information related to Points of Interest – name, description, location, photo, etc. Each Point of Interest in this table has a direct relationship with a village – relating the *pois* table to the *villages* table. The *events* table has a similar relationship to the previous table, with the particularity of having the record of the start date and the end date of the event. Like the *pois* table, the *events* table also relates to the *villages* table, thus ensuring the existence of an association of an event with a village. In addition, there is the *categories* table that allows the categorization of Points of Interest and events within a pre-defined set of categories.

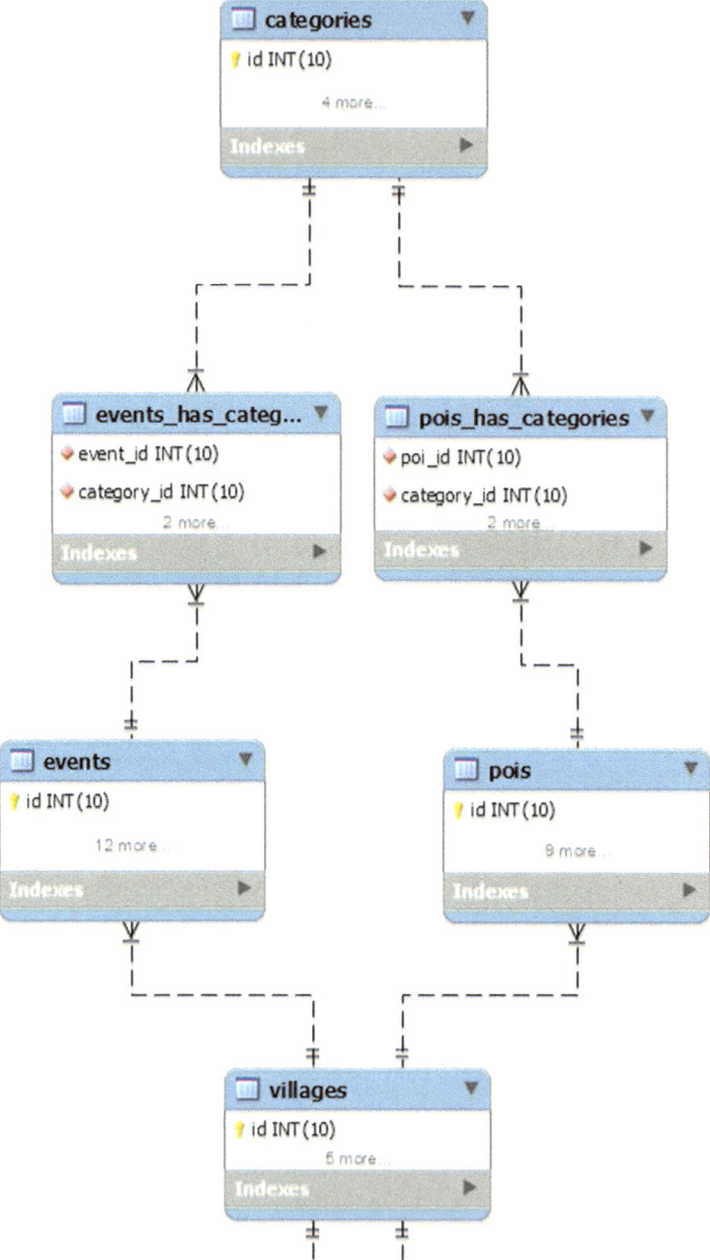

Fig. 2 Excerpt 1 of the database – useful information for tourists (exported from MySQL WorkBench) (Marques et al. 2018)

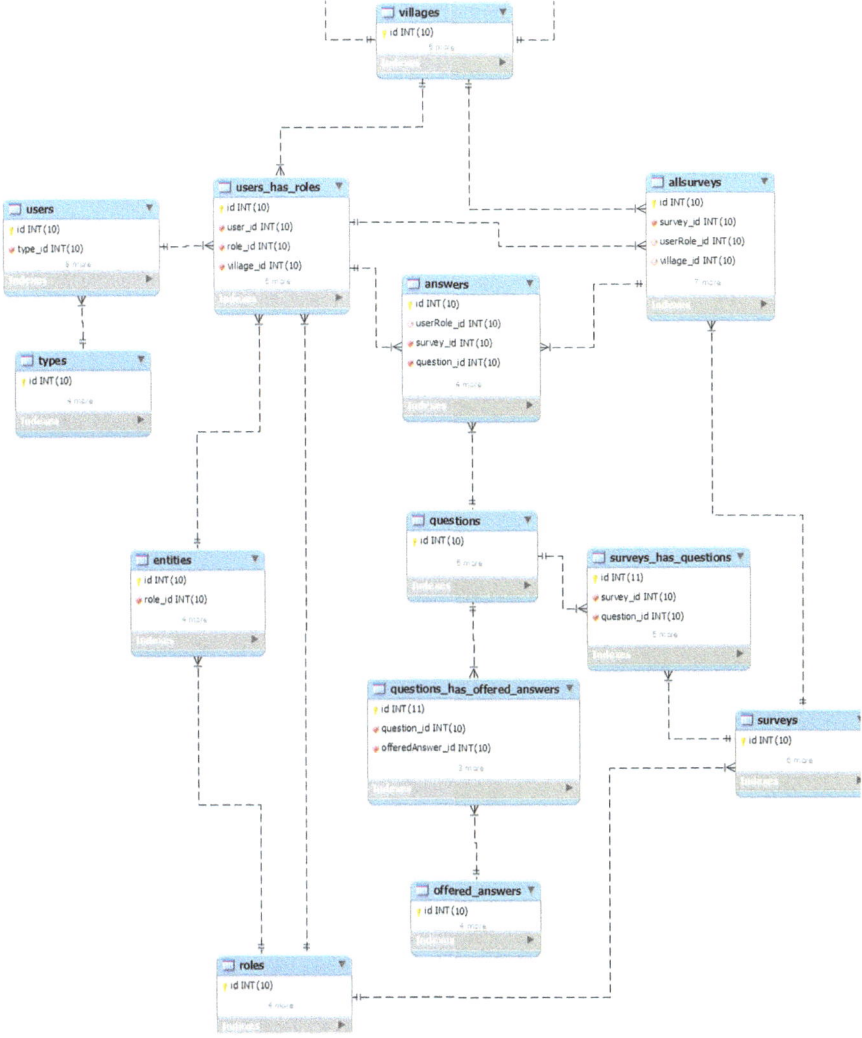

Fig. 3 Excerpt 2 of the database – collection and analysis of indicators (exported from MySQL WorkBench) (Marques et al. 2018)

For the management of the data collected to produce the indicators, tables and relationships were created according to the logical view of Fig. 3.

This figure shows the second part of the structure of the database, in terms of the relationships between the villages (*villages*), the users (*users*), the roles (*roles*) and the questionnaires (*surveys*).

Users have roles in the villages and, optionally, there may be an entity in that relationship – for example, user X is resident in village Y, or user Z is an accommodation agent in village W by entity H. These relationships are stored in the *user_has_roles* table.

In turn, each of these relationships implies participation in a set of questionnaires aimed at all stakeholders in a given role. The table of the questionnaires (*surveys*) is related to the table of questions (*questions*) which, in turn, is related to the table of possible answers (*offered_answers*), which allows saving the answer options for multiple-choice questions. The *allSurveys* table will be partially filled automatically, on the first of each month, by a script that generates a record for each relationship between users, roles and villages (and optionally entities) and corresponding questionnaires to be filled out for the previous month. On the first day of each year, a similar script runs, but this time with the aim of generating the records related to annual surveys. This table allows informing each user of the inquiries that still have to be answered. Regarding the responses to the questionnaires, these are stored in the *answers* table, which stores the information related to the questionnaire and the question, which is the registration ID of the *user_has_roles* table, as well as the response value.

4.4 Deployment of the Digital Platform

In this section, steps 4, 5 and 6 of the design science methodology are briefly described, namely, the application, evaluation and dissemination of the digital platform.

The platform was deployed and tested in some villages which integrate the AHP network. Firstly, a pre-test was carried out, including the dissemination of the ILDA digital platform in 9 of the 12 villages, with participants from the different types of users. This pre-test aimed at providing clarifications regarding the access to the ILDA platform, user registration, profile creation and, finally, response to surveys on the platform. Participants tested access to the platform, filling out the appropriate surveys, indicating errors, inconsistencies and proposing improvements. A user manual was also made available to the participants in the pre-test. In each iteration, two sessions were organized, one aimed at municipal agents, and another at economic agents and residents, in an attempt to bring together the largest number of participants. After these pre-test sessions, the necessary adjustments were made in order to improve the digital platform.

Another method to validate the framework and the platform was carried out at the end of the pre-tests conducted in some villages. This last validation consisted of two Focus Groups that included academics, economic agents, policy makers and residents. The participants of the Focus Groups gave some more suggestions regarding the conceptualization and the definition of the objectives and requirements of the solution. The solution presented in this chapter has already included these suggestions.

Throughout the implementation period, the collection of data and the calculation of the indicators also made it possible to validate the effectiveness of the digital platform in its different dimensions, showing that it is a useful tool for maintaining continuous data collection over time, for automatic calculation of the indicators, as well as for the dissemination of the indicators to the different stakeholders (Santos et al. 2020a).

Finally, the disclosure of this solution was made in conjunction with the disclosure of the project and its results: in workshops with the main stakeholders of the AHP network (Santos et al. 2020a); through marketing strategies regarding how visitors could use the mobile application (Santos et al. 2020a); through conference papers and scientific publications (Marques et al. 2018); and in a final event, aimed at publicizing the results of the the PLowDeR project and all its components (including this digital platform) to the community.

5 Final Considerations

This chapter presents the research methodology and some aspects regarding the design and development of a digital platform to support the purposes of the PLowDeR project, which aims to devise a set of indicators organised within a theoretical framework that enables the assessment of the impact of tourist activities in low-density territories.

From the validations carried out, it is worth highlighting the contribution obtained in the Focus Groups, composed of different stakeholders (economic agents, policy makers, residents, academics). These enabled the understanding of their expectations, needs and experiences and the validation of the architecture previously thought of. As such, it is possible to state that this solution proposal is feasible and corresponds to the AHP stakeholders' expectations.

Data were collected through the platform and stored. Data from the mobile application were also stored in the database. These data relate to the visitor's profile, as well as to the route they have followed within the AHP network. Several resources were used for this purpose, namely beacons and georeferencing. Each tourist was invited to complete a questionnaire made available on the digital platform, aimed at assessing its overall level of satisfaction with the visit.

It should also be noted that, before the final implementation of the platform in the AHP network, a pilot study was conducted in 9 of the 12 AHP. This was important to validate the feasibility of the indicators devised and of the digital platform.

The platform enables the collection of information by various stakeholders, regarding the indicators that are most useful for monitoring the impact of tourist activities within the AHP network, namely, the evolution of the businesses and the profile and the satisfaction of visitors, making it possible, if necessary, to adjust the strategy devised to their profile. The data collected also enables the characterization of the remaining agents, which may be useful in terms of introducing improvements that will attract more visitors and investment, both public and private. Moreover, data will allow for the characterization of each AHP's residents, which may help the development of policies aimed at promoting the establishment of more people in the low-density territories under analysis.

From the data collected and available in the platform, it is also possible to carry out statistical analyses, testing namely the relationship between some variables, in order to better understand the territory under study. This possibility is particularly useful in identifying the variables that affect the satisfaction levels of both residents, visitors and economic agents.

Finally, the importance of the work presented in this chapter is not in the technological innovation of the platform, but is related to the innovative character of the main purpose of the PLowDeR project, which is intensified with the digital transformation provided by the application of the platform.

References

Alexieva S (2014) Sustainable tourism development between innovative competitiveness of the industry and effective communications in the digital era. J Sci Res 9:215

Borges L (2017) Criação de uma Geo-Aplicação para Dispositivos Móveis – Rotas de Turismo em Lisboa. Universidade de Lisboa, Lisbon

Chen CC, Tsai JL (2019) Determinants of behavioral intention to use the personalized location-based mobile tourism application: an empirical study by integrating TAM with ISSM. Futur Gener Comput Syst 96:628–638. https://doi.org/10.1016/j.future.2017.02.028

Dorcic J, Komsic J, Markovic S (2019) Mobile technologies and applications towards smart tourism – state of the art. Tour Rev 74:82–103. https://doi.org/10.1108/TR-07-2017-0121

Efraimidis P, Drosatos G, Arampatzis A et al (2016) A privacy-by-design contextual suggestion system for tourism. J Sens Actuator Netw 5:10. https://doi.org/10.3390/jsan5020010

European Commission (2010) EUROPE 2020: a strategy for smart, sustainable and inclusive growth. European Commission, Brussels

Gonçalves F, Martins AL, Ferreira JC et al (2020) Tourism guidance tracking and safety platform. In: Lecture notes of the Institute for Computer Sciences, social-informatics and telecommunications engineering. LNICST, Springer, Cham, pp 162–171

Gustavsson M (2017) Digital platforms as dislocators on digitalization and limits of discourse. University of Gothenburg, Gothenburg

Hashim NL, Isse AJ (2019) Usability evaluation metrics of tourism mobile applications. J Softw Eng Appl 12:267–277. https://doi.org/10.4236/jsea.2019.127016

Hein A, Schreieck M, Riasanow T et al (2019) Digital platform ecosystems. Electron Mark 30:1–12. https://doi.org/10.1007/s12525-019-00377-4

Hevner AR (2007) The three cycle view of design science research. Scand J Inf Syst 19:87–92

Hevner A, Chatterjee S (2010) Design science research in information systems. In: Design research in information systems. Springer US, New York, pp 9–22

Ivanovic S, Milojica V, Roblek V (2016) A holistic approach to innovations in tourism. Int Conf Econ Soc Stud Reg Econ Dev Entrepneursh Innov 3:367–380

Jarvenpaa SL, Markus ML (2018) Data perspective in digital platforms: three Tales of genetic platforms. Proc 51st Hawaii Int Conf Syst Sci:4574–4583

Kennedy-Eden H, Gretzel U (2012) A taxonomy of mobile applications in tourism a taxonomy of mobile applications in tourism a taxonomy of mobile applications for tourism. E-Rev Tour Res 10:47–50

Kenney M, Zysman J (2016) The rise of the platform economy. Issues Sci Technol 32:61–69. https://doi.org/10.17226/21913

Korže SZ (2019) From industry 4.0 TO tourism 4.0. Innov Issues Approaches Soc Sci 12:1855. https://doi.org/10.12959/issn.1855-0541.iiass-2019-no3-art3

Lee D-I, Lee H, Yi J, Lim S (2017) How do we change our apprenticeships for dealing with industry 4.0? Krivet, Yeongi-gun

Lewandowski CM (2013) Choosing a future in platform economy. J Chem Inf Model 53:1689–1699. https://doi.org/10.1017/CBO9781107415324.004

Liberato P, Alén-González E, Liberato D (2016) A importância da tecnologia num destino turístico inteligente: o caso do Porto. Xix Congr Aecit 5:1–19

Liberato P, Liberato D, Abreu A et al (2018) Generation Y: the competitiveness of the tourism sector based on digital technology. In: Advances in intelligent systems and computing. Springer, Cham, pp 227–240

Madureira L, Gamito T, Ferreira D, Portela J (2013) Inovação em Portugal Rural – Detetar, Medir e Valorizar, 1ªEdição. Princípia Editora, Lda, Cascais

Marques R, Duarte R, Ferreira A et al (2018) Industry 4.0: facilitator of the low density territories sustainability. CAPSI 2018 Proc 21:10–20

Martins ML, Malta C, Costa V (2015) Viseu Mobile: a location based augmented reality tour guide for mobile devices. Dos Algarves a Multidiscip E J 26:8–26. https://doi.org/10.18089/DAMeJ.2015.26.1.1

Myers MD (1997) Critical ethnography in information systems. In: Information systems and qualitative research. Springer US, New York, pp 276–300

Natário M, Melo AI, Biscaia R et al (2019) The impact of the tourism of the historical villages of Portugal: a framework of analysis. Finisterra 54:21–36. https://doi.org/10.18055/finis14861

Peffers K, Tuunanen T, Gengler CE, et al (2006) The design science research process: a model for producing and presenting information systems research. Proceedings of the first international conference on design science research in information systems and technology (DESRIST 2006). pp. 83–106

Pereira FS (2013) Desenvolvimento de uma Aplicação Móvel para o Turismo. Universidade de Coimbra, Coimbra

Pereira DB (2016) Jogo Baseado na Localização para a Otimização da Experiência Turística Jogo Baseado na Localização para a Otimização da. Universidade do Porto, Porto

Pina A (2016) La usabilidad del sitio web de un destino turístico y sus efectos en la demanda: una aproximación a un índice de satisfacción digital turística. Universidad de Extremadura, Extremadura

Roblek V, Meško M, Štok ZM (2016) Digital sustainability in the fourth industrial revolution. In ENTRENOVA – Enterprise Research Innovation Conference. Rovinj, Croatia

Rodrigues S (2016) Quando a Tecnologia Falha: a figura da falha tecnológica no contexto da experiência turística. Instituto Politécnico de Leiria, Leiria

Rong K, Lin Y, Shi Y, Yu J (2013) Linking business ecosystem lifecycle with platform strategy: a triple view of technology, application and organisation. Int J Technol Manag 62:75. https://doi.org/10.1504/IJTM.2013.053042

Santos L, Pereira D, Beça P et al (2017) Aplicação móvel para divulgação do património natural no turismo Mobile app for natural heritage dissemination in tourism. Tur Desenvolv 1:1461–1473

Santos C, Melo A, Ferreira A et al (2020a) Projeto PlowDeR: Relatório Final, 1st edn. UA Editora – Universidade de Aveiro, Aveiro

Santos C, Melo A, Ferreira A et al (2020b) Projeto PLowDeR – Manual de Formação Avançada, 1st edn. UA Editora – Universidade de Aveiro, Aveiro

Schwab K (2018) The global competitiveness report 2018. Geneva

Schwab K (2019) The global competitiveness report 2019. Geneva

Silva J (2014) Gamificação em aplicações móveis para atividades turísticas baseadas em geolocalização. Universidade do Minho, Minho

Souza V d S, Varum CMDA, Eusébio C (2017) O Potencial da Gamificação Para Aumentar a Competitividade dos Destinos Turísticos: revisão de literatura baseada na Scopus/the potential of gamification to increase the competitiveness of tourist destinations: literature review based on

Scopus/El potenci. Rev Tur em Análise 28:91–111. https://doi.org/10.11606/issn.1984-4867.
v28i1p91-111

Tiwana A, Konsynski B, Bush AA (2010) Platform evolution: coevolution of platform architecture,
governance, and environmental dynamics. Inf Syst Res 21:675–687. https://doi.org/10.1287/
isre.1100.0323

Vassilakopoulou P, Skorve E, Aanestad M (2016) A commons perspective on genetic data
governance: the case of BRCA data. Proc 24th Eur Conf Inf Syst ECIS

Yıldız E, Davutoğlu NA (2019) The transition from industry 4.0 to tourism 4.0: smart hotels,
artificial intelligence and improvements in robotics. In: Efe R, Koleva I, Öztürk M, Arabacı R
(eds) Recent advances in social sciences. Cambridge Scholars Publishing, Newcastle, pp
229–242

Zysman J, Kenney M (2017a) Intelligent tools and digital platforms: implications for work and
employment. Intereconomics 52:329–334. https://doi.org/10.1007/s10272-017-0699-y

Zysman J, Kenney M (2017b) The next phase in the digital revolution: platforms, automation,
growth, and employment. Commun ACM 61(2):54–63

Releasing Cultural Tourism Potential of Less-privileged Island Communities in the Mediterranean: An ICT-enabled, Strategic, and Integrated Participatory Planning Approach

Dionisia Koutsi and Anastasia Stratigea

1 Introduction

In contemporary societies, culture constitutes an inseparable part of the urban and regional policy agenda, perceived by some as a sector that crosscuts all three pillars of sustainability (economy, society, and environment), while by others as the fourth pillar of sustainable development (Hawkes 2001; Astara 2014). Due to the culture's prominent position in communities, it also plays, in the one or the other way, a pivotal role in the fulfillment of each single goal of the Agenda 2030 (UCLG 2018). The realization of the exceptional role of culture in the twenty-first century has rendered it a critical resource and a key driver for achieving future development objectives (Pita da Costa 2017). Such objectives are strongly oriented toward the sustainable and resilient exploitation of *cultural resources* for maintaining cultural integrity, preserving local values and ecosystems, and generating new opportunities for employment and income; while giving rise to the experience-based *cultural tourism paradigm* (UNTWO 2018; Stratigea and Katsoni 2015, 2016). The latter seems to be an already quite noticeable and dynamic trend in the evolving tourism market—the supply side—in response to demand-driven patterns as to new, meaningful, and authentic tourism experiences (UNWTO 2018), roughly presented as a combination of four *'e'* words, namely, *e*ntertainment, *e*xcitement, *e*ducation, and *e*xperience of tourists (Stratigea and Katsoni 2015).

But what is exactly meant by culture and its content, namely, cultural resources or cultural heritage (CH)? This question has not a clear-cut answer. CH is created over thousands of years ago and is inherited to current generations, while it continuously

D. Koutsi (✉) · A. Stratigea
Department of Geography and Regional Planning, School of Rural and Surveying Engineering, National Technical University of Athens, Athens, Greece

© Springer Nature Switzerland AG 2021
R. P. Marques et al. (eds.), *The Impact of Tourist Activities on Low-Density Territories*, Tourism, Hospitality & Event Management,
https://doi.org/10.1007/978-3-030-65524-2_4

evolves through the perpetual *human–nature interaction*. It thus represents the past and the present, while demarcates the future of each single community. It encompasses the *tangible*, e.g., human settlements, industry, agriculture, but also the *intangible* elements of this interaction, e.g., aesthetics and spirituality, cultural identity and value systems, to name a few. As Harrison (2010) claims, for each tangible part of heritage, an intangible one "wraps" around it, creating an integral and indivisible whole that is experienced by people or managed by tourism managers. In his effort to clarify the meaning of culture, Richards (1999) reveals the close relationship between tourism and culture or cultural resources. According to his view, cultural resources can be grasped as the outcome of the social structure (e.g., perceptions, beliefs, values), what people do (e.g., behavioral patterns, traditions, lifestyle), and what they produce (e.g., cultural products, gastronomy). Thus, consumption of cultural resources by tourism, marking the *culture and tourism complex*, is not just about visiting cultural sites and monuments, i.e., the tangible footprint of CH, promoted by traditional cultural tourism models; but it also involves the consumption of the intangible elements of areas visited. This delineates the current view of *cultural tourism*, perceiving tangible and intangible elements of a certain tourist destination as a consolidated and coherent whole. This view is also reflected in the definition of cultural tourism by the World Tourism Organization, portraying this as "*a type of tourism activity in which the visitor's essential motivation is to learn, discover, experience and consume the tangible and intangible cultural attractions/products in a tourism destination. These attractions/products relate to a set of distinctive material, intellectual, spiritual and emotional features of a society that encompasses arts and architecture, historical and cultural heritage, culinary heritage, literature, music, creative industries and the living cultures with their lifestyles, value systems, beliefs and traditions*" (Richards 2018: 3). Such a definition unveils the strong relationship of culture and tourism and the tight linkages of cultural products, consumed by tourists, to the everyday life and habits of destinations' population (UNWTO 2018).

Counting over 39% of tourism arrivals in 2014 (UNWTO 2018), *cultural tourism* constitutes currently a *major trend* and an essential feature in many tourist destinations' profiles (Katsoni and Stratigea 2016), but also an attractive element that firmly influences visitors' destination choice. Rising interest in cultural tourism as well as relevant policy initiatives has resulted in its further specialization into several distinct place- and resource-based alternative forms, e.g., historical, natural, maritime, monument, and diving tourism, to name a few. A particular type of cultural tourism form, recently receiving much attention in terms of both attractiveness to visitors and concerns as to the CH preservation and sustainable exploitation, refers to the *dark tourism*. This form is associated with tourist activities intimately related to death and/or war disaster sites. Destinations falling into the "dark tourism" category are nowadays proliferating in the global tourist realm and are also varying in content, taking forms of concentration camps, sites of major human disasters, etc. (Sharpley 2009). Of rising importance is also a subset of dark tourism, the *battlefield tourism* that is linked to battlegrounds where historical martial events have occurred, e.g., incidents of World War I or II, and are witnessed through, e.g., martial installations' sites, sites of sunken ship and plane wrecks (Kunwar and Karki 2020). It should also be noted here that although land cultural resources and cultural tourism have been extensively explored during last decades, the same does not hold for maritime cultural resources. However, the latter are nowadays attracting interest in terms of both their preservation and sustainable exploitation as CH objects, in alignment with respective interest in maritime cultural or diving tourism, and policy developments addressing the multiple benefits expected by their sustainable exploitation (Koutsi and Stratigea 2019).

One distinguishable example of areas endowed with exquisite tangible and intangible, land and maritime, natural and cultural resources are small islands in the *Mediterranean Region* (Manera and Taberner 2006). Based on these resources, some of these islands are by far the most attractive and highly appreciated destinations in the world (Koutsi and Stratigea 2019). However, apart from some exceptions, small island regions in general but also a large number of Mediterranean island regions in particular are distinct examples of underdeveloped spatial entities. Moreover, they seem to face severe barriers in strengthening their position as tourist destinations in a rapidly evolving and highly demanding tourism market. *Insularity*, in this respect, causes a range of inadequacies and bottlenecks that result in a certain deficit as to the effectiveness of islands' developmental endeavors. Removal of insularity constraints and the tracking of more promising as well as place- and people-centered developmental trails of these peculiar spatial entities in the Mediterranean is the *motive* of this work.

The specific *goal* to be served, along these lines, is the sustainable exploitation of cultural resources in remote, lagging-behind insular territories in the Mediterranean Region; and the flourishing of these astonishing areas as distinct, authentic and qualitative, experience-based cultural tourism destinations. The structure of this work has as follows: in Sect. 2, insularity repercussions of Mediterranean island territories and cultural tourism perspective as a means for dealing with them are discussed; in Sect. 3, current concerns and planning streams are delineated and are integrated into the steps of a strategic participatory planning framework; in Sect. 4, the implementation of this framework in a specific case study—island of Leros, Greece—is exemplified, coupled with key empirical results produced, while finally in Sect. 5 some conclusions are drawn.

2 Insularity and Cultural Tourism Potential in Remote and Less-privileged Mediterranean Islands

The geographical borders of many European states, especially of the Mediterranean ones, incorporate island regions in their jurisdiction. Many of these regions, based on their cultural and natural assets, are by far some of the most attractive and highly appreciated tourist destinations, owning an international brand name, e.g., the island state of Malta, Ibiza in the Balearic Islands-Spain or Mykonos in the Aegean

Sea-Greece, to name a few. However, there are also a large number of islands that do not share the glory of the previous examples, they remain underdeveloped, and they are confronted with severe difficulties in their efforts to gain competitiveness as tourist destinations (Koutsi and Stratigea 2019). In most of the cases, small island regions are perceived as disadvantaged, fragmented and isolated, lagging-behind areas. The reason for that lies in a range of inadequacies that are summed up under the term *"insularity"* and confine successful outcomes of their developmental efforts (European Parliament 2019). Various researchers link insularity with *"smallness"* and *"remoteness"* or *"peripherality,"* emphasizing thus the limited geographical space and the water-based discontinuity, i.e., the natural barriers (sea) separating insular territories from the mainland, as the most distinguishable characteristics of island territories (Rontos et al. 2012), and the reason behind their unsuccessful developmental pattern. At this point, however, it should be noted that although insularity is a common attribute of almost all islands, its intensity is highly dependent on their proximity to the mainland (Mannion and Vogiatzakis 2007; Pungetti 2012).

According to Stratigea et al. (2017), insularity consequences are summarized as follows: location of islands in the state's periphery; confined geographical space and related availability of natural resources; a demographic pattern that is characterized by low density and an ageing, of low educational profile and digitally illiterate population, mainly employed in the agricultural or tourist sector (Chatziefstathiou et al. 2005); lack of economies of scale, delimiting the flourishing of local economy; bottlenecks that are due to geographical fragmentation and are mostly associated with the insufficient infrastructure for serving basic population needs (e.g., health and transport infrastructure). Furthermore, isolation and accessibility constraints are often causing difficulties for younger population groups in accessing educational opportunities, with higher education studies being usually associated with migration to the mainland. Limited labor market opportunities are also a defining factor and one that reinforces migration of youth and productive age groups to the mainland, further weakening the strength of the population pyramid. In addition to the above weaknesses, European islands and especially the Mediterranean ones are confronted with significant challenges as host regions of a large number of immigrants during the last few years. Greek islands, for example, being at the forefront of this immigrants' wave, are nowadays coping with severe consequences in social, economic, cultural, and environmental terms.

Flourishing of local economies in insular territories is constrained by the lack of economies of scale. Moreover, scarcity of natural resources (e.g., water, land or primary resources) leads, in most cases, to a certain shortage in agricultural and industrial products, thus increasing islands' reliance on more costly imports from distant larger markets. Higher transportation costs that are due to insularity also affect competitiveness of economic sectors and place severe barriers to the efforts of local businesses to become competitive counterparts in the European and international markets (Chatziefstathiou et al. 2005). A certain deficit also appears in skilled and highly educated human resources, resulting in low innovation rates and discourage of investments (Carbone 2018). This, in turn, prevents the flourishing of local economic sectors and causes the further loss of human power (Rontos et al. 2012). These constraints have so far led to an occasional and seasonal (summer period) mono-sectoral developmental pattern, largely based on mass tourism activities. This pattern is the source of significant environmental and social burden which, most importantly, goes beyond the carrying capacity of these limited geographical entities at certain time slots, while leaving island economies highly exposed to a volatile and sensitive to external shocks economic sector, i.e., tourism.

Insular territories in general are hosts of unique *natural features* (e.g., coastline configurations, NATURA 2000 regions, wetlands). However, many of these are quite fragile and vulnerable to drought and land degradation, rising sea level and coastal erosion (Margaras 2016). These pressures, being usually the outcome of unplanned decisions or thoughtless human activities, but also of disturbing developments of the external environment, e.g., climate change, when coupled with the low capacity of these regions to deal with them, place islands' communities and economies at risk of losing part of their scarce resources (e.g., water, arable land, or valuable ecosystems and coastal areas). Consequently, there is an urgent need to address the challenges that need to be dealt with in island regions and seek alternative pathways for achieving sustainability and resiliency objectives.

Apart from their exquisite natural attributes, island regions are hosts of extraordinary tangible and intangible *cultural resources*, both in land and maritime environments (Pungetti 2012). This holds especially true in small islands of the Mediterranean Region (Manera and Taberner 2006) and is the outcome of their exceptional geopolitical position at the intersection of three continents—Europe, Africa, and Asia—and their location at the crossroad of commercial sea routes (Stratigea et al. 2017). This has enabled a strong physical and cultural interaction among various places, civilizations, and cultures throughout the centuries. The overexploitation of these resources but also exogenous factors can place them at risk of loss, an issue that is currently gaining importance especially in the case of underwater cultural heritage (UCH) laying at the bottom of the Mediterranean Sea (Argyropoulos and Stratigea 2019a).

Speaking of the *Mediterranean scenery*, this is formed by approximately 5000 islands of different shapes and sizes (Mannion and Vogiatzakis 2007), which are marked by a highly contrasting topography and are exhibiting a unique topographical diversity and altitudinal differences, coupled with spectacular mainland and coastal backgrounds (Stratigea et al. 2017). A majority of these islands present a remarkable richness in natural heritage, with many of them being currently under protected areas' regime. From a *cultural resource* perspective, Mediterranean islands, as the settlements of some of the most significant civilizations, are disposing unique and multicultural remains (ENPI-CBC-MED 2015). Indeed, Mediterranean island landscapes have a great symbolic and historical value, while historical monuments and mediaeval settlements are preserved in most islands, bearing witness to their glory past (Vogiatzakis et al. 2008). Furthermore, the involvement of many of these islands in a range of historical events of European or even global significance, e.g., World War I and II, but also remains of their recent historical trajectories, renders them historical places of global reach. This involvement, in case of various Greek islands for example, took the form of foreign occupation or fatal war events taking place in the islands' territory and has left important evidence in the form of intangible (e.g., habits, language idioms, gastronomy, values), but also tangible remains (e.g., architecture and buildings, batteries and military installations, ship and plane wrecks) in their land and maritime environment (Koutsi and Stratigea 2019).

The aforementioned attributes of Mediterranean islands are perceived differently by *visitors* and their *inhabitants* (Vogiatzakis et al. 2008). The former consider the coastline as the great advantage of these areas; and they are keen on their remoteness, being translated into a chance to escape from noisy, polluted, and stressful urban environments, and combine entertainment with cultural authentic experiences. The latter realize insularity as a major constraint and a source of unenviable socioeconomic and environmental repercussions. And the question is: how can we combine natural and cultural heritage of endowed island territories in building attractive and authentic cultural tourism products? How win-win solutions can be produced, i.e., meeting visitors' desires and expectations as well as exploiting land and maritime resources for reaching sustainability and resilience objectives and wealth of these territories and their population? What should be the most suitable steps for planning the transition from remoteness to advantage and increase attractiveness of insular regions to local population and the external world? How can local population be engaged in such a planning exercise in order to manage own resources in alignment with own expectations? How can Mediterranean islands' cultural heritage of European or global reach be preserved and its messages be spread out to a wider audience? An attempt to properly respond to these questions is presented in the next sections.

3   The Methodological Framework

Current evolutions in the planning discipline that are relevant to cultural resource management endeavors and can partially deal with the previously raised questions are discussed in this section and are integrated into the steps of a strategic participatory methodological approach for carrying out relevant planning exercises.

3.1   Key Concerns Relevant to Cultural Heritage Planning Endeavors

Planners nowadays have to deal with wicked problems within a rapidly changing, globalized, and wired environment, key aspects of which are uncertainty and complexity. In accomplishing their tasks, they need a repertoire of *tools and approaches* that will allow them to (Stratigea 2015):

- Grasp potential future developments of the external to the study region/problem environment and the future world images these can produce, i.e., delineating the *decision environment*, within which solutions of planning problems need to be implemented.
- Sketch *community- and place-based solutions* of planning problems within each single decision environment.
- Delineate *policy pathways* that are plausible, gather consensus, and can steer the smooth transition from the current state to a desired end.

For dealing with uncertainty and complexity, planners are largely supported by evolutions in the planning discipline, among which the context of *strategic planning* is falling (Cooper 1995; David 2003; Cornish 2004; Boškovic et al. 2010). Strategic planning seeks to identify desired end states for a certain region and/or problem at hand and related policy paths leading to these states that are better adjusted to diversified external decision environments. *Key aspects* of strategic planning are as follows (Stratigea et al. 2016):

- *External environment*, where potential evolutions of a range of different fields, such as population and income patterns, market developments, technological concerns, climate change issues, political framework at the national and international level, etc., are explored. A combination of different developments in each specific field sketches distinct future images of the external environment, forming the decision context within which planning problems for a specific region need to be dealt with.
- *Internal environment,* referring to the study region and/or problem at hand, where key issues for getting further insight are as follows: (1) *Current state* of the study region and planning problem at hand or stated differently "where we currently stand.", implying a detailed exploration of socio-economic, environmental, technological, cultural, political, and value aspects. (2) *Desired future state* or "where we want to be in the future," usually expressed through a *vision* that is built upon views, desires, and expectations of local community groups. This introduces the need for a participatory vision-building process, aiming to identify the interests of the various societal groups and reach a compromise among them in order for a *consensus* to be built as to the desired end state or the vision to be pursued. (3) *Policy paths* that are capable of linking current to visionary state, namely, policy directions, measures, and actions that are adjusted to local value systems and can steer developments toward the desired end state.
- Strengths and weaknesses of the internal environment (study region) that are critical for coping with rising opportunities but also threats emerging from the external environment. Or stated differently, how developments of the external decision environment can affect progress and problem-solving in the study region. This is grasped by conducting a *SWOT analysis* as an integral part of each strategic planning exercise.

Managing the *culture-tourism complex* necessitates a multi-dimensional, cross-sectoral, and interdisciplinary approach, while bringing to the forefront the issue of cultural governance, i.e., a multi-spatial level and multi-stakeholders' consideration (Baltà Portolés et al. 2014; Argyropoulos and Stratigea 2019a, b). Such a management perspective needs also to be undertaken within a *decision environment—the external one*—demarcated by a number of international conventions and policy directions, with reference to both the global and the European levels. This unveils as a prevailing feature the issue of preservation and protection of cultural resources for current and future generations and stresses the importance of participatory, sustainable, and resilient cultural resource management for cultural tourism purposes (Ahmad 2006). The most important aspects of this decision environment, explored for the purposes of the empirical part of this work, are emerging from the following:

- "Protection of the World Cultural and Natural Heritage" and the "Safeguarding of the Intangible Cultural Heritage," stressing the value and interpretation of intangible cultural heritage for establishing place identity, social cohesion, cultural diversity, and creativity (UNESCO 1972, 2003)
- "International Cultural Tourism Charter," defining communities' involvement in cultural resource management, synergies' creation among stakeholders and adoption of sustainable tourism models that promote cultural identity (ICOMOS 1999)
- European Convention on the "Protection of the Archaeological Heritage (Revised)," addressing the protection of archaeological heritage as a source of the European identity and a resource of historical/scientific wealth, tackling also issues of archaeological interests in spatial planning endeavors (Council of Europe 1992)
- Convention on the "Protection of Underwater Cultural Heritage," defining UCH types of cultural importance and disentangling issues of ownership and public access (UNESCO 2001)
- European Agenda for "Culture in a Globalizing World," exploring the significance of culture with respect to tourism and providing input for the articulation of the objectives of a new EU Agenda for Culture and the drafting of innovative models of cooperation and partnerships' creation (European Commission (EC) 2007a)
- "Agenda for a Sustainable and Competitive European Tourism," placing sustainable tourism at the heart of policy agenda; stressing issues of protection and preservation of non-renewable cultural resources and the unbreakable links between culture and tourism; and adopting a holistic and integrated approach of tourism with the rest of the economic sectors and society (European Commission (EC) 2007c)
- "Europe, the World's No 1 Tourist Destination—A New Political Framework for Tourism in Europe," focusing on sustainable tourism issues and the promotion of a sustainable, responsible, competitive, resilient, and of high-quality European destinations' image (European Commission (EC) 2010)
- "European Strategy for more Growth and Jobs in Coastal and Maritime Tourism," promoting sustainable development and competitiveness of coastal and maritime tourism; and innovative alternative tourism forms for addressing economic

growth, social cohesion and environmental concerns (European Commission (EC) 2014)

Regarding the maritime cultural environment and particularly the UCH, additional policy considerations, related to the blue economy and Maritime Spatial Planning, need to be taken into account. Furthermore, in 1992 the issue of Integrated Coastal Zone Management (ICZM) came to the forefront in order for significant pressures, exerted on coastal areas, to be addressed. At the European Union (EU) level in this respect, of crucial importance is the creation of new, innovative, and effective ways of sustainable exploitation of maritime resources, a fact that is reflected in several policy documents, such as the EU Integrated Maritime Policy (IMP) (EC 2007b), the Blue Growth Strategy (EC 2012), and the Maritime Spatial Planning (MSP) (Directive 2014/89/EU). From a cultural resource perspective, it is worth noting here that although the role of UCH in pursuing sustainable heritage-led local development has not gained adequate attention, all three previously mentioned EU directions present a certain opportunity for its spatial delineation, preservation, and sustainable exploitation toward maritime cultural tourism directions.

An integral part of strategic planning is *scenario building*, with scenarios falling into a group of planning tools that are capable of effectively addressing uncertainty and complexity of spatial systems and their evolution (Lindgren and Bandhold 2003; Cornish 2004). The use of scenarios in planning exercises actually reflects a shift from the view that "the future is there to be predicted" to the one of a "socially-constructed future," where a systematic study of potential future developments is perceived as a way for creating "the most desirable end state." Key attributes of a scenario building process are *system-thinking* and *actor-thinking*. System-thinking is about thinking in layers of change, dependencies and interdependencies. It implies a deep insight into a (spatial) system and its components (subsystems) as well as their interrelationships, potentially revealing the key variables that can drive a system's change (Cornish 2004). *Actor-thinking* is taking for granted that the future is shaped by *actors' decisions and actions*, both inside and outside the study system (Godet et al. 2004). A thorough analysis of the actors' interests can thus provide a deeper understanding of potential future developments, based on power relationships, strategic moves, motives and attitudes, personal profiles, alliances, strengths, and weaknesses, to name a few (Lindgren and Bandhold 2003).

Speaking of strategic planning and the deployment of future scenarios for serving developmental goals, *community engagement* becomes an indispensable dimension of relevant endeavors (Healey 1997; Allegretti 2006; Boškovic et al. 2010; Abdalla et al. 2015; Stratigea 2015; Stratigea et al. 2018; Somarakis and Stratigea 2019). This emerges from the very nature of these tools as the means for gathering collective intelligence from a variety of actors, but also from the current understanding that community engagement in developmental planning studies is no longer optional, but it is imperative (Nalbandian et al. 2013). This holds even truer in case of planning exercises addressing the issues of *cultural resource management*, where communities' *right* but also *responsibility* to take part in decision-making processes are stressed (Trau and Bushell 2008; Rössler 2012; Panagiotopoulou et al. 2018a, b;

Koutsi and Stratigea 2019; Argyropoulos and Stratigea 2019a). Community engagement was rather underestimated in many relevant studies in the past (Jimura 2011), which had rated lower issues such as self-determination, cultural survival, and pride stimulation of local communities (Dyer et al. 2003). On the contrary, prominence was given to the integration of regions into a globalized trading system for reaping the economic benefits out of it (Higgins-Desbiolles 2003; Jamal and Dredge 2014). However, the convergence of the rising interest in cultural tourism and respective destinations (Richards 2014; Katsoni et al. 2017) on the one hand and the enriched planning repertoire of recent decades on the other has fueled new approaches in integrated and sustainable cultural tourism studies (Jamal and Dredge 2014; Stratigea and Katsoni 2015; Katsoni et al. 2017). These are mainly characterized by their *focus on people* in local contexts and small-scale bottom-up strategies for cultural tourism development (Scheyvens 2002). As Jureniene and Radzevicius (2014) notice, currently the world seems to realize the three powerful components of cultural tourism, being heritage protection, heritage management, and local community.

Currently, *community engagement* in planning cultural tourist development gains ground. Indeed, the number of studies that take into account the voices of local communities is proliferating, in order for tourism models that are respecting carrying capacity of destinations; are in alignment with visions, expectations, and needs of local communities; and are conforming to local value systems to be promoted (Buono et al. 2012; Bello et al. 2016). In shifting from a historically top-down, mainly driven by governments and tour operators, to a bottom-up approach targeting sustainable and resilient cultural tourism trails in destinations, *empowerment* of local communities and *participation* in relevant planning endeavors are of decisive importance (Sofield 2003). Such endeavors place local community groups as equals to policy makers and planners for: embedding indigenous knowledge in decision-making processes; and ending up with cohesive, authentic, experience-, and value-driven cultural tourism narratives as well as locally adjusted strategies to promote them. At the same time, they contribute to *community awareness raising* as to the imperative of safeguarding scarce, precious, sensitive, and non-renewable cultural resources.

Management of cultural resources for cultural tourism purposes is largely an issue of proper *spatial data management and communication / interaction*.

Spatial data management aims at collecting, analyzing, and visualizing qualitative and quantitative data on cultural resources and sketching, out of these data, attractive cultural tourism products or routes. Geographical Information Systems (GIS) are extremely important in this respect. Furthermore, empowerment and participation imply access to information that is strongly dominated by visual media in the form of *maps and images*, with textual description being an important subcomponent of such information (Hudson-Smith et al. 2002; Kahila and Kyttä 2009; Panagiotopoulou and Stratigea 2017). Maturity of GIS technology has allowed its extensive use beyond very technical environments and has broadened its potential for spatial data management and visualization of planning proposals in a GIS environment. This, coupled with Web developments, has brought forward *interactive Web-based GIS* exploitation as a bidirectional interactive approach that is capable of (Hansen and Prosperi 2005; Stratigea 2015; Panagiotopoulou and Stratigea 2017; Panagiotopoulou et al. 2018a): ensuring equal access to information; rendering participation more wide and substantial due to the better grasping of spatial data and problems; creating new perspectives for social inclusion; and strengthening democratic procedures that support efficiency of spatial decision-making.

Communication / interaction is largely facilitated by the use of Information and Communication Technologies (ICT) and their applications, enabling a number of actions, such as: digital cultural content creation, visualization, and managing; mapping of cultural resources and crowdsourcing (Brabham 2008; Oomen and Aroyo 2011; Duxbury et al. 2015; Panagiotopoulou et al. 2018a, b); effective marketing of cultural tourism products (Panagiotopoulou and Stratigea 2017), to name a few. Due to their potential, such tools are nowadays considered an integral part of *cultural tourism planning initiatives*, while marking the emerging *smart tourism development* paradigm (Gretzel et al. 2015).

Within the currently ICT-enabled environment and the plethora of applications for gathering, management, and communicating planning information, the concepts of *participatory e-planning* and *community e-engagement*—i.e. technology-mediated interaction in the planning context—are born, marking a newly emerging stream of research and practice in planning endeavors (Klessman 2010; Saad-Sulonen 2012). e-Planning and e-engagement are inherent to a digitally enabled planning process, effectively integrating spatial planning approaches, public participation, and visualization techniques; and steering new opportunities as well as innovative and inclusive solutions for dealing with wicked planning problems and ensuring wide engagement and thus commitment to planning outcomes (Panagiotopoulou and Stratigea 2017; Somarakis and Stratigea 2019).

Empowerment and engagement of local communities is nowadays largely enhanced by the Internet and Web-based applications, bringing to the forefront the concept of *digital citizenship*, i.e., online participation in societal issues (McNeal et al. 2007). Digital citizenship is largely supported, among others, by *social media*, perceived as quite popular means for interaction for a number of purposes; and a means that embeds actors in glocal (global and local) networks by using ICT-enabled and non-mediated networking for a shared purpose (Horelli and Wallin 2010). A broad and comprehensive definition of this new communication pattern is provided by Kaplan and Haenlein (2010), defining *"social media"* as a group of Internet-based applications that is grounded on ideological but also technological foundations of Web 2.0. From the perspective of e-planning, social media and networking allow the provision of e-services for community revitalization, the creation of community groups sharing the same concerns, the enlargement of space of people activity, the potential to map and transmit information about things happening in their neighborhood, and the e-engagement in dedicated e-planning exercises, to name a few.

The remarkable changes and innovations related to the maturity and wide use of GIS technology, the potential offered by ICT, and the advent of Web 2.0 and interactive Web-based GIS as well as the explosion in the use of social networks are currently penetrating the political, economic, cultural, and social realm and are expected to considerably alter the scenery of Web-enabled participation and a variety of e-planning exercises (Stratigea 2015), but also the demand and supply side evolutions of cultural tourism in the years to come.

3.2   Building up a Strategic ICT-enabled Participatory Framework for Planning Cultural Tourism

The aforementioned streams, prevailing in the planning discipline nowadays, have fed the development of a strategic ICT-enabled participatory framework for planning cultural tourism (Fig. 1).

Step 1 refers to the delineation of a *place- and community-based vision*, i.e., the end state of the strategic planning exercise. This is further specialized into a *goal* and related *objectives*, i.e., priority axes for planning interventions in order for the vision to be reached.

Step 2 is associated with the exploration of trends or policy directions—the external decision environment—as well as the internal one, i.e., the study region. With respect to the *external environment*, culture- and tourism-related dominant trends and interdependencies at the global and European scene are identified, as decisive factors that frame decision-making toward cultural resource management. This is combined with an in depth analysis of the *internal environment*, i.e., the study region, incorporating the survey of the *current state* of the area of concern (social attributes, local economic structure, infrastructures, natural characteristics, comparative advantages, problems, etc.); and the assessment of its strengths and weaknesses as well as opportunities and threats emerging from the external environment through a SWOT analysis. Furthermore, this step involves a thorough identification and GIS-mapping of cultural resources.

Based on the exploration of the external and internal environment as well as the mapping of cultural resources, in *Step 3*, *alternative cultural tourism future development scenarios* of the region under study are structured, each one accompanied by the description of a diversified *scenario narrative*. Particular emphasis, at this step, is placed on the spatial pattern of cultural resources and the building of scenario narratives that can effectively integrate these resources.

Step 4 forms the core of *community engagement* in the context of the case study. Its goal is to engage local community in assessing the proposed scenarios. More specifically, *participatory assessment*, conducted at this step, aims at gathering opinions as to the proposed scenarios as well as preferences of local communities for scenarios' prioritization and supports the choice of the prevailing one that embeds local expectations. Furthermore, community is engaged in rating priority axes that are set in Step 1. The outcome of this step is a certain planning decision, i.e., selection of the *dominant scenario* for serving sustainable, inclusive and

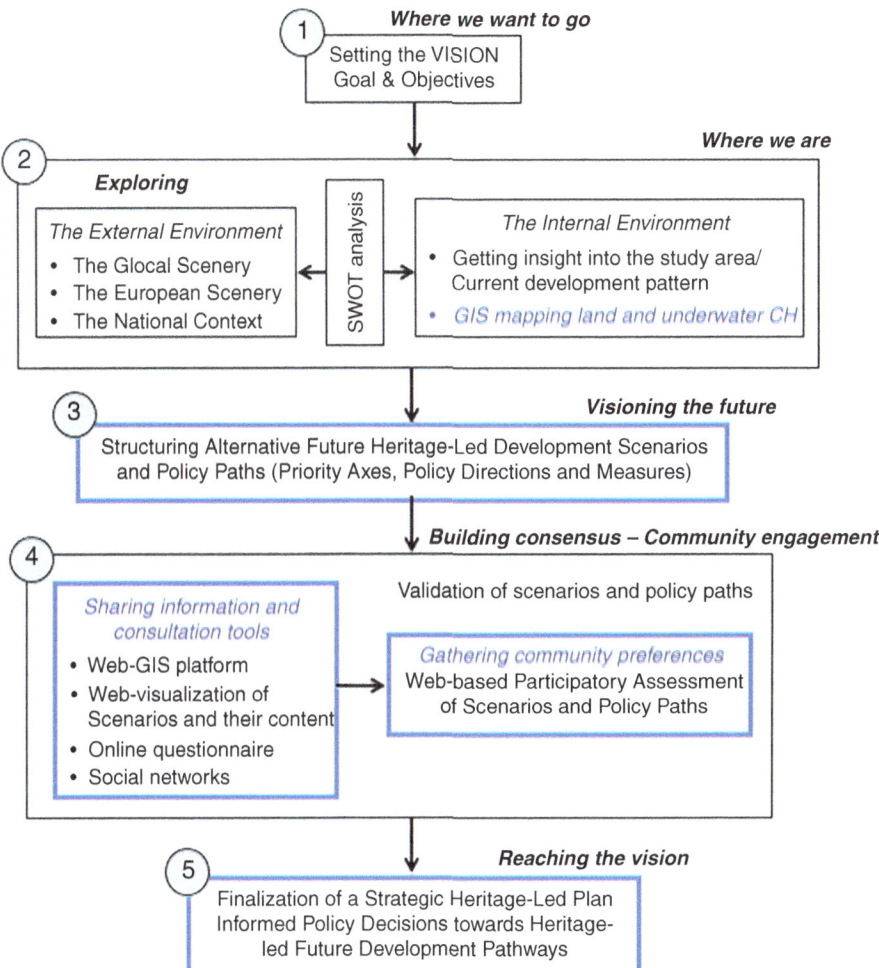

Fig. 1 Steps of the proposed strategic participatory planning framework for planning cultural tourism. Source: Adapted from Koutsi and Stratigea (2019)

resilient cultural tourism futures; and prioritization of policy directions for implementing this scenario that are in alignment with community preferences and expectations.

Finally, *Step 5* of the proposed participatory planning framework relates to the finalization of a strategic cultural tourism development plan, comprising the detailed description of the prevailing scenario and related policy paths, in order for more cohesive and informed policy decisions to be made for its implementation.

4   The Leros Island Region

A short description of the Leros case study is provided in the following, coupled with discussion on the results obtained from the implementation of the proposed methodological framework of Fig. 1.

4.1   Setting the Scenery: The Leros Case Study

Before embarking on the implementation of the proposed methodological framework for cultural tourism planning in the specific case study of Leros, it is important to realize the very peculiar nature and attributes of this specific remote, fragmented, and less-privileged Mediterranean island territory.

Leros, although part of the complex of the south-eastern Aegean Region (Fig. 2), has not followed developmental pathways of other islands of this region, being tourist destinations of global reach (e.g., Rhodes, Kos). On the contrary, various historical events and political choices through time have rendered this island *a place of isolation and abandonment*; and a *lagging-behind* small island in developmental terms, compared to other Aegean or Dodecanese counterparts.

A distinguished feature of this region in its historical trajectory is *foreign occupation*, rendering Leros the crossroad of various civilizations and cultures in different time slots. This was mainly due to its attractive location as a strategic natural fortress in the Aegean Sea, a privileged location though loading the island with many traumatic events (Koutsi and Stratigea 2019). Indeed, the historical trajectory of

Fig. 2 Geographical location of Leros Island. Source: Leros (2020), Areianet (2020)

Leros was marked by Turkish occupation for more than one and a half centuries (1648–1821); Italian occupation until World War II period (1912–1943); and German occupation during 1943–1948, beyond which Leros was annexed to the Greek state.

The most remarkable of these occupation time slots was the Italian one, which had transformed Leros into a heavily fortified aeronautical base for serving Italian dominance over the Mediterranean Sea (Koutsi and Stratigea 2019; Argyropoulos and Stratigea 2019b). This was due to the excellent, deep water port of Lakki, the largest natural port in the Eastern Mediterranean. The role of Leros as an Italian aeronautical base had a catalytic effect on the island's spatial organization and development pattern, marked by: the construction of a number of military installations across the island, such as fortifications, firearm locations, gun emplacements, to name a few; and the establishment of the Lakki harbor as a base for the Italians' supremacy in the Mediterranean in general and the Dodecanese island complex in particular. Many remains of this time slot are still intact and today yet accessible, constituting an outstanding ensemble of history and culture and a bedrock for cultural tourism, if adequately preserved and properly promoted to potential market niches. Large infrastructural projects were also deployed in this period, such as the central road network, linking diverse areas of Leros Island and serving transportation needs even today. Of great cultural interest are also the particular architectural buildings in the city of Lakki, exuberantly exuding the scent of Italian architecture in the island (Kostopoulos 2005). The end of the Italian occupation and the transition to the German one was accomplished through a quite notable, for its human and arms' loss, event of World War II, the famous naval battle widely known as *"The Leros Battle'* or *'Operation Typhoon"* (November 1943). Lasting 22 days, the Leros Battle resulted in a significant amount of underwater historical remnants (Mentogiannes 2004). Indicative land and underwater remains of this period are depicted in Fig. 3.

It is worth noting here that the World War II period (1939–1945) was marked by extensive naval warfare and military operations, many of which took place in the *"Mediterranean Theater"* (Argyropoulos and Stratigea 2019a, b). However, and despite the abundance of UCH as remnants of famous battlefield scenes, witnessing historical events of this period in the Mediterranean (e.g., in Croatia, southern France, Greece, Italy, and Malta, including North Africa), the *narratives* of many of these Mediterranean scenes and sunken heritage (ship and plane wrecks) are largely unknown today; while many of them still lie underexplored or fully unexploited and, most importantly, unprotected by international conventions and, in many cases, national laws (Argyropoulos and Stratigea 2019b). Leros is one of these scenes, the ground for *"The Battle of Leros,"* which has left behind important and of multiple origin (Greek, Italian, German, etc.) remnants, some of which were holding iconic status for the Greek nation, e.g., RHNS Vasilissa (Queen) Olga (Thoctarides and Bilalis 2015).

In its recent history in the second half of the nineteenth century and beyond, the "image" sent out by Leros Island is the one of a *"Soul House."* This is the outcome

Fig. 3 Indicative land and underwater cultural heritage—(U)CH—in Leros Island—World War II remnants. (**a**) War museum "Deposito di Querra" (Lerosisland.gr 2020) (**b**) Destroyer 'Queen Olga', sunk in 26 September 1943 in Lakki Bay (Collings 2008) (**c**) JUNKERS JU 52, sunk in the Battle of Leros, 13 November 1943 (Collings 2008) (**d**) ARADO 196, German hydroplane (Collings 2008)

of notably *political choices* that had rendered Leros (Koutsi 2018; Koutsi and Stratigea 2019):

- A *concentration camp* for mentally disturbed people (1957–1992), taking over the extensive military installations left on the island by the Italian occupation time slot ("The Europe's guilty secret" or a "hidden scandal" for human rights, as noticed by Observer in 1989)
- An *exile camp* for dissidents during the Greek dictatorship period (1967–1974)
- A *"hot spot"* for hosting part of the refugees' wave, embarking on the Easter Aegean islands' complex (2016–today)

This "image" has largely traumatized Leros' destiny and developmental trajectory, leaving unexploited the extraordinary cultural but also natural local assets. It has also negatively affected the local economic structure through time (unemployment rates rise to 11% in 2011) and social cohesion, while local population (7917 inhabitants in 2011 census) and administration are struggling for altering this image toward more promising future developmental pathways.

Taking into consideration the drawbacks and constraints emanating from Leros historical course, but also comparative advantages drawn from *insularity* (Spilanis 2012), the cultural tourism planning exercise in Leros Island is a quite challenging effort. In fact, it aims at combining goals related to both: the *"big picture,"* i.e., preserving European cultural heritage remains and integrating their tangible and intangible aspects in order for their meanings to be effectively conveyed to future generations, thus safeguarding European history, identity, and memory; and the *more partial but equally important* one, i.e., the integrated, sustainable, and resilient exploitation of tangible and intangible, natural and cultural, land and maritime resources for reversing the unpleasant destiny of Leros Island and reaping the benefits of current cultural tourism market trends.

In seeking to achieve this twofold goal, a strategic planning exercise is conducted based on the aforementioned methodological framework (Fig. 1), with work carried out in each step and results obtained being discussed in the following subsection.

4.2 Implementation of the Proposed Framework and Results

The starting point of this exercise is the realization that Leros Island constitutes an extraordinary and unique example in the Mediterranean Region that disposes historically significant land and maritime as well as tangible and intangible cultural remains of *glocal (global and local) importance*. It is host of a remarkable natural beauty (NATURA 2000 regions and wildlife shelters, landscapes of outstanding beauty and wetlands) and a rich World War II land CH and especially UCH, counting for fourteen well-located sunken ship and plane wrecks in the island's maritime environment, all linked with World War II fatal events.

4.2.1 Vision, Goal, and Objectives

For handling the Leros exquisite cultural wealth toward a cultural tourism perspective, a *vision* is created. As such is perceived the shift of the island's image from a place of isolation, abandonment, underdevelopment, and social banishment to a place of multi-nature, experience-based cultural tourism activities. The *goal* is delineated as the "sustainable and resilient exploitation of natural and cultural, land and underwater, tangible and intangible CH." Furthermore, a number of objectives or priority axes are outlined at this step, emanating from identified key challenges of this particular case study and tracing out key directions for policy action in order for the vision and goal to be reached. These are (Koutsi and Stratigea 2019):

- Designation of local cultural identity as a pillar for sustainable cultural tourism through GIS mapping of natural and cultural resources, and realizing their very essence and value

- Treatment of land CH and UCH in an integrated way, since both are parts of the same narrative, i.e., Italian occupation and World War II fatal events
- Integrated view of natural and cultural resources, co-existing in many parts of the island and enriching the value and experience gained out of them
- Development of alternative, authentic, experience-based, cultural tourism products in alignment with the globally noticeable tourism trends and policy priorities as to the "culture-tourism" complex
- ICT-enabled promotion of land CH and UCH as a key factor for dealing with fragmented and geographically isolated areas, such as the lagging-behind island regions; and providing direct access to specific tourism niches
- Enhancement of local entrepreneurship and creation of value chains for strengthening local economy and boosting extroversion of local authentic cultural tourism products
- Raising awareness of local community on the value of natural and cultural resources, stressing preservation and sustainable exploitation concerns
- Spatially balanced cultural tourism development and removal of internal inequalities by promoting an evenly dispersed cultural tourism pattern

4.2.2   Exploring the External and Internal Environment

Having sketched the vision, goal, and objectives of the Leros planning exercise, a deep insight is acquired with respect to the external and internal (study region) environment. As to the *external environment*, the global tourism market trends from the demand and supply side, cultural heritage preservation policies and international conventions (see subsection 3.1), policies promoting "culture-tourism complex" at the national and European level, regional policies related to developmental aspects of fragmented insular communities, European directions as to the protection of natural resources, sustainability and resilience objectives, etc., are explored. Speaking of the *internal environment*, a thorough analysis of socio-economic, demographic, educational, cultural, environmental, technological, and infrastructural aspects is conducted. The study of both the external and the internal environment has provided the ground for conducting a SWOT analysis of the study region, reflecting the identification of its strong and weak points as well as the way these can be used or improved respectively in order to effectively cope with opportunities and threats of the external environment.

Furthermore, of critical importance at this stage is the use of *GIS technology* for mapping cultural assets that can set the ground for building strategies and effective policies towards specific forms of cultural tourism products and related activities. In the present study, GIS mapping and content creation of cultural (Fig. 4) and natural resources is accomplished, in order for a *twofold goal* to be served, namely, to: provide *geospatial information* as to the distribution of these resources in the land and maritime part of the study area and thus facilitate the planning endeavor; and form the ground for the development of a *Web-GIS platform* and related application

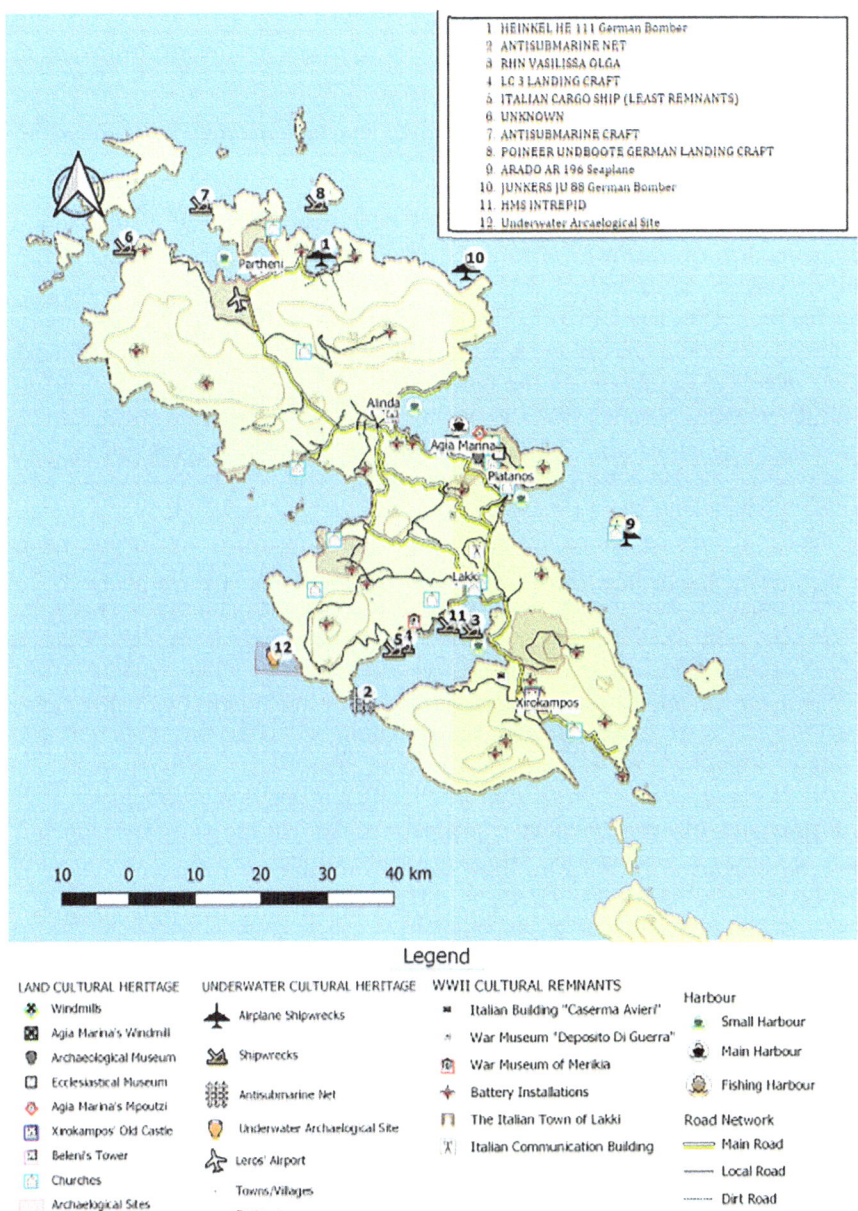

Fig. 4 Leros Island—GIS mapping of cultural resources, Source: Koutsi (2018)

for engaging Leros local community in the assessment and prioritization of planning proposals.

4.2.3 Visioning Alternative Future Trails

Building up the image of an attractive, sustainable, and competitive cultural tourist destination is the outcome of a successful planning endeavor (Hudson et al. 2004). This endeavor aims at capitalizing on local assets, while it also has to promote sustainable and resilient forms of cultural tourism that are both consistent with local aspirations and well-adjusted to global tourism as well as other prevailing trends or policy directions (Stratigea and Katsoni 2015).

In this respect, planning needs to explore a number of strategic policy options ahead that can effectively establish the "link" between the local and the global context, assuring that communities and regions can compete, in a successful way, in the evolving global scene (Stokes and Wechler 1995; David 2003). It also implies a meaningful balance among different stakes and expectations of various stakeholders' groups (Stratigea 2015), while embodying in the planning outcome the current social and environmental concerns, as tourism is an industry heavily capitalizing on nature's endowments and society's cultural heritage (Stokes and Wechler 1995; Cooper 1995).

Based on the previous mentioned work, such a multi-objective balance was sought in Leros case study through the structuring of *alternative scenarios* that constitute a portfolio of possible and plausible future states, fulfilling goals and objectives of the specific study region within different decision environments.

Effort is also placed on the mild exploitation of the valuable local assets, in order for a compromise between their role as a vehicle for local economic development and social cohesion on the one hand; and their protection for serving cultural resilience purposes on the other, to be attained. Finally, special care is also taken for reaching a *spatially balanced exploitation pattern*, fulfilling thus equity developmental aspects and revocation of socio-economic disparities in the study region.

In structuring these scenarios, the *"two uncertainty axes"* scenario building methodology was applied (Jäger et al. 2007). As key uncertainty axes were perceived the (Koutsi and Stratigea 2019) (Fig. 4):

- *Spatial pattern* of cultural tourism development, hypothesizing either a concentrated or a de-concentrated spatial pattern.
- *Thematic approach* of scenarios, being either *mono-thematic*, exclusively linking the island's cultural tourism narrative to World War II events and remains, i.e., building up a 'story' that presents the region's specialization in World War II cultural heritage or battlefield tourism; or *multi-thematic*, integrating multiple cultural heritage themes inherent in Leros Island, which represent the multifarious past of the island—various occupations through time—and reveal trails left in the built and social environment.

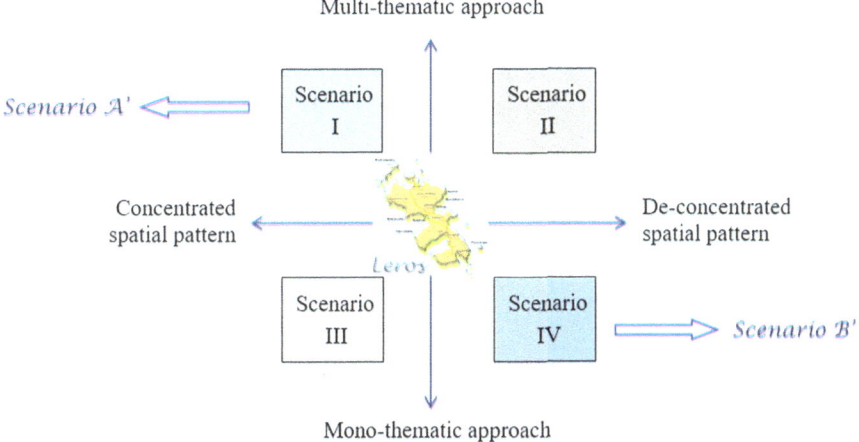

Fig. 5 "Two uncertainty axes" scenario building approach for exploring potential future trails of cultural tourism development in Leros Island. Source: Koutsi and Stratigea (2019)

In a rough pre-evaluation of the four distinct future images of Fig. 5 on the basis of a range of criteria (e.g., competitiveness of Leros in the Dodecanese islands' complex, relevance of cultural resources to World War II, spatial distribution of cultural resources in land and maritime regions, rising trends toward maritime cultural and/or diving tourism, to name a few), it seems that scenarios I and IV take precedence and are selected for further specialization as the most challenging and relevant options for Leros region. Based on this scenarios' choice, the spatial deployment and the respective narratives accompanying them are shortly outlined. For simplicity reasons, in the following text, Scenario I is referred to as Scenario A' and Scenario IV as Scenario B'.

4.2.4 Scenario A': "Leros: From a 'Soul-House' to a Place of Multiple-Opportunities"

The scope of Scenario A' is to shift the image of Leros from a "Soul House" to a place of multiple opportunities. This is to be achieved by a *multi-thematic, spatially concentrated model* of future cultural tourism development, with emphasis on balanced, heritage-led, local development concerns. As to its spatial formulation, a *polycentric spatial deployment* is predicted by establishing *four distinct nodes*, evenly dispersed throughout Leros Island (Fig. 6). Each of them bears a specific cultural identity, thus sending out positive development impulses to its areas of influence. The scenario follows a *multi-thematic* cultural tourism development perspective integrating, in a structured way, aspects of the strong World War II cultural heritage message into other important natural and cultural attributes of the study area. Each of the four prevailing nodes, i.e., "vehicles" for spreading cultural development in their surrounding spatial entities, is crosscut by respective *cultural*

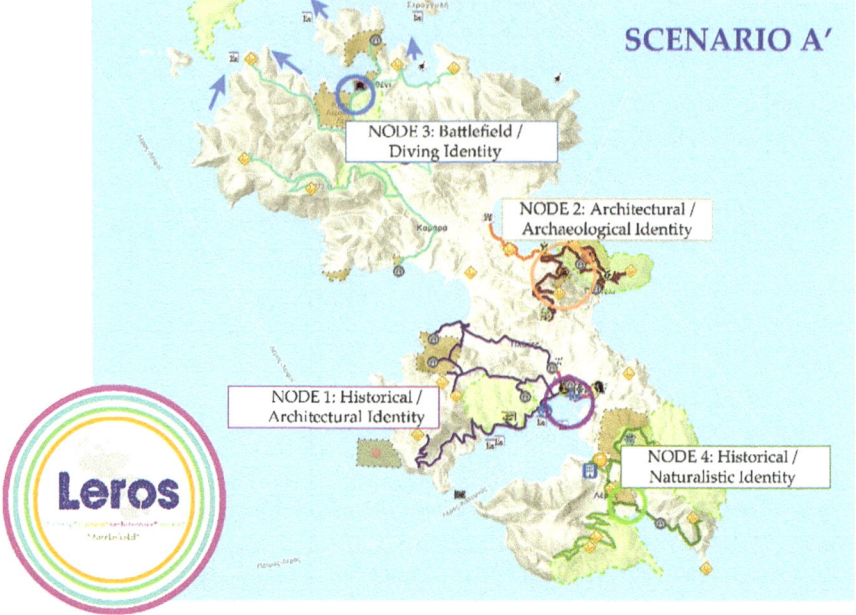

Fig. 6 Narrative and spatial delineation of cultural tourism development in Scenario A'—Four cultural tourism nodes and related routes surrounding each node. Source: Koutsi (2018); Koutsi and Stratigea (2019)

routes, each of which links and promotes tangible and intangible cultural heritage attributes of both land and underwater parts of the island. Scenario A' promotes a *variety of alternative tourism forms*, such as religious tourism, nature tourism, cultural tourism, diving tourism, etc., thus opening up a range of cultural tourism opportunities and providing the chance to encounter a wide range of diversified cultural tourism experiences.

4.2.5   Scenario B′: "Leros: An 'Open Museum' of the European Cultural Heritage and Identity"

In Scenario B′ (Fig. 7), a mono-thematic approach is adopted, having as prevailing feature the Italian occupation (1912–1943) and the World War II historical events. This choice is grounded on the strong and decisive influence these have had on the socio-cultural, economic, and spatial development of the island through time and the important remains of this period in both the land and marine environment, witnessing trails of the foreign occupation, important military actions of the European but also global history, and, ultimately, the confrontation of different political ideologies and civilizations on the land of Leros.

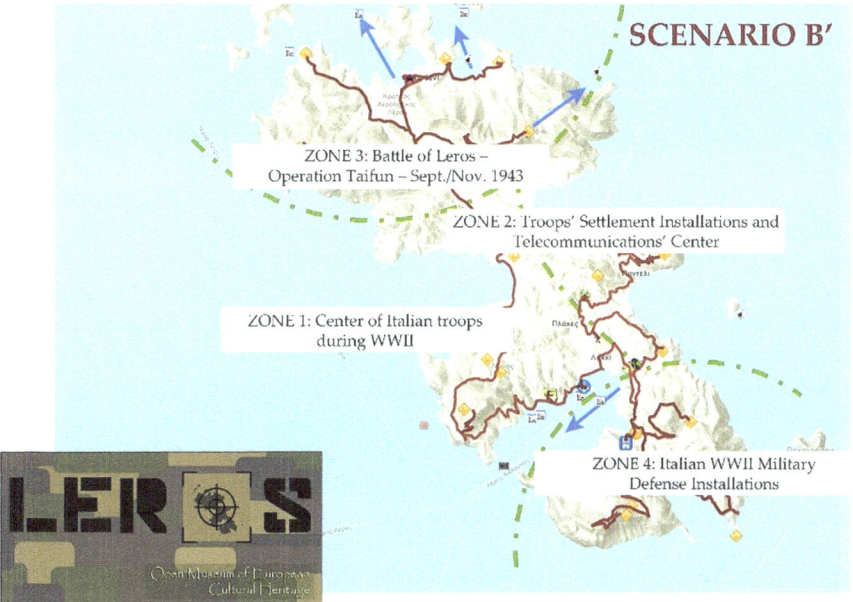

Fig. 7 Narrative and spatial delineation of future cultural tourism development in Scenario B′—Zones (green intermittent lines) and the Unified Cultural Route (continuous dark red line) crossing Leros as a whole. Source: Koutsi (2018); Koutsi and Stratigea (2019)

Sustainable and resilient exploitation of these tangible and intangible land and maritime World War II cultural remains attempts to place Leros in the rapidly evolving geography of "Battlefield/Dark" tourism destinations, a remarkable node in the Aegean, but also in the Mediterranean Region and Europe as well. The narrative of Scenario B′ has at its heart the development of Leros as an 'Open Museum' of the European Cultural Heritage and Identity. This 'Open Museum' tale is realized through the establishment of a 'History and Culture Route' which traverses the island as a whole, both in the land and maritime environment; incorporates particular locations and places, where historical facts took place; and represents a painful but also constructive trajectory of Leros Island per se, and a "lessons learnt" footprint of the European and world's history. In such a context, the area of the island was divided into four distinct zones, which comply with the narrative of the island's history (Fig. 7).

4.2.6 Building Consensus: Community Engagement

Building consensus or more specifically rating scenarios' preferences and priority axes for reaching the vision is pursued at this stage by engaging Leros community through digitally enabled interaction. In support of this e-participatory assessment process, a Web-GIS application was deployed (Koutsi 2018) by the use of the ESRI Story Maps, complemented also by its counterpart mobile phone application for further impacting community engagement. This aimed at fully delineating the scenarios' narratives, the natural and cultural resources addressed to each narrative (e.g., location, type, content), and the way these resources were integrated into cultural tourism nodes and routes.

Members of the Leros community were invited to use the Web-GIS application and, by means of an online questionnaire (Google Docs' form), express their views with respect to the: assessment of the current state of the island's cultural development; rating of preferences as to the proposed scenarios; selection of most relevant priority axes (selection of three out of the eight proposed) for implementing the proposed scenarios; suggestion of scenarios and related narratives' improvements.

Promotion actions notifying local community of the Leros cultural planning exercise and Web-GIS application and attracting people to engage incorporated targeted communication through cultural associations, local press (E-Leros and Leros news), diving schools, and travel agencies; but also a campaign through Facebook and Instagram, addressing an audience that fulfilled certain criteria, namely: being residents of Leros Island or persons originated from there, falling into the 18-65+ age groups, and being interested in themes associated with World War II, diving, Leros island, cultural tourism, wrecks, tourism, Aegean Sea islands, and/or alternative tourism.

The online questionnaire was available for three months (June to August 2018), while the targeted campaign through Facebook and Instagram was carried out for the time span 17 June–17 August 2018 and attracted 799 interactions/likes and 8038 views. Out of this Web interaction, *204 questionnaires* were reaped, a crop that was perceived as satisfactory, taking into consideration the profile of population of the study region, i.e., educational and communication skills as well as experience in relevant e-participation endeavors.

Respondents' gender profile was balanced, both in total and within age groups considered, with a slight precedence of women (54%). The majority of respondents fell into the 18–35 (52%) and 36–50 (30%) age groups that exhibit a greater familiarization and skills for handling internet applications and social media. People engaged had a high (57% possess PhD, MSc, or University Degree) or medium educational profile (42% are high or technical school graduates), while 11% of respondents were unemployed and 9.8% university students.

As far as the very essence of responses is concerned, this sums up as follows (Koutsi 2018; Koutsi and Stratigea 2019):

- A large share of respondents perceived land and underwater cultural resources in Leros Island as largely underexploited.
- Respondents realized the uniqueness of the island's World War II cultural heritage and its potential for serving sustainable local development and cultural tourism objectives; while they also pointed out the need for a more systematic and integrated cultural tourism planning approach, addressing long-term prosperity objectives of the region in a sustainable and resilient way.

- Respondents appraised the narrative presented by Scenario B′—a narrative of local but also European and global reach—as more relevant and one sustaining a unique identity and a competitive advantage of this small island in the Aegean Sea; while revealing the value attached by the local community to World War II events and their remnants, sealing the "body" (land and maritime), the history, and the people of Leros in the past and present, and eventually in the future, in case this plan is successfully implemented.
- Highest precedence was given to three priority axes, namely, "designation of local cultural identity as a pillar for economic development and social cohesion," "development of alternative, experience-based, cultural tourism products," and "balanced cultural tourism development for removing local inequalities."
- Finally, of great importance were replies of people in the open question, requesting proposals for improvement of the designed narratives. These, although small in number (nine replies), have revealed the passion of people for their history, identity, and values and their concern for keeping them alive for the future generations.

4.2.7 Reaching the Vision

Based on the outcomes of the e-participatory process, a Heritage-Led Local Development Plan was developed, accompanied with a policy path, i.e., a set of policy directions, measures, and targeted policy actions for implementing this plan. This policy path aims at achieving a sustainable, integrated, durable, and innovative exploitation of available natural and cultural resources, while also coping with obstacles imposed by the geographical and social isolation of Leros Island.

5 Conclusions

"Culture is the fountain of our progress and creativity" (von Droste 2012:14). This wording unveils the outstanding importance of cultural heritage for the global community and the obligation to handle it with discretion and in a sustainable and resilient way so that the messages this carries to remain intact and be successfully handed out to future generations. It also reveals, in a rather unconditional way, that concern should be addressed to both tangible and intangible, in land or submerged, cultural and natural elements of this heritage, considering these as: indispensable parts of keeping spiritual values, identity, tradition, and memory; and a motor for promoting creativity and progress. This statement becomes extremely important in times of globalization that favor branding and cultural standardization, within which cultural heritage is becoming a pillar for keeping alive *identity, historical memory*, and *roots* of local communities.

Concurrently, cultural heritage is perceived as a valuable resource and a bedrock for *sustainable & resilient urban and regional development*. This is largely grounded on the integration of culture with tourism—the culture-tourism complex—and is justified by the noticeable global tourist trend towards the "consumption" of authentic cultural and aesthetic products. Such a development perspective has fueled a *"cultural turn"* of cities and peripheral regions; and has recently attracted planners and policy makers' attention in seeking *place- and people-centered options and policy paths* for exploiting cultural assets in a *sustainable, durable, creative and resilient way*. This cultural turn and related focus on cultural tourism planning endeavors embeds cultural resources as an integral part in the way planners and policy makers evaluate the past and plan for the future. It thus renders culture an overarching and underpinning aspect for durable heritage-led development that is enriched by *intrinsic spiritual and unique values* of *societal knowledge* and *identity*. Additionally, it initiates lasting improvements in cities and communities by transforming, in a sustainable and resilient way, cultural heritage assets into market-driven commodities, with multiple benefits that touch upon the economic, the social, the spatial and the individual realm.

The evolving planning repertoire arms nowadays planners with appropriate means for effectively realizing this turn, i.e., tools and approaches needed to shift to more community- and place-based strategic and participatory planning endeavors when dealing with cultural resource management issues. This is a promising advancement, taking into consideration the peculiarities of each single study region; the vulnerability of these resources in a turbulent and unstable environment, calling for more long-term planning approaches; and the necessity to grasp the relevance of cultural heritage for society.

In the cultural wealthy Mediterranean islands, rating though high as to a variety of risks, e.g., climate change impacts, loss of biodiversity, urbanization, and immigration, to name a few, sustainable and resilient exploitation of tangible and intangible, land CH and exceptional UCH is of major importance in seeking to weaken insularity bottlenecks and pursue long-term prosperity objectives. The proposed methodological approach addresses these concerns and attempts to establish a mutual learning platform for all three planning counterparts, namely, planners, decision makers, and local population; while it also increases cultural resource awareness and responsibility of local population. By integrating current planning streams with powerful and limitless ICT-enabled tools, such as Web-GIS and social networks, communication of cultural planning outcomes to a large audience is achieved; and an interaction is established that allows local 'flavor' to be embedded in technically prescribed planning outcomes. Empirical results of this effort in Leros case study, though reflecting that part of population that disposed the necessary skills, indicate that the new, mature and of low cost, ICT and Web 2.0 arsenal and related applications need to be factored into cultural heritage management and interpretation, provided that digital readiness of island communities is improved. However, the experience of authors shows that precedence of face-to-face interaction can further improve e-engagement results, being a prerequisite in order for trust, necessary for people to engage, to be established. Worth noting is also the eagerness of those engaged to become agents of change of Leros destiny, challenging insularity drawbacks and using heritage as their own single "weapon."

References

Abdalla S, Elariane S, El Defrawi S (2015) Decision-making tool for participatory urban planning and development: residents' preferences of their built environment. J Urban Plan Dev 142 (1):04015011

Ahmad Y (2006) The scope and definitions of heritage: from tangible to intangible. Int J Herit Stud 12(3):292–300

Allegretti U (2006) Verso una nuova forma di democrazia: la democrazia partecipativa. Democrazia e Diritto 3:7–13. (in Italian)

Areianet Leros Map. http://www.hri.org/infoxenios/english/dodecanese/leros/ler_map.html. Accessed 15 Jan 2020

Argyropoulos V, Stratigea A (2019a) Sustainable management of underwater cultural heritage: the route from discovery to engagement – open issues in the Mediterranean. Heritage 2:1588–1613. https://doi.org/10.3390/heritage2020098

Argyropoulos V, Stratigea A (2019b) Linking WWI and II underwater cultural heritage to sustainable development in the Mediterranean: an integrated participatory strategic planning approach. In: International conference on the Management of accessible underwater, cultural and natural heritage sites: dive in blue growth, Athens, October 2019

Astara OH (2014) Culture as the fourth pillar of sustainable development. SDCT J 1a–2a:93–102

Baltà Portolés J, Čopič V, Srakar A (2014) Literature review on cultural governance and cities. Kultur 1(1):183–200

Bello FG, Lovelock B, Carr N (2016) Enhancing community participation in tourism planning associated with protected areas in developing countries: lessons from Malawi. Tour Hosp Res 18(3):309–320. https://doi.org/10.1177/1467358416647763

Boškovic D, Saftic D, Trošt K (2010) Planning and organizing tourist destinations – the example of the rural Istria cluster. In: Proceedings of the 20th Biennial international congress tourism & hospitality industry, Opatija, 6-8 May 2010

Brabham DC (2008) Crowdsourcing as a model for problem solving: an introduction and cases. Convergence 14:75–90

Buono F, Pediaditi K, Carsjens GJ (2012) Local community participation in Italian national parks management: theory versus practice. J Environ Policy Plan 14(2):189–208

Carbone G (2018) Expert analysis on geographical specificities. cohesion policy 2014-2020. Final report. Available via Europa.eu. https://ec.europa.eu/regional_policy/sources/docgener/studies/pdf/expert_analysis_geographical_specificities_en.pdf. Accessed 5 Mar 2020

Chatziefstathiou M, Spilanis I, Charalambous A (2005) Sustainable development of island regions and the role of aquaculture. In: Proceedings of the EcoForum – 1st international conference for environmental management, policy and technology, Nicosia, Cyprus 28-30 June

Collings P (2008) Leros shipwrecks. Available via Leros active. http://lerosactive.com/main/images/2014-LEROSACTIVE-EBOOK.pdf. Accessed 30 Jan 2020

Cooper C (1995) Strategic planning for sustainable tourism: the case of the offshore islands of the UK. J Sustain Tour 3(4):191–209. https://doi.org/10.1080/09669589509510726

Cornish E (ed) (2004) Futuring: the exploration of the future. World Future Society, Maryland

Council of Europe (1992) European convention on the protection of the archaeological heritage (Revised), Valetta, Italy. 16 January 1992. Available via coe.int. https://rm.coe.int/168007bd25. Accessed 28 Feb 2020

David F (ed) (2003) Strategic management: concepts and cases. Prentice Hall, Upper Saddle River, NJ

Directive 2014/89/EU (2014) Establishing a framework for marine spatial planning. Available via EUR-Lex. https://eur-lex.europa.eu/legal-content/EN/TXT/PDF/?uri=CELEX:32014L0089&from=EN. Accessed 8 Mar 2020

Duxbury N, Garrett-Petts WF, MacLennan D (2015) Cultural mapping as cultural inquiry – introduction to an emerging field of practice. In: Duxbury N, Garrett-Petts WF, MacLennan D (eds) Cultural mapping as cultural inquiry. Routledge, New York, pp 1–42

Dyer P, Aberdeen L, Schuler S (2003) Tourism impacts on an Australian indigenous community: a Djabugay case study. Tour Manag 24:83–95

ENPI-CBC-MED (2015) Mediterranean stories, cultural heritage and sustainable tourism. Available via enpicbcmed.eu. https://issuu.com/andaluciasolidaria/docs/mediterranean_stories_cul tural_heri. Accessed 11 Mar 2020

European Commission (EC) (2007a) COM (2007)242 final: the "European agenda for culture in a globalizing world. Available via EUR-Lex. https://eur-lex.europa.eu/LexUriServ/LexUriServ. do?uri=COM:2007:0242:FIN:EN:PDF. Accessed 8 Mar 2020

European Commission (EC) (2007b) COM (2007)575 final: an integrated maritime policy for the European Union. Available via EUR-Lex. https://ec.europa.eu/maritimeaffairs/policy_en. Accessed 5 Mar 2020

European Commission (EC) (2007c) COM (2007)621: agenda for a sustainable and competitive European tourism. Available via EUR-Lex. https://eur-lex.europa.eu/legal-content/EN/TXT/? uri=CELEX%3A52007DC0621. Accessed 8 Mar 2020

European Commission (EC) (2010) COM(2010)352: Europe, the world's no 1 tourist destination – a new political framework for tourism in Europe. Available via EUR-Lex. https://ec.europa.eu/ growth/tools-databases/vto/policy/europe-worlds-no1-tourist-destination. Accessed 6 Mar 2020

European Commission (EC) (2012) COM(2012)494 final: blue growth—opportunities for marine and maritime sustainable growth. Available via EUR-Lex. https://ec.europa.eu/maritimeaffairs/ publications/blue-growth-opportunities-marine-and-maritime-sustainable-growth_en. Accessed 6 Mar 2020

European Commission (EC) (2014) COM(2014) 86 final: a European strategy for more growth and jobs in coastal and maritime tourism. Available via EUR-Lex. https://eur-lex.europa.eu/legal-content/EN/ALL/?uri=CELEX:52014DC0086. Accessed 8 Mar 2020

European Parliament (2019) Mediterranean insularity: challenges and future. Available via YouTube. https://www.youtube.com/watch?v=nTWy-0WY4bE&feature=youtu.be. Accessed 11 Mar 2020

Godet M, Monti R, Meunier F, Roubelat F (eds) (2004) Scenarios and strategies: a toolbox for problem solving. Cahiers du LIPSOR, Laboratory for Investigation in Prospective and Strategy, Paris

Gretzel U, Sigala M, Xiang Z, Koo C (2015) Smart tourism: foundations and developments. Electron Mark 25(3):179–188

Hansen HS, Prosperi D (2005) Citizen participation and internet GIS – some recent advances. Comput Environ Urban Syst 29(6):617–629. https://doi.org/10.1016/j.compenvurbsys.2005.07. 001

Harrison R (2010) What is heritage? In: Harrison R (ed) Understanding the politics of heritage. Manchester University Press, Manchester, pp 5–42

Hawkes J (ed) (2001) The fourth pillar of sustainability – culture's essential role in public planning. Cultural Development Network, Melbourne

Healey P (ed) (1997) Collaborative planning. Shaping places in fragmented societies. McMillan, London

Higgins-Desbiolles F (2003) Globalization and indigenous tourism: sites of engagement and resistance. In: Shanahan M, Truren G (eds) Globalization: Australian regional perspectives. Wakefield Press, Kent Town, pp 240–262

Horelli L, Wallin S (2010) The future-making assessment approach as a tool for e-planning and community development – the case of ubiquitous Helsinki. In: Silva CN (ed) Handbook of research on e-planning: ICTs for urban development and monitoring. Hershey, New York, pp 58–79

Hudson S, Ritchie B, Timur S (2004) Measuring destination competitiveness: an empirical study of Canadian ski resorts. J Hosp Tour Res 1:79–94. https://doi.org/10.1080/1479053042000187810

Hudson-Smith A, Evans S, Batty M, Batty S (2002) Online participation: the Woodberry down experiment. Centre for Advanced Spatial Analysis – CASA. University College London, London. Working Paper 60

ICOMOS (1999) Cultural tourism charter adopted by the 12th General Assembly in Mexico. Available via icomos.org. https://www.icomos.org/en/newsletters-archives/179-articles-en-francais/ressources/charters-and-standards/162-international-cultural-tourism-charter. Accessed 29 Feb 2020

Jäger J, Rothman D, Anastasi C, Kartha S, van Notten P (2007) Scenario development and analysis. GEO resource book, a training manual on integrated environmental assessment and reporting. United Nations Environment Programme (UNEP). International Institute for Sustainable Development (IISD), Winnipeg, pp 15–16

Jamal T, Dredge D (2014) Tourism and community development issues. In: Sharpley R, Telfer D (eds) Tourism and development. Channel View, Bristol, pp 178–204

Jimura T (2011) The impact of world heritage site designation on local communities – a case study of Ogimachi, Shirakawa-mura. Japan Tour Manag 32:288–296

Jureniene V, Radzevicius M (2014) Models of cultural heritage management. Transform. Bus Econ 13(32):236–256

Kahila M, Kyttä M (2009) SoftGIS as a bridge-builder in collaborative urban planning. In: Geetman S, Stillwell J (eds) Planning support systems best practice and new methods, The GeoJournal Library, vol 95. Springer, Amsterdam, pp 389–311

Kaplan AM, Haenlein M (2010) Users of the world, unite! The challenges and opportunities of social media. Bus Horiz 53:59–68

Katsoni V, Stratigea A (eds) (2016) Tourism and culture in the age of innovation. Springer, New York

Katsoni V, Upadhya A, Stratigea A (eds) (2017) Tourism, culture and heritage in a smart economy. In: Proceedings of the 3rd International Conference IACuDiT, Athens, May 2016. Springer, Berlin. https://doi.org/10.1007/978-3-319-47732-9

Klessman J (2010) Portals as a tool for public participation in urban planning. In: Silva CN (ed) Handbook of research on e-planning. ICTs for urban development and monitoring. IGI Global, Hersey, pp 252–267. https://doi.org/10.4018/978-1-61520-929-3

Kostopoulos D (ed) (2005) Leros' travel guide. Toubis Publications, Athens

Koutsi D (2018) Integrated management of land and underwater cultural resources as a pillar for the development of isolated insular islands. Master's thesis, National Technical University of Athens, Athens, Greece

Koutsi D, Stratigea A (2019) Unburying hidden land and maritime cultural potential of small islands in the Mediterranean for tracking heritage-led local development paths – case study Leros-Greece. Heritage 2(1):938–966. https://doi.org/10.3390/heritage2010062

Kunwar RR, Karki N (2020) A study of dark (disaster) tourism in reconstructed Barpak, Nepal. The Gaze J Hosp Tour Res 11(1):140–180

Leros. http://leros.homestead.com/geographyGR.html. Accessed 15 Jan 2020

Lerosisland.gr. https://lerosisland.gr/. Accessed 22 Jan 2020

Lindgren M, Bandhold H (eds) (2003) Scenario planning: the link between future and strategy. Palgrave Macmillan, New York

Manera C, Taberner J (2006) The recent evolution and impact of tourism in the Mediterranean: the case of island regions, 1990-2002. Available via FEEM, Working Paper No. 108.06. https://ssrn.com/abstract=927743. Accessed 9 Mar 2020

Mannion AM, Vogiatzakis IN (2007) Island landscape dynamics: examples from the Mediterranean. Available via Geographical Paper No.183. https://www.reading.ac.uk/web/files/geographyandenvironmentalscience/GP183_Island_Landscapes_AMMINV_1Aa.pdf. Accessed 8 Mar 2020

Margaras V (2016) Islands of the EU: taking account of their specific needs in EU policy. Available via EPRS | European parliamentary research service. https://www.europarl.europa.eu/thinktank/en/document.html?reference=EPRS_BRI(2016)573960. Accessed 10 Mar 2020

McNeal SR, Mossberger K, Tolbert JC (eds) (2007) Digital citizenship. The Internet, Society, and participation. The MIT Press, Cambridge

Mentogiannes B (2004) 52 days 1943 – the Queen Olga and the battle of Leros: underwater filming and research. Kastaniotes, Athens

Nalbandian J, O'Neil R, Wilkes JM, Kaufman A (2013) Contemporary challenges in local government: evolving roles and responsibilities, structures, and processes. Public Adm Rev 73(4):567–574

Oomen J, Aroyo L (2011) Crowdsourcing in the cultural heritage domain: opportunities and challenges. In: Proceedings of the 5th international conference on communities and technologies. Brisbane-Australia, 29 June–2 July 2011

Panagiotopoulou M, Stratigea A (2017) Spatial data management and visualization tools and technologies for enhancing participatory e-planning in smart cities. In: Stratigea A, Kyriakides E, Nicolaides C (eds) Smart cities in the Mediterranean – coping with sustainability objectives in small and medium-sized cities and island communities. Springer, Berlin, pp 31–57

Panagiotopoulou M, Somarakis G, Stratigea A (2018a) Smartening up participatory cultural tourism planning in historical city centres. J Urban Technol:1–24. https://doi.org/10.1080/10630732.2018.1528540

Panagiotopoulou M, Somarakis G, Stratigea A (2018b) Participatory spatial planning in support of cultural-resilient resource management: the case of Kissamos-Crete. In: Stratigea A, Kavroudakis D (eds) Mediterranean cities and island communities: smart, sustainable, inclusive and resilient. Nature Springer, Cham, pp 181–211. https://doi.org/10.1007/978-3-319-99444-4_8

Pita da Costa D (2017) Mapping of cultural heritage actions in European Union policies, programmes and activities. Interpret Europe Newslett 3:21

Pungetti G (2012) Islands, culture, landscape and seascape. J Mar Island Cult 1(2):51–54

Richards G (ed) (1999) Culture, cultural tourism and identity. Tilburg University, Tilburg

Richards G (2014) Tourism trends: the convergence of culture and tourism. Working Paper, Academy for Leisure. NHTV University of Applied Sciences, Brenda

Richards G (2018) Cultural tourism: a review of recent research and trends. J Hosp Tour Manag 36:12–21

Rontos K, Kitrinou E, Lagos D, Diakomihalis M (2012) Islands and tourism development: a viewpoint of tourism stakeholders of Lesvos Island. In: Kasimoglu M (ed) Visions for global tourism industry-creating and sustaining competitive strategies. IntecOpenTech, London, pp 461–478

Rössler M (2012) Partners in site management – a shift in focus: heritage and community involvement. In: Albert MT, Richon M, Viñals MJ, Witcomb A (eds) Community development through world heritage, World heritage papers, vol 31. UNESCO, Paris, pp 27–31

Saad-Sulonen J (2012) The role of the creation and sharing of digital media content in participatory e-planning. Intern J e-Plan Res 1(2):1–22

Scheyvens R (ed) (2002) Tourism for development: empowering communities. Pearson Education, Essex

Sharpley R (2009) Shedding light on dark tourism: an introduction. In: Sharpley R, Stone PR (eds) The darker side of travel: the theory and practice of dark tourism. Aspects of tourism. Channel View Publications, Bristol, pp 3–22

Sofield T (2003) Empowerment for sustainable tourism development. Emerald Group, Bingley

Somarakis G, Stratigea A (2019) Guiding informed choices on participation tools in spatial planning: an e-decision support system. Intern J e-Plan Res 8(3):38–61

Spilanis J (2012) European islands and political cohesion. Gutenberg, Athens. (In Greek)

Stokes FB, Wechler B (1995) State agencies' experiences with strategic planning: findings from a national survey. Public Adm Rev 55:159–168. https://doi.org/10.2307/977181

Stratigea A (2015) Theory and methods of participatory planning. Greek Academic Electronic Books Kallipos Program, Athens. (in Greek)

Stratigea A, Katsoni V (2015) A strategic policy scenario analysis framework for the sustainable tourist development of peripheral small island areas – the case of Lefkada- Greece Island. Eur J Futures Res 3(5):1–17. https://doi.org/10.1007/s40309-015-0063-z

Stratigea A, Katsoni V (2016) A strategic policy scenario analysis framework for the sustainable tourist development of peripheral small island areas. In: Katsoni V, Stratigea A (eds) Tourism and culture in the age of innovation. Springer, New York, p 331-349. https://doi.org/10.1007/978-3-319-27528-4

Stratigea A, Marava N, Alexopoulos A (2016) A guide of good practices for participatory cultural planning at the local level, Report III.2, "DemoCU" research project, program «we are all citizens», EEA Grants 2009-2014 (in Greek). https://doi.org/10.13140/RG.2.1.2908.8884

Stratigea A, Leka A, Nicolaides C (2017) Small and medium-sized cities and island communities in the Mediterranean: coping with sustainability challenges in the smart city context. In: Stratigea A, Kyriakides E, Nicolaides CH (eds) Smart cities in the Mediterranean – coping with sustainability objectives in small and medium-sized cities and island communities. Springer, Berlin, pp 31–57

Stratigea A, Kikidou M, Patelida M, Somarakis G (2018) Engaging citizens in planning open public space regeneration: PEDIO-AGORA framework. J Urban Plan D 144(1):1–10. https://doi.org/10.1061/(ASCE)UP.1943-5444.0000418

Thoctarides K, Bilalis A (2015) Shipwrecks of the greek seas, dive into their history. Aikaterini Laskaridis Foundation, Peraias

Trau A, Bushell R (2008) Tourism and indigenous people. In: McCool SF, Moisey RN (eds) Tourism, recreation and sustainability. CAB International, Oxfordshire, pp 260–282

UCLG (2018) Culture in the sustainable development goals: a guide for local action. Available via United Cities and Local Governments – UCLG. https://www.uclg.org/sites/default/files/culture_in_the_sdgs.pdf Accessed 8 Mar 2020

UNESCO (1972) Convention concerning the protection of the world cultural and natural heritage. Adopted by the General Conference at its 7th Session Paris, France. Available via UNESCO. https://whc.unesco.org/archive/convention-en.pdf Accessed 18 Feb 2020

UNESCO (2001) Convention on the protection of the underwater cultural heritage. Adopted at the General Conference of UNESCO in Paris, France. Available via UNESCO. http://unesdoc.unesco.org/images/0014/001429/142919e.pdf. Accessed 1 Mar 2020

UNESCO (2003) Safeguarding of the intangible cultural heritage. Adopted at the General Conference of UNESCO in Paris, France. Available via UNESCO. https://ich.unesco.org/en/convention. Accessed 8 Mar 2020

UNWTO (2018) Tourism and culture synergies. Available via UNWTO. https://www.e-unwto.org/doi/book/10.18111/9789284418978. Accessed 6 Mar 2020

Vogiatzakis I, Mannion AM, Pungetti G (2008) Introduction to the Mediterranean island landscapes. In: Vogiatzakis I, Mannion AM, Pungetti G (eds) Mediterranean island landscapes series, vol 9. Springer, Dordrecht, pp 1–14. https://doi.org/10.1007/978-1-4020-5064-0

von Droste B (2012) World's heritage and globalization: UNESCO's contribution to the development of global ethics. In: Albert MT, Richon M, Viñals MJ, Witcomb A (eds) Community development through world heritage. UNESCO, Paris

Sustainable Tourism, Young Entrepreneurship, and Social Innovation in Peripheral Rural Areas: Case Studies from Southern Italy

Rita Salvatore, Emilio Cocco, and Anna Farrell Mines

1 Theoretical Framework

The theoretical framework behind this research is based on the relation between sustainable tourism and social innovation, and moves up through innovative dynamics between economy, society, and the environment. Innovation is meant as the bridging element between economic growth and a wider territorial requalification, and primarily references Bock's work and her definition of social innovation as "a motor of change rooted in social collaboration and social learning, the response to unmet social needs as a desirable outcome, and society as the arena in which change should take place" (2016, p. 555).

The study presented here focuses on the benefits sustainable tourism may generate in rural economies not only in terms of direct tourist spending and income but also from increased awareness from local residents and local resource enhancement, to new job opportunities, increased quality of life, and changes in lifestyle (Maretti

The fieldwork activities that allowed the data collection for this research were financed by the Faculty of Communication Sciences, under the fund "Poseidon 2008" (chair: Prof. Emilio Cocco).

R. Salvatore (✉)
Faculty of Biosciences, Food and Environmental Technology, University of Teramo, Teramo, Italy
e-mail: rsalvatore@unite.it

E. Cocco
Faculty of Communication Sciences, University of Teramo, Teramo, Italy
e-mail: ecocco@unite.it

A. F. Mines
Department of Food Studies, The American University of Rome, Rome, Italy
e-mail: a.mines@aur.edu

© Springer Nature Switzerland AG 2021
R. P. Marques et al. (eds.), *The Impact of Tourist Activities on Low-Density Territories*, Tourism, Hospitality & Event Management,
https://doi.org/10.1007/978-3-030-65524-2_5

and Salvatore 2012; Williams and Ponsford 2009; Wallace and Russell 2004). These post-agricultural trajectories of rural development have met the interests of academic research, and in the last 20 years scholars have conceptualized them along interesting lines, such as the New Rural Paradigm—NRP (Milone and Ventura 2011; OECD 2006), multifunctional agriculture (Halfacree 2006; Wilson 2007), nexogenous networked development (Murdoch 2000; Murdoch 2006; Woods 2007; Bock 2016), and the rural web (Van der Ploeg and Marsden 2008; Van der Ploeg et al. 2010; Messely et al. 2013). Accordingly, academics and policy makers have assessed the capacity of rural areas to play upon their local identity and reach a "double coherence," that is to say to mobilize social capital in order to turn their territorial resources into symbolic capital recognized both by insiders and outsiders alike (Bourdieu 1984, Bourdieu and Richardson 1986; Putnam 2000).

While the concept of innovation has gained popularity in this ongoing debate, it is far from being framed in a clear and consensually accepted way (Barbera and Parisi 2019). Social innovation is both a "vague" and "dark" buzzword and a supposed "inspirational," "magic word" to solve the wicked problems of contemporary capitalism. For example, policy-oriented literature addresses social innovation in compensatory terms, such as by recognizing its "compassionate" action in the (neo)liberal framework of increased deregulation and flexibility (Moulaert et al. 2013). The academic literature on the other hand focuses more on the changing modes of value production and the way this is culturally legitimated (Nicholls et al. 2015; Scott 2007). In other words, academics tend to be more critical, by investigating the symbolic and structural changes that improve collective well-being, with special regards to social movements and the local development of "weak territories" (Moulaert and Nussbaumer 2005; Borghi 2017; Bortoletto and Grignoli 2019). From this point of view, innovation studies emerge as a promising perspective when they concentrate on the new "cooperative" approaches to production and distribution of goods and services, namely, on-demand and sharing economy (Pais and Provasi 2015) or commons-based peer production (Benkler and Nissembaum 2006).

However, independent of the type of approach, we think that the point of a critical reading of social innovation should be to cast light on the role of social change agents. What we refer to as social innovators are not exceptionally skilled heroes inspired by redemptive goals but rather a specific population that enacts individual and collective social actions which, embedded in specific contexts, tackle unsorted problems through a hybrid, applied knowledge (Barbera and Parisi 2019).

For the scope of our investigation, and in some relevant literature, social innovation in weak territories is often coupled with the regenerative features of leisure activities, for instance in the context of gentrification policies (Evans and Foord 2008) or in the frame of a "New Rural Paradigm" (Horlings and Marsden 2014). Therefore, with special regards to inner rural areas, the assumption is generally shared that in weak territories (i.e., contexts particularly affected by loss of economic opportunities, depopulation, and population aging, as most rural peripheral areas are), sustainable tourism is a potential tool to support local development (Maretti and Salvatore 2012; Salvatore et al. 2018). Furthermore, several studies have shown that rural tourism, and ecotourism in particular (Ceballos-Lascuràin 1991; Beaumont

2011), when combined with cultural capital can offer an important tool kit to activate the different assets of local economies, thus revitalizing low-density territories (Sharpley and Jepson 2011; Beaumont and Brown 2018).

As it is widely known, most Italian peripheral rural areas (PRAs) have been characterized by deep social and economic problems such as depopulation, aging, lack of job opportunities, and lack of basic services (De Rossi 2018). Because of this situation, they have often been referred to as "left behind" places, with their social atmosphere often depicted as passive and inactive. As a matter of fact, a complex whole of concurrent causes characterizes the post-crisis situation, such as a higher digital and analogical literacy, a wider availability of ethical knowledge, a deeper environmental consciousness, and a growth of post-materialistic values. Therefore, these areas are now facing some important challenges, which also relate to new sustainability-oriented tourist practices that may trigger big changes on a socio-economic and cultural level (Carrosio 2019).

Due to the environmental crisis on one side, to the more recent global finance failures and public health concerns on the other, and in turn to a wider demand of post-materialist values, these areas may represent "safer" regions for experimentation, according to both environmental and socio-economical sustainability. For instance, they can aim at pursuing new, integrated territorial approaches to local development with the ambition of shaping alternative interconnected geographies. From this standpoint, it is possible to gain back places once lost in the deployment of a unidimensional, globalized paradigm of neo-liberal market-driven development (Wiskerke 2009). Thus, rural peripheral areas are primed for trying renovated ways of doing post-crisis development starting from a greener idea of quality of life. After being victims of abandonment, these small rural towns of the Apennines might now turn into spaces of debate and social experimentation where both the residents and the tourists may share the same sense of place and may think of a new way of making local society, in a more inclusive and sustainable way. In short, what were originally deemed to be problems are now potential opportunities, and these "left behind" places may find themselves as spatial socio-cultural labs, or places that are "moving ahead" (see Fig. 1).

Some of these opportunities are actually related to the possibilities sustainable tourism can offer as a kind of bridging field among different socio-economic sectors. Thanks to the involvement from a new generation of young entrepreneurs, tourism has become an important means to change the way people can actually live and perceive the quality of life in these towns and, in turn, the proximal relations within local communities. We have attributed this change with social innovation in the frame of sustainable tourism, which seems to work quite well in some inner areas, such as the Alpine mountain districts (Kuščer et al. 2017). To what extent that might actually be realized in relation to the hospitality and tourism sector in a peripheral Southern Italian inner area, which is nonetheless rich in natural and cultural heritage, is the main objective of our research.

We hypothesize that thanks to an increased "life project" investment of social innovation-oriented young entrepreneurs, these places can change through experiment and find themselves as prepositive, rather than passive, places. Against this

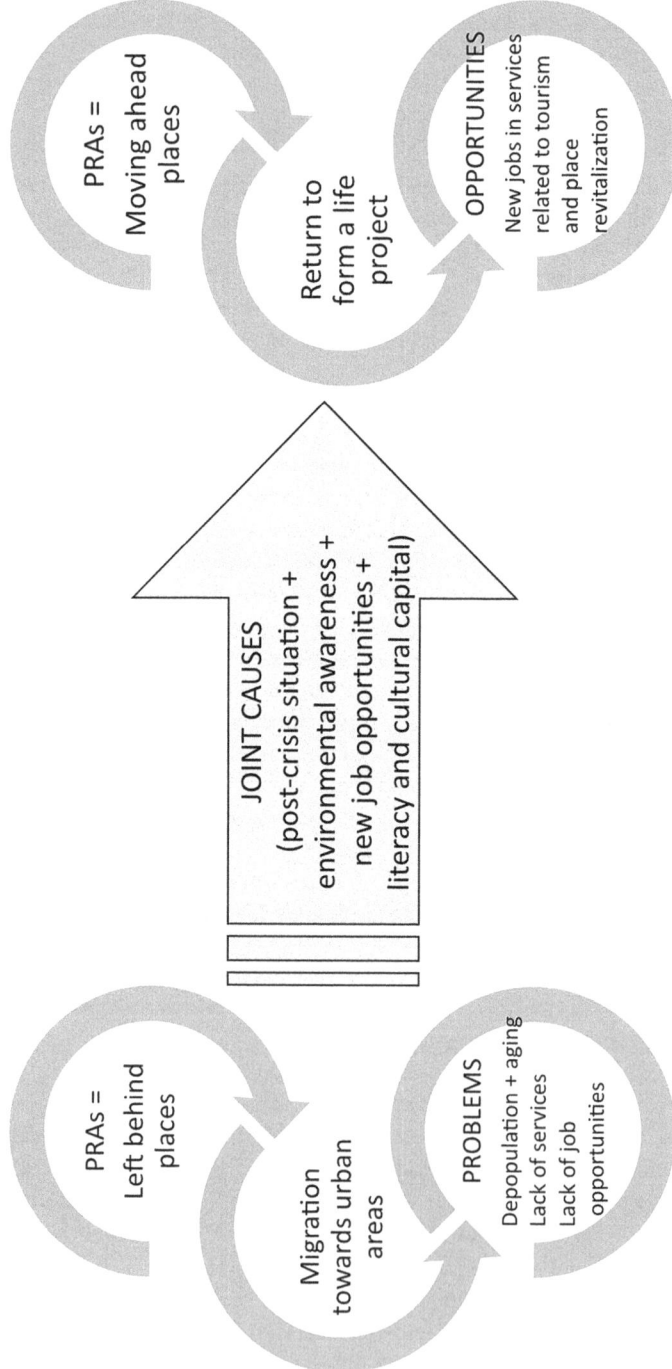

Fig. 1 Theoretical background

idea, sustainable tourism might catalyze all the different endogenous resources, perhaps not previously recognized, and organize them into a local tourist offer (local cuisine, agricultural products, rural settlements, cultural experiences, natural landscape, etc.). A key turning point in the framework is represented by the role of these young entrepreneurs that we refer to as "reflexive selves," that is as subjects carrying on a place-centered vision by paying particular attention to the human impact on both society and nature in a wider sense. We derive the notion of "reflexive selves" first from the sociological works that were mostly influenced by the phenomenological and existentialist tradition. In particular, we bear in mind the following ideas: "intentionality" as a central feature of the experience of reality (Brentano 1874/1973); the *Lebenswelt* or "lifeworld," the empathic connections with the lifeflow and the consciousness of "things" after the suspension of judgment (Husserl 1989); and the existence of only subject-dependent, relatively natural world as opposed to the objectified representation of the world coming from positivist tradition (Scheler 1980). In this context, we refer in particular to the contribution made by Alfred Schutz and his attempt to expand and improve the category of comprehension of social life derived from Dilthey and Max Weber (Schutz 1967).

Schutz follows the "interpretative" tradition by narrowing the focus on the meaning of social action but, in addition to that, brings the examination of the making of sense—a precondition of any authentic social action—to a further level by distinguishing a subjective, intentional sense and a "second order," an objective typification of the sense. Namely, Schutz describes the lifeworld in terms of inter-subjective structuration and claims that any social action makes sense only when inscribed within a "project." In other words, it is possible to grasp the sense of a social action only when one can think of it as "already done"—the social action has meaning as an anticipation of a project to be deployed. Only under these conditions can we rightfully talk of "social action" as distinguished from behavior or routine because the action is performed in the lifeflow as part of an existential unity. In these conditions, it can also be observed *ex-post* as a "reproduction," with the result of attaching different patterns of sense depending on the viewpoint and the time of observation. From here we understand that selves are reflexive as they act intentionally but are also subject to self-observations in the frame of an ongoing structuration of projects within an inter-subjective social world. As a result, we witness an explosion of "sense" through multiple "typizations" and "observation levels" (Wagner 1970).

Among the more recent interpretations of the "subject in the world" theme, a quite successful one has been proposed in the 1990s by Ulrich Beck with his understanding of the individual self-accomplishment in terms of "own life" (*das Eigene Leben*) (Beck and Ziegler 1997). Interestingly, Beck brings forward a long-term investigation of the process of differentiation and autonomization of the individual actors as part of the shift from first to second modernity. However, he progressively moves away both from an individualistic (utilitarian and hedonistic) and a normative (emancipatory and anti-systemic) notion of the "self" that belongs to a long-established European and Continental tradition, dating back to Durkheim and Simmel and still popular with the Frankfurt School (Privitera 2015). In a different fashion, Beck does not focus on the unsolved tensions between the individual and the collective, but rather turns the perspective upside down by looking at the individual subject as an agent of social integration through increased individualization. Here, Beck draws on the lessons of Talcott Parsons and his distinction between utilitarian and institutional individualism (Parsons 1978), and, therefore, he does not conceive the subjective pursuit of the individual interest as contradictory to the collective interest. Conversely, Beck reconnects with the tradition of democratic individualism, more popular in the American scholarship and revived by authors such as Rawls and Habermas. In this perspective, an increased individualization happens within the system and expresses the interiorization of the institutional norms by the individualized subjects.

Moreover, Beck suggests that the ability of the actors of the social "lifeworld" to differentiate and liberate from traditional roles brings about an innovative potentiality to achieve new and aware forms of social integration. In other words, Beck's reflexive modernity shows that although an increased individualization means both a loss of empathy as a sensory guide to interpret reality and a progressive disconnection from the traditional norms of the lifeworlds (living through secondhand non-experience) (Beck 1986), the destiny of the self is not necessarily written in terms of psychological fragmentation, anonymity, or a-critical integration into the functional logic of the political and economic systems. On the contrary, to pursue a life project as a form of free self-accomplishment makes the individuals the true builders of their "own life" and turns them from passive recipients of societal transformations into active subjects of social change in the eve of second modernity.

When combined with personalized forms of post-mass tourism, the notion of reflexive self appears as a very promising research tool and, as a matter of fact, it has already been applied in some intriguing ways. For instance, Pritchard et al. discuss reflexive selves as "responsible tourism intellectuals" concerned with pursuing "tourism knowledge which directly relates to the challenge of creating a more just and sustainable world" (2011, p. 942). They call this Hopeful Tourism and claim that it is

> a values-based, unfolding transformative perspective (imbued by principles of partnership, reciprocity and respect). It offers a 'reflexive accounting' (Seale 1999) of the development of hopeful tourism, a pause for reflection which aspires to stimulate debate on the philosophical scope of tourism enquiry and the potential role of tourism scholars as change agents. (p. 942)

In a similar fashion but perhaps with less ambitious goals, the young entrepreneurs of the two case studies presented in this chapter are acting as agents of civic transformation through innovative tourism practices. The reflexivity of their selves is manifested in life projects aimed at pursuing one's "own life" by reshaping tourism practices around the concepts of sustainability, responsibility, and quality of life. Thus, they are not consuming new land in order to build big hotels but they are promoting the idea of "dispersed hospitality" by requalifying the old abandoned houses; they offer open-air activities and encourage slow mobility; they invite the tourist to rediscover a "peasant way" of doing agriculture as van der Ploeg has defined it (2009) where the use of the resources is balanced with their future regeneration; and finally, they work in order to shorten the tourist and gastronomic supply chain. A still preserved natural environment, high quality agricultural products, the uniqueness of the historical and cultural heritage, and the architectural style of the settlement are just some of the many elements they may refer to, to both decide for a new project of life away from urban contexts and to plan a place-based tourist offer. Thanks to these subjects' actions, tourism, sustainability, and social change interrelate with the place's inner vocations.

2 Methodology

A three-month fieldwork was conducted in spring-summer 2019 in several small towns of the Basilicata and Calabria regions, specifically located within the Gallipoli Cognato—Piccole Dolomiti Lucane Regional Park and the Pollino National Park. The main research task was to understand how the particular environmental, cultural-historical and architectural assets of these towns may be interacting in order to favor sustainable tourism and social innovation within small rural towns and low-density areas. The selection of the cases, their identified assets, and a theoretical framework have been built upon the successful case of the town of Matera (Basilicata region), where the unique anthropological-historical value of the site has allowed for a large cultural and tourism transition (Salvatore et al. 2018) and lately received recognition as the European Capital of Culture 2019 (Aquilino et al. 2018).

In this research period, during a preliminary visit and an explorative two-week visit, several small rural towns were visited in the inner areas across the Basilicata region (Castelmezzano, Grottole, Rotonda, San Costantino Albanese, San Paolo Albanese, Senise, Terranova del Pollino) and the Calabria region (Acquaformosa, Cerchiara di Calabria, Civita, Morano Calabro, Mormanno, San Basile, Saracena) (see Fig. 2). The places were selected because each one of them had interesting elements to be investigated in relation to the theoretical framework, whether it was the tourist enhancement of the cultural dimension (i.e., the Arbëreshë towns of San Costantino Albanese, San Paolo Albanese, Acquaformosa and Civita or Grottole), the young generation commitment (i.e., San Basile, Castelmezzano, Civita), the regional food (i.e., Mormanno, Cerchiara di Calabria, Saracena, Rotonda, Senise, Terranova di Pollino), or the environmental context (i.e., Terranova di Pollino, Civita, Castelmezzano). In this phase, about 40 key informants were interviewed including tourist operators (both guides and B&B owners), farmers, administrators, association members, and other local entrepreneurs.

On the basis of this first exploratory research experience and of direct observation, two case studies (Castelmezzano in the Lucanian Gallipoli Cognato—Piccole Dolomiti Lucane Regional Park, and Civita in the Calabrian side of the Pollino National Park) were chosen in order to more deeply reveal the relation between the local tourist offer within a protected area and the ongoing social change within the towns (Hammer et al. 2007). The reasons why these two cases were studied more

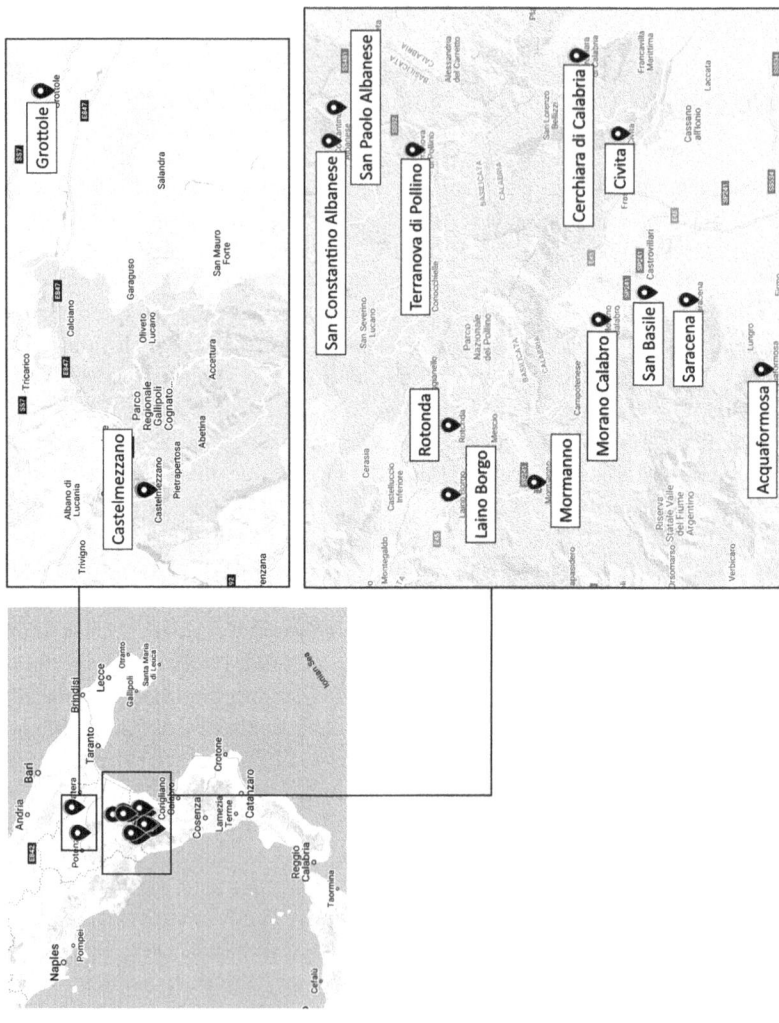

Fig. 2 Map of case areas (Basilicata and Calabria) rendered with Google My Maps tool

Table 1 Structure of the population in the area under study (2002–2018)

Municipality	Province	Population			2002–2018 variation %	Average age 2018
		2002	2013	2018		
Castelmezzano	Potenza	970	835	789	−18.7	50.3
Grottole	Matera	2607	2327	2116	−18.8	45.1
Matera	Matera	57,785	60,009	60,403	4.5	43.9
Rotonda	Potenza	3888	3475	3435	−11.7	55.6
San Costantino Albanese	Potenza	884	754	686	−22.4	44.1
San Paolo Albanese	Potenza	416	280	260	−37.5	51.2
Senise	Potenza	7182	7077	6995	−2.6	44.5
Terranova di Pollino	Potenza	1534	1291	1141	−25.6	51.1
Basilicata (whole region values)		**597,768**	**576,194**	**567,118**	**−5.1**	**45.3**
Acquaformosa	Cosenza	1295	1158	1108	−14.4	47.3
Cerchiara di Calabria	Cosenza	2942	2439	2344	−20.3	47.8
Civita	Cosenza	1125	926	912	−18.9	49.9
Morano Calabro	Cosenza	4966	4606	4413	−11.1	46.9
Mormanno	Cosenza	3729	3186	2955	−20.8	48.6
San Basile	Cosenza	1285	1058	1034	−19.5	50.5
Saracena	Cosenza	4309	3908	3744	−13.1	48.1
Calabria (whole region values)		**2,011,466**	**1,958,238**	**1,956,687**	**−2.7**	**43.6**

Data source: Authors' own elaboration on ISTAT (National Institute of Statistics) data
The bold values are related to the whole regions of Basilicata and Calabria

deeply is related to several conditions they showed to have in common, despite their differences and uniqueness:

- As the following secondary data has clearly stressed (see Tables 1 and 2), despite their loss in population and their high average age, both have had a recent and noteworthy increase in the number of tourist establishments, particularly in the Defert's tourist function index (DFTI) (Defert 1967; Marković et al. 2017) (see Figs. 3 and 4).[1]
- Both are situated in protected areas that require economic development based on sustainability principles.

---

[1]This index is focused on researching the relation between the accommodation capacity and the population size within a specific destination. It determines the tourist function of a place by indicating its capacity to satisfy tourists' needs in terms of hospitality and it is calculated by putting into relation the number of beds and residents.

Table 2 Tourist capacity and DFTI in the area under study (2002–2018)

Municipality	Province	Tourist capacity						DFTI		
		2002		2013		2018		2002	2013	2018
		Acc. est.	Beds	Acc. est.	Beds	Acc. est.	Beds			
Castelmezzano	Potenza	2	18	13	138	23	170	1.9	16.5	**21.5**
Grottole	Matera	1	16	3	27	7	39	0.6	1.2	1.8
Matera	Matera	20	1140	160	2747	639	4739	2.0	4.6	7.8
Rotonda	Potenza	8	220	18	269	22	281	5.7	7.7	8.2
San Costantino Albanese	Potenza	8	171	6	95	6	66	19.3	12.6	9.6
San Paolo Albanese	Potenza	0	0	0	0	0	0	0.0	0.0	0.0
Senise	Potenza	3	82	6	202	7	136	1.1	2.9	1.9
Terranova di Pollino	Potenza	7	160	12	241	11	197	10.4	18.7	17.3
Basilicata total		450	32,595	749	39,113	1409	36,306	**5.5**	**6.8**	**6.4**
Acquaformosa	Cosenza	1	6	3	19	5	37	0.5	1.6	3.3
Cerchiara di Calabria	Cosenza	5	72	10	124	11	113	2.4	5.1	4.8
Civita	Cosenza	3	40	16	107	17	113	3.6	11.6	**12.4**
Morano Calabro	Cosenza	9	173	36	353	37	399	3.5	7.7	9.0
Mormanno	Cosenza	4	40	21	223	24	276	1.1	7.0	9.3
San Basile	Cosenza	0	0	1	7	1	7	0.0	0.7	0.7
Saracena	Cosenza	1	12	8	86	8	87	0.3	2.2	2.3
Calabria total		1263	193,245	2888	187,845	3512	192,797	**9.6**	**9.6**	**9.9**

Data source: Authors' own elaboration on ISTAT (National Institute of Statistics) data
The bold values are related to the whole regions of Basilicata and Calabria

Fig. 3 DFTI
Castelmezzano
(2002–2018). Data source:
Authors' own elaboration on
ISTAT (National Institute of
Statistics) data

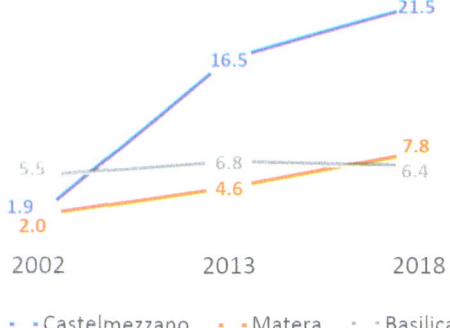

Fig. 4 DFTI Civita
(2002–2018). Data source:
Authors' own elaboration on
ISTAT (National Institute of
Statistics) data

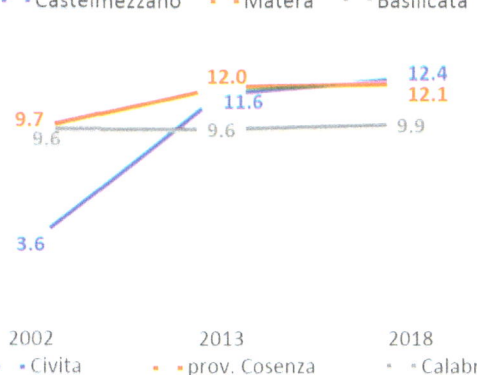

- Services and hospitality are run and managed by young entrepreneurs and administrators.
- Both have a particular and remarkable historical-architectural structure working as an effective pull factor.
- The tourist offer is strongly based on ecotourism activities.[2]

Because of these features, it was possible to study the conditions under which sustainable ecotourism may trigger social innovation processes thanks to the specific commitment from innovative entrepreneurs (reflexive selves), in accordance with our starting hypothesis. Are Castelmezzano and Civita actually shaping up to be proactive places in which new modalities of living can be experimented especially by young entrepreneurs? If so, is that happening in close relation with their innermost vocations (cultural heritage, environmental habitat, rural/urban landscape)? These have been the central questions and issues addressed in our research. To what extent this is actually going on was the focus of our fieldwork.

Given that the phenomenon under observation (the tourism transition of low-density rural towns) is still in progress and closely related to a contemporary context, we have chosen a particularly flexible research method in terms of research

---

[2]This is in reference to The International Ecotourism Society definition of ecotourism (www.ecotourism.org).

techniques and data collection. Therefore, the research has been taken on according to the multiple case studies methodology (Yin 2017; Barkley 2006) with the double role of exploratory/descriptive tasking and hypothesis testing. The objective of this study is clearly far from showing any statistical representativeness but at the same time it looks for a theoretical meaningfulness by highlighting new elements of qualitative interest (such as the role of the "reflexive selves," the contemporary revitalization of local heritage through tourism, the social impact of the innovations, the integration among different tourist assets, and the commitment from institutions) that are worth being analyzed in depth.

For these reasons, a second phase of the research project was entirely dedicated to these two cases in which the border between new entrepreneurship and the way of life characterizing the context was not clearly distinguishable. For this reason, the data and the information gathered in the field during a second visit have referred mainly to qualitative techniques (such as direct observation, field notes, photos, document collection, and interviews) whose application has relied on multiple sources of evidence based on the main theoretical propositions and categories. Overall, the case study research design has revealed itself as a "comprehensive research strategy" (Barkley 2006) particularly suited to the aims of this study, including the development of a theoretical framework, data collection, and data analysis.

The main findings of the research have come out of two overlapping stages: secondary data analysis and qualitative data analysis. The former was used to better understand how both the tourist offer and the tourist demand have changed and increased in more recent years, with meaningful changes. In order to analyze their condition, the main tourist indicators were taken into consideration (tourist capacity and occupancy, and tourist function).

The second stage has involved a code-based analysis (Ryan 2004) realized through the use of the Computer Assisted Qualitative Data Analysis Software (CAQDAS) Nvivo. This analysis has been realized on the basis of 10 in-depth interviews of "key informants" selected from private tour operators, local administrators, farmers, business owners, and tour guides living in one of the two case studies examined for their theoretical representativeness. The pieces of their statements related to the main categories used within the theoretical framework have been selected and categorized under a "node" whose name synthesizes the content of the reference. These nodes were then grouped when applicable as "child nodes" under "mother nodes," which indicated analytical categories to be used for the themes during the reporting phase of the research, hereafter to be referred to as "codes." Nvivo was also used to produce a word cloud for each case based on the most repeated relevant terms found in the interviews (see Fig. 6 in the conclusions). The word clouds visually represent word frequency which, with the elimination of common words such as auxiliary parts of speech, might indicate the core themes of the interviews. The abstraction and compilation of these words occurred at the end of the secondary data analysis stage to gauge how our codes aligned with these themes.

Fig. 6 Word clouds for interviewees residing in Civita (left) and Castelmezzano (right)

2.1 The Cases

2.1.1 Castelmezzano and the "Volo dell'Angelo"

Castelmezzano (750 m a.s.l.) is one of the most representative places within the Gallipoli Cognato - Piccole Dolomiti Lucane Regional Park. Due to its unique biotope, this area was first identified by the National Research Council (CNR) for protection, and then in 1997 instituted as a regional park. The park falls entirely in the region of Basilicata, partly in the province of Matera and partly within the municipalities of Castelmezzano and Pietrapertosa, in the province of Potenza. In the latter two municipalities, geological sandstone formations evocatively stick out of the landscape. The site is unique to the Mezzogiorno because of its resemblance to the Alpine dolomites.

Like most of the Italian inner areas, Castelmezzano is a low-density town, with a total of 789 inhabitants and an average of 23.3 inhabitants per km^2. It also has an older population, with an average age of 50.3, and over one-third over 65. During the period from 2002 to 2018, it lost almost 20% of its population (see Table 1).

However, despite these deep criticalities, Castelmezzano now shows one of the highest values (21.5) in the DFTI within the region and definitively the highest of the area under study. Compared with the entire territory of Basilicata, this indicator was over three times higher. Therefore, by observing this value and how it has changed over time (see Fig. 3), we can assume that—in a relatively short time—Castelmezzano went from a place practically with no tourist activity (sixth and last position in the scale of the tourist function proposed by Pearce) (Pearce 1995; see also Borzyszkowski et al. 2016 for application) to a municipality with an important, if not predominant, tourist activity (fourth position in the same scale). The analysis of the processes and the dynamics that eventually led to this important change have been the main interest of this study during the collection of the qualitative data in Castelmezzano.

For the uniqueness of its settlement, Castelmezzano was one of the first Italian towns to be included in the club of *I Borghi Più Belli d'Italia* ("the most beautiful villages of Italy"). The urban structure is medieval, with sandstone slab roofs and homes built into the rocks.

> When the club I Borghi Più Belli d'Italia was instituted in 2001 due to an initiative of some small Italian municipalities, Castelmezzano was among the founders. It was 37 of us spread across the national territory. Now we have reached 270 to 280 members all across Italy! [...] That was the beginning of this small town's development path! (Administrator 02)

However, what most contributed to the widespread popularity of this small town is the *Volo dell'Angelo* (flight of the angel, hereafter to be referred to as the Volo), an innovative experiential tourism attraction that sends participants flying on a zip line over the wilderness of rocks and forest located between Castelmezzano and the neighboring town of Pietrapertosa. Realized in 2007, the Volo has evolved over the years and has meaningfully contributed to the economic growth of the local community. This major attraction has also been a driving force for other minor attractions, such as the Via *Ferrata* (fixed rope routes for climbers), *Il Percorso delle Sette Pietre* (the path of the seven stones), and *Il Ponte Nepalese* (the Nepalese bridge), making Castelmezzano a popular ecotourist destination in the south of Italy. Our interview with the mayor of Castelmezzano elaborated on this history:

> Before we got all the permits needed both from the Park and from the EU, it took more than 7 years to realize the Volo and it cost one million euros which were funded by the EU. When we first opened it, I met all the young people and invited them to work for free during the first period because it was going to be a great challenge for our community on the whole. I thought we would need at least a one-year time to assess whether it was going to be an economic success or not... but it boomed from the beginning, also because it quickly spread on YouTube worldwide. Some of the videos shot from the zip line have been watched by over 400,000 people! [...] We managed the attraction through a public company owned by the two municipalities of Castelmezzano and Pietrapertosa. Today this company invoices about €650,000 a year and it has employed 22 young people. [...] Something like 200 beds have been realized out of the restructuring of previously abandoned houses and three new restaurants and two bars have opened. (Administrator 02)

These actions have had an impact even in terms of tourist fluxes and growth. Due to the lack of data availability in the previous period, we can only look at what happened in the four years from 2014 to 2018. According to these data, there has been a widespread meaningful growth all over the Basilicata region (+54% in arrivals; +24% in the overnight stays). Compared to these regional rates, Castelmezzano shows a slightly lower growth rate than the regional one (+44.9% in the arrivals) (but still a noteworthy growth) and a decline in overnight stays (−21%). The average stay in fact has decreased from 2 days to 1. This suggests that more people are visiting Castelmezzano but are spending less time there. This may also suggest that tourists spend just enough time in Castelmezzano to take the Volo dell'Angelo and then leave to spend the rest of their holidays in the nearby places of

Basilicata, maybe Matera which, in the same period, saw an increase of 125.4% in the number of arrivals and of 123.6% in the number of nights spent.

2.1.2 Civita: An Arbëreshë Town in Pollino National Park

Civita (450 m. a.s.l.) is one of the ten Arbëreshë towns on the Calabrian side of the Pollino National Park, making it part of one of the most important linguist islands whose origins date back to the fourteenth century (Fiorini et al. 2007). In that period, groups of Albanian refugees settled in this area of Southern Italy in several flows of migration which went on for centuries, following the establishment of the Kingdom of Albania, the death of the Albanian national hero Skënderbeu, and the gradual conquest of Albania by the Ottomans. Their history has always strongly characterized their cultural identity in terms of language, religion, traditions, and gastronomy and is now recently turning into an important tourist pull factor in this area of Pollino, in addition to the environmental draw.

Pollino National Park, whose defining trait is the mountain range from which it takes its name, covers 192,565 hectares of land, is located between two regions, Basilicata (or Lucania) and Calabria, and is the largest protected area in Italy. The Pollino area was first recognized as a regional park by L.R. n. 3/1986 and then as a national park four years later. It took three years for the establishment of the park authority and another for the management bodies, finally taking off in 1994. The tourism pull of the park includes natural attractions, food, culture, natural history, and landscape beauty. The latter includes the mountains but also picturesque views from several points in the park, such as Civita and Cerchiara di Calabria, both of which have access to views of the sea.

Thanks to the above elements, and also for the unique architectural structure of its historical hamlet, Civita has been included in the Club of *I Borghi Più Belli d'Italia,* was awarded the Orange flag from the Italian Touring Club (a quality brand for the tourist rural towns), and is recognized as an important setting within the UNESCO Geopark site. Therefore, the tourist offer is integrated and based on a variety of assets which might host tourists all year round to participate in non-seasonal related activities (food and culture) and enjoy both the summer months (hiking, canyoning, river rafting, etc.) and the winter months (skiing, snowshoeing, etc.).

> Tourists come to Civita because we have unique natural attractions such as the Ponte del Diavolo (the Devil's Bridge) and the Gole del Raganello (Raganello River Gorges) but also because they can eat good food and experience Arbëreshë culture and its Greek Orthodox rite. So, if we set a value scale, I would say nature is the first pull factor. The territory of Civita goes from 400 meters to 1200 a.s.l. so you can do ecotourism activities in the river in the spring-summer and walk on the snow in the winter season. Then, once tourists arrive here, they discover our Arbëreshe peasant culture with its food, its museum, its colors and costumes... (Administrator 03)

Drawn by these potentialities, several young entrepreneurs have started up new businesses in town, in the hospitality sector, as well as in tourist services (there is one travel agency/tour operator in the town and there are also several ecotourist guides), in agriculture, in restaurants, and in small shops, thus in some way revitalizing the socio-economic fabric.

> Most of the B&Bs we have in Civita are managed by young people. I personally know a girl who moved from Milan to come back here. As soon as she had sufficient economic resources, she restored her grandparents' house and opened a B&B. She now lives here and works in the tourism sector. But there are also new young farmers… two young guys started a new farm and opened a small shop in the central square to sell their products and other unique regional products. Two other guys have become farmers and they go around the towns and in markets with a small truck to sell their products. The ones who had the chance to stay and start up a new business, they did it! (Tour Operator 03)

These young people continue to face the big challenge of living in a population that is both decreasing in size and aging. Civita currently has 912 inhabitants with an average age of 50 (6.5 years over the regional score), and since 2002, it has lost almost 20% of its population (see Table 1). Moreover, almost one third is over the age of 65. Notwithstanding these criticalities, Civita—although less evidently than Castelmezzano—has shown a noteworthy increase in its DFTI which peaks in 2013, passing from 3.6 in 2002 to 12.4 in 2018. This is even more meaningful when compared to the regional trend which, even if in 2002 showed a much higher score (9.6), has remained almost unchanged within the considered time period (see Fig. 4). Thus, even if Civita lost an important percentage of its population, it seems to have invested in the availability of new accommodation in the hope to host more tourists. In 2003 it only had 3 accommodation establishments which became 16 in 2013 and 17 in 2018, with an overall increase of 73 beds (see Table 2).

Unfortunately, because of the unavailability of more recent data in some municipalities of the Calabria region, we cannot say exactly what kind of impact this increase in tourist capacity has had in a significant time lapse. We can only see that, compared to Castelmezzano, Civita managed to obtain a higher average stay by keeping its tourists sleeping in the town for an average time of three days. This may be related to a more integrated tourist offer: ecotourism activities alongside a rich gastronomy and a particular cultural offer related to the Arbëreshë identity. Moreover, looking at the occupancy data in the time period going from 2014 to 2016, we realize that Civita's tourist performance in relative terms has been definitively more positive than that of the province and the region. As shown in Fig. 5, its growth rate (both in the arrivals +17.9% and in the nights spent +23.1%) is higher than the Cosenza province rate (+15.2% and 16.2%) and Calabria regional rate (+14.3% and 9.7%).

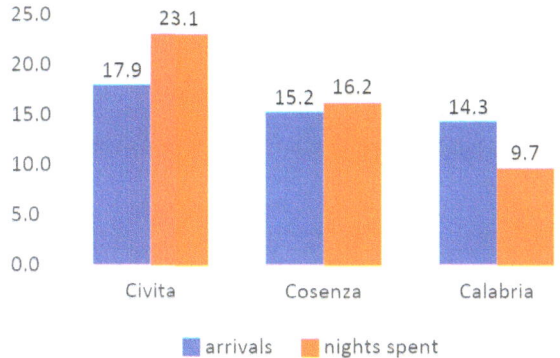

Fig. 5 Growth rate in arrivals and nights spent (2014–2016) %. Data source: Authors' own elaboration on ISTAT (National Institute of Statistics) data

Table 3 Motivations for remaining/returning/moving from elsewhere for Castelmezzano (case 1) and Civita (case 2)

Case	Respondent appellation	Age	Status	Motivations: No. of references		
				Roots	Rural idyll	Self-realization
1	Administrator 01	48	Returned	1	1	3
1	Administrator 02	50	Returned	1	0	1
1	Agri-tour Operator 01	32	Returned	1	1	1
1	Tour Operator 01	30	Returned	0	2	4
1	Restaurant Owner	41	Never moved away	3	1	3
2	Administrator 03	38	Never moved away	1	2	2
2	Agri-tour Operator 02	23	Never moved away	0	3	1
2	Tour Operator 02	47	Moved there from elsewhere	3	0	3
2	Tour Operator 03	40	Never moved away	1	0	0
2	Tour Operator 04	26	Moved there from elsewhere	0	2	0
Total no. references				11	12	18

3 Thematic Findings

3.1 *Who Are the Actors of Tourism Development in these Two Cases?*

The actors of tourism development in our two case studies include administrators, tour and agri-tour operators, and a restaurant owner. These actors were demarcated by their migration status, having moved away from the town and returned, having moved to the town from elsewhere, or having never moved away (see Table 3). The actors themselves are between the ages of 26 and 50, and can be considered young actors, given their present age or their age at the time of their initial involvement in the tourism development process, and the average age of the inhabitants of these towns (one third of the inhabitants are over the age of 65, see Table 1). When we look at the profile of the community members who have chosen to live in these "left behind" places and involve themselves in socially innovative projects, we find that their age is the most commonly shared characteristics, with eight interviews referencing young people as having an important role with a total of 13 references.

In Civita, the administration is "comprised of young people" (Administrator 03) and the "majority of B&Bs are managed by [young people]," mentioned Tour Operator 03, a young person who also cited how three of their peers either returned to or stayed in Civita to grow tourism-related businesses. In Castelmezzano, young people are encouraged to take on an active role. A young person involved in the Volo dell'Angelo at the onset while still in high school (and continued to work there at the time of this research) expressed that a senior administrative official of Castelmezzano made the effort to involve young people since the beginning and reimburse them as quickly as possible for their contribution (Tour Operator 01). This was confirmed by that official who remarked that the success of the Volo allowed for all volunteers of young people (25 to 30 years old) to be paid within the first year after its launch, and today employs 22 young people (Administrator 02).

Of course, both cases continue to depopulate with young people as the first to go. This was also well noted in the interviews, but not without reference to the impact of the loss. For example, both in Civita and Castelmezzano young people contribute to the success of tourism through filling physically demanding jobs required of such outdoor excursions that both towns offer, canyoning and zip-lining, respectively (Administrator 03, Tour Operator 01). Their absence is also noted in a more general sense with comments such as, "B&Bs aren't made by elderly people, it's young people that invest" (Administrator 03), "this town needs young people [. . .] otherwise it will become a ghost town" (Tour Operator 04), and "there could be more" (Agri-tour Operator 02, regarding involving young people in the tourism offer to meet the growing demand). Both in their presence and their absence, young people are acknowledged as critical actors in the growth of these towns.

3.2   What Makes these Actors Social Innovators?

It was the decision by these actors to remain, return, or move to Castelmezzano or Civita that initially informed us of their reflexive tendencies. These young people were actively deciding to live in a place that was rapidly depopulating (and continues to do so today), and with limited access to services and leisure activities. This conscious effort to live in a place considered to be "left behind" required a decision-making process weighing the challenges and the benefits of such a move. The challenges included the economic costs of remaining (Tour Operator 01, Restaurant Owner, Agri-tour Operator 02), limited access to necessities such as schools (Tour Operator 01, Restaurant Owner, Agri-Tour Operator 01, Administrator

02, Administrator 03, Tour Operator 03, Tour Operator 04), and the limits to self-realization (Tour Operator 01, Tour Operator 02, Tour Operator 04, Restaurant owner).

The emotional response to these challenges came out naturally in the interviews, with frequent comments: "We chose to live and work here, even if there's a ton of difficulties. There are few consumers, so lots of difficulties" (Agri-tour Operator 02), "Here, if you want to live well, you have to make a lot of sacrifices, I mean a lot" (Restaurant Owner), and "I have my limits to staying here, I'm not in a creative context, I'm not able to find people that give me input or feedback for developing an idea, and so I have to get out of here, two weeks in Milan, two weeks out of here" (Tour Operator 02).

For the benefits, we analyzed and coded every interview for references to this decision-making process to remain, return, or move from elsewhere. The codes were then subdivided into varying motivations behind this decision, and the three most cited were "roots," "rural idyll," and "self-realization" (see Table 3) to be explained in detail below. Analyzing these three motivations, while recognizing the interviewees' affirmation that these challenges exist, begins to show us in practice what Pritchard et al. have referred to as the "collaborators in tourism storying" and "co-creators of tourism knowledge" (Pritchard et al. 2011, p. 952). They are the reflexive selves both very aware of the challenges they face and hopeful in addressing those challenges.

3.2.1 Roots

First, seven of the interviewees spoke about family or their connection to the town as a reason to return and participate in its reclamation, referenced 11 times. Two of these interviewees used the term *radici* or "roots" to describe this connection, while others referred to attachment of place and family, all of which were ultimately categorized under the "roots" code. In our first case, when asked what aspects of Castelmezzano convinced them to return, one interviewee said, "I don't know how to explain it... it's a love for the territory, for the town, the roots of my own land" (Administrator 01). Another answered, "new perspectives, because having my own business I preferred to go out a bit and visit everything in order to gain inspiration to bring back to the family business" (Agri-tour Operator 01). A third spoke more about the obligation to their family:

> I thought about leaving many times, but we put the brakes on that idea because my husband had a farm here in town. Before having married me, he invested a lot of money [...] so it would have been a shame to abandon it all. [...] Later, [after the financial crisis] we didn't think any more about leaving. We stayed here because the kids were young, so we had... we relied a bit on the family. We stayed here. (Restaurant Owner)

Three interviewees of Civita carried similar sentiments. The first, who never thought about leaving to begin with said, "I've always had this connection to Civita. My idea was always that I must do everything I can to stay and work here" (Tour Operator

03). The second, "My grandparents were farmers, so I come from a family of farmers and they transmitted that passion to us. More than anything it started as a hobby, and then instead it became an actual job" (Agri-food Tour Operator 02). The third, an interviewee who had moved to Civita from elsewhere, nevertheless referred to this attachment:

> When I arrived here, it was a choice to live in the town of my paternal grandparents because I hadn't lived here before. I came on Sundays to spend a few hours with my grandparents. [...] Then, over the years, 12 years in Rome, I always felt more strongly the need to reintegrate something that was inside of me, still yet in an unconscious way. But I was above all connected to this place. I mean, my roots were here. Actually, I call it father land and father tongue because my grandfather always represented the person that I visualized whenever I was in hard times... I was always very attached to him and I didn't know it [laughs]. (Tour Operator 02)

For Civita, both Tour Operators 02 and 03 spoke of this attachment regarding their Arbëreshë heritage. Tour Operator 03 boasted direct ties, having been born and raised in Civita and speaking fluent Arbëreshë. The former spoke of their paternal ties to the Arbëreshë culture, how their father opened the Arbëreshë museum in Civita, and how "there is Arbëreshë blood inside of me, but I really really live in Arbëreshë music more than the language because my mother wasn't Arbëreshë" (Tour Operator 02).

3.2.2 Rural Idyll

The second motivation, what we have referred to and coded as "rural idyll," was referenced 12 times in seven interviews. Five traits were found to make up this code, and were added as sub-codes: "social proximity" (Restaurant Owner, Agri-tour Operator 02, Administrator 03, Tour Operator 04), "access to nature" (Administrator 03, Tour Operator 04), "quality food" (Agri-Tour Operator 02, Tour Operator 04), "a sense of tranquility" (Tour Operator 01, Agri-tour Operator 01, Administrator 03, Tour Operator 04), and an "overall healthier lifestyle" (Administrator 01, Tour Operator 01, Tour Operator 04).

Rural idyll is a motivation particularly valuable to understanding the reflexive self and the subjective side of sustainability, both to be considered fundamental to stimulating social innovation. As mentioned above, there are many economic and social challenges of living in these small towns, but when analyzing the rural idyll motivation, we saw that interviewees were not only considering the draw of these villages, such as family and roots, but also the drawbacks of living elsewhere: rural as alternative to urban. This was especially true for sub-codes "sense of tranquility" and "overall healthier lifestyle." One interviewee recounted their time living in Rome where they were happy up to a point and then, "I didn't like living there anymore, I noticed the disorganized life, the problems with public transportation, always full... so the tranquility of the countryside... you live it differently when you're born in that place" (Tour Operator 01). Later they said, "The elderly, in respect to those who live in the city, maybe have a more accentuated physical strength [. . .] they walk so much!" (Tour Operator 01). An administrator from Civita also made a direct comparison to Rome, "Every time I go up to Rome for a meeting, I get a headache. The tranquility here allows you to also work in a serene way" (Administrator 03). Other comparisons included, "It's a small town so there isn't the stress of the city" (Tour Operator 04), and "there's tranquility, plus there's no traffic, no metro, it's the countryside" (Agri-tour Operator 01). In their words, Civita and Castelmezzano are represented as the opposite choice to Rome, a place symbolizing the urban/metropolitan context with all its chaotic and stressful qualities, and a polarized choice to the rural idyll.

3.2.3 Self-Realization

Of all the motivations for staying, returning, or moving from elsewhere, the most prevalent (18 references, eight interviews) was coded as "self-realization." This code refers to the comments made by interviewees who found that, by deciding to live in Civita or Castelmezzano, they had the opportunity to form their identity, most commonly through their profession. This is closely related to the issue of social innovation, because in order to realize their life project, they had to invest their professional knowledge in finding possible solutions to improve the social situation of these places and to favor the needed changes.

The previous citations regarding the roots code also carry a connotation of self-realization, such as Tour Operator 02 who wanted to follow a feeling inside of them or Agri-food Operator 02 who turned a hobby into a career. These three motivations (roots, rural idyll, and self-realization) are not mutually exclusive and often overlap. Finding self-realization to be a prominent motivation for our interviewees is in accordance with our theoretical framework, where we refer to how Beck's reflexive modernity allows for such individuals to seek out their life project while still contributing to collective action towards social innovation in these towns, in non-contradictory terms.

In Castelmezzano, as mentioned, the Volo dell'Angelo employed local young people who were not only motivated by the economic benefit of employment, but also saw it as a chance for self-realization. For one interviewee, the Volo kickstarted their career in tourism. They said, "My entire path revolved around the Volo, because when I started this training [for the Volo] I was still in high school. But after, I decided to go to university and so also decided to study Tourism Science" (Tour Operator 01). They said that this decision to return was strong because "I have an attachment to the Volo, maybe because, yeah, I was there when it was born and saw it grow. But not only me, all of us who work there. Especially those who have been there since the start." They continued on, adamant about their early decision to return, "People told me, 'what are you going to do with a degree?' and I always responded, 'but sorry why can't there be a qualified person working in the Volo ticket office?'" (Tour Operator 01).

For the administrators involved in the establishment of the Volo, they also saw a benefit to developing their career in Castelmezzano. Adding on to their comments about *radici* (see above), one administrator said:

> I don't know how to explain it... it's a love for the territory, for the town, the roots of my own land... to believe in an economic-touristic development project, even if it's in a small town... it's like a challenge. It's a challenge because everyone thinks that in small towns, you can't do it. Maybe we in Castelmezzano are an example that even in small places, de-centered and with less services, you can develop. (Administrator 01)

They went on to say that after living in Milan, a city where all the services, essential or otherwise, can be found:

> At a certain point, one of the reasons I returned was because [in Milan] I found myself in the Piazza del Duomo one Sunday, very sad... you are one number, only one, a drop in the middle of the ocean of people who pass by. You have all the services you need but... I don't know... better to be an integral part of an economic and social project in a small town than to be one number in a city of three million people. (Administrator 01)

The second administrator, the mayor of Castelmezzano during the establishment of the Volo, said, "Being a mayor is the most gratifying thing, even if you do it in a place so small, because whatever you think up you can realize, if you are lucky, consistent, resilient and also supported. If all of these elements are combined, what happened at Castelmezzano could happen again" (Administrator 02). Choosing to live in a small town meant that our interviewees had an opportunity to make more of an impact, for the resources available per capita and for the opportunity that arises from need in these "left behind" places. One young agri-tour operator spoke about choosing to start a business in a completely new sector for them and their family:

> My father and my brother started with a construction company, but this sector was in crisis right away. About ten years ago, the sector was already in decline [...] so they thought to create, let's say, an activity parallel to that one, changing to a completely different sector. There was this land here, left fallow by our grandparents, about two hectares, and from there we set off to cultivate it. (Agri-tour Operator 02)

This interviewee's family invested in a business completely unrelated to their original family business, yet chose to do so given that they already had the land. This again checks out with the theoretical framework, where we find risk-taking as characteristic of the reflexive self who tends to take these risks in rural peripheral areas as they represent "safer" regions of experimentation specifically for post-crisis development based on greener ideas of quality of life (Wiskerke 2009).

For our interviewees on the whole, the decision to stay, return, or move from elsewhere was motivated primarily by roots, rural idyll, and self-realization, meaning that they were considering their place attachment, the beauty of rurality, and their life project potential in these towns. Partaking in sustainable tourism ventures from this standpoint fulfills that vision of a greener quality of life, but above all requires hope to turn these challenged "left behind" places into places that are moving ahead (Pritchard et al. 2011). The appeal of returning to the roots, along with the desire for self-realization and the realization of a shared project among different actors (both private and public) who work as a leading group, seems to be the basic ingredient for opening the way to social innovation and to the transformation of the rural idyll into a working reality.

3.3 From Sustainable Tourism to Social Innovation and Back

The CAQDAS analysis of the interviews revealed that sustainable tourism in Civita and Castelmezzano has changed the socio-cultural status of these towns fostering a wider territorial requalification. Over time, these social changes have allowed tourism itself to develop. However, the purpose of this research is to look beyond the economic status and toward the dynamics between economy, culture, society, and environment. The findings presented here show the benefits tourism may generate in rural economies not only in terms of direct tourism spending and income but also from increased awareness from local residents and local resource enhancement, to new job opportunities, increased quality of life, and changes in lifestyle. The interaction between these two different levels (the purely economic one and the immaterial one) leads to and is fed in return by what we identify as social innovation.

Accordingly we identified the four most prominent codes of social innovation (Table 4): (1) "nexogenous networking," coded at any mention of networking between businesses or individuals in the case with external actors; (2) "tourist encounter," coded at any mention of exchanges between residents and tourists and/or what effect this exchange has on residents; (3) "community involvement," coded at any mention of efforts made to involve the community in social change processes with success; (4) "local networking," coded at any mention of networking between businesses or individuals within the case.

By definition, social innovation is rooted in collective citizen action across places and fostered by social collaboration and social learning (Bock 2016), so it is no surprise that our interviewees spoke about networking, community involvement, and interactions with tourists in reference to the success of these social innovation processes. To start, the community was involved both formally and informally when requalifying Castelmezzano and Pietrapertosa around the Volo dell'Angelo. Formally, the Volo was managed by a *società pubblica* or public enterprise, "that was constituted by the two municipalities, and also before by the mountain community, a consortium with exclusively public participation" (Administrator 02). The requalification on the whole for Castelmezzano also formally saw community members convert spaces into touristic places, such as places for lodging and eating,

	Codes	# Interviews	# References
Table 4 Codes related to social innovation	Nexogenous networking	8	18
	Tourist encounter	7	12
	Community involvement	7	11
	Local networking	6	11
	Total no. references		52

as we saw in the description of the cases above. However, some community members would take part in other, less formal ways:

> In Pietrapertosa, you will see some small houses in the Arabic district, almost all of them uninhabited. Among the last, literally way up at the top there is a 90-year-old woman [. . .] She waits for people, dressed in the clothes as we say from once upon a time, so the woman with the black scarf on her head. She's behind her door, waiting for people to pass by and then, when they do, she opens the door. Since there are all these empty houses, the people don't expect it. So, they start to speak with her right away, "how are you able to live up here? How do you bring the bags?" [. . .] They start to ask the standard questions, and she starts to speak about everything. She tells them about what she cooks, about her clothes [. . .] It's as if she is waiting behind her door to give a personal interview. It's very beautiful. (Tour Operator 01, coded at *community involvement*)

In Civita, one tour operator described their community as very hospitable, and "a bit sentinel." They went on to say, "They willingly provide information" (Tour Operator 02). In the same town, another tour operator attributed the cleanliness and order of the streets to involvement of the community, rather than to the municipality: "Everything here is beautiful and perfect, but when you live here every day, you know that the streets are cleaned thanks to the citizens that clean and cut the weeds" (Tour Operator 04). The behavior is similar in Castelmezzano, as noted by an administrator who said,

> You've seen the flowers. . . at the beginning we [the administration] planted them, but with the heat they dried up... However, today if you take a look, on every balcony there are flowers. It's become a value to decorate the front of your own home, and before it wasn't like this, it wasn't at all like this. (Administrator 02, coded at *community involvement*)

These informal tourist activities represent the towns' dependence on civic self-reliance and self-organization that Bock proffers as distinctive of rural social innovation (2016). She adds that another distinction is its "cross-sectoral and translocal collaborations" (p. 554) or *nexogenous* development (p. 569). In the case of sustainable tourism, the relevant actors are not only the residents of the rural areas but also their urban and peri-urban counterparts, the tourists themselves (the exogenous resource), who are linked to rural spaces thanks to the enhanced capital of that space (the neo-endogenous resource). Referring to our interviewees, other examples of nexogenous development tools may include: brands and certifications (such as the club *I Borghi Più Belli d'Italia*), social networking sites (mentioned by Agri-tour Operator 01, Tour Operator 01, Tour Operator 02, Tour Operator 03, Tour Operator 04), alternative food networks that shorten the supply chain (mentioned by Agri-tour Operator 02), extra-regional tour collaborations (mentioned by Agri-tour Operator 01, Tour Operator 01, Tour Operator 03, Tour Operator 04), and film (mentioned by Administrator 02).

The revitalization for Castelmezzano and Civita is then twofold. Through innovative collaborative structures, tourism flows and the responding hospitality have been enhanced, but another process is occurring at the same time: our interviews expose not only the observation by interviewees of an increased number of encounters between residents and tourists, but also the positive effect this has on the community (Tour Operator 01, Administrator 01, Administrator 02, Agri-tour

Operator 01, Restaurant Owner, Agri-tour Operator 02, Tour Operator 03). Comments include "the work is great. You wind up getting to know so many people" (Tour Operator 01) and "tourism brings culture and it opens your mind" (Administrator 01). The outlook that residents had on tourists had not always been so positive:

> The people like having tourists. I notice it also when I hear them speak with them, when they respond to their questions. At the start maybe they were bothered by the continuous questions, [. . .] a bit fed up by them. Instead now I really see that there's an opening, even with the elderly, to converse and speak, to recount lots of things, so I think there was an evolution. Actually, I would say maybe an education of the inhabitants [laughs]. (Tour Operator 01, coded at *tourist encounter*)

A similar observation was made about Civita:

> In the last few years even them, the elderly, are seeing tourism in a different light. They are way more open to conversing with [tourists], also passing down old traditions and their ways of cooking. Today cuisine is a very vast cultural exchange. So, this is opening up a lot, this aspect of understanding between the tourist and the resident [. . .] Sometimes [the elderly] literally organize demonstrative kitchens, like in B&Bs. They show you, like how to make our traditional pasta or how to make bread. (Agri-tour Operator 02, coded at *tourism encounter*)

The relationship between the resident and tourist is fostered by a sense of hospitality and the pre-existing tendency for these rural areas to favor social proximity, but at the same time the encounter itself and the investment from young people to believe in change has prompted for the actual tourist development. Our sustainable tourism actors and community members on the whole are sharing in this reciprocal tourism exchange. As mentioned, these subjects have a place-centered vision, one that requires a positive outlook in order to ultimately transmit the place to the tourists as desirable to visit. While some of our actors perceived this positive on the outset, which may have motivated their decision to stay, return or remain in their respective towns, other actors, like the above-mentioned elderly folk, acquired that outlook over time, largely in part thanks to the actions of young people, our reflexive selves.

4 Conclusions

The purpose of this research is to address the links between sustainable tourism and social innovation by looking beyond the pure economic status of the case areas and casting a light on the dynamics between economy, culture, society, and environment. The role of young entrepreneurs as innovators, the actors who have chosen to live in these peripheral areas, is pivotal for the development strategies of such areas, and the reflexive approach to one's "own life" is what makes it possible to steer the trajectories of these areas away from abandonment.

In both Castelmezzano and Civita, towns situated in a regional and national park respectively, sustainable tourism has favored social innovation, mainly through the manmade and natural landscape beauty which has allowed for tourism to prosper both directly (for visitors who want to escape the city and enjoy the views) or indirectly (for visitors who benefit from the natural beauty through the availability of ecotourism activities such as hiking, rock climbing, canyoning, zip lines, etc.). The word clouds below (Fig. 6) indicate that the core themes in the interviews align with these resources, with some shared points between towns ("tourism," "young people," "park," "food," "community," "territory") and their unique defining points: "Arbëreshë," "Pollino," and "anthropomorphic" (referring to the homes that resemble faces) in Civita, and the "Volo dell'Angelo," the "Dolomites," and "honey" in Castelmezzano.

Peripheral rural areas can act as a sort of incubator for social innovation experiments where our actors can unfold their life projects with low risk, utilizing a tourism development based on the need to change the living conditions of these places.

Italian natural protected areas are even more primed for such experimentation when it comes to sustainable tourism given their intrinsic ability to combine economic growth, environmental sustainability, and protection of common goods (Phillips 2002; Cassola 2005; Consorzio Aaster 2013). With the longstanding recognition that these natural areas also contain a built environment valuable to the identity, economy, and wellbeing of the Italian people, parks have more recently applied strategies capable of combining conservation and enhancement, with the involvement of local communities (Salvatore and Chiodo 2017). We named the formal and informal involvement of community members in our thematic findings and identified how revitalization processes that engage the community create a sort of feedback loop: sustainable tourism feeds social innovation (such as innovative networking strategies, community-based development, and changes in lifestyle through encounters with tourists [see Table 4]) which in turn enhances the tourism offer. The impact on the observed towns was increased awareness from local residents, local resource enhancement, new job opportunities, and increased quality of life.

Furthermore, our investigation reveals a new approach to mobility and community that is taking shape in our selected cases. Staying, leaving, or returning are incorporated into people's "own life" trajectories as a realistic but impermanent choice, often giving way to circular movements that affect the "sense of place," even for the permanent dwellers. This new sense of community is particularly important in the perspective of resilience because these peripheral inner areas display strategic resources to mobilize in times of economic, environmental, and, more recently, public health crises. For instance, more recently the outcomes of the COVID-19 pandemic are revealing to us the importance of resources such as clean air, open spaces, and low population density to create sustainable alternatives for development.

In this context, tourism's role has yet to be clearly outlined. After our fieldwork and data elaboration, it seems that tourism could be an important, strategic tool to improve life quality and sustainability through resource mobilization. On the other hand, it is not clear how and when this might happen. We do know, however, that a fundamental part is played by the community members old and new, and by their ability to pursue shared paths of innovation. Thus, continuing a critical read into the role of these actors will remain pertinent to following the socio-cultural and economic change that social innovation, in the framework of sustainable tourism, is bringing to these peripheral rural areas.

References

Aquilino L, Armenski T, Wise N (2018) Assessing the competitiveness of Matera and the Basilicata Region (Italy) ahead of the 2019 European Capital of Culture. Tour Hosp Res. https://doi.org/10.1177/1467358418787360

Barbera F, Parisi T (2019) Innovatori sociali. La sindrome di Prometeo nell'Italia che cambia. Il Mulino, Bologna

Barkley DL (2006) The value of case study research on rural entrepreneurship: useful method. In Presented Joint ERS-RUPRI conf., exploring rural entrepreneurship: imperatives opportunities res., Washington, DC

Beaumont N (2011) The third criterion of ecotourism: are ecotourists more concerned about sustainability than other tourists? J Ecotour 10:135–148

Beaumont E, Brown D (2018) It's the sea and the beach more than anything for me local surfer's and the construction of community and *communitas* in a rural Cornish seaside village. J Rural Stud 59:58–66

Beck U (1986) Risikogesellschaft. Suhrkamp, Frankfurt

Beck U, Ziegler U (1997) Eigenes Leben. Ausflüge in die unbekannte Gesellchaft, in der wir leben. Beck'sche Verlagsbuchhandlung, München

Benkler Y, Nissembaum H (2006) Commons-based peer production and virtue. J Polit Philos 14 (4):394–419

Bock BB (2016) Rural marginalisation and the role of social innovation; a turn towards nexogenous development and rural reconnection. Sociol Rural 56(4):552–573

Borghi E (2017) Piccole Italie: le aree interne e la questione territoriale. Donzelli, Roma

Bortoletto N, Grignoli D (eds) (2019) Dal locale al globale e ritorno: nuovi paradigmi e nuovi modelli di azione. FrancoAngeli, Milano

Borzyszkowski J, Marczak M, Zarębski P (2016) Spatial diversity of tourist function development: the municipalities of Poland's West Pomerania Province. Acta Geogr Slov 56(2):267–276

Bourdieu P (1984) Distinction: a social critique of the judgement of taste. Routledge, London

Bourdieu P, Richardson JG (1986) Handbook of theory and research for the sociology of education. The forms of capital. Greenwood Press, New York, pp 241–258

Brentano F (1973) Psychology from an empirical standpoint (A.C. Rancurello, D.B. Terrell, and L. McAlister, Trans.). Routledge, London. (Original work published 1874)

Carrosio G (2019) I margini al centro. L'Italia delle aree interne tra fragilità e innovazione. Donzelli, Roma

Cassola P (2005) Turismo sostenibile e aree naturali protette. ETS, Pisa

Ceballos-Lascuràin H (1991) Tourism, ecotourism and protected areas. Parks 2:31–35

Consorzio Aaster (2013) Parchi come luogo di incontro tra green economy e green society. Federparchi, Ministero dell'Ambiente e della Tutela del Territorio e del Mare

De Rossi A (ed) (2018) Riabitare l'Italia. Le aree interne tra abbandoni e riconquiste. Donzelli, Roma

Defert P (1967) Le Taux de Fonction Touristique: Mise au Point et Critique. In: Aix-en-Provence: Centre des Hautes Etudes Touristiques. du Tourisme, Les Cahiers

Evans G, Foord J (2008) Cultural mapping and sustainable communities: planning for the arts revisited. Cult Trend 17(2):65–96

Fiorini S, Tagarelli G, Boattini A, Luiselli D, Piro A, Tagarelli A, Pettener D (2007) Ethnicity and evolution of the biodemographic structure of Arbëreshe and Italian populations of the Pollino area, southern Italy (1820–1984). Am Anthropol 109:735–746

Halfacree K (2006) Rural space: constructing a three-fold architecture. In: Cloke P, Marzden T, Mooney P (eds) Handbook of rural studies. Sage, London, pp 44–62

Hammer T, Mose I, Siegrist D, Weixlbaumer N (2007) Protected areas and regional development in Europe: towards a new model for the 21st century, protected areas and regional development in Europe. Towards a new model for the 21st century, pp 233–246

Horlings LG, Marsden TK (2014) Exploring the "new rural paradigm" in Europe: eco-economic strategies as a counterforce to the global competitiveness agenda. Eur Urban Reg Stud 21 (1):4–20

Husserl E (1989) The crisis of European sciences and transcendental phenomenology: an introduction to phenomenological philosophy. Northwestern University Press, Evanston

ISTAT (Istituto Nazionale di Statistica) (2020) Microdata Available at https://www.istat.it/en/services?data-and-indicators

Kuščer K, Mihalič T, Pechlaner H (2017) Innovation, sustainable tourism and environments in mountain destination development: a comparative analysis of Austria, Slovenia and Switzerland. J Sustain Tour 25(4):489–504

Maretti M, Salvatore R (2012) The link between sustainable tourism and local social development. A sociological reassessment. Sociologica Ital J Sociol 2. https://doi.org/10.2383/38271

Marković S, Perić M, Mijatov M, Doljak D, Žolna M (2017) Application of tourist function indicators in tourism development. J Geograph Ins "Jovan Cvijić" SASA 67(2):163–178

Messely R, Rogge E, Dessein J (2013) Using the rural web in dialogue with regional stakeholders. J Rural Stud 32:400–410

Milone P, Ventura F (2011) Networking the rural. Royal Van Gorcum, Assen

Moulaert F, Nussbaumer J (2005) The social region – beyond the territorial dynamics of the learning economy. Eur Urban Reg Stud 12(1):45–64

Moulaert F, MacCallum D, Mehmood A, Hamdouch A (eds) (2013) The international handbook on social innovation: collective action, social learning and transdisciplinary research. Edwar Elgar, Cheltenham

Murdoch J (2000) Networks—a new paradigm of rural development? J Rural Stud 16(4):407–419

Murdoch J (2006) Networking rurality: emergent complexity in the countryside. In: Cloke P, Marsden T, Mooney P (eds) Handbook of rural studies. Sage, London, pp 174–181

Nicholls A, Simons J, Gabriel M (2015) New Frontiers in social innovation research. Palgrave Macmillan, London

OECD (2006) The new rural paradigm: policies and governance. OECD Publishing, Paris

Pais I, Provasi G (2015) Sharing economy: a step towards "re-embedding" the economy? Stato e Mercato 105(3):347–377

Parsons T (1978) Action, theory and the human condition. Free Press, New York

Pearce D (1995) Tourism today: a geographical analysis. CABI, Wallingford

Phillips A (Ed) (2002) Sustainable tourism in protected areas. Guidelines for planning and management. IUCN, WCPA, Best practice protected areas guidelines series, No. 8, UK

Pritchard A, Morgan N, Ateljevic I (2011) Hopeful tourism: a new transformative perspective. Ann Tour Res 38(3):941–963

Privitera W (2015) Ulrich Beck. Un percorso intellettuale. Sociologia Ital-AIS J Sociol 6:11–26

Putnam RD (2000) Bowling alone: the collapse and revival of American community. Simon & Schuster, New York

Ryan GW (2004) Using a word processor to tag and retrieve blocks of text. Field Methods 16 (1):109–130

Salvatore R, Chiodo E (2017) Non più e non ancora. Le aree fragili tra conservazione ambientale, cambiamento sociale e sviluppo turistico, 1st edn. Franco Angeli, Milano, IT

Salvatore R, Chiodo E, Fantini A (2018) Tourism transition in peripheral rural areas: theories, issues and strategies. Ann Tour Res 68:41–51. https://doi.org/10.1016/j.annals.2017.11.003

Scheler M (1980) Problems of a sociology of knowledge. Routledge, London

Schutz A (1967) The phenomenology of the social world. Northwestern University Press, Evanston, IL

Scott R (2007) Prefatory chapter: institutions and social innovation. In: Hamalainen TJ, Heiskala R (eds) Social innovations, institutional change and economic performance. Edward Elgar, Cheltenham, pp viii–xxi

Sharpley R, Jepson D (2011) Rural tourism: a spiritual experience? Ann Tour Res 38(1):52–71

Van der Ploeg JD (2009) The new peasantries: struggles for autonomy and sustainability in an era of empire and globalization. Routledge, London

Van der Ploeg JD, Marsden TJ (eds) (2008) Unfolding webs. The dynamics of regional rural development. Van Gorcum, Assen

Van der Ploeg JD, Jingzhong Y, Schneider S (2010) Rural development reconsidered: building on comparative perspectives from China, Brazil and the European Union. Riv Econ Agrar 2:163–190

Wagner A (1970) Alfred Schutz: on phenomenology and social relations. Chicago University Press, Chicago, IL

Wallace G, Russell A (2004) Eco-cultural tourism as a means for the sustainable development of culturally marginal and environmentally sensitive regions. Tour Stud 4:235–254

Williams PW, Ponsford IF (2009) Confronting Tourism's environmental paradox: transitioning for sustainable tourism. Future 41:396–404

Wilson GA (2007) Multifunctional agriculture: a transition theory perspective. CABI, Wallingford

Wiskerke JSC (2009) On places lost and places regained: reflections on the alternative food geography and sustainable regional development. Int Plan Stud 14(4):369–387

Woods M (2007) Engaging the global countryside: globalization, hybridity and the reconstitution of rural place. Prog Hum Geogr 31(4):485–507

Yin RK (2017) Case study research and applications: design and methods. Sage, Los Angeles, CA

Transformation to Seasonal Villages: Second-Home Tourism as Initiator of Rural Diversification

Aleksandra Terzić and Biljana Petrevska

1 Introduction

The core objective of this study is to examine the process of transforming low-density rural areas from permanent to seasonal (second-home tourism) settlements. Tourism is considered a powerful tool in the substitution of an ongoing abandonment process with seasonal vitality. Small peripheral villages from Southern and Eastern Serbia (SES) were used as the case study, in line of contributing to the literature on the general phenomenon of depopulation of rural areas. Further, possibilities for prolonging rural vitality by second-home tourism expansion were examined. In this manner, the study clarifies that some peripheral villages have good preconditions for using tourism as a sort of sustainable development strategy. However, tourism development may also become an initiator of gentrification process in rural areas.

A common characteristic of rural communities is their adaptation ability concerning survival. They seem to be able to change their way of living due to the circumstances they face: income system vulnerability, resiliency, and sensitivity (Ellis 2000). So, by coping with their bare existence and searching for a way out from the economic collapse and global changes (depopulation, migration, the decline in agricultural production, unemployment, rural poverty, climate change, etc.), tourism is seen as a chance. Introducing tourism in impoverished rural

A. Terzić (✉)
Geographical Institute "Jovan Cvijić", Serbian Academy of Sciences and Arts, Belgrade, Serbia
e-mail: a.terzic@gi.sanu.ac.rs

B. Petrevska
Faculty of Tourism and Business Logistics, "Goce Delčev" University – Štip, Štip, North Macedonia
e-mail: biljana.petrevska@ugd.edu.mk

© Springer Nature Switzerland AG 2021
R. P. Marques et al. (eds.), *The Impact of Tourist Activities on Low-Density Territories*, Tourism, Hospitality & Event Management,
https://doi.org/10.1007/978-3-030-65524-2_6

communities of Southeastern Europe is frequently regarded as grasping at straws (Petrevska and Terzić 2020). Small-scale agricultural activity as dominant faced the need for finding productive alternatives in fighting low production and incomes, abandonment, and contamination (Petrevska and Terzić 2020), starting the diversification process (Brandth and Haugen 2011). Besides, peripheral rural areas are often resided in an attractive natural environment, possessing specific capital in terms of uniqueness, traditional setting, and socioeconomic potential. As such, small rural communities may prolong their vitality, by taking their chances in tourism development.

There is an extensive literature on seasonal migrations and second-home tourism development in amenity-rich areas of Western countries while being limited in terms of the same process in peripheral rural areas of transitional countries of Southeastern Europe (SEE). This makes the generalization of some findings quite challenging. Tuulentie (2007: 287) outlines that since the 1970s the number of second-homes has grown fast in the peripheral regions. The same study notes a decrease in the proportion of *natives* (due to depopulation and aging) in favor of *semi-locals*. There is a lack of evidence addressing the impact of empty or irregularly occupied property on community sustainability and the effectiveness of policy interventions (Wallace et al. 2005). Growing awareness for second-home ownership was seen in many studies to deliver a valuable contribution to local economies as part of the tourism industry (Wallace et al. 2005).

Tourism is introduced as a specific diversification strategy in underdeveloped regions and counties, thus becoming part of many national strategic plans (Iorio and Corsale 2010, 2014). As such, increased attention was placed on development issues encouraging diversification of rural economy (Brotherton 1989). Tourism represents a source of alternative income for rural communities to escape from poverty and possibly accelerate social progress. Improving the conditions for alternative business (non-agricultural) is the main precondition for introducing other economic activities and generating jobs in the rural area (Orboi 2012). Quite recently, national and local governments in many SEE countries posed some serious initiatives for practicing small-scale rural tourism as the developmental goal for the future. Therefore, some villages activated their amenities and began providing seasonal tourist services. Consequently, the traditional rural economy started a shift from productive (agriculture) to the service sector (recreation and leisure).

2 Literature Review

This literature review deals with the main concepts and issues related to the research: loss of vitality, second-home tourism, and rural tourism, particularly for the case of low-density territories.

2.1   Loss of Vitality of Rural Areas

Low-density territories worldwide are considered to be less favored and least developed, faced with drastic changes, being politically insignificant and economically disadvantaged (Blackman et al. 2004). As such, peripheral areas are faced with many challenges and uncertainties and acquire an urgent need for economic reconstruction. Aside from its geographical location, the term *periphery* carries social, political, and economic implications. It frequently becomes a synonym for marginalization, disadvantage, lack of technological infrastructure, and political weakness (Brown and Hall 2000). With the disappearance of the principal economic activity (agriculture), limited production, lack of markets, and low prices eventually caused the demographic decline and abandonment (Salvatore et al. 2018).

Rural vitality reflects the positive characteristics of certain places that make them suitable and desirable for living. It is strongly affected by migration, population change, age, household structure, employment, labor market, income per capita, poverty level, availability of social services and facilities, cultural and environmental aspects of the settlement, community cohesion, etc. (Turcanu and Koomen 2012). The vitality of rural areas nowadays becomes a concern for policymakers in most countries, being a result of depopulation trends and abandonment of the countryside in search of jobs, amenities, or services (Turcanu and Koomen 2012). Regrettably, many peripheral areas in Europe are experiencing the loss of vitality. This is particularly the case for the developing countries (in transition), specifically within the Southeastern Europe. Therefore, countries, in which agricultural production remains a major part of the economy, must find a way to revitalize declining countryside and ensure possibilities for a more sustainable future (Naghiu et al. 2005).

Rural areas, being economically underdeveloped and structurally weak, are considered problematic from the developmental point of view. They are being permanently dependent on state support and lacking service centers, infrastructure, sociability, and cultural performances (Lampič and Potočnik-Slavič 2007). Vujicic et al. (2013) emphasize the role of human resources at the local level as a key factor of development, contributing to the diversification of the economy and increasing the welfare of rural communities. According to Mihai et al. (2019), intensification of agricultural and non-agricultural activities, investments in infrastructure, higher income levels, and improvement of living conditions imply the rising of vitality. Also, Crull and Cook (2000) outline that quantity and quality of rural housing and available services are important to retain current residents and draw potential workers and retirees, therefore having a significant impact on the economic vitality of rural areas. In particular, local housing and local government decisions reflected in strong leadership and entrepreneurship may positively affect community vitality (Cook et al. 2009). Therefore, specific development perspectives using existing local potential by activating human capital and various natural and cultural resources are needed to provide more sustainable rural livelihoods.

On top of that, there is a common stand that second-homes are slowly becoming the dominant real-estate type in peripheral rural areas of Europe. Moreover, the expansion of second-homes remains to be generally perceived as a local phenomenon. Early studies note that demand for second-homes was expressed in the reuse of surplus housing left by the effects of rural depopulation, especially in the coastal and upland locations of attractive natural beauty (Wallace et al. 2005). Recently, many studies considered how empty or irregularly occupied properties (second-homes) were part of wider social and economic transformations affecting rural communities. Yet, it is little known how it affects the sustainability aspect.

2.2 Second-Home Tourism in Low-Density Territories

Tourism is commonly considered the act or process of spending time and money away from home in pursuit of unknown places, recreation, relaxation, and pleasure. It is reflected in principles of displacement, return, motivation, and hospitality while making use of the commercial provision of services at tourist destinations (Netto 2009).

Second-home tourism, on the other hand, represents a particular phenomenon interconnected with an intense emotional attachment to a place (Borge 2007; Hall 2014). Some tourists may even transcend their typical positions and make a place or a region their regular haunt or even home, in a form of *settled tourists*. They are becoming part-time dwellers (second-homers) representing a kind of hybrid between tourists and locals (Tuulentie 2007). Ties to the seasonal residence are most likely associated with the origin and emotional attachment to the place, but it may also be amenity-related (depending on cultural patterns and traditions of different societies and specific timing of life). Various circumstances determine these migrations, like age, retirement, financial and health status, family, and friendship relationships. As McHugh (1990: 231) outlined "as long as ties to the primary home community remain strong, a permanent move to a seasonal residence is unlikely, while seasonal movement is a substitute for permanent migration."

The occurrence of second-homes in low-density territories seems to be a direct consequence of the human migration patterns. Thus, the *era of mobility* took the central place in urbanization and recently counter-urbanization process (Halfacree 2012). As Löfgren (1999) outlines, rural second-homes may represent the territory of rooting in an era of increasing careers of urban mobility. Indeed, in contemporary society, there is a trend of possessing multiple homes, while at least some of these are related to leisure and tourism (Tuulentie 2007). There is vast scholarship on second-homes, mostly related to strong national traditions. However, the recent upsurge in academic interest reflects more their increased spatial reach (Williams et al. 2004) and recognition of their significance in the sense of mobility and place affiliation (Halfacree 2012; Hall and Müller 2004; Williams and McIntyre 2012).

Generally, second-homes are representing occasional residence of a person that usually lives elsewhere, which is primarily used for leisure and recreation purposes (Shucksmith 1983; Wong and Musa 2014). Therefore, these dwellings may be considered specific tourism-like facilities, having in mind deep relations to leisure and tourism (Hall and Page 2014). Such housing types are found across the world (Hall and Müller 2004), occurring in urban, suburban, and rural environments, being present commonly at the intranational but also at international levels (Halfacree 2012). Their use may also be considered as a normative type of tourism characterized by recurrence, both on time and spatial scale (Jaakson 1986). It is reflected in short- or long-term migration patterns and practicing of rural lifestyles.

Vacation homes, compared to weekend homes, are characterized by a greater distance, occasional but longer visits. As such, they are being relatively independent of the location of the primary home but highly dependent on the geography of amenity-rich landscapes and accessibility (Müller 2004). Second-homes may increasingly be seen as comprising an integral element of home. Thus, refining the traditional concept of home and home culture (Støa 2007) in line with the *era of mobility* (Halfacree 2012; Hall and Müller 2004). It further introduces a concept of dynamic *heterolocalism* (reflected in the second-home practices) which denies dependence on the core *sedentarism* assumption of a single settled home place. It equally disturbs a core concept of tourism as a continuous escape and an extraordinary realm outside the home and everyday life (Tuulentie 2007).

2.3   Rural Tourism as a Way Out for the Low-Density Territories

Increased complexity of tourism trends offers peripheral low-density areas the chance to reconsider their position (Salvatore et al. 2018) and consider tourism as part of an integrated system of rural development (Naghiu et al. 2005). From places of dependency and/or abandonment, peripheral rural areas were currently experiencing tourism transition making their cultural transformation into territories for symbolic consumption (Jepson and Sharpley 2015). The very same attributes that were previously considered to be disadvantageous (isolation and remoteness, rurality, and traditional lifestyles) are now being valued as a new opportunity for low-density areas (Salvatore et al. 2018). This is particularly important for the revitalization and enhancement of rural capital (Garrod et al. 2006) and rural community renewal and survival (Knowd 2006).

Recently, the world experienced saturation with old destinations and the expansion of fresh ones adapted to satisfy the requirements of special interest groups of travelers. In this line, rural tourism offer suits perfectly the contemporary needs of predominantly urban European travelers, having in mind its expansion particularly in Europe. Accommodation establishments in rural areas within the European Union (EU-28 countries) make about a 5.4% share in all tourism establishments. Recent figures show that the overnights spent in such establishments increased by 12% (2012–2015) and represent roughly 15% of the entire accommodation capacity of Europe (Ana 2017). However, it must be noted that rural tourism is primarily focused on domestic travel and second-home tourism (visits to friends and relatives) generating low expenditure on accommodation, only 10% (Bel et al. 2015). Hence, second-home visitation in many rural regions is actually a dominant activity.

Second-home expansion can be perceived as a symptom of the declining countryside on one hand. On the other, it provides opportunities to be used as a valuable source in the tourism development process. For rural communities that suffered an extreme loss of local population, second-homes may be the additional economic contributor, where other development alternatives are lacking (Hall 2014).

3 A Case Study

Region of Southern and Eastern Serbia is chosen as a case study due to its predominantly rural character and agrarian production. This region is considered the poorest, demographically, and economically least developed in Serbia, but with substantial tourism development potentials. Since the 1950s, it has experienced extreme levels of migratory flows and demographic drain, particularly in the rural areas. According to official statistics, out of 745,819 housing units, more than half (53.6%) are located in rural areas (Statistical office of the Republic of Serbia 2011). Furthermore, 17.2% of all registered housing units in this region are temporarily unoccupied (greater level compared to national 14.7%). About 6.6% of rural housing units are abandoned houses (also higher than the national level of 3.5%) indicating that many small peripheral rural areas of SES may be considered depopulated most of the time during the year around. About 7.7% of total housing units in Serbia are used occasionally, mostly for vacation, leisure, and recreation purposes (secondhomes). It is interesting to note that, in rural areas of SES, second-homes make 10.4% of all housing units. The dominant type of property ownership in SES is personal (85.6%) as a result of tradition but also a typical situation of postponing the property-ownership transfer to avoid taxes. About 3.5% of rural houses represent the property of two and more people (spouses or relatives), while the public property represents only 0.8% of the total number of housing units.

Furthermore, this region is well-recognized for a large number of temporary foreign workers, periodically coming back home and do some investing, particularly in their family real estates. Since 2010, the number of returnees to rural villages of SES region has rapidly increased, due to returnees from Serbian diaspora, the first generation of so-called *Gastarbeiter* (temporary workers mostly in German-speaking countries). The second-homeowners seem to be unwilling or unable to sell their old rural houses due to profound emotional attachment to the homeland. This is also influenced by extremely low real-estate prices, low demand market, or due to some legal obstacles (multiple owners due to inheritance, avoiding timely transfer of ownership, avoiding paying taxes, existing debts or mortgage placed on the house, etc.). In the case of picturesque small villages, good position, solid infrastructure, and quality of natural ambiance, low real-estate prices may create a growing demand market for cheap rural houses. Therefore, such rural areas might provide a much-needed escape for the urban business class who are in search for second-homes or for returnees from towns and abroad.

3.1 Methodology and Data

The research applied a multistage methodology. The sample was created based on geographical data, demographic data, data on socioeconomic status, data on housing units, and natural amenities index (Josipović 2018; Statistical Office of the Republic of Serbia 2011), along with the following additional criteria:

- To have a population density less than 100 inhabitants per km^2, indicating a low-density rural area (Dijkstra and Poelman 2014)
- To be distanced from an urban center with over 50,000 inhabitants measured in travel time by the road of 30 min or more (Jonard et al. 2009)
- To be positioned near established tourist center, with good connectivity and existing resource base (outlined in national strategic documents: Strategy of rural tourism development in Serbia 2012; Government of Republic of Serbia 2011, 2016)

Based on the set criteria, the following 55 villages from the SES were chosen for evaluation (Fig. 1) in several micro-regions:

1. Lower Danube area
2. Homolje and Negotin wine region
3. Sokobanja region (spa, Mt. Ozren, Mt. Rtanj)
4. Mt. Stara Planina (prosperous ski center and natural park)
5. Lake Vlasina (nature reserve) and Jerma Canyon (protected nature reserve)
6. Kuršumlija area (Prolom Spa, Lukovska Spa, Kuršumlija spa, and Djavolja Varoš geo-heritage site)

A mixed methodology has proceeded in three stages. In the first stage, a qualitative approach included an extensive review of the literature and analysis of relevant publications. This generally covered the issue of tourism development in low-density territories. Discussion on tourism contribution for prolonged vitality of the rural areas and interconnecting it with the second-home expansion was done. This enabled discussion if the theoretical nature of the research is coherent and consistent with the defined national/regional/municipal socioeconomic goals outlined in relevant strategic and planning documents.

The second stage applied the scholarship research approach (Martin 2010; Van de Ven 2007) and the action research approach (Zuber-Skerritt 1996). This allowed combining the overall academic thinking and the practical knowledge gained from a 2-year-long research on the low-density rural areas in the SES. Extensive data were collected during May–November 2019 when observations and semi-structured

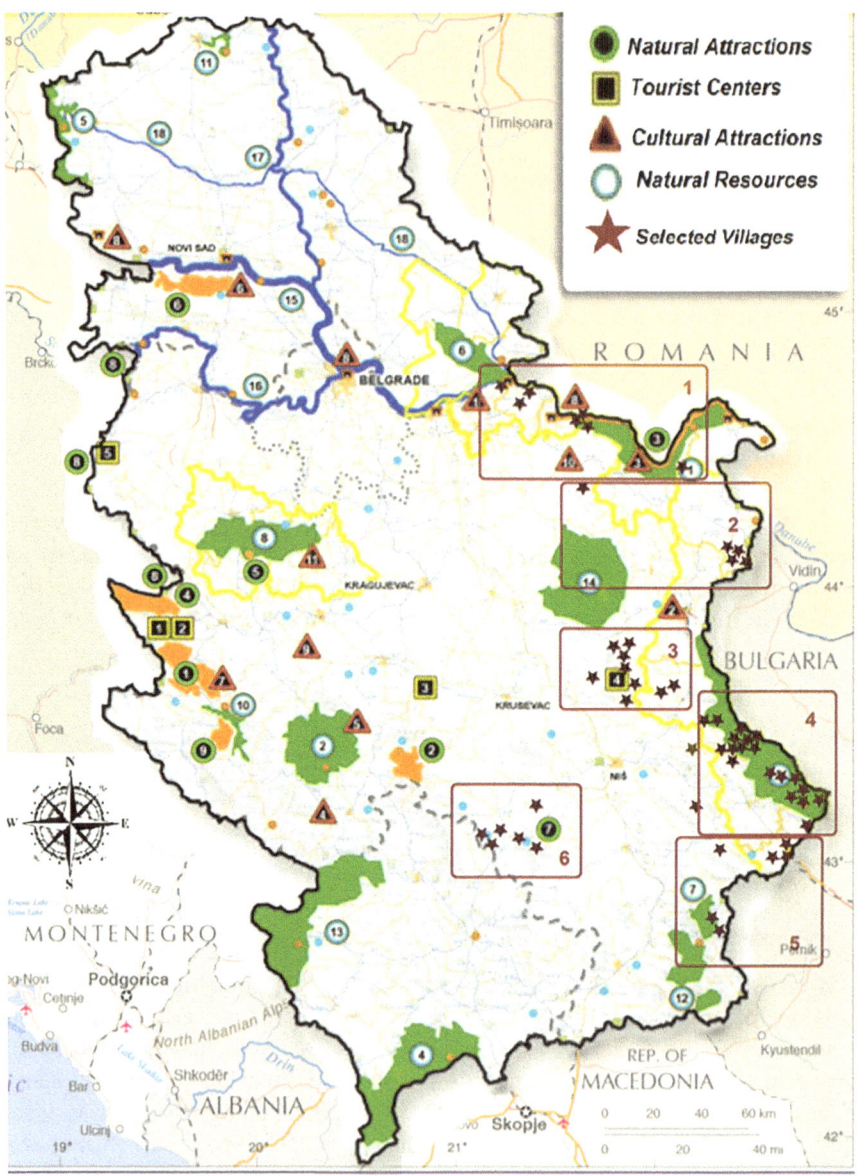

Fig. 1 Sampled villages in selected tourist areas within SES region (Reproduced and adapted from Strategy of Rural Tourism Development in Serbia 2012)

interviews were conducted on casual passers (permanent and seasonal residents) in 55 sampled villages. Before collecting data, an interview protocol was developed. It was designed to serve as a framework for evaluating tourism development potential and the current rural capital of sampled villages (Bogdanov and Janković 2013;

Mahdavi et al. 2013; Terzić et al. 2019; Dimitrov et al. 2020). As such, data on social, economic, environmental, infrastructural, and rural tourism structure was collected. Besides, understandings on how the rural diversification is applied and what individual farm activities were adapted was based on a set of questions related to the personal preferences and attitudes of the interviewees, their household composition, age, and educational and activity level (Meert et al. 2005; Jongeneel et al. 2008; Lange et al. 2013). Furthermore, this stage also incorporated a practical understanding of the current situation in the sampled villages. Based on collected data (from primary and secondary sources), an in-depth evaluation was made upon which the extensiveness of second-home tourism in sampled villages was indicated.

These findings were further tested in the third stage, when a quantitative approach was included with data from secondary sources (Statistical Office of the Republic of Serbia 2011). According to Crull and Cook (2000) for estimation of the economic vitality of rural areas, various indicators may be extracted from the official census data. Those are geographical location (proximity to urban areas and tourist centers), human capital investments (population size, education), economic activities (labor force activity level, diversification level, and economic dependency ratio), demographic characteristics (gender, age), and housing characteristics (household structure and occupancy). In addition, the census provides a readily accessible source in the attempt to measure the number of empty, second (vacation) homes, as well as a possibility to interrelate it with other standard socioeconomic data (Wallace et al. 2005). By standard statistical analysis, the Pearson's correlation coefficient was calculated, and the simple regression models (Moore 2000) were performed, thus directly investigating the connections between the rural diversification and the second-home expansion in the sampled villages. This stage provided statistical support to the previous indications from the field research findings related to the factors that may determine the general patterns and relationships between the second-home development and socioeconomic determinants in the sampled villages. The following hypotheses were developed and tested:

Hypothesis 1
The level of diversification of the rural economy in the low-density territories directly depends on tourism development.

Hypothesis 2
Tourism development (reflected in rural diversification process) in the low-density territories directly depends on the second-home expansion.

Hypothesis 3
There is interconnectivity between the diversification of the rural economy and second-home tourism in low-density territories.

3.2 Results

Table 1 presents various socioeconomic indicators for sampled villages of the SES region, as the expansion of second-homes may be influenced by different factors. Also, it shows main characteristics of the sample, indicating to similarities and differences between observed villages.

Table 2 presents the test of the expansion of second-homes in terms of seasonal vitality by conducting a Pearson correlation method to selected indicators. Second-home expansion is strongly interrelated to the dominance of other types of housing, showing strong negative relationship to permanently occupied ($r = -0.727$, sig. = 0.000), temporarily unoccupied ($r = -0.582$, sig. = 0.000), and abandoned dwellings ($r = -0.540$, sig. = 0.000) (Table 2). Also, the share of second-homes in total housing is positively correlated to the share of single-member households ($r = 0.292$, sig. = 0.031) and the diversification level ($r = 0.388$; sig. = 0.003). Opposite to this, it is negatively correlated to the activity level of the population ($r = -0.343$, sig. = 0.010) and the share of daily migrants ($r = -0.289$, sig. = 0.032) but at moderate level (Newbold et al. 2007).

Table 3 presents the rural diversification level, which is based on the development of service and manufacturing industry in rural areas, measured in the relative share of

Table 1 Descriptive statistics on the sampled villages in SES region

$N = 55$	Min	Max	Mean	Std. dev.
Population[a]	15.00	511.00	159.93	120.79
Population change (1981–2011) (%)[a]	−51.88	−2.72	−31.79	11.86
Population density[a]	0.57	45.51	10.57	10.59
Single-member households (%)[a]	13.43	73.68	35.61	12.32
Elders 65+ (%)[a]	21.77	91.30	48.08	18.30
Daily migrants (%)[a]	0.00	100.00	54.02	32.14
Activity level (%)[a]	5.00	268.75	80.41	58.68
Economic dependency (%)	0.14	174.00	11.11	25.83
Diversification level (III, II)[a]	0.00	100.00	13.70	23.73
University education (%)[a]	0.00	13.11	3.37	3.08
Secondary education (%)[a]	0.00	44.83	23.09	11.70
Total number of dwellings[a]	31	1196	208.6	215.40
Permanently occupied dwellings (%)[a]	7.40	88.20	39.85	20.03
Temporarily unoccupied dwellings (%)[a]	0.30	52.60	14.80	13.38
Second-homes (%)[a]	0	90.00	30.42	30.22
Abandoned dwellings (%)[a]	1	53	16.94	13.53
Distance from municipal center (km)	4.00	40.00	19.29	10.02
Physical capital (infrastructure quality)[c]	0	5	1.07	1.32
Natural amenities index[b]	−0.14	2.57	0.51	0.85

Note: [a]Census (2011), calculated; [b]Josipović (2018) (relates to climate, landscape, tourist infrastructure, and outdoor activity offer at district level); [c]Drobnjaković (2019) (evaluation of quantity and quality aspects of existing communal infrastructure at settlement level on Linkert scale)

Table 2 Factors influencing expansion of second-homes in selected villages

N = 55	Mean	Std. deviation	Pearson correlation	Sig. (two-tailed)
Second-homes (%)	30.42	30.22	1	.
Permanently occupied dwellings (%)	39.85	20.03	−0.726	0.000
Temporarily unoccupied dwellings (%)	14.80	13.38	−0.591	0.000
Abandoned dwellings (%)	16.94	13.53	−0.544	0.00
Population (2011)	159.93	120.79	−0.18	0.18
Population change (1981–2011)	−31.79	11.86	−0.056	0.69
Population density	10.57	10.60	−0.033	0.810
Single-member households (%)	35.61	12.32	0.292	0.031
Share of elders, 65+ (%)	48.08	18.30	0.102	0.458
Daily migrants share (%)	54.02	32.14	−0.289	0.032
Activity level (%)	80.41	58.68	−0.343	0.010
Economic dependency ratio	11.11	25.83	0.182	0.182
Diversification level (III, II, %)	13.69	23.73	0.388	0.003
University education (%)	3.37	3.09	0.213	0.119
Secondary education (%)	23.09	11.71	0.97	0.482
Distance from municipal center (km)	19.29	10.02	0.144	0.295
Physical capital (infrastructure quality)	1.07	1.317	0.208	0.128
Natural amenities index	0.51	0.85	0.17	0.208

Note: Author's calculations

the population with professional orientation to secondary and tertiary sector compared to total employed, used to measure the level of decrease of the agricultural orientation of rural settlements (Drobnjaković 2019). The study indicated factors interrelated to the rural diversification process. Those are activity level ($r = -0.41$, $p < 0.01$), daily migrant share ($r = -0.37$, $p < 0.01$), share of university ($r = 0.50$, $p < 0.001$) and secondary education ($r = 0.41$, $p < 0.01$) among residents, share of single-member households ($r = 0.40$, $p < 0.01$), and second-home share in total housing ($r = 0.39$, $p < 0.001$).

The predictive model of rural diversification toward tourism development was constructed by hierarchical regression. The summary of the model results is presented in Table 4. The control of the second-home expansion effects was entered in the first block (following the presumption that expansion of second-homes initiated the process of rural diversification), followed by increased educational level (university education among "new residents").

Various socioeconomic factors (single-member households share, activity level, and daily migrants share) were added to the equation. As such, the regression analysis estimates the explanatory power of predictive variables on a criterion measure (diversification). Regression results (Tables 4 and 5) indicated that

Table 3 Factors in interrelation to the rural diversification level

$N = 55$	Mean	Std. deviation	Pearson correlation	Sig. (two-tailed)
Diversification level (%)	13.69	23.73	1.00	0.00
Activity level (%)	80.41	58.68	−0.412	0.002
Daily migrants share (%)	54.02	32.14	−0.371	0.005
University education (%)	3.37	3.08	0.502	0.000
Secondary education (%)	23.09	11.70	0.408	0.002
Economic dependency ratio (%)	11.11	25.83	0.15	0.27
Population size (2011)	159.93	120.79	−0.121	0.380
Population change (1981–2011)	−31.79	11.86	0.007	0.957
Population density	10.57	10.59	−0.116	0.400
Single member households (%)	35.61	12.32	0.403	0.002
Share of elders, 65+ (%)	48.08	18.30	−0.053	0.703
Second-homes (%)	30.42	30.22	0.39	0.000
Distance from municipal center (km)	19.29	10.02	0.175	0.202
Physical capital (infrastructure quality)	1.07	1.32	0.210	0.124
Natural amenities index	0.51	0.85	0.217	0.111

Note: Author's calculations

Table 4 Hierarchical regression analysis

Model	R	R^2	Adjusted R^2	R^2 change	Std. error
1	.388[a]	0.151	0.135	0.151	22.08
2	.579[b]	0.335	0.310	0.184	19.72
3	.743[c]	0.552	0.506	0.217	16.68

[a]Predictors: (Const.), second-homes (%); [b]Predictors: (Const.) second-homes (%), university education (%); [c]Predictors: (Const.) second-homes(%), university education (%), single-member households (%), activity level (%), daily migrants (%); [d]dependent variable: diversification level (service and manufacturing, %)

second-home expansion is a significant predictor of the diversification process in peripheral rural areas ($r^2 = 0.15$, $p < 0.005$), but with rather modest effects. On the other hand, the share of university education among locals is a very significant predictor, explaining additional variance ($r^2 = 0.34$, $p < 0.001$) and significantly straightening the model. Furthermore, the share of single-member households, activity levels, and daily migrants share also explained the additional variance (about 21.7%) in the rural diversification process ($r^2 = 0.552$, $p < 0.001$). In total, these factors explained 55.2% of the variance.

According to Tables 5 and 6, each step of the regression equation was significant and in line with the hypotheses. First, second-home share predicted rural diversification process F(1, 55) = 9.59, $p < 0.01$; second, university education among locals was added and positively affected the diversification process $F(2, 55) = 13.33$, $p < 0.001$, with strong effects ($\beta = 3.24$); while single-member household share

Table 5 ANOVA results

Model		Sum of squares	df	Mean square	F	Sig
1	Regression	4591.07	1	4591.07	9.42	.003[b]
	Residual	25287.63	53	487.31		
	Total	30418.7	54			
2	Regression	10307.21	2	5097.31	13.11	.000[c]
	Residual	20111.49	52	388.93		
	Total	30418.7	54			
3	Regression	16781.46	5	3356.29	12.06	.000[d]
	Residual	13637.24	49	278.31		
	Total	30418.70	54			

[a]Predictors: (Const.), second-homes (%); [b]Predictors: (Const.) second-homes(%), university education (%); [c]Predictors: (Const.) second-homes(%), university education (%), single-member households (%), activity level (%), daily migrants (%); [d]Dependent variable: diversification level (service and manufacturing industry %)

Table 6 Coefficients

Model 3	Unstandardized coefficients			T	Sig.	Collinearity test	
	B	Std. error	Std. beta			Tolerance	VIF
Constant	−0.50	11.49		−0.04	0.97		
Second-homes (%)	0.04	0.09	0.05	0.45	0.66	0.75	1.34
Higher education (%)	3.24	0.79	0.42	4.09	0.00	0.86	1.16
Daily migrants (%)	−0.19	0.08	−0.25	−2.3	0.03	0.78	1.29
Single-member households (%)	0.58	0.21	0.3	2.76	0.01	0.78	1.29
Activity level (%)	−0.11	0.04	−0.26	−2.42	0.02	0.79	1.27

[a]Predictors: (Constant), A-Predictors: (Const.), single-member households (%), higher education (%), second-homes (%); [b]Dependent variable: diversification

($\beta = 0.58$), a decrease of daily migrants share ($\beta = -0.19$), and decrease of activity level ($\beta = -0.11$) also contribute to the rural diversification process, F $(5, 55) = 12.07$. The bootstrapped 95% confidence interval for the slope to forecast the diversification level based on university education share among locals ranges from 1.66 to 4.83.

3.3 Findings and Discussion

Generally, the study confirmed that the diversification of selected rural areas is being in direct relation to tourism-related activities initiated by seasonal population. Namely, the study outlined the factors of significant influence on general tourism development in these peripheral rural areas. As such, it was found that the diversification of the economy in remote rural areas is based mostly on tourism development, thus confirming H1.

Furthermore, shrinking rural areas offer a good basis for tourism development expressed through the expansion of second-home houses in rural areas, predominately used for vacation and leisure purposes. This suggests that the diversification of the rural economy, and, therefore, tourism development in rural areas, is directly affected by second-home expansion (confirming H2). A connection was found between the second-home tourism and diversification of the rural economy. This could be used as a pattern (predictor) for rural development in demographically endangered but amenity-rich areas (with high-quality natural and cultural resources), thus confirming H3.

3.3.1 Findings from the Field Research

The on-site research revealed many interesting findings. Upon the demographic status of the sampled villages, secondary sources cover official data only for permanent residents, while the demographics on seasonal residents remain hidden. All sampled villages record a seasonal migratory pattern. This leads to a symbiotic relationship between tourism and migration, implying to the conclusion that tourism may also generate migration flows (Williams and Hall 2000:8). Seasonal residents are mainly returnees from big cities (Belgrade, Novi Sad, Niš, Pirot) and abroad. Their extreme concentration is noted in the summertime, while the villages have dormitory characteristics during the winter season. They possess stronger capital and entrepreneurship capacities (sense of business) than locals, own additional housing space available for rent (due to their flexibility), seek additional income, and enjoy providing traditional hospitality to tourists. This is a result of being in rather isolated areas with rather different living conditions and cultural patterns, along with present social distancing between humble peasants and urban second-homeowners. On the other hand, permanent residents tend to be rather poor, elder, and mainly single or couples, poorly educated, and simple-minded. The active ones are working in small-scale agriculture and cattle breeding, as simple workers in the industry in neighboring towns and just a few in the service sector. Permanent residents are aware of the tourism development perspective in their village, but they are incapable to strongly engage in it. Simply, they rather see it as a possibility to sell some agricultural products to tourism-oriented households (predominantly owned by second-homeowners). It is also suggested that, within the early stages of tourism development, host communities show more favorable attitudes toward tourism development (Hao et al. 2011), which is also confirmed in the sampled villages.

There is a need for understanding sustainability from different perspectives, while reaching sustainability means meeting the needs and requirements of all stakeholders (local communities, tourists, operators, and regulators) (Petrevska et al. 2020). In reaching a more sustainable development path, various impacts tourism has on destinations must be taken into consideration. The concept of sustainable rural development is based on creating favorable conditions for the progress of various sectors and the business environment while respecting local cultural and environmental values (Orboi 2012). Understanding stakeholders' perceptions is essential in minimizing potential negative effects and maximizing benefits (Petrevska et al. 2020). The low level of demographic vitality significantly influences the people's ability to identify key development problems and opportunities on the local level (Lampič and Potočnik-Slavič 2007). Therefore, the role of the local community is especially important in reaching sustainability, directing activities in organizing the community environmentally, socially, and economically. Moreover, the local community should benefit and not have its role marginalized in the process (Terzić et al. 2014).

Some villages retained the image of residential areas with common architectural style, sense of place, and strong community relationships (Gostuša, Visočka Ržana, Poganovo). Others suppressed the old "rural image" by creating unplanned weekend zones with building new oversized houses, spatially dispersed and architecturally diverse (Usije, Vinci, Vlasina Okruglica, and Vlasina Rid). Also, the second-home dwellings in selected villages may be divided as:

1. Those used for leisure and recreation (dominant type)
2. Those periodically used for seasonal agricultural works (evident in 11 villages)

Villages where second-homes are used for seasonal agriculture (Gostuša and Visočka Ržana) evidence lower level of diversification compared to those with predominant "leisure and recreation" function. This further indicates that agriculture is still the only activity of permanent and seasonal residents. Thus the tourism development initiative is still lacking.

In some cases, it was apparent that tourism initiatives contributed significantly to the village revitalization process. Yet, examples of severe suppression of locals by seasonal residents have become obvious, initiating the sort of gentrification process. The observations confirmed the findings of Hao et al. (2011) and Stedman and Hammer (2006) that the perception of seasonal and permanent residents differs in terms of place attachment. A distinction is made between seasonal residents who originate from the area that highly appreciates the social dimensions (Gostuša and Visočka Ržana). On the other side, outcomers are generally either led by the high-quality natural ambiance and recreation-oriented (Poganovo, Slavinja, and Dojkinci) or economically focused (quite rarely). Permanent residents tend to be more supportive of economic development than second-home owners. However, they are sharing a high degree of place attachment and common views on community values and overall needs (Hao et al. 2011).

Furthermore, the field research revealed the obvious expansion of second-homes. Broadly, this is a direct consequence of the extreme depopulation process present for a considerably long period in the whole SES region (Drobnjaković 2019). As such, second-home expansion may be explained by various spatial and socioeconomic factors. Namely, the beneficial impact of second-homes tourism in rural diversification from the residents' viewpoints refers to a possibility for achieving sustainable development of villages exposed to depopulation (Einali 2014). Sampled villages, due to its favorable geographical position, provide a solid base for examination of second-home expansion trends and changes from residential to seasonal (leisure and recreation) settlements. The findings of Bieger et al. (2007) and Hall (2014) that second-home expansion may be associated with potential retirement planning and the long-term migration pattern of the urban population were confirmed. Second-homes are also adaptable to a specific tourist function, forming common rural tourist accommodation facilities. They are commonly used for exclusive tourist purposes of its owners and their friends and family, but also for establishing tourism business (accommodation), depending on the entrepreneurial capacities of its owners. On-site observations provided insight into the fact that all sampled villages lack some vital resources that are needed for ensuring quality of living. These are related to availability of public services, as well as good transport and communal infrastructure (Glaeser et al. 2001).

Second-homes often represent converted former permanent rural housing (Müller 2004) and may be seen as a base for further development of rural areas. Second-home ownership has a positive impact on the built environment in the village, particularly with regard to conservation, as many properties are renovated (Wallace et al. 2005). Yet, their extreme expansion in an attractive rural setting may contribute to the development of elite landscapes and start the gentrification process (Hall and Müller 2004; Hall 2014). The impact of second-home tourism is dependent on the extent to which second-home ownership displaces permanent residents or complements them by utilizing otherwise empty houses (Müller 2004).

Residents seem to be aware of the existing problems within their community, seeking suitable measures in providing sustainability and vitality. However, the general awareness is not sufficient. Local initiatives and real possibilities for participation of local community members in the decision-making process are generally lacking (Terzić et al. 2014). This urges the importance to understand the perceptions of locals, but also that of a growing number of second-home owners, regarding tourism development possibilities along with general communal problems (Hao et al. 2011; Mason and Cheyne 2000; Williams and Lawson 2001). Public care and direct investments in rural amenities within these peripheral areas, as well as tourism development, depend mostly on the economic strenghts and entrepreneurship potential of local communities and individuals, and only in rare cases on nonrefundable governmental support.

3.3.2   Findings from Statistical Tests

Based on the population census data, one may see the overall demographic picture of the sampled villages. Yet, considering the general vitality of selected rural areas, in some cases, such data may be somewhat misinterpreted. Namely, the official data might be considered unreliable and to some extent even conceiving. This was particularly related to the marking of certain rural areas as "abandoned," while the on-site observations found them to be more likely described as "seasonal." Only 18 sampled villages have over 50% permanently inhabited dwellings. These villages are still functioning as relatively stable residential settlements, but with a constant population decrease. Among them, seven villages have over 10% share of second-homes each (Dojkinci, Donja Kamenica, Radejna, Trubarevac, Vina, Vrelo, and Miroč). Consequently, due to their proximity to well-developed tourist centers, many have shifted their activity from traditional agriculture to tourism. In some rural areas (villages: Brnjica, Donja Kamenica, Gulijan, and Miroč), we evidence a certain level of diversification. The high level of daily migrants indicates that most of the active population is working in the industrial sector in nearby urban centers. Among the sampled villages, seven have over 30% of housing units that are permanently abandoned: Janja, Šuman Topla, Mehane, Djake (with less than 50 people), Rudare, Novo Korito, and Ćuštica (over 100 residents).

Besides abandonment, the common characteristic for these villages is extremely poor infrastructural capacities and full orientation toward agricultural production. Certain diversification level is noted in the villages Djake and Rudare in Kuršumlija area, where tourism is expanding due to attractive tourist resources (geo-heritage site *Đavolja varoš* and spa centers *Prolom and Lukovska Banja*). Other interesting case is Ćuštica village, which, despite being labeled as residential, records the high level of abandonment. Moreover, the village possesses a favorable position in terms of tourism development, being settled on the main route toward ski center of Mt. Stara Planina. Even though the village shows a high level of economic activity, 100% of the workforce is represented by daily migrants (many working in the hotel complex and ski resort "Stara Planina"). Only 9% of housing units in this village are being used seasonally, but this is likely to alter soon, toward the greater expansion of second-homes. Villages that have over 50% second-homes (Bela, Brlog, Gostuša, Ostrovo, Poganovo, Prolom, Rsovci, Rtanj, Senokos, Slavinja, Trnski Odrovci, Usije, Vinci, Visočka Ržana, Vlasi, Vlasina Okruglica, and Vlasina Rid) and those with the proportional ratio between permanent and second-home dwellings (Inovo, Mokra, and Ram) show seasonal character and changed perception of vitality and functionality.

The share of the active population and daily migrants decreases the share of second-homes in favor of residential functionality of the village (those close to towns) or permanent abandonment (continuous migration to distant places in search of job). Namely, young just want to escape from the village, while elders hope to return eventually. The higher the share of temporarily unoccupied dwellings of foreign or urban workers, the greater the chances they will eventually represent part of a future retirement comeback plan. However, the likelihood that some village may become eventually abandoned depends on the overall abandonment level. The higher the share of abandoned dwellings, the overall rural ambiance becomes devastated, and, eventually, the village becomes labeled as unpleasant (ghostly and ghastly) for living. To understand this, one must add other additional indicators (spatial, economic, and social). Such indicators should address not only local communities but incorporating characteristics of seasonal residents as well, which seems hardly manageable, extremely costly, and time-consuming process.

With regard to the expansion of second-homes, the study found that their share in total housing is positively correlated to the share of single-member households and the diversification level. On the opposite, they are being negatively correlated to the activity level of the population, and the share of daily migrants, but quite modestly. Logically, single-member households, having in mind high share of elders in sampled villages, are likely to become second-homes. Due to the tradition, elders tend to change their residence and start living in towns with their children or go to specialized homes and transfer the property ownership to their descendants (common cultural pattern of Balkan people and patriarchal rural communities). The diversification level indicates the possibility to improve the economic status of villagers by their engagement in the secondary and tertiary economic sectors. Because of the collapse in the Serbian industry in peripheral areas, most villagers were forced to orient themselves toward the service sector (tourism). This is why diversification of the economy is not prior to "seasonal vitality" but a result of it.

As hypothesized (H2, H3), second-home expansion and the increase of educational level among locals, along with the increase of single-member households (retirement homes) and the decrease of activity levels and daily migrants share, were associated with the rural diversification process directed toward tourism development. Hierarchical regression indicated that indeed expansion of second-homes enables predictability of rural diversification process but at modest levels (explaining about 15% of variance). The best possible results were provided by adding factors such as second-home share, university education, single-member household share, activity level, and daily migrants share, providing the predictability for about 55.2% of the variance. Expansion of the second-home share was not able to provide high predictability on an individual but only in a cumulative manner (jointly with other factors) to the rural diversification process, while the increase of the educational levels among local population shows the strongest effects of the model predictability. Thus, for each one unit (%) of the increase of the university-educated people's share in the total population of the village, the diversification level is likely to increase for an average of 3.24%. As outlined in Jovičić Vuković et al. (2018), there is the evident significance of the educational background in the hospitality sector, which significantly influences entrepreneurship and innovation potentials, indicating that educated people can enhance the probability of innovation and organizational learning. On the other hand, the contribution of second-homes expansion to diversification is statistically insignificant (or showing rather small effects compared to other predictors). According to Josipović and Molnar (2018), human capital is more strongly linked to the rural economy which has a high volume of entrepreneurial activities, reflected in knowledge, innovation, and talent of human capital. In this line, human capital seems to remain the main predictor of the rural diversification process, while the expansion of second-homes is inducing the changes of socioeconomic profile of local communities and influences reorientation to the service sector, therefore improving the predictability of the model.

In particular, several villages that already established tourism, characterized by a relatively high share of second-homes in total housing (Prolom 77%, Slavinja 52%, Rtanj 51%, Vinci 82%, Vlasina Okruglica 74%, Vlasina Rid 69%, Poganovo 90%) and higher diversification levels (Prolom 52.4%, Slavinja 100%, Rtanj 34.4%, Vinci 19.8%, Vlasina Okruglica 64.7%, Vlasina Rid 60.9%, Poganovo 50.0%), also have significantly higher educational levels among locals (Prolom 13.3%, Slavinja 10.3%,

Rtanj 9.8%, Vlasina Rid 9.5%, Vlasina Okruglica 7.2%, Vinci 6.5%, Poganovo 6.5%) compared to other villages in the region. These villages have clearly changed their functionality to seasonal tourist villages due to their attractive natural setting and proximity to established tourist centers, while similar fate is expected in other villages as well.

The contribution of second-home expansion might be seen in the prospects of changing general characteristics of local communities in favor of seasonal residents (characterized by higher educational levels, urban habits, and strong entrepreneurship potentials). This is believed to be the consequence of the common seasonal migratory patterns in these peripheral areas that are mostly associated with repeated migration of a predominantly elderly population (second-home owners), which, in some cases, may indicate seasonal migration as a substitute or precursor to permanent migration (McHugh 1990). This seems to be the main precondition for inducing successful tourism development patterns in peripheral rural areas by providing needed entrepreneurship potential and stimulate local initiative.

4 Conclusions

Poverty, abandonment, and general loss of vitality are considered a predominantly rural phenomenon, typical for peripheral high-mountain areas. The study investigated the features of tourism development in low density peripheral rural areas of the SES region. Sampled low-density villages are located relatively nearby main tourist centers, and dispersion of tourists in the surrounding rural areas provides sustainability development patterns. Regardless, the perspective of such rural communities ranges from gradual abandonment to the market inclusion of innovative products and services (reserved for those with strong human capital and high diversification levels). There are also a series of transitional solutions in the form of "seasonal villages" (seasonal agriculture, second-home tourism). Rural areas featured prominently to the development of sustainable tourism to ensure higher levels of livelihood (short or long term) (Petrevska and Terzić 2020), while tourism seems to provide at least prolonged vitality of peripheral villages, even though mostly *seasonal*.

As of 2011, with the proclamation of the national master plan for rural tourism in Serbia and governmental support, the process of diversification of economy was initiated, thus boosting expansion and promotion of rural development in Serbia. The focus was placed on investigating the initiation of rural tourism development in selected areas that emerged as a government-induced strategy for the prevention of abandonment and stimulation of the diversification process. The study found that the diversification level over 10% is present in only 18 villages (of 55 total sampled villages). This was fully expected since sampled villages are located in underdeveloped peripheral areas. With regard to the interrelations with daily migrant share and other demographic indicators, only 10 villages may already have integrated tourist function. The symbolic income generated from the small number of tourists and visitors cannot substantially contribute to the rural economy in general and the local community. It rather provides an additional income to individual households and might create spillover effects. Representing an added value to the government support, it may contribute to a somewhat better vitality of the village and better quality of life, at least temporarily and strictly seasonally.

The study confirmed that tourism-related activities in the SES region are at the moment in its initial stage. Namely, diversification of the rural economy in Serbia is a recent process, especially in peripheral areas. However, due to the current circumstances, rural diversification toward service sector has experienced high levels of growth since 2000. Principally, tourism initiatives were supported by the local government. Small-scale entrepreneurship and hospitality in these small pastoral communities are still mostly based on the self-initiated activities and entrepreneurship potential of "second-home owners." The spillover effects were also detected in numerous cases, where locals directly engaged in or accepted good-business practices and slowly started up their businesses. This situation contributed to the rural diversification process, which was previously unknown in the area (significantly lower diversification levels were present in the observed villages in the previous census) (Statistical Office of Republic of Serbia 2011). Due to second-home tourism expansion in peripheral rural areas, reorganization of traditional agriculture towards supplying tourism-related facilities is expected, representing common effect as discussed by Fiorello and Bo (2012) and Salvatore et al. (2018). Also, severe environmental, economic, social, and tourism-related pressures are expected. Rural communities may also experience huge cultural changes in their traditional living patterns (Gallent, et al. 2003; Sznajder et al. 2009). There is an uprising trend of seeking the untouched natural environment (as a getaway from crowded urban space) and traditional values (experiencing different cultures, travel to the past in search for origins). Such trends boost the process that peripheral attractive rural areas become places of intensive tourist visitation. Here, the providers of tourist services are mainly second-home owners (as hosts). Since domestic visitors are still by far the most dominant, a need is raised for providing tailor-made activities and services that may fulfill broader tourists' expectations (Fiorello and Bo 2012; Salvatore et al. 2018).

Currently, the prospects of sampled peripheral villages are likely to be improved, based on recent governmental decisions and financial support, generally through subventions and various nonrefundable funds. Newly capital investments and infrastructural improvements stimulated the entrepreneurship potential which provides hope for prolonged vitality and functionality of low-density rural areas.

Limitations During the research, several limitations occurred, simultaneously representing opportunities that may be addressed in future research work. First, the sample is limited (55 villages), with extremely low diversification levels influencing that certain demographic and economic factors might not provide greater statistical significance. Second, due to data inconsistency (data census from 2011, tourism startup in these areas after 2012, conducted interviews in 2019), the investigated effects must be carefully interpreted. A further concern about the census data is that it only provides data every 10 years. Third, there are no available data evidencing sociodemographic characteristics and economic activity of the seasonal population (in many cases predominant population of small peripheral villages) due to their different permanent residences. Therefore, the diversification of rural economy among the local population is considered a "spillover" effect. The low to medium correlation coefficients for explaining the phenomenon do not diminish the attempt to extract factors influential to future tourism development in peripheral rural areas. Namely, this research confirms, supports, and explains on a real case study. The ongoing trend of rural tourism development in the low-density territories, as a survival strategy, is foreseen in the second-home expansion and rural diversification process.

Acknowledgments This research is part of the project *Evaluation of preconditions for tourism activities in rural depopulated areas—a comparative study between Macedonia and Serbia*, carried out by the Academy of Sciences and Arts of the Republic of North Macedonia and the Geographical Institute "Jovan Cvijić" of Serbian Academy of Sciences and Arts.

References

Ana MI (2017) Ecotourism, agro-tourism and rural tourism in the European Union. In Conference paper. Conference: CACTUS 2017-contemporary approaches and challenges of tourism sustainability, Predeal, Romania

Bel F, Lacroix A, Lyser S, Rambonilaza T, Turpin N (2015) Domestic demand for tourism in rural areas: Insights from summer stays in three French regions. Tour Manag 46:562–570. https://doi.org/10.1016/j.tourman.2014.07.020

Bieger T, Beritelli P, Weinert R (2007) Understanding second-home owners who do not rent: insights on the proprietors of self-catered accommodation. Int J Hosp Manag 26(2):263–276. https://doi.org/10.1016/j.ijhm.2006.10.011

Blackman A, Foster F, Hyvonen T, Jewell B, Kuilboer A, Moscardo G (2004) Factors contributing to successful tourism development in peripheral regions. J Tour Stud 15(1):59–70

Bogdanov N, Janković D (2013) Territorial capital of rural areas: an example of analysis of the potential for rural tourism development in Serbia. In: Škorić D, Tomić D, Popović V (eds) Agri-food sector in Serbia: state and challenges. Serbian Association of Agricultural Economics, Belgrade, pp 201–233

Borge JH (2007) Linked population and second-homes in Galicia. Bol AGE 43(73):375–377

Brandth B, Haugen M (2011) Farm diversification into tourism: Implications for social identity. J Rural Stud 27:35–44. https://doi.org/10.1016/j.jrurstud.2010.09.002

Brotherton I (1989) Farmer participation in voluntary land diversion schemes: some observations from theory. J Rural Stud 5(3):299–304. https://doi.org/10.1016/0743-0167(89)90008-9

Brown F, Hall D (2000) Introduction: the paradox of peripherality. In: Brown F, Hall D (eds) Tourism in peripheral areas: case studies. Channel View Publications, Clevedon, pp 1–6

Cook CC, Crull SR, Bruin MJ, Yust BL, Shelley MC, Laux S et al (2009) Evidence of a housing decision chain in rural community vitality. Rural Sociol 74(1):113–137. https://doi.org/10.1526/003601109787524124

Crull SR, Cook CC (2000) Housing and economic vitality in rural midwestern counties. Housing and Society 27(1):16–32. https://doi.org/10.1080/08882746.2000.11430442

Dijkstra L, Poelman H (2014) A harmonised definition of cities and rural areas: the new degree of urbanization. European Commission (WP 01/2014). https://ec.europa.eu/regional_policy/sources/docgener/work/2014_01_new_urban.pdf. Accessed 15 February 2019

Dimitrov N, Terzić A, Petrevska B (2020) Rural capital in small villages: an analysis of selected rural areas in Eastern Serbia and North Macedonia. J Appl Econ Bus 8(1):18–26

Drobnjaković M (2019) Methodology of typological classification in the study of rural settlements in Serbia. J Geograph Inst "Jovan Cvijić" SASA 69(2):157–173. https://doi.org/10.2298/IJGI1902157D

Einali J (2014) The assessment of the role of second-homes tourism in rural economic diversification. J Res Rural Plan 3(5):97–107. https://doi.org/10.22067//jrrp.v3i5.27065

Ellis F (2000) Rural livelihoods and diversity in developing countries. Oxford University Press, Oxford

Fiorello A, Bo D (2012) Community-based ecotourism to meet the new tourist's expectations: an exploratory study. J Hospital Market Manag 21(7):758–778. https://doi.org/10.1080/19368623.2012.624293

Gallent N, Shucksmith M, Tewdwr-Jones M (eds) (2003) Housing in the European countryside: rural pressure and policy in Western Europe. Routledge, Abington

Garrod B, Wornell R, Youell R (2006) Re-conceptualising rural resources as countryside capital: the case of rural tourism. J Rural Stud 22(1):117–128. https://doi.org/10.1016/j.rurstud.2005.08.001

Glaeser EL, Kolko J, Saiz A (2001) Consumer city. J Econ Geogr 1(1):27–50. https://doi.org/10.1093/jeg/1.1.27

Government of the Republic of Serbia (2011) National Program for rural development of the Republic of Serbia, Official Gazette, 5/11

Government of the Republic of Serbia (2016) The Strategy for the development of tourism of the Republic of Serbia from 2016 to 2025. http://mtt.gov.rs/download/3/strategija.pdf, (20 February 2019). Assessed 15 Feb 2019

Halfacree K (2012) Heterolocal identities? Counter-urbanisation, second-homes, and rural consumption in the era of mobilities. Popul Space Place 18:209–224. https://doi.org/10.1002/psp.665

Hall MC (2014) Second-home tourism: a international review. Tour Rev Int 18(3):115–135. https://doi.org/10.3727/154427214X14101901317039

Hall CM, Müller DK (eds) (2004) Tourism, mobility, and second-homes: Between elite landscape and common ground. Channel View Publications, Bristol

Hall MC, Page SJ (2014) The geography of tourism and recreation: environment, place and space, 4th edn. Routledge, Abington

Hao H, Long P, Kleckley J (2011) Factors predicting homeowners' attitudes toward tourism: a case of a coastal resort community. J Travel Res 50:627–640. https://doi.org/10.1177/0047287510385463

Iorio M, Corsale A (2010) Rural tourism and livelihood strategies in Romania. J Rural Stud 26 (2):152–162. https://doi.org/10.1016/j.jrurstud.2009.10.006

Iorio M, Corsale A (2014) Community-based tourism and networking: Viscri, Romania. J Sustain Tour 22(2):234–255. https://doi.org/10.1080/09669582.2013.802327

Jaakson R (1986) Second-home domestic tourism. Ann Tour Res 13(3):367–391. https://doi.org/10.1016/0160-7383(86)90026-5

Jepson D, Sharpley R (2015) More than sense of place? Exploring the emotional dimension of rural tourism experiences. J Sustain Tour 23(8-9):1157–1178. https://doi.org/10.1080/09669582.2014.953543

Jonard F, Lambotte M, Ramos F, Terres JM, Bamps C (2009) Delimitations of rural areas of Europe using criteria of population density, remoteness and land cover. JRC-IES, Luxembourg: Europan Commission

Jongeneel RA, Polman NBP, Slangen LHG (2008) Why are Dutch farmers going multifunctional? Land Use Policy 25:81–94. https://doi.org/10.1016/j.landusepol.2007.03.001

Josipović S (2018) Pogodnosti ambijenta, preduzetnistvo i ruralni razvoj Srbije. Doktorska disertacija, Beograd: Ekonomski fakultet. https://fedorabg.bg.ac.rs/fedora/get/o:18930/bdef: Content/download. Accessed 7 Feb 2019

Josipović S, Molnar D (2018) Human capital, entrepreneurship and rural growth of Serbian economy. Acta Econ 16(29):39–62. https://doi.org/10.7251/ACE1829039

Jovičić Vuković A, Gagić S, Terzić A, Petrović MD, Radovanović M (2018) The impact of organisational learning on innovation: case study of the Serbian hotel industry. J East Eur Manage Stud 23(4):673–692. https://doi.org/10.5771/0949-6181-2018-4-673

Knowd I (2006) Tourism as a mechanism for farm survival. J Sustain Tour 14(1):24–42. https://doi.org/10.1080/09669580608668589

Lampič B, Potočnik-Slavič I (2007) Demographic vitality and human resources as important factors for rural areas development. Glasnik srpskog geografskog drustva 87(2):103–114. https://doi.org/10.2298/GSGD0702103L

Lange A, Piorr A, Siebert R, Zasada I (2013) Spatial differentiation of farm diversification: how rural attractiveness and vicinity to cities determine farm households' response to the CAP. Land Use Policy 31:136–144. https://doi.org/10.1016/j.landusepol.2012.02.010

Löfgren O (1999) On holiday: a history of vacationing. University of California Press, Berkeley

Mahdavi D, Parishan M, Hasar A (2013) Practical model for measuring progress towards sustainable rural tourism development (SRTD) in rural area of Iran. Int Res J Appl Basic Sci 5(8): 1073–1082. http://irjabs.com/files_site/paperlist/r_1558_130928150057.pdf. Accessed 7 Feb 2019

Martin S (2010) Co-production of social research: strategies for engaged scholarship. Publ Money Manag 30(4):211–218. https://doi.org/10.1080/09540962.2010.492180

Mason P, Cheyne J (2000) Residents' attitudes to proposed tourism development. Ann Tour Res 27 (2):391–411. https://doi.org/10.1016/S0160-7383(99)00084-5

McHugh KE (1990) Seasonal migration as a substitute for, or precursor to, permanent migration. Res Aging 12(2):229–245. https://doi.org/10.1177/0164027590122005

Meert H, Van Huylenbroeck G, Vernimmen T, Bourgeois M, van Hecke E (2005) Farm household survival strategies and diversification on marginal farms. J Rural Stud 21:81–97. https://doi.org/10.1016/j.rurstud.2004.08.007

Mihai C, Ulman SR, David M (2019) New assessment of development status among the people living in rural areas: an alternative approach for rural vitality. Sci Annals Econ Bus 66 (2):167–192

Moore DS (2000) Statistics: concepts and controversies, 5th edn. W.H. Freeman & Company, New York

Müller DK (2004) Mobility, tourism and second-homes. In: Lew AA, Hall CM, Wiliams MA (eds) A companion to tourism. Blackwell Publishing, Oxford, pp 387–398

Naghiu A, Vázquez JL, Georgiev I (2005) Rural development strategies through rural tourism activities in Romania: chance for an internal demand? Int Rev Publ Nonprofit Market 2 (1):85–95. https://doi.org/10.1007/BF02893253

Netto AP (2009) What is tourism? Definitions, theoretical phases and principles. In: Tribe J (ed) Philosophical issues in tourism. Channel View Publications, Bristol, pp 43–62

Newbold P, Carlson WL, Thorne B (2007) Statistics for business and economics, 5th edn. Pearson Prentice Hall, New York

Orboi MD (2012) Development of rural communities by diversification of rural economy in the context of sustainable development. Sci Papers Animal Sci Biotechnol 45(1):450–453

Petrevska B, Terzić A (2020) Sustainable rural livelihoods: can tourism-related activities contribute? In: Vasile J, Subic J, Grubor A, Privitera D (eds) Handbook of research on agricultural policy, rural development, and entrepreneurship in contemporary economies. IGI Global, Pensilvania, pp 354–377

Petrevska B, Terzić A, Andreeski C (2020) More or less sustainable? Assessment from a policy perspective. Sustainability 12(8):3491. https://doi.org/10.3390/su12083491

Salvatore R, Chiodo E, Fantini A (2018) Tourism transition in peripheral rural areas: theories, issues and strategies. Ann Tour Res 68:41–51. https://doi.org/10.1016/j.annals.2017.11.003

Shucksmith M (1983) Second-homes – a framework for policy. Town Plan Rev 54:174–193. https://doi.org/10.3828/tpr.54.2.n62238775vj83560

Statistical Office of the Republic of Serbia (2011) Census of population, households and dwellings in the Republic of Serbia. https://www.stat.gov.rs/sr-Latn/oblasti/popis/popis-2011/. Accessed 15 Feb 2019

Stedman RC, Hammer RB (2006) Environmental perception in a rapidly growing, amenity-rich region: the effects of lakeshore development on perceived water quality in Vilas County, Wisconsin. Soc Nat Resour 19(2):137–151. https://doi.org/10.1080/08941920500394733

Støa E (2007) Urban cottages – rural homes? Changing home cultures: challenges towards sustainable development. European network for housing research international conference "sustainable urban areas", Rotterdam

Strategy of rural tourism development in Serbia (2012) Master plan of sustainable rural tourism development in Serbia. https://futurehospitalityleaders.files.wordpress.com/2012/11/master-plan-odrzivog-razvoja-ruralnog-turizma-u-srbiji.pdf. Accessed 15 June 2015

Sznajder M, Przezbórska L, Scrimgeour F (2009) Agritourism. Cabi, Wallingford

Terzić A, Simeunović-Bajić N, Jovičić A (2014) Community role in heritage management and sustainable tourism development: case study of the Danube region in Serbia. Transyl Rev Admin Sci Special Issue:183–201

Terzić A, Petrevska B, Petrović M (2019) Evaluation methods for sustainable rural tourism development: issues to be addressed. Agri 48(84):55–64

Turcanu L, Koomen E (2012) Rural vitality in the Netherlands. VU University of Amsterdam, Amsterdam

Tuulentie S (2007) Settled tourists: Second homes as a part of tourist life stories. Scandinavian Journal of Hospitality and Tourism 7(3):281–300

Van de Ven AH (2007) Engaged scholarship: a guide for organizational and social research. Oxford University Press, Oxford

Vujicic M, Ristic L, Ciric N (2013) Local initiatives for rural vitality and social inclusion: some experiences from Serbia. Eastern Eur Countryside 19(1):105–125. https://doi.org/10.2478/eec-2013-0006

Wallace A, Bevan M, Croucher K, Jackson K, O'Malley L, Orton V (2005) The impact of empty, second and holiday homes on the sustainability of rural communities – a systematic litterature review. The Centre for Housing Policy and University of York, York

Williams AM, Hall CM (2000) Tourism and migration: new relationships between production and consumption. Tour Geogr 2(1):5–27. https://doi.org/10.1080/146166800363420

Williams J, Lawson R (2001) Community issues and resident opinions of tourism. Ann Tour Res 28 (2):269–290. https://doi.org/10.1016/S0160-7383(00)00030-X

Williams DR, McIntyre N (2012) Place affinities, lifestyle mobilities, and quality-of-life. In: Uysal M et al (eds) Handbook of tourism and quality-of-life research. Springer, Dordrecht, pp 209–231

Williams A, King R, Warnes A (2004) British second-homes in Southern Europe: shifting nodes in the scapes and flows of migration and tourism. In: Hall C, Müller D (eds) Tourism, mobility and second-homes. Channel View Publications, Clevedon, pp 97–112

Wong KM, Musa G (2014) Retirement motivation among 'Malaysia my second-home' participants. Tour Manag 40:141–154. https://doi.org/10.1016/j.tourman.2013.06.002

Zuber-Skerritt O (1996) New directions in action research. Taylor & Francis, Abigdon

Tourism, Immigrants and Lifestyle Entrepreneurship: The (In)coming of People as a Key Factor for Sustainability of Low-Density Territories—A Case Study in Portugal

Anabela Dinis

1 Introduction

In a global economy dominated by large urban centres that concentrate a great part of the population and economic activities, there is a vast geographical extension of rural territories. Although these rural areas are highly diverse, a large part of them are lagging regions characterized by progressive abandonment of the traditional activities linked to the primary sector and continuous exodus which translates into lower population densities and an aging population. In these circumstances the viability of health and education infrastructures, as well as of other services associated with quality of life, are quite low, as well as the prospects of economic development and communities' sustainability.

Entrepreneurship is often considered as an engine for regional economic development, as it generates growth and serves as a vehicle for innovation and change (e.g. Henderson 2002; Dinis 2006; Huggins and Thompson 2015). However, the promotion of the business phenomenon seems particularly difficult in low-density areas that normally present greater limitations on human, material and financial levels as well as in market demand, when compared to urban areas (Dinis 2006).

In the academic sphere, several studies have sought to examine the factors that promote entrepreneurship in rural and peripheral areas as well as the relationships between the creation of new activities and the local populations (Dinis 2002, 2006; North and Smallbone 2006). Nevertheless, several works have reported that the main actors of rural economy diversification were from outside the local community, associating the establishment of small businesses in rural areas to progressive counterurbanization processes (Gorton et al. 1998; Paniagua 2002; Bosworth

A. Dinis (✉)
Management and Economics Department, University of Beira Interior, Covilhã, Portugal
e-mail: adinis@ubi.pt

© The Author(s) 2021
R. P. Marques et al. (eds.), *The Impact of Tourist Activities on Low-Density Territories*, Tourism, Hospitality & Event Management,
https://doi.org/10.1007/978-3-030-65524-2_7

149

2006; Kalantaridis and Bika 2006; Stockdale 2006; Kalantaridis 2010; Akgün et al. 2011; Herslund 2011; Pallarès-Blanch et al. 2014). This is explained because migrants from urban to rural areas tend to have significant business know-how and the capital to invest in their destination rural areas but also have higher qualifications and larger world perspectives (Marchant and Mottiar 2011; Dinis 2009; Klapper et al. 2018). Specifically, rural tourism is an attractive sector for urban immigrants because it gives them the opportunity of living in the countryside, whilst the cost of setting up the business is relatively low, especially when they can invest the profits from the sale of an urban residence (Hoggart and Buller 1995; Iversen and Jacobsen 2016; Mitchell and Shannon 2018; Möller and Amcoff 2018). However, the relationship between tourism and immigration is not limited to the above, i.e. immigrants as tourism entrepreneurs. Williams and Hall (2000, 2002) highlighted the overlaps between both fields of inquiry and also the symbiotic relationship between them. In 2002, these authors classified the studies that explored the tourism-migration nexus in three main themes: (i) tourism and labour migration (e.g. migrants that are attracted by tourism labour opportunities); (ii) tourism and consumption migration (e.g. tourists that turn into lifestyle migrants); and (iii) visiting friends and relatives tourism—which is an outgrowth of migration but also has the capacity to generate new migration and mobility flows. In spite of this classification, these authors also claim the need to have a holistic approach to the study of tourism-migration relationships.

In the European context, there are some empirical studies exploring the nexus between tourism and migration; however, they are mainly concentrated in northern Europe (e.g. Lundmark 2006; Iversen and Jacobsen 2016; Lundmark et al. 2014; Eimermann 2015; Eimermann et al. 2017) or in touristic places in southern Europe (e.g. Williams et al. 1997; O'Reilly 2003). To date, with some exceptions (e.g. Paniagua 2002; Cunha 2018; Barbosa et al. 2020), there is very little empirical evidence of the participation of urban immigrants in diversification activities and also about the motivations, processes and impacts of settlement of international immigrants in very low density and peripheral rural areas in southern Europe. The relative paucity of studies about migrants in these rural areas may be explained by the fact that research into rural development tends to fail at distinguishing the geographical origin of those involved (Paniagua 2002) but also by the fact that, in several regions, this kind of mobility is a new phenomenon.

In Portugal the most rural and peripheral regions are located in the interior of the country. For several decades these regions have suffered a continuous exodus of population and the consequent aging of the remaining population. Contrary to what happens in other countries, with similar problems (see, for instance, the case of Sweden as described by Cassel (2008), Eimermann (2015) and Eimermann et al. (2017)) no rural place marketing efforts have been made, and other political actions have not been able to reverse this situation. Despite this, recently, there has been a spontaneous phenomenon of foreign population coming to some of these territories. This phenomenon has already started to attract the attention of the media and some researchers, but still very little is known about who these immigrants are, why they migrate and what the impact of such mobilities on local communities is.

The Portuguese municipality of Penamacor, being one of the less densely populated municipalities and, according to the last census (INE 2011), the most aged in Portugal, is a paradigmatic case of this phenomenon. In 2012, one of the most widely circulated newspapers in the country reported "the death" of some villages in this municipality (*Público*, 16 July 2012). However, in recent years, there has been a very significant increase in foreign immigrants. Today, it is the municipality that has the highest rate of foreign residents in the interior: almost 10% of the population. A previous empirical study (Cunha 2018) showed that these incomers have lifestyle motivations. However, they are treated as a homogenous group, and little is said about their mobility patterns or their impact in the territory, namely, through their entrepreneurial activities. Also, as highlighted by Cunha (2018: 75), "another dimension of the phenomenon to be explored is to assess the impacts that inevitably the establishment of these expats have on local communities in all areas".

Thus, through the lens of the new patterns of mobility and lifestyle entrepreneurship, the case of Penamacor is analysed seeking to further explore the following questions: Who are these migrants, and what are their motivations for mobility and to settling in the territory? Are they all the same? How do they differ concerning their lifestyle motivations, their demographic characteristics, their occupations and their patterns of mobilities and spatial frame of action? How do they make a living in Penamacor? In particular, it seeks to understand whether entrepreneurship (in tourism or other sectors) is a possibility of income generation for these immigrants. Furthermore, it intends to understand what the impact of these immigrants in the territory is, namely, in the creation of wealth and well-being in the community. Do they act as community entrepreneurs? Does their presence in the territory generate other mobility flows, through the attraction of other (family and friends) tourists or immigrants?

This case study (Stake 1995; Yin 2009) has an exploratory nature and applies an abductive methodology (Dubois and Gadde 2002) based in a literature review, primary data (an interview with a key informant) and secondary data (TV and other media documentaries, written reports and statistics)—see Appendix for more details. Qualitative data, from primary (personal interview) and secondary sources of information (interviews to Penamacor's immigrants in the media and in the work of Cunha 2018), were analysed through content analysis: first reviewing the interviews and all the media information and then, based in the research questions, selecting (and transcribing) the relevant statements, following a process of condensation, coding and categorization that allowed to define the themes (underlying meanings) presented in the paper.

After this introduction, the chapter continues with a literature review about the new mobilities, besides tourism and traditional immigrants. It follows with a discussion about lifestyle entrepreneurship in rural areas and its relation with tourism, travellers and migrants. In Sect. 4, Penamacor's case is presented and discussed in light of the questions raised. Finally, some concluding remarks are made under a development perspective.

2   New Mobilities: Between Tourism and Migration

In 2000, Allan Williams and Michael Hall, argued that there was a weak conceptualization of the differentiation between migration and tourism, which contributed to neglecting the relationship between both. In their work they distinguish and discuss both concepts.

Migration is usually defined spatially as a movement from one territory to another that implies some permanence or an intention of settling permanently or temporarily. Tourism, in turn, is generally defined by three main features: (i) it occurs outside the normal place of residence, (ii) it is of a temporary short-term character, and (iii) destinations are visited for purposes other than taking up permanent residence or remunerated employment (Williams and Hall 2000). Thus, being both tourism and migration forms of mobility, *tourism* is traditionally associated to non-permanent mobility to other areas, usually by motives of leisure (or non-remunerated work) and associated to pleasure, adventure, discovery or other "positive" sensations/experiences, whilst traditional *migration* is related with a mobility for long permanence/settling, usually by motives of work, i.e. associated with lack of work opportunities in the region/country of origin.

However, demographic, social, economic, technological and political changes[1] resulted in an increase of mobility lifestyles in all ages, young adults and seniors and in mobilities mixing different rationalities, as economic with recreational or even ideological or humanitarian motives. This is the case of lifestyle migrants who choose to pursue a new life in the new locale by motives that often involves a new work-life balance, a better quality of life and freedom from prior constraints (Benson and O'Reilly 2009, 2016; O'Reilly and Benson 2009; Ibrahim and Tremblay 2017; Sun and Xu 2019). Lifestyle migration has been increasing in recent years and has been grounded on changes in value systems and facilitated by teleworking (Williams and Hall 2000). Benson and O'Reilly (2016) refer to lifestyle migration as a conceptual framework that focusses specifically on the motivations behind migrations, broadly described as the search for a better way of life whilst also considering it "a process rather than a one-off act completed upon arrival at the destination" (p. 21). In this sense and according to Hoey (2005), for lifestyle migrants, the choice made of *where* to live is, in fact, also one about *how* to live. But lifestyle migrants are not a homogeneous category. Benson and O'Reilly (2009) define lifestyle migration as the migration of "relatively affluent individuals, moving either part-time or full-time, permanently or temporarily, to places which, for various reasons, signify for the migrants something loosely defined as quality of life" (p. 621). Thus, concerning the permanence, lifestyle migrants include those that decided to stay permanently in the chosen location and those who, as "nomads," lead a peripatetic lifestyle shifting between two or more homes—a form of mobility that Williams and Hall (2002: 7) denominated "circulation" as opposed to migration.

---

[1]See Williams and Hall (2002) who explain how each of these factors contributed for increasingly mobile societies.

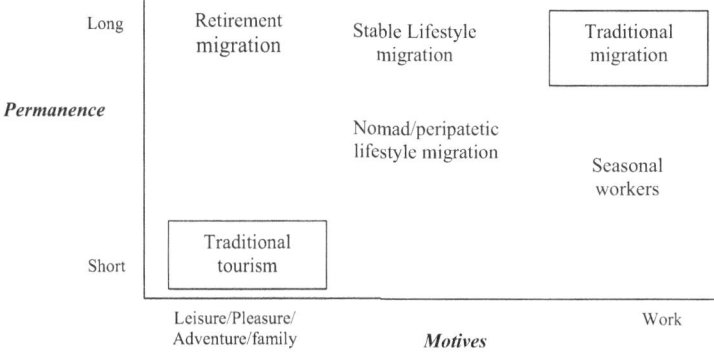

Fig. 1 Forms of mobility and the evolving tourism-migration nexus. Source: Elaborated by the author

Summing up, new forms of mobility have emerged, besides traditional tourism and traditional migration, located along a two-dimensional *continuum* that shaped the evolving tourism-migration nexus, as shown in Fig. 1.

The nexus between tourism and migration is not restricted to the areas of overlapping described above. It also exists in the form of symbiotic relationships, as noted by Williams and Hall (2000). In fact, many forms of migration generate tourism flows through the geographical extension of friendship and kinship networks. These flows are, often, bidirectional, i.e. friends and family travel to visit the new place of migrants' residence; migrants, in turn, become tourists in returning to visit friends and relatives in their areas of origin. The inverse may also happen, i.e. tourism generate migration. This is the case of touristic places that generate labour demand that is not met locally, stimulating labour migration (Lundmark 2006). In addition, tourism may contribute/help to find the right place to settle as immigrant, whether for motives of work, lifestyle or retirement. These links, not being new in the history of mankind in the current era of a globalized world and increasingly mobile societies, are not only becoming more important and relevant but also more and more expressed on the international scale.

Williams and Hall (2002) presented a typology of five main forms of migration related with tourism (see Table 1). The main purpose of this typology is to differentiate whether the migrant aims to work in the tourism industry (production-led migration) or to enjoy the same environment as tourism (consumption-led migration).

The typology recognizes the existence of both temporary mobility and permanent migration. It also distinguishes the several types of migration along two other dimensions: migrants' age and property ownership in the destination. It includes three forms of *production-led migration*, differentiated by the direction of the flow (emigration or return) and position in the economic structure (worker or entrepreneur), and two forms of *consumption-led migration*, differentiated in relation to whether individuals are still economically active or retired. Their links with tourism are in many ways similar to those for retirement migrants: search of spaces for

Table 1 Tourism-related migration: selected characteristics

	Mobility		Age		
	Temporary	Permanent	Younger	Older	Property Ownership
Production-led migration					
Labour	x	x	x		
Entrepreneurial		x	x		x
Return		x	x	x	x
Consumption-led migration					
Economically active		x	x		x
Retirement	x	x		x	x

Source: Williams and Hall (2002:26)

tourism/life experiences and amenity seeking. Both cases of consumption-led migration can be related with lifestyle migration.

In spite of the important advance in the discussion of the tourism-migration nexus, Williams and Hall's typology (Williams and Hall 2002) does not explicitly consider the possibility of consumption-led migrants (e.g. lifestyle migrants) being also entrepreneurs. This blurring of the borders between production-led migration and consumption-led migration was already studied by Williams et al. (1989) and has also received attention from other authors, as will be discussed in the next section.

3 Tourism, Travellers, Migrants and Lifestyle Entrepreneurship in Rural Areas

3.1 Lifestyle Entrepreneurship: Around Definitions and Typologies

Many researchers and policymakers have noted and encouraged entrepreneurial ventures as a mean of economic growth (Acs 2006; Acs et al. 2018; Baumol and Strom 2007; Braunerhjelm et al. 2010; Schumpeter 1934; Wennekers and Thurik 1999). However, in recent years, an increasing number of research studies analysed the phenomena of lifestyle entrepreneurs as the opposite of the growth-oriented or typical Schumpeterian entrepreneurs (Ateljevic and Doorne 2000; Peters et al. 2009; Cederholm and Hultman 2010; Claire 2012; Bredvold and Skålén 2016; Cunha et al. 2018; Sun et al. 2020). The contrast between entrepreneurs who develop businesses for profit and those who are motivated by lifestyle has been the focal point of much discussion in research focused on tourism entrepreneurship (e.g. Williams et al. 1989; Shaw and Williams 1998; Getz and Carlson 2000) but also on entrepreneurship in rural areas (e.g. Henderson 2002; Dinis 2009) as well as on migrant entrepreneurship (e.g. Bosworth 2006; Hedfeldt and Lundmark 2015).

Lifestyle entrepreneurs have been defined as a specific type of entrepreneurs whose aim is finding a sufficient and comfortable way of living and less focussed on profit and growth. In other words, they are primarily motivated by the need to succeed at living a certain quality of life by maintaining an income which allows them to survive (Marcketti et al. 2006; Marchant and Mottiar 2011; Bredvold and Skålén 2016). This quality of life could be defined by the possibility to maintain or practice a hobby and/or to balance work, family and social needs. In some cases, as those described by Ateljevic and Doorne (2000), lifestyle entrepreneurs consciously reject economic and business growth opportunities as an expression of their socio-political ideology, which "do not subscribe to the inevitable path of 'progress' as an end in itself" (p. 381). In these cases, the "market ethos" (p. 379) is rejected in favour of personal values, beliefs, interests and passions, usually related with sustainability and connection with nature, as motivating factors for doing business.

But, as also argued by Bredvold and Skålén (2016), this kind of dichotomy between commercial and lifestyle entrepreneurship is a simplification, because it is possible to find "hard-core" lifestyle entrepreneurs, entrepreneurs motivated by economic factors and entrepreneurs motivated by both lifestyle and economic factors (e.g. Shaw and Williams 1998, 2004).

One of the most well-known typologies of lifestyle entrepreneurs that make evident this diversity is that of Shaw and Williams (1998) that distinguishes between "non-entrepreneurship" and "constrained entrepreneurs". The first group shows similarities with the "pure" lifestyle entrepreneurship, as they have moved into tourism destinations for non-economic reasons; they have established enterprises (mainly with personal savings) and enjoy being their own boss. Many of these non-entrepreneurs are owners who have retired from former professions and perceive tourism and hospitality small businesses as a way to enjoy a nice destination whilst generating some income to sustain their lifestyle. This group is often characterized by ageing owners or retirees and were labelled "non-entrepreneurs" because they showed a lack of business experience and "entrepreneurial activity was extremely limited" (Shaw and Williams 2004, p. 102). The second group of "constrained entrepreneurs" constitute younger people with economic growth motives, but they demonstrate many lifestyle motives to explain their activities. The capital required is family raised and have former professional experience in tourism and other industries. They also demonstrate some entrepreneurial attitudes towards innovation and product development, as well as towards customer values and needs. They are "constrained" by their desire for a certain lifestyle as well as the business, but, contrary to non-entrepreneurs, they are willing to grow the business given the right training and support.

Another typology distinguishing entrepreneurs with lifestyle motivations is the typology presented by the author in a previous study. In that study, Dinis (2009) identified two types of entrepreneurs in rural areas. One type is the "owner-entre-preneurs", usually native people, whose main motivation is providing a family income. They do not have the desire to leave the rural place, neither the desire (or capability) to build high-growth business. In these cases, the creation of self-employment and the generation of an income source (exclusive or supplementary) are seen as the success criterion. This kind of entrepreneurship also often allows to preserve or valorize local/endogenous resources (e.g. natural resources, traditional arts, other aspects of local culture, etc.). The benefits of the existence of these kind of entrepreneurs relates with the quality of life in local communities, providing many of the services needed by local residents but also, given "personality and charm", to local economy that attracts many people to shop and live in rural communities (Henderson 2002:49). The other type of entrepreneurs, called "entrepreneurial-entrepreneurs", are those who enjoy and choose to live in a rural place but they are more innovative, more aware of the rural resources in the global market and develop a strategic vision of the business. They also differ from the previous mainly for their "expanded life experience". Many of them have lived experiences outside the local scope, such as studying or living in other places (in a city or abroad), traveling frequently and/or interacting with a larger social network (reaching individuals in urban/international contexts and/or in central positions). Besides that, they are usually younger and with a higher level of education (not necessarily higher education) than the "owner-entrepreneurs" type.

3.2   The Impact of Lifestyle Entrepreneurship in Rural Areas: A Discussion Around Tourism, Travellers and Migrants

Adopting the economic theory perspective, Peters et al. (2009) define lifestyle entrepreneurs as those entrepreneurs that accept suboptimal levels of production. These authors, based in a literature review, also point several characteristics of lifestyle entrepreneurs such as limited capital, lack of skills, irrational management, low innovation, and unwillingness to cooperate. This definition helps to understand why some authors claim that this type of entrepreneurs constrains regional economies and create problems for firm survival (e.g. Williams et al. 1989; Getz and Carlson 2000; Peters et al. 2009). However, others maintain that despite the fact that lifestyle entrepreneurs do not follow economic motives, their contribution to economic welfare and customer satisfaction should not be underestimated (e.g. Ateljevic and Doorne 2000; Dinis 2009; Marchant and Mottiar 2011). As noted by Peters et al. (2009) lifestyle entrepreneurs often get involved in business because they are experienced consumers, who either make a profession out of their hobby or seek optimal customer oriented solutions still not provided by the market. Thus, many lifestyle entrepreneurs can be seen as lead users who can be important sources of product/service innovations. The business creation can happen by "coincidence", i.e. a situation "evolving organically with one incident leading to another" (Cederholm and Hultman 2010: 21) or meant to make that settling choice economically viable. Furthermore, as concluded by Ateljevic and Doorne (2000), even in the cases of "ideological" lifestyle entrepreneurs, the conscious rejection of a profit-driven orientation does not necessarily result in financial suicide or developmental stagnation but rather provides opportunities to engage with "niche" market consumers who share the same values of the lifestyle entrepreneur. These consumers, with values embracing environmental and sociocultural integrity, identify themselves as "travellers", as a distinct identity from the more traditional "tourist" (the "others") whose activities are pre-planned and packaged by the industry, who seek hedonistic and frivolous experiences. These authors also concluded that the lifestyle entrepreneurs of their study were immigrant. As they state:

> These 'outsiders' are often individuals who previously visited the area as 'independent travellers', yet in making this move seek an opportunity to engage in extended lifestyle experiences, which reflect the traditional motivations of the 'backpacker'. (p. 386)

The relevance of past experience of travel is also highlighted by Marchant and Mottiar (2011). In some cases, the travel facilitated experiences that influence individuals' decisions about what they wanted to (or can) do with their lives. In other cases, experiences and knowledge from one place made individuals aware of the potential for offering the same service or product in other places. So, in many ways, travel has been a catalyst for their entrepreneurial journey. Thus, it was no coincidence that many of the lifestyle entrepreneurs were "travellers" themselves, motivated by their experiences and/or values often inscribed in the sustainability paradigm.

In the "ideological" cases, paradoxically, the search to escape from a "suffocating" market environment has provided a niche opportunity to engage with that market on their own terms and to sustain their businesses. Furthermore, despite their efforts to limit the growth of their own businesses, the innovative and creative attributes of these individuals make them dynamic elements in the economy, as those entrepreneurs described by Schumpeter (1942). This paradox illustrates the extent to which consumption and production are intertwined and provides research opportunities to disentangle the conventional polarization of entrepreneurship in terms of production and consumption.

Besides that, often lifestyle immigrant entrepreneurs have levels of education higher than native people, and their life experiences make them good communicators, enjoying interacting with people (Marchant and Mottiar 2011). Also, they have relied at the start-up phase on imported financial capital, albeit largely their own. They have also brought with them internalized skills, ways of thinking, priorities and preferences (Klapper et al. 2018). These attributes can provide potential benefits for the local destination areas and community. Some of them are very much involved in the local community, coming together to run local initiatives and being actively involved, for instance, in local chambers of commerce or business organizations. Thus, in addition to personal satisfaction, lifestyle entrepreneurship can also enhance well-being at the community level (Ateljevic and Doorne 2000; Marcketti et al. 2006), making them, also, communitarian entrepreneurs (Cornwall 1998; Johannisson and Nilsson 1989), i.e. important parts of community building and a powerful element in processes of social change.

But the relationship with community has a symbiotic nature. In fact, as pointed by Klapper et al. (2018) in a context of tight resource constraints, i.e. of limited availability of financial capital, accumulation of social capital (Bourdieu 1980;

Putnam 1993) is fundamental to the survival and prospering of the businesses. That is, lifestyle entrepreneurs are able to survive commercially, partly, because their financial expectations are relatively low and, partly, because they can rely on each other and are able to deploy a range of coping practices. As noticed by Ateljevic and Doorne (2000, 386) "the growth of many of these businesses (. . .) has been via the facilitation of community, family and friendship relationships based on a common set of values".

4 The Case of Penamacor

4.1 Characterization of the Territory

The municipality of Penamacor is located in Centro region (NUTS II), in Beira Baixa (NUTS III). It is limited, in the east, by the Spanish Extremadura region. The municipality included 12 villages: Águas, Aldeia do Bispo, Aldeia de João Pires, Bemposta, Pedrógão, Aranhas, Benquerença, Meimoa, Meimão, Penamacor, Salvador and Vale da Senhora da Póvoa (see Fig. 2). All together, they possess a population of less than 5000 inhabitants, making Penamacor one of the municipalities with the lowest population density in Portugal. It is also one of the Portuguese municipalities with the highest aging rate (see Table 2). For this reality contributed a strong and continuous emigration flow of the local population, since the end of the 1950s of the last century, with special incidence in the decades from the 1960s and 1970s, essentially targeting Europe, in a first phase, and then the national coast, mainly Lisbon, in search of better living conditions. In 2012, one of the most popular newspapers (*Público*, edition of July 16), in a report about this municipality, announced the death of its small villages, declaring them "in extinction".

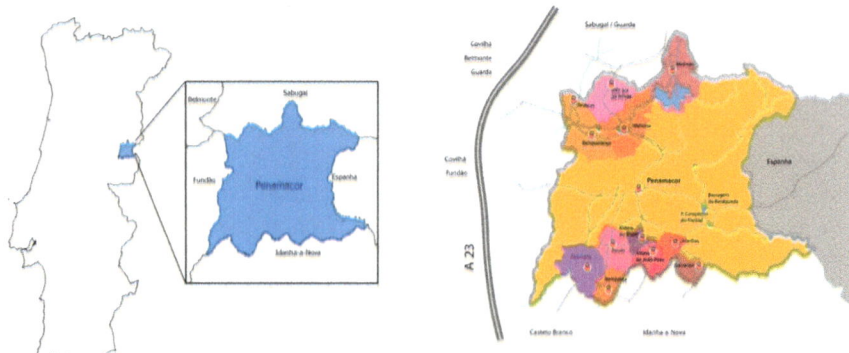

Fig. 2 Municipality of Penamacor: classification in the national territory and main localities. Source: Vilas Boas et al. (2015) and http://www.cm-penamacor.pt/cmp/index.php/conhecer/caraterizacao

Table 2 Resident population, population density and aging index in Portugal, Centro Region, Beira Baixa and Penamacor municipality (estimates at December 31, 2018)

Territory		Resident population Individual	Population density[a]	Aging index[b] Ratio—%
NUTS I	Portugal	10,276,617	111,5	157,4
NUTS II	Centro	2,216,569	78,9	196,6
NUTS III	Beira Baixa	80,782	17,6	281,9
County	Penamacor	4831	8,6	630,4

[a]Average number of individuals per km^2
[b]The relationship between the number of elderly people and the young population in a certain region. More specifically, it is the ratio of the number of elderly persons aged 65 and over (when they are generally economically inactive) to the number of young persons (from 0 to 14).
Source: PORDATA, Data Sources: INE—Annual Estimates of the Resident Population; Data Sources: IGP—National Cartographic Series at 1:50,000 scale and Official Administrative Letter of Portugal—CAOP 2009.0. Last updated: 2020-02-07

In view of this demographic scenario, economic activity naturally suffers, conditioned by the lack of entrepreneurship and qualified labour and by the weak expression of the local market. Trade is unable to compete with the nearest urban centres (Fundão, Covilhã and Castelo Branco[2]), and the most relevant productive sector is usually related to local resources, with particular emphasis on forestry and the small agrifood industry based in the olive grove and in the breeding of cattle, sheep and goats. However, agriculture tends to assume subsistence characteristics in the region, due not only to the demographic characteristic of the local population but also to the land tenure characteristics of the farms, which are very parcelled and often abandoned.

4.2   The Immigration Phenomena

Despite this reality, since 2017 the municipality of Penamacor made headlines again, first in the local press, and, soon after, also in the national press and on television. But this time to deal with a striking phenomenon alluded in the headings of the media: "Foreigners are giving life to Penamacor" (*Reconquista*, 23 March 2017), "Penamacor has the highest rate of foreign residents in the interior" *(TVI24,* 2 October 2018), and "The fugitives Brexit are invading the oldest municipality in Portugal" (*Diário de Notícias*, 14 October 2018). In this news, the subtitle advances:

> Penamacor was the oldest municipality in the country. Today, it has the highest rate of foreign residents in the interior—almost 10% of the population. They are mainly English, working age and fleeing Brexit. They are buying abandoned farms, they opened an international school, they work online for the whole world. There is a new world in Beira Interior.

---

[2]The distances from Penamacor to this places are all less than 50 km.

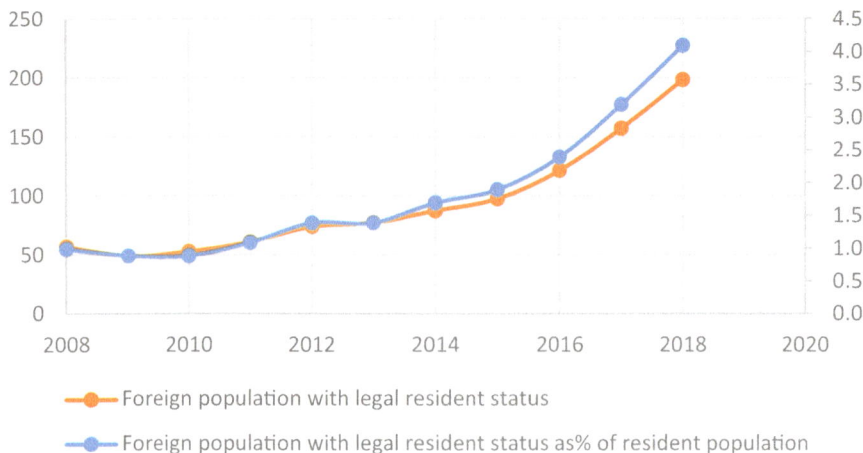

— Foreign population with legal resident status

— Foreign population with legal resident status as% of resident population

Fig. 3 Evolution of foreign people in Penamacor county (2008–2018). Source: Elaborated by the author based in INE, Portugal—Resident Population Annual Estimates I SEF/MAI—Foreign Population with Legal Resident Status. Data provided by PORDATA (last update 2020-02-07)

In 2019, this phenomenon was the subject of a large television report on one of the most popular news channels in Portugal, entitled "Good Morning Penamacor"[3] (*SIC Notícias*, 27th March), showing and giving a voice to the community of foreigners living in the villages of Penamacor. This situation is also highlighted in the official statistics. Data show that between 2008 and 2018, and especially since 2016, year of the *Brexit* referendum, the percentage of foreign residents in Penamacor increased from 1 to 4.1, corresponding to a 243% increase in the foreign population in this territory (Fig. 3).

And if the accentuated presence of foreigners in interior and less densely populated territories in Portugal is not so usual (the vast majority is located in urban or coastal centres), what makes the case of Penamacor particularly impressive is the strident growth in the last 4 years and the origin of these new inhabitants. In fact, this sharp increase is mainly due to the income of immigrants from the United Kingdom that, in 2018, already represented the majority of the foreign population in the municipality (56. 6%), a much higher weight of British than that registered in any other municipality in Beira Baixa (13.8%), in Algarve (18.3%)—the traditional destination of British people in Portugal—and even more when compared to the average weight of these emigrants in the Centro Region (7%) and in Portugal (5.5%) (Pordata; 2020/INEl SEF/MAI).[4]

---

[3]In English in the original.

[4]PORDATA; Data Sources: INElSEF/MAI – Foreign Population with Legal Resident Status (last update: 2019-07-30).

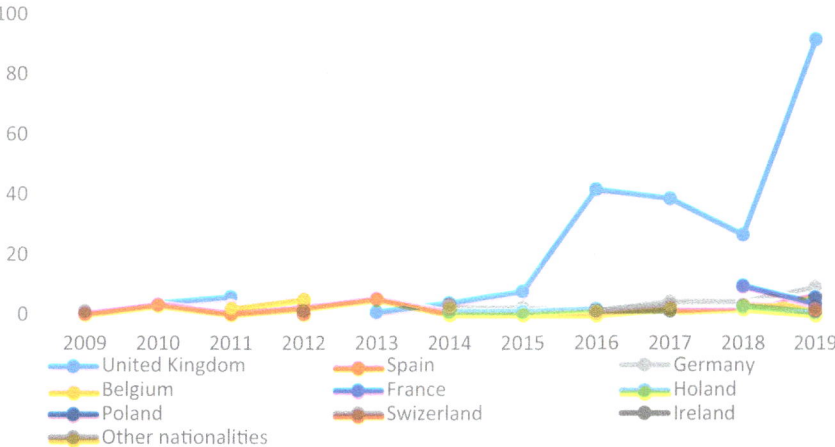

Fig. 4 Evolution of registration certificates for foreign residents issued by SEF for the municipality of Penamacor (2009–2019). Elaborated by the author. Source: Serviço de Estrangeiros e Fronteiras (SEF)/Foreigners and Borders Service

Data provided by the municipality of Penamacor, collected from the Foreigners and Borders Service (SEF), provide more accurate and updated information (see Fig. 3). In the period considered, 359 foreign immigrants were registered in the municipality of Penamacor, the majority (65.5%) being immigrants from the United Kingdom.[5] Figure 4 shows the weight of the different nationalities of foreign immigrants. It should be noted that around 90% of foreign immigrants are from northern and central Europe, with no entries from other continents (e.g. Brazil, Cabo Verde and China) revealing a *sui generis* pattern of immigration in this county.

4.3   Profiles of Foreign Immigrants in Penamacor: Searching for a Typology

Besides the national profile of the foreign immigrants in Penamacor presented in the previous section, it is now intended to further understand who they are and what reasons stand behind their decisions. Cunha et al. (2018), in his work carried out between 2017 and 2018[6], concluded that the reasons of these new inhabitants for

---

[5]As Cunha (2018: 13) states, "it should be noted that these numbers are official, that is, they reflect only the expats who formally requested the residence certificate. In fact, the actual number of those residing in Penamacor may be higher. (. . .). The explanation for this difference may be that the majority of those who arrive with retired status and income do not apply for the SEF document, presumably because it is not rewarding for them for fear of losing the social support benefits in their country of origin".

[6]Study based on 38 questionnaires, applied to European foreign residents installed for more than 1 year in the municipality of Penamacor, including different nationalities and residing in rural areas

moving to the countryside are related to lifestyle, clearly integrating with the so-called counterurbanization (Gorton et al. 1998). Jammie Malloy (identified as #9 in Appendix), one of the first movers to Penamacor and that nowadays represents a central figure in this foreign community, described the incomers as:

> Young people, young families, retired people, people that have businesses online, people who have houses back in their own country that are renting out or have sold to find a better life or a more tranquil life and peaceful. (SIC Notícias, 25/03/2019)

This statement makes it evident that, in spite of the fact that they have their lifestyle motivations in common, they are not all the same, showing differences in their demographic characteristics, personal motivations and, eventually, occupations and patterns of mobility and spatial frames of action, which will be analysed below.

4.3.1 Demographic Characteristics

As showed by Cunha (2018) and as evidenced by the other empirical sources (see Appendix), there are immigrants of all ages in Penamacor. According to Cunha (2018) the most represented age groups are those between 22 and 60 years old[7] and in most cases, the household is composed not only for the couple but also by several children. These characteristics are in sharp contrast to the characteristics of the local population, as shown in Table 1.

4.3.2 Motivations

A closer look at the results obtained by Cunha (2018) shows that lifestyle motivations are not homogenous. In fact, a considerable group (44% in his study) expressed the search for an alternative way of living as the main reason, similar to those "pure lifestyle" immigrants described by Ateljevic and Doorne (2000). The lifestyle choice of this type of immigrants is associated with a sociopolitical ideology that both reject the "market ethos and economic rationalities" (Cederholm and Hultman 2010: 17), i.e. the "capitalist world" and is based on a strong commitment with sustainability and connection with nature. However, other immigrants mention reasons with less ideological factors envolved and eventually more self-centered, related with the individual concern of searching for a better way of living either by living a more peaceful life away from the urban fuss or by the possibility of realizing a personal project (agricultural or other) more in line with the reasons described by Benson and O'Reilly (2009) and Ibrahim and Tremblay (2017). This distinction—between

---

(outside urban areas) and also a qualitative analysis, based on six interviews with expats (which involved nine people).

[7]That represent more than 65% of individuals, and only 11% are older.

socio-ideological motivations vs better-quality life motivations—is also evident in diverse statements of this new immigrants as the examples shown in Box 1.

Box 1 Evidences of distinct motivations of Penamacor lifestyle foreign immigrants

Socio-ideological motivation	Better quality of life motivation
"Sweden is a country that, in my opinion, is moving a bit more to the right than I am comfortable with, and that's one of the reasons why we feel very much at home here in Portugal, because Portugal is a country that is very including" (former leader of the Swedish ecological party) (# 11, SIC Notícias, 25/03/2019) *"...the ability to make my own choices in line with my own ethics. To be able to practice natural farming without interference from governments which are little more than mouthpieces for corporations which are destroying this world with great success. This is not the kind of 'success' that I am looking for. I could not achieve this in 'Great' Britain so I came here". (...) "The ugly face of corporatism and how it has insidiously taken over virtually every aspect of modern life; this is true of nearly every western democracy At least it seemed to me that Portugal with its rich rural tradition would be a good place to pursue my dreams" (#6, Cunha 2018: 65–66)* *"this is the beginning of the Research Development Center [for sustainability and alternative cities], right here in Village João Pires, center of Portugal". (...) (# 15, SIC Notícias, 25/03/2019)* *"[U.K.] it's a mess. Nobody thought that this would be the results [of the Brexit referendum] and this tipped my hand as to think: 'O.k. This is it now; I'm gonna stay because it's becoming hostile back home, I feel...'" (#14, SIC Notícias, 25/03/2019)*	*"...I made the decision to radically change my life. And to be honest, I just felt ready for a new adventure! (...) Following the recession in England, where property prices plummeted, I realised that in order to follow my dreams, I would need to find somewhere cheaper to live'" (...) "I love the countryside here – this year in particular there have been so many spring flowers and so many beautiful birds. I also enjoy seeing snakes, lizards and terrapins in the river" (#5, Cunha 2018: 65–66)* *"It's peaceful, is nice landscape, is not so crowed, not so touristic, it's green, but not so MUCH... (We lived in Pedrogão Grande before and it's dangerous because of the fires and here is more calm)" (# 16, SIC Notícias, 25/03/2019)* *"The people are very welcoming and it is a pleasant, simple life 'tranquilito'". (#9, TVI24, documentary 01-11-2018)* *"Here you can live a very peaceful, quiet, rural life but you are not isolated" (#7b, Diário de Notícais, 19/10/2018)* *"...now we have our own land, where we can live together as a family"(...) "I feel happier here. And I like my children to grow in the freedom of the countryside and in nature..."(#4a, Cunha 2018:64, 66)* *"The weather is one of the main reasons, at least why I pick Portugal" (#14, SIC Notícias, 25/03/2019)*

4.3.3 Occupations, Mobilities and the Spatial Frames of Action

According to Cunha et al. (2018), in their country of origin, immigrants predominantly had professions linked to intellectual and scientific activities (47%), which includes artists, teachers, health professionals, etc., followed by skilled workers in industry, construction and craftsmen (18%) and intermediate technicians and professions (11%), which reflects relatively high levels of qualification, which tend to be superior than native people.

Unlike what happens in the Algarve region[8] (Guerreiro 2019), most of this population is in working age and still maintains an occupation. The study by Cunha (2018) found that almost all respondents (92%) are engaged in agricultural activities.[9] However, these activities are often combined with other professional activities, developed locally (see Box 2) or globally (see Box 3), in this later case, making large use of information technologies.

Box 2 Local occupations

"He is an Australian graduate in Physical Education, who was an international hockey player for many years. (...). Now here he is teaching kids of 11, 12 years old" (#8, Diário de Notícias-14/10/2018)

"At the Jamie Molloy Hamburgers bar and van, it is the meeting point for the foreign community that lives in Penamacor. In addition to this business, Jamie owns the first real estate agency in town". (#9 TVI 24-02/11/2018)

"I'm a carpenter and a builder and I like working with the stone and wood and I do have other forms of trade work but my specialty is carpentry. There are many beautiful buildings out there that need restoration and there's a lot of people that came out here to set up a home and lots of them abandon places like this and it takes a lot of work to get it in a beautiful place... Yes. I think there should be enough work on here". (#18b, SIC Notícias-27/03/2019)

Box 3 International/global occupations

*"From here she continues to **write for a Pakistani** magazine and also his books. This at night because the day is spent looking after the vegetable garden where she has everything she needs".* (# 19 TVI 24-01-11-2018)

*"A **professional truck driver**, he **regularly returns to England** to work for short periods and obtain some savings that will allow him to return to his farm*

(continued)

---

[8]Touristic region in the south of Portugal where the largest English community in the country lives.
[9]Organic farming is practiced by 71% of respondents, 45% exclusively and 26% together with conventional farming.

Box 3 (continued)

the rest of the year, always taking advantage of the trip to transport and sell some profitable products such as olive oil that he himself produces with the olives of its 100 olive trees but also with all the olives that its neighbors offer it on the tree for not wanting to harvest it". (#3, Cunha 2018: 64)

*"I teach English **on-line** and I teach people from **all over the world**. I tend to teach business professional from Asia, Northern Europe, from Spain, Italy, from Africa and Mexico: I have one student that lives in Congo" (#5, Diário de Notícias, 19/10/2018)*

*"[He is] a computer engineer who does 3D projects **for the whole world**" (#7 Diário de Notícias-14/10/2018). "I use to work in a university and I was a computer programmer leading with virtual reality applications (. . .) Technology, in my point of view is good. In a lot of ways, it's an enabler (. . .) makes the world a smaller place, in a lot of ways, it allows people to work on internet. Make possible to live in a rural place like Penamacor and still **access to wider world** and make a living" (#7 Diário de Notícias-19/10/2018)*

*"I'm psychologist, **I work on-line** and **I have clients all over the world**, and run a company with 15 team members, and so that's why I can stay everywhere". (#16, SIC Notícias, 25/03/2019)*

Not only for their international occupations but also because of their mobility experiences (see Box 4), the foreign community in Penamacor tends to be "citizens of the world". Considering their lifestyle attitude and values, as the connection with nature, the concern with sustainability and the need to move away from urban and (massive) touristic areas, they also fit the notion of "travellers" as defined by Ateljevic and Doorne (2000). This is also the perception of the mayor of the county, António Beites when saying "we can see that they are highly travelled people, with a lot of world and a high cultural level" (#1, Diário de Notícias, 19/10/2018).

Box 4 Mobility experiences

*"At about 30 years of age they experienced the extraordinary adventure of crossing the Atlantic Ocean in a 6-meter boat, without motor or radio. Leaving **Tenerife** in the Canaries, for 33 days they only saw sea and sky until they docked on the island of **Saint Martin** where they stayed for about 35 years and where they had a small sewing business making upholstery for boats, canvas and candle repairs, and collection systems of sunshade / water for yachts. Their decision to move from a small Caribbean island to a small village in the interior of Portugal, in a remote area, is seen as another adventure in their lives, probably the last, they recognize, but just another adventure. (#2, Cunha 2018: 63) They meet in south of France. "I'm not certainly a major patriotic person, Like I said, **I've been more than half of my life out of the country**, I've been back to England for four weeks in 40 years". (#2, SIC Notícias 25/03/2019)*

(continued)

Box 4 (continued)

*"I've played football **Uzbekistan, England and Australia**. (...) I have a Portuguese wife and I met her in Hong Kong when I was professionally athlete in Hong Kong" (#2, SIC Notícias 25/03/2019)*

*"The fight against the Taliban in Afghanistan and Pakistan forced this 62-year-old journalist into exile, refused to stay in **Scotland** from where she left in 1983 and 30 years later took refuge in Penamacor (#19, SIC Notícias, 25/03/2019) 'It was necessary for me to leave from **Pakistan** and I wasn't sure where I was going to go. So I was going to go first in **Portugal**, then in **Spain**, then in **Corsega**, and **Italy** and **Turkey**, but I came to Portugal and I didn't go any further'" (#19, TVI24, 01-11-2018)*

*"**I've travelled all over the world, it was my dream**, I worked as a flight attendant, then on a cruise and then I met my partner and he always wanted to have land, take care of the land, have animals and then we had a son and everything changed..." (#18 SIC Notícias 25/03/2019)*

*"I've spoke to a lot of my friends who voted to leave because I was shocked they did because they knew that it would hurt me in trying to stay here, because **it was beautiful before to travel between [the two countries]** and not having any issues, and now who knows"? (#14, SIC Notícias, 25/03/2019)*

Both characteristic of higher qualifications associated with liberal and skilled professional backgrounds and the relevance of past travel experience are consistent with other studies (e.g. Marchant and Mottiar 2011; Dinis 2009; Klapper et al. 2018).

The lifestyle characteristics of these migrants configure what Williams and Hall (2002) called *consumption-led migration*, including both economically active and retired migrants. Concerning the patterns of mobility of the active migrants, it is possible to identify at least two patterns: those that oscillate between Portugal and their country of origin [or other countries where they work], as is the case of Ian (see #3 in Box 2), and those who decided to settle permanently in Penamacor.

The first situation, in a "circulation" mode (Williams and Hall 2000), corresponds to *nomad* or the *peripatetic lifestyle migration*, shifting between two or more homes. This form of mobility was also mentioned by Cunha (2018:13) in their work about Penamacor immigrants[10]:

According to [SEF and Penamacor Municipality] (...), these expats adopt a 'new nomad' scheme (...), that is, they remain relatively long periods both in Portugal and in the country of origin, first because their financial situation allows them to have this 'nomadism' but also, due to the combination of other factors such as the family connections and commitments they maintain at the origin, or the advantages and benefits attributed to the health system and plan that they already had at the time of acquiring the 'secondary' property in Portugal.

---

[10]In a footnote.

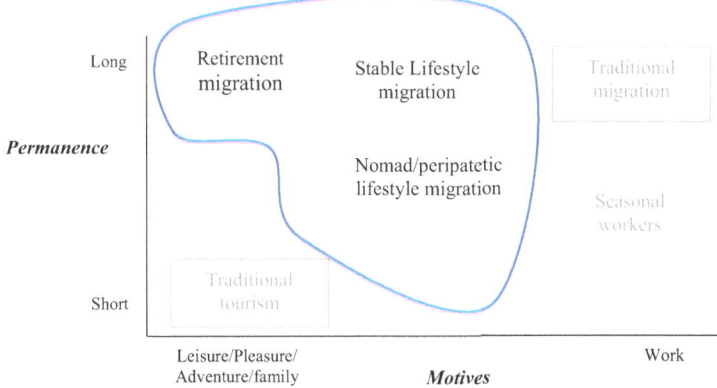

Fig. 5 Forms of mobility of Penamacor immigrants. Source: Elaborated by the author

The second situation corresponds to those earlier described as *stable lifestyle migration* which might be the majority of the immigrants. In fact, Cunha (2018) found that most immigrants (53% of the respondents) intend to stay and live forever in the territory with only about 1/5 with intention of leaving.

Therefore, in spite of the fact that foreign immigrants in Penamacor have in common their lifestyle motivations and "travellers" characteristic, they are not homogenous in what refers to the motives/concerns and permanence of the stay, fitting in three of the types previously identified: *retired migrants, stable migrants* and *nomad migrants* (Fig. 5).

These differences can be better understood in a multidimensional scheme, along four dimensions: (i) age/situation in the labour market (active vs retired); (ii) individual or family lifestyle vs social/ideological motives; (iii) frame of action (occupation); and (iv) duration of permanence in the territory, as follows (Table 3).

In spite of their global perspective, these citizens are also closely linked to the local territory, right away, in the physical sense, since the practice of agriculture implies a connection to the land, but also in the sense of community. According to Cunha (2018), a significant number of immigrants (32% of respondents) expressed a desire to be more involved with the local community, probably the group of immigrants who have already taken the decision to settle definitely in Penamacor.[11]

---

[11]In fact, the number that expressed that desire is exactly the same of those that already decided to stay for living in Penamacor.

Table 3 Incomers in rural and low-density areas: selected characteristics

	Retirement migration	Stable lifestyle migration	Nomads
Age			
Older/retired	x	x	x
Younger/economically active		x	x
Concerns			
Individual/family lifestyle	x	x	x
Social/ideological	x	x	x
Frame of action/occupation			
Local		x	
Global		x	x
Mode of the presence			
Permanent	x	x	
Circulation	x		x

Source: Elaborated by the author

4.4 The Impact of Lifestyle Immigration in Penamacor: Between Accidental/Casual Entrepreneurs and Community Entrepreneurs

As discussed before, entrepreneurship has been considered a central process for economic development. Concerning lifestyle entrepreneurship—here defined as the process of creation of new ventures by people motivated to find a sufficient and comfortable way of living and less focussed on profit and growth—the impact on local economy may be less evident, even though, as shown by several authors (e.g. Paniagua 2002; Dinis 2009; Peters et al. 2009; Pallarès-Blanch et al. 2014), lifestyle immigrants with entrepreneurial ventures can have a significant impact in rural areas.

In Penamacor, the economic impact of the coming of these immigrants was felt immediately in the acquisition of properties that were not occupied. This is evident in the testimonies collected from all sources and also explained by Cunha et al. (2018) in his study:

> As a result of the emigration movements registered in the last 4 decades, a significant abandonment of the lands is visible and notorious, with the prospects of reoccupation by their owners being practically null, the overwhelming majority of whom will have remade their lives in the places of destination. Nor is it expected that the second and third generations will reoccupy those same lands, from which they did not derive any economic benefit—on the contrary, if we consider some fiscal obligations—, as well as the nonexistent affective connection that, in many cases, would make return, albeit sporadically, their ancestors. It is mainly these abandoned lands that are now occupied by these new inhabitants, also attracted by their low price. (Cunha 2018: 75)

In fact, this demand for properties created a business opportunity that Jamie Malloy (#9), an immigrant with previous business experience, ended up exploring creating

Quintamaior, the first State Agency in Penamacor. This started as an informal activity that grew organically and became a firm with two partners in 2018 and generated, in 2019, a new job (see Box 5), a process similar to that described by Cederholm and Hultman (2010). As mentioned by Pedro Agapito[12] "this could have been created for any people from Penamacor, but it was by them" alluding to their entrepreneurial spirit or "alertness" (Kirzner 1973). This entrepreneurial attitude towards innovation combined with their lifestyle values fits the figure of "constrained entrepreneurs" described by Shaw and Williams (2004) or, considering also their "expanded (global) life experience", the rural "owner-entrepreneurs" identified by Dinis (2009). This case also illustrates, as stated by several authors, how lifestyle entrepreneurs, being lead users, became promoters of service innovations.

Box 5 Jamie Malloy entrepreneurial ventures

"At the Jamie Molloy Hamburgers bar and van, it is the meeting point for the foreign community that lives in Penamacor. In addition to this business, Jamie owns the first real estate agency in town (. . .) We [with is partner #10] have the estate agency 'Quintamacor' because so many people come in now". (#9, TVI 24, 01-11-2018)

"[He] was one of the first foreigners to emerge in the village. 'In my other life I was an engineer, responsible for the safety of a gas exploration in Australia. One day I got fed up and opened a bar in Melbourne, but I ended up going bankrupt and going back to Europe. (. . .) I came here five years ago because I was told that there was really cheap land here. I bought a farm and started to tell some friends, especially English, that there were fantastic opportunities here". (#9, Diário de Notícias-14/10/2018)

"Three years ago he sold the farm to an English couple, bought another. And that was when he created a website to sell properties. 'In the meantime I decided to make things official and create an agency. Last week I made the sale number one hundred. All farms, and everything to foreigners.' (. . .) The Irishman also has a bar, the JCJ, which serves as a meeting point for the foreign community. It serves beef, chicken or vegetarian burgers and fills up in the late afternoon like an English pub. 'Now I've just bought a store and I'm going to open a laundry. Most foreigners live on farms that run on solar energy and can't get enough energy for a washing machine'". (#9, SIC Notícias, 25/03/2019)

"I'm starting to work to Quintamacor, at the moment, with the guys (. . .)". (#17, SIC Notícias, 25/03/2019)

---

[12]Employee of the municipality of Penamacor and professor of Portuguese foreign community in Penamacor, in a personal interview.

The impact on the local economy is also extending to small service providers in construction and in agriculture, as testimonies in Box 6 make evident, and, based on Cunha (2018), this impact tends to grow. In fact, this author found that in the near future, a significant number of immigrants (50% of respondents) expected to start an entrepreneurial activity.

Box 6 Other entrepreneurial ventures by immigrants
"I'm a carpenter and a builder and I like working with the stone and wood and I do have other forms of trade work but my specialty is carpentry. There are many beautiful buildings out there that need restoration and there's a lot of people that came out here to set up a home and lots of them abandon places like this and it takes a lot of work to get it in a beautiful place... Yes. I think there should be enough work on here". (#18b, SIC Notícias, 25/03/2019)

"There is not enough work for me around here as an electrician because there are already local electricians and I don't want to take any work away from the guys who already established here themselves. I'm trying to get away from that and sort up and to make some progresses with the farming". (#20, SIC Notícias, 25/03/2019)

As described by several authors (Ateljevic and Doorne 2000; Marcketti et al. 2006; Kapler 2018), these immigrants have a set of skills and abilities that translate into a benefit for the local community, translating in some cases in new services or innovative activities, as the cases presented above, but also resulting in the promotion of other communitarian initiatives such as the creation of a school with an innovative curriculum (the international school) (see Box 7) or the carrying out of cultural activities such as the collaboration in Penamacor intercultural fair. Being actively involved in local initiatives and "actively seeking closer relationships and initiate inclusive community relationships which emphasise social worth" as described by Ateljevic and Doorne (2000, 386), they, in fact, also act as communitarian entrepreneurs (Cornwall 1998; Johannisson and Nilsson 1989), i.e. they became important parts of community building and a powerful element in processes of social change.

However, the testimonies presented also show that lifestyle entrepreneurs are able to survive commercially partly because they can rely on each other and develop mechanisms of integration within the foreign community (e.g. Hub association but also Jamie Malloy's JCJ bar) and also between the foreign and local community, and as described by Cunha et al. (2018):

> It seems that the culture of promoting sharing, exchange and, in many cases, the sale of surpluses from their small production is relatively established in their own organization and organization of short marketing channels. The search for mutual assistance in agricultural work—and others—is a current practice. (p.72)

This is consistent with Ateljevic and Doorne (2000) and Klapper et al. (2018) conclusions that the foreign immigrant community is significantly reliant on their own resources and those of the group, making evident the importance of social capital for the success of their ventures.

But the presence of these immigrants with new habits and more purchasing power has created a demand that also impacts the economic activities promoted by local people, originating new businesses and making the existing ones more viable, as shown in Box 7.

Box 7 Impact of lifestyle immigrants in local businesses

"In the center of Penamacor there is a gourmet grocery store that had to adapt to the arrival of outsiders. 'Do you know what they buy most?' asks Érica Bargão, who has occupied the space behind the counter since the store opened three years ago. 'Dog food. Here, we give the animals the leftover food, but they prefer it that way. So we had to reinforce the orders. That, the tea, the bacon. And then we started introducing new products that were not used here, like oats and lentils'. (. . .) This store opened when the first foreigners started to arrive, Érica knows that it was this impetus that came from outside that is making the business profitable". (#9L Diário de Notícias-14/10/2018)

"It is noticeable! In the morning, it's almost double . . . it's 50/50: 50 Portuguese, 50 English. And, at night, you can also notice (. . .) because they have no problems about spending money. (. . .) I think it will be our future, because the people get old, the new ones don't stay and so, I think they will be our hope in Penamacor". (#11L, TVI24, 01-11-2018)

"I don't know how to speak. . . I only know how to speak Portuguese, but I have already transported them, that I am a taxi driver . . . they are more . . . hum . . . how can I say they are more 'thing' than the Portuguese. . .the Portuguese are always haggling over the price and they are not, what the taximeter mark is what they pay". (#12L, TVI24, 01-11-2018)

These new inhabitants in Penamacor county also generated a demand for other basic services, such as health, education and information technologies, which created a "critical mass" (Dinis 2006) that justify/make viable the creation/development of these infrastructures in the territory. For instance, in September 2017, the first English curriculum school in the country opened here. Being fundamental to the quality of life of families, the existence of those services became elements of attraction for more immigrants, particularly for the active and younger ones (see Box 8).

Box 8 Impact of lifestyle immigrants in local infrastructures

"The health center not only gained more than one hundred of users but also strengthened valences: 'increased maternal health, because some have

---

(continued)

Box 8 (continued)

already become pregnant, some women (. . .) and the family planning. . .it all increased". (#4L, SIC Notícias, 25/03/2019)

"At the health center, the head nurse Vítor Fernandes explains the impact of the arrival of children: 'Until now, we were almost a palliative unit. We served almost exclusively old people who need continued care. And now we have children again, we can already do prevention campaigns, vaccinations, teach healthy habits. And this is what we really are for". (#5L, Diário de Notícias-14/10/2018)

"The [former] day school of Our Lady of Incense [closed since the 90s for lack of students] gave way to the only school in English in the interior of Portugal [The international school of Penamacor."(. . .) 'There were 33 students now, from 4 and 12 years old and from more than 10 different countries: Israel Canada, America, England, Germany, Italy, France . . .' "(#21 [teacher/director of the school], TVI24, 01-11-2018)." The school began two years ago with a lady call Zoe Burgess who had a home tuition school in the U.K and she moved to Portugal and wanted to continue that for her children. Other local foreign children joined her and she was very successful, and then needed a larger building and the municipality provided her this building (. . .) I imagine that in the next couple of years, with the people that I'm talking to and that are coming to the area, the school will probably reach 60 students in the (. . .) and then will increase after that" (#21 Diário de Notícias-19/10/2018)

"I have a Portuguese wife (. . .) she is from Oporto. We are both teachers and we were looking for the right school (we have two children) to put them and then we found this school that was here in Penamacor. . ." (#8, Diário de Notícias-19/10/2018)

"There are also three dozen foreign children attending Portuguese education, and this allows in some cases to open two classes for the same year, something that was not mentioned in Penamacor for decades". (Diário de Notícias-14/10/2018)

"Today we have in most of our villages and in our parishes, a fiber optic network, that is, working here in the village of João Pires is perfectly the same as working in the center of the capital or there is not a climate of differentiation in terms of job opportunities. (#1L, SIC, 25/03/2019) "We are about to tender for the opening of a technological center. Basically, we will have rooms with internet with fiber, so that it is possible to work in this land with high speed internet". (#1L, Diário de Notícias-14/10/2018)

Furthermore, the presence of these global citizens in the territory also generates other mobility flows, attracting others—mainly family and friends—as tourists (for short periods) or as immigrants (for longer periods or for life) (see Box 9), generating a virtuous cycle, i.e. reinforcing the local dynamic of economic growth and social development. It should also be noted that in the study of Cunha (2018), from the first phase (January 2017) to the second phase of data collection (which includes questionnaires from April and May 2018), the answer "I was advised by friends" increased from 3% to 17% of respondents, showing a marked growth in the "word of mouth".

Box 9 The generation of new influxes of people

"I came here five years ago because I was told that there was really cheap land here. I bought a farm and started to tell some friends, especially English, that there were fantastic opportunities here. And some came along". (#9, DN, 2018)

"11 years ago he bought a farm with about 1.3 hectares, near Aldeia de João Pires where he lives alone most of the time, except when he is visited by one of his 4 children and 3 grandchildren who live in England". (#3, Cunha 2018:64)

"She bought a 2.2-hectare farm near the village of Pedrógão, rebuilt the house in ruins to the minimum conditions and lives there alone, except when she receives a visit from his son who lives in England and his friends. Recently, the son launched on social media a request for volunteering to help with the farm and rebuilding the house, and now he is preparing to receive, during next summer, groups of 4 volunteers out of a total of 14 who responded to the request". (#5, Cunha 2018: 64)

---

5   Conclusions

The purpose of this study was to explore the nexus between tourism and migration and, through the lens of the lifestyle entrepreneurship, to assess the impact of the new patterns of mobility in rural and low density territories. The case of Penamacor, one of the most lagging regions in Portugal, represents a paradigmatic case of this new motilities, presenting a recent and overwhelming influx of young (and not so young) people to the territory. Thus, this case was instrumental to further understand *who these migrants* are and what their motivations are for mobility and to settle in the territory and also if *entrepreneurship is a possibility of income generation for these immigrants and for the creation of wealth and well-being in the community*. It was also intended to understand whether the presence of these new incomers in the territory *generates other mobility flows*, through the attraction of others, mainly, family and friends or acquaintances, as tourists, immigrants or travellers.

Results show that in spite of their lifestyle motivations, they are not all the same, showing differences in their demographic characteristics, specific motivations, occupations and their patterns of mobilities and spatial frames of action. They differ in their ages, including retired people and—mostly—young people, who came alone or with family. They also differ in their motivations with some of them mainly concerned with their (and their family) quality of life, not necessarily implying a radical detachment from the capitalist/market system, whilst others are clearly motivated by socio-ideological beliefs associated with the rejection of the mainstream neoliberal order, looking for alternative ways of living. Also, in spite of the fact that most practice agriculture, it seems that there are also differences in the weight that this activity represents in their income and working hours. In some cases, they abandoned their previous professional occupations to dedicate themselves to agriculture in full time or complementary to other local activities. However, in other cases, agriculture seems to be a hobby, in the sense that their professional occupation and what their source of income are, mainly, connected to the same (or similar) jobs as before migration, working globally and making extensive use of information technologies and telework. In general, these new inhabitants have in common the extended/international "life experiences" and often a history of international mobilities, making them "citizens of the world" and "travellers" (as defined by Ateljevic and Doorne 2000), with different perspectives and attitudes, from tourists and traditional immigrants, in regard to mobility. However, in addition to the above finer distinction concerning lifestyle motives and age (and thus in concerning their position in the market labour—active/inactive), they also differ in the patterns of permanence in the territory, with some presenting a stable permanence in the territory (some for life) and others presenting a circulation/shifting mode between one or several international locations. These differences can be aggregated in different types of lifestyle migration: *retirement migration*, *stable migration* and *nomad* or *peripatetic migration*. These typologies can be better understood in a multidimensional scheme, along four dimensions: (i) age/situation in the labour market (active vs retired); (ii) individual or family lifestyle vs social/ideological motives; (iii) frame of action (occupation); and (iv) duration of permanence in the territory. *Retired immigrants* are distinguished from the rest by the fact that they are no longer active in the labour market and, therefore, there is no need to balance work with quality of life. For the same reason, it makes no sense to talk about the spatial frame of their (professional) occupations. *Stable lifestyle immigrants* differentiate from nomad by their permanence in the territory, corresponding to a more stable pattern (possibly definitive) in opposition to the "circulation" mode of the "nomad". Associated with the nomad's circulation mode is their professional global/non-local work context.

For what concerns their impact on the community, results show that immigrants' characteristics, namely, their global experience and perspectives, their (younger) age and higher qualifications than native population, can make them more aware of business opportunities and also agents of social and cultural change, acting both as commercial and communitarian entrepreneurs. Furthermore, the success of their ventures is strongly supported by their own (foreign) community, as both clients and partners. Besides that, their presence in territory increased the demand for local products and services and create a "critical mass" (Dinis 2006) needed for the viability of essential infrastructures as health and education. Finally, through their social networks—family, friends and acquaintances—other mobility flows to the territory are generated whether for long or short periods of time, reinforcing the local dynamic of economic growth and social development.

From the theoretical point of view, the study provides more in-depth understanding of emigrant lifestyles, showing that they do not constitute a homogeneous group and designing new differentiated profiles. It also confirms the relevant economic and social impact that these new inhabitants have on a territory that suffers from depopulation problems. The study further relates literature with different traditions, namely, exploring the tourism-migration nexus and associating it with the field of entrepreneurship, providing, at the same time, important clues for rural studies and the field of regional development. Finally, the study reinforces and extends to other sector besides tourism, the conclusion of Williams et al. (1989) about the blurring borders between consumption (lifestyle)-led and production (entrepreneurial)-led migration. From a practical point of view, the study advances knowledge about the characteristics, motivations, capacities and (potential) impacts of these new settlers, which is essential to design policies aimed at attracting new settlers, supporting their projects and leveraging their impact on the territory.

In spite of these contributions, this study had an eminently qualitative and exploratory nature, so, more than providing definitive answers, it allowed to further understand *why* these immigrants come and *how* they impact the territory. However, more studies of descriptive and quantitative nature are needed in order to provide more conclusive evidence concerning the profiles and the impact. For instance, future research should measure the relative weight of each type of immigrant and to quantify the impact of their presence and activities and, also, to assess if different migrant profiles have different impacts in the territory.

Furthermore, other questions can be deepened in further studies. For instance, as noted by Marchant and Mottiar (2011), "as life changes so do motivations and desires"; thus, along their life cycle, an individual can move from being one type of immigrant to another or from being one type of entrepreneur to another, for instance, if a "nomad" become "stable" or a "lifestyle" entrepreneur become commercial one. Why does it happen? What are the implications of such changes? How often does it happen? These are also questions to be answered in future research.

The present work focusses on a chapter of the migrations (hi)story in a low-density territory that will be succeeded by other chapters that are important to follow. For example, in Penamacor, the academic year 2019–2020, the international school did not open due to problems in the internal dynamics. What impact will the closure of the school have on the sustainability and growth of the immigration? If the migratory flow continues to increase significantly, how is it support the integration of these foreign immigrants preserving also the identity of the local community? Additionally, in 2020 we are facing the pandemic of COVID-19, which profoundly affected the mobility and the relationship with spaces. What will the future impact of this threat (or similar ones) in these territories be? Will containment of mobility have longer term effects, restraining the globalization process and consequently also the international migratory movements? Or, on the contrary, will it accentuate the counterurbanization movement, by people searching for greater health security in less densely populated areas? These are some of the challenges that these territories face and for which it is worth looking for answers.

Acknowledgements I would like to thank Pedro Salvado for personally sharing his perspective about this new community of residents in Penamacor and Anselmo Cunha for kindly providing me with his work about these new rurals.
This work has the support of FCT through P- RIDE Project (PTDC/ATP-DEM/0441/2014).

Sources of Empirical Data

Personal Interview
Exploratory personal interview with Pedro Agapito, employee of the municipality of Penamacor and professor of Portuguese foreign community in Penamacor

Studies/Reports
Report of the Foreign Community Monitoring Working Group presented at the Municipal Assembly of Penamacor February 2017

Cunha, Anselmo (2018). Neoruralidades em territórios de baixa densidade—o caso do concelho de Penamacor, Dissertação de mestrado em Antroplogia de Iberoamérica,/(Neoruralities in low-density territories—the case of the municipality of Penamacor, Master's Dissertation in Anthropology of Iberoamerica), Universidad de Salamanca, June 2018

Vilas Boas, M. De Carvalho, C., Rodrigues, J. e Valente, A. (2015): Património Geológico de Penamacor: Inventário Geossítios e propostas para a sua valorização, *AÇAFA* On Line, n° 10 Associação de Estudos do Alto Tejo

Statistical Data
Foreign and Borders Service (SEF), Number of registration certificates Issued for the municipality of Penamacor between November 2008 and February 2020

PORDATA, Data Sources: INE—Annual Estimates of the Resident Population; Data Sources: IGP—National Cartographic Series at 1:50,000 scale and Official Administrative Letter of Portugal—CAOP 2009.0. Last updated: 2020-02-07

PORDATA, Data Sources: INE—Annual Estimates of the Resident Population I SEF/MAI—População Estrangeira com Estatuto Legal de Residente, Last updated 2020-02-07

Sites/Blogs

Municipality of Penamacor site: http://www.cm-penamacor.pt

Blog of Pedrogrão de S. pedro (Small village of Penamacor County): http://pedrogaosaopedro.blogspot.com/2017/03/penamacor-estrangeiros-estao-dar-vida.html

News/Documentaries in Media

In the Local Press

Furtado, J (2017, 23 March). Estrangeiros estão a dar vida a penamacor [Foreigners are giving life to Penamacor]. *A Reconquista*, p. 22

In the National Press

Araújo, A. (2019, 3 March) Preço das casas na cidade empurra procura para aldeias do interior [Price of houses in the city pushes demand for rural villages] availabel in *Expresso,* Cadernos de Economia, https://expresso.pt/economia/2019-08-03-Preco-das-casas-na-cidade-empurra-procura-para-aldeias-do-interior

Faria, N. (2012, 16 July). A Aldeia de Martim está condenada [The Village of Martim is doomed]. *Público*, available in https://www.publico.pt/2012/07/16/jornal/a-aldeia-de-martim-esta-condenada-24898186

Rodrigues, R. (2018, 14 October) Os fugitivos do brexit estão a invadir o concelho mais envelhecido de Portugal [Brexit fugitives are invading Portugal's oldest municipality], *Diário de Notícias*, available in https://www.dn.pt/edicao-do-dia/14-out-2018/os-fugitivos-do-brexit-estao-a-invadir-o-concelho-mais-envelhecido-de-portugal-9996873.html

Documentaries (Video/TV)

Ferreira, M. (journalist) & Ramos, A. (Coord) (2019, 27 March). Good Morning Penamacor. *SIC Notícias, Sic Notícias*, available in https://sicnoticias.pt/programas/reportagemsic/2019-03-27-Good-Morning-Penamacor [Duration:29m:46′)

Rodrigues, R. (2018, 19 October) Fugir do Brexit para Penamacor [Escape from Brexit to Penamacor], *Diário de Notícias*, https://www.dn.pt/galerias/videos/vida-e-futuro/fugir-do-brexit-para-penamacor-10027837.html (Duration:9m:11′)

(s/a., 2018, 2, November). Penamacor tem a maior taxa de residentes estrangeiros do interior [Penamacor has the highest rate of foreign residents in the interior], *TVI 24*, available in https://tvi24.iol.pt/videos/sociedade/penamacor-tem-a-maior-taxa-de-residentes-estrangeiros-do-interior/5bdca6a10cf2223b6a7ae10d   (Duration: 4m:05′)

All together, these sources allowed access to statements of 27 foreign immigrants, corresponding to 21 households (Table 4) and 12 local inhabitants (Table 5), that constituted key informants for the empirical study.

Table 4 Foreign community key informants

#	Name	Gender	Age	Nationality	Source
1a	Jacques[a]	Male	44	French	Cunha (2018: 62–69)
1b	Brigitte[a]	Female	41	French	Cunha (2018: 62–69)
2a	Sílvia[a]/Flora van Heteren	Female	69	Dutch	Cunha (2018: 62–69) *SIC Notícias-27/03/2019*
2b	Eric[a]/Dudley Campling	Male	69	English	Cunha (2018: 62–69) *SIC Notícias-27/03/2019*
3	Ian[a]	Male	57	English	Cunha (2018: 62–69)
4a	Loorena[a]	Female	34	Iranian/English	Cunha (2018: 62–69)
4b	Chris[a]	Male	32	English	Cunha (2018: 62–69)
5	Sandy[a]/Sophia Mars	Female	51	English	Cunha (2018: 62–69) *Diário de Notícias-14/10/2018* (press) *Diário de Notícias-19/10/2018* (video)
6	Jack[a]	Male	48	Scottish	Cunha (2018: 62–69)
7a	Peter Siedle	Male	51	English	*Diário de Notícias-14/10/2018* (press) *Diário de Notícias-19/10/2018* (vídeo)
7b	Dawn Siedle	Female	51	English	*Diário de Notícias-14/10/2018* (press) *Diário de Notícias-19/10/2018* (vídeo)
8	Andrew Smith	Male	37	Australian	*Diário de Notícias-14/10/2018* (press) *Diário de Notícias-19/10/2018* (vídeo) *SIC Notícias-27/03/2019*
9	Jamie Molloy	Male	38/40	Irish	*Reconquista-27/03/2017* (press) *Diário de Notícias-14/10/2018* (press) *Diário de Notícias-19/10/2018* (vídeo) *TVI 24-02/11/2018* *SIC Notícias-27/03/2019*
10	Joshua Laurent	Male	36	English	*SIC Notícias-27/03/2019*
11	Tira Noren	Female	50	Swedish	*SIC Notícias-27/03/2019*
12	Helen Morgen	Female	57	Wales	*SIC Notícias-27/03/2019*
13	Peter Russeu	Male	47	English	*SIC Notícias-27/03/2019*
14	Shaun Kenny	Male	45	Wales	*SIC Notícias-27/03/2019*
15	Jesus Mathias	Male	33	American	*SIC Notícias-27/03/2019*
16a	Stephanie Bruns	Female	38	German	*SIC Notícias-27/03/2019*
16b	Janus Bruns	Male	44	German	*SIC Notícias-27/03/2019*
17	Carly Bennet	Female	43	English	*SIC Notícias-27/03/2019*
18a	Noélia Rodrigues	Female	32	Spanish	*SIC Notícias-27/03/2019*
18b	Richard Stonechild	Male	32	English	*SIC Notícias-27/03/2019*

(continued)

Table 4 (continued)

#	Name	Gender	Age	Nationality	Source
19	Zahrah Nasir	Female	62	Pakistani/ Scottish	*TVI 24-02/11/2018* *SIC Notícias-27/03/2019*
20	Figgs	Male	33	Zimbabwean	*SIC Notícias-27/03/2019*
21	Paul Large	Male	50	English	*Diário de Notícias-14/10/2018* (press) *Diário de Notícias-19/10/2018* (video) *SIC Notícias-27/03/2019*

[a]Fictitious names

Table 5 Local community key informants

#	Name	Identification	Sources
1L	Luis Bates	Mayor of Penamacor	*Diário de Notícias-14/10/2018* (press) *Diário de Notícias-19/10/2018* (vídeo) *TVI 24-02/11/2018* *SIC Notícias-27/03/2019*
2L	Pedro Agapito	Employee of the municipality of Penamacor and professor of Portuguese foreign community in Penamacor	Personal Interview (February 2020) *Reconquista-27/03/2017 (Press)* *SIC Notícias-27/03/2019*
3L	Anselmo Cunha	Sociologist from a Penamacor village (Aldeia do Bispo)	Master Dissertation (2018) *Reconquista-27/03/2017 (Press)* *SIC Notícias-27/03/2019*
4L	Elizabete Rato	Doctor at Penamacor Health Center	*SIC Notícias-27/03/2019*
5L	Vitor Fernandes	Head nurse at Penamacor Health Center	*Diário de Notícias-14/10/2018 (Press)*
6L	António Pinto	President of Pedrógrão de S. Pedro and Bemposta townships union (small villages of Penamacor county)	*SIC Notícias-27/03/2019*
7L	Gonçalo Martins	Kid from Penamacor (football player)	*SIC Notícias-27/03/2019*
8L	Cristina Canaveiro	Shopkeeper	*SIC Notícias-27/03/2019*
9L	Érica Bargão	Shopkeeper	*Diário de Notícias-14/10/2018 (Press)*
10L	Ilda Tavares	Local inhabitant	*SIC Notícias-27/03/2019*
11L	(Young man)	Bartender	*TVI 24-02/11/2018*
12L	(Old man)	Taxi driver	*TVI 24-02/11/2018*

References

Acs Z (2006) How is entrepreneurship good for economic growth? Innovations 1(1):97–107

Acs ZJ, Estrin S, Mickiewicz T, Szerb L (2018) Entrepreneurship, institutional economics, and economic growth: an ecosystem perspective. Small Bus Econ 51(2):501–514

Akgün A, Baycan-Levent T, Nijkamp P, Poot J (2011) Roles of local and newcomer entrepreneurs in rural development: a comparative meta-analytic study. Reg Stud 45:1207–1223

Ateljevic I, Doorne S (2000) "Staying within the fence": lifestyle entrepreneurship in tourism. J Sustain Tour 8(5):378–392

Barbosa B, Santos C, Santos M (2020) Tourists with migrants' eyes: the mediating role of tourism in international retirement migration. J Tour Cult Chang. February

Baumol WJ, Strom RJ (2007) Entrepreneurship and economic growth. Strateg Entrep J 1(3–4):233–237

Benson M, O'Reilly K (2009) Migration and the search for a better way of life: a critical exploration of lifestyle migration. Sociol Rev 57(4):608–625

Benson M, O'Reilly K (2016) From lifestyle migration to lifestyle *in* migration: categories, concepts and ways of thinking. Migr Stud 4(1):20–37

Bosworth G (2006) Counterurbanisation and job creation: entrepreneurial immigration and rural economic development. Centre for rural economy discussions paper series, 4. Tyne and Wear: Centre for Rural Economy, University of Newcastle upon Tyne

Bourdieu P (1980) Le capital social. Actes de la Recherche en Sciences Sociales 31:2–3

Braunerhjelm P, Acs ZJ, Audretsch DB, Carlsson B (2010) The missing link: knowledge diffusion and entrepreneurship in endogenous growth. Small Bus Econ 34(2):105–125

Bredvold R, Skålén P (2016) Lifestyle entrepreneurs and their identity construction: a study of the tourism industry. Tour Manag 56:96–105

Cassel S (2008) Trying to be attractive: image building and identity formation in small industrial municipalities in Sweden. Place Brandind Publ Diplom 4:102–114

Cederholm EA, Hultman J (2010) The value of intimacy – negotiating commercial relationships in lifestyle entrepreneurship. Scand J Hosp Tour 10(1):16–32

Claire L (2012) Re-storing the entrepreneurial: lifestyle entrepreneurs as hero? Tamara 10(1):31–39

Cornwall JR (1998) The entrepreneur as a building block for community. J Dev Entrep 3 (2):141–148

Cunha A (2018) Neoruralidades em territórios de baixa densidade – o caso do concelho de Penamacor, Dissertação de mestrado em Antroplogia de Iberoamérica,/ (Neoruralities in low-density territories – the case of the municipality of Penamacor, Master's Dissertation in Anthropology of Iberoamerica), Universidad de Salamanca, June

Cunha C, Kastenholz E, Carneiro MJ (2018) Lifestyle entrepreneurs in rural tourism: motivations, management practices and sustainability issues. Revista Turismo e Desenvolvimento 8 (2):53–55

Dinis A (2002) Rural entrepreneurship: individual or collective phenomena. Estudos de Gestão – Portuguese J Manag Stud VII(2): 111–126

Dinis A (2006) Rural entrepreneurship – an innovation and marketing perspective. In: Nijkamp P, Morgan E, Vaz T (eds) The New European rurality: strategies for small firms. Ashgate, New York, pp 157–178

Dinis A (2009) Who are the rural entrepreneurs? A perspective from institutional support agents. Proceedings of 32nd annual institute for small business & entrepreneurship (ISBE) conference. Liverpool on the 3–6 November

Dubois A, Gadde L-E (2002) Systematic combining: an abductive approach to case research. J Bus Res 55:553–560

Eimermann M (2015) Promoting Swedish countryside in the Netherlands: international rural place marketing to attract new residents. Eur Urban Reg Stud 22(4):398–415

Eimermann M, Agnidakis P, Åkerlund U, Woube A (2017) Rural place marketing and consumption-driven mobilities in Northern Sweden: challenges and opportunities for community sustainability. J Rural Commun Dev 12(2/3):114–126

Getz D, Carlson J (2000) Characteristics and goals of family and owner-operated businesses in rural tourism and hospitality sectors. Tour Manag 2(1):547–560

Gorton M, White J, Chaston I (1998) Counterurbanisation, fragmentation and the paradox of the rural idyll. In: Boyle P, Halfacree K (eds) Migration into rural areas. Wiley, Chichester, pp 215–235

Guerreiro J (2019) Mobilidades, estilos de vida e autenticidade: os estrangeiros residentes na zona histórica de Olhão [Mobility, lifestyles and authenticity: foreigners residing in the historic area of Olhão], Master Dissertation in Sociology, Universidade do Algarve

Hedfeldt M, Lundmark M (2015) New firm formation in old industrial regions – a study of entrepreneurial in-migrants in Bergslagen, Sweden. Norsk Geografisk Tidsskrift–Norwegian J Geogr 69(2):90–101

Henderson JR (2002) Are high-growth entrepreneurs building the rural economy? The main Street Economist. Centre for Study of Rural America, Federal Reserve Bank of Kansas City, Kansa, August, 2–5

Herslund L (2011) The rural creative class: counterurbanisation and entrepreneurship in the Danish countryside. Sociologica Ruralis 52:235–255

Hoey B (2005) From Pi to Pie: moral narratives of noneconomic migration and starting over in the postindustrial midwest. J Contemp Ethnogr 34(5):586–624

Hoggart K, Buller H (1995) British home owners and housing change in rural France. Hous Stud 10 (2):179–198

Huggins R, Thompson P (2015) Entrepreneurship, innovation and regional growth: a network theory. Small Bus Econ 45:103–128

Ibrahim Z, Tremblay T (2017) Lifestyle migration and the quest for a life-long vacation. Téoros [Online], 36, 2 | 2017, Online since 08 September 2017, connection on 03 May 2019. http://journals.openedition.org/teoros/3074

INE (2011) Censos 2001, INE-Instituto Nacional de Estatística, Lisboa

Iversen I, Jacobsen J (2016) Migrant tourism entrepreneurs in rural Norway. Scand J Hosp Tour 16 (4):484–499

Johannisson B, Nilsson A (1989) Community entrepreneurs: networking for local development. Entrepr Region Dev 1(1):3–19

Kalantaridis C (2010) In-migration, entrepreneurship and rural-urban interdependencies: the case of East Cleveland, North East England. J Rural Stud 26:418–427

Kalantaridis C, Bika Z (2006) In-migrant entrepreneurship in rural England: beyond local embeddedness. Entrep Reg Dev 18:109–131

Kirzner IM (1973) Competition and entrepreneurship. University of Chicago Press, Chicago

Klapper R, Upham P, Kurronen K (2018) Social capital, resource constraints and low growth communities: lifestyle entrepreneurs in Nicaragua. Sustainability 10

Lundmark L (2006) Mobility, migration and seasonal tourism employment: evidence from Swedish Mountain Municipalities. Scand J Hosp Tour 6(3):197–213

Lundmark L, Ednarsson M, Karlsson S (2014) International migration, self-employment and restructuring through tourism in sparsely populated areas. Scand J Hosp Tour 14(4):422–440

Marchant, B. & Mottiar, Z.: Understanding (2011). Lifestyle tourism entrepreneurs and digging beneath the issue of profits: profiling surf tourism lifestyle entrepreneurs in Ireland. Tour Plann Dev, 8 (2): 171–183

Marcketti SB, Niehm LS, Fuloria R (2006) An exploratory study of lifestyle entrepreneurship and its relationship to life quality. Family Consum Sci Res J 34(3):241–259

Mitchell C, Shannon M (2018) Establishing the routes to rural in-migrant proprietorship in a Canadian tourism region: A mobilities perspective. Popul Space Place 24:e2095.

Möller P, Amcoff J (2018) Tourism's localised population effect in the rural areas of Sweden. Scand J Hosp Tour 18(1):39–55

North D, Smallbone D (2006) Developing entrepreneurship and enterprise in Europe's peripheral rural areas: some issues facing policy-makers. Eur Plan Stud 14(1):41–60

O'Reilly K (2003) When is a tourist?: The articulation of tourism and migration in Spain's Costa del Sol. Tour Stud 3(3):301–317

O'Reilly K, Benson M (2009) Lifestyle migration: escaping to the good life? In: O'Reilly K, Benson M (eds) Lifestyle migrations: expectations, aspirations and experiences. Ashgate, London, pp 1–13

182 A. Dinis

Pallarès-Blanch M, Prados Velasco M, Tulla Pujol A (2014) Naturbanization and Urban – rural dynamics in Spain: case study of new rural landscapes in Andalusia and Catalonia. Eur Countryside 6(2):118–160

Paniagua A (2002) Urban-rural migration, tourism entrepreneurs and rural restructuring in Spain. Tour Geogr 4(4):349–371

Peters M, Frehse J, Buhalis D (2009) The importance of lifestyle entrepreneurship: a conceptual study of the tourism industry *PASOS*. Revista de Turismo y Patrimonio Cultural 7(2):393–405

Putnam RD (1993) Making democracy work. Civic traditions in modern Italy. Princeton University Press, Princeton

Schumpeter JA (1934) The theory of economic development: an inquiry into profits, capital, credit, interest, and the business cycle. Transaction Publishers

Schumpeter JA (1942) Capitalism, socialism and democracy (3rd ed). George Allen and Unwin London, 1976

Shaw G, Williams AM (1998) Entrepreneurship, small business culture and tourism development. In: Ioannides D, Debbage KG (eds) The Economic Geography of the Tourist Industry. Routledge, London, pp 235–255

Shaw G, Williams AM (2004) From lifestyle consumption to lifestyle production: changing patterns of tourism entrepreneurship. In: Thomas R (ed) Small firms in tourism: international perspectives. Elsevier, Amsterdam, pp 99–113

Stake R (1995) The art of case study research. Sage, Thousand Oaks, CA

Stockdale A (2006) Migration: a pre-requisite for rural economic regeneration? J Rural Stud 22:354–366

Sun X, Xu H (2019) Role shifting between entrepreneur and tourist: a case study on Dali and Lijiang, China. J Travel Tour Market, April, 1–15

Sun X, Xu H, Köseoglu MA, Okumus F (2020) How do lifestyle hospitality and tourism entrepreneurs manage their work-life balance? Int J Hosp Manag 85(February):1–8

Wennekers S, Thurik R (1999) Linking entrepreneurship and economic growth. Small Bus Econ 13 (1):27–56

Williams AM, Hall CM (2000) Tourism and migration: new relationships between production and consumption. Tour Geogr 2(1):5–27

Williams AM, Hall CM (2002) Tourism, migration, circulation and mobility: the contingencies of time and place. In Hall H, Williams A (eds) Tourism and migration: new relationships between production and consumption, pp 1–52

Williams AM, Shaw G, Greenwood J (1989) From tourist to tourism entrepreneur, from consumption to production: evidence from Cornwall, England. Environ Plan A 21(12):1639–1653

Williams A, King R, Warnes T (1997) A place in the Sun: international retirement migration from Northern to Southern Europe. Eur Urban Region Stud 4(2):115–134

Yin R (2009) Case study research: design and methods, vol 5. Sage, London

High-Speed Rail and Tourism in Spanish Low-Density Areas: Not Always a Solution

Daniel Albalate, Javier Campos, and Juan Luis Jiménez

1 Introduction

The provision of new and major interurban transport infrastructure often raises high economic and social expectations, especially in territories with low-population density and limited or even declining opportunities for alternative socioeconomic development. The tourism industry has a singular interest in this type of investments, as they generate the prospect of greater accessibility and increased attractiveness for new visitors. In Spain, greater tourism opportunities have been commonly associated with the deployment of its high-speed rail (HSR) network which, due to a radial design that departs from a central hub in Madrid toward the most populated and tourist-oriented cities on the coast, makes it particularly possible to connect intermediate sparsely populated areas along its route.

Despite these ex ante expectations, there is a lack of disaggregated empirical evidence on the real impacts of HSR infrastructure on the tourism performance of these areas, and additional empirical research is largely needed. This chapter aims to

D. Albalate
Department of Econometrics, Statistics and Applied Economics (GiM-IREA) & Observatori d'Anàlisi i Avaluació de Polítiques Públiques (OAP-UB), Universitat de Barcelona, Barcelona, Spain
e-mail: albalate@ub.edu

J. Campos
Department of Applied Economics and EITT, Universidad de Las Palmas de Gran Canaria, Las Palmas de Gran Canaria, Spain
e-mail: javier.campos@ulpgc.es

J. L. Jiménez (✉)
Department of Applied Economics, Universidad de Las Palmas de Gran Canaria, Las Palmas de Gran Canaria, Spain
e-mail: juanluis.jimenez@ulpgc.es

© Springer Nature Switzerland AG 2021
R. P. Marques et al. (eds.), *The Impact of Tourist Activities on Low-Density Territories*, Tourism, Hospitality & Event Management,
https://doi.org/10.1007/978-3-030-65524-2_8

examine the effects of the arrival and consolidation of the high-speed rail services on the tourism industry of some of the most depopulated provinces in Spain, focusing on their main municipalities (province capitals). Using the Spanish experience, a leader in Europe in investment and length in this transportation mode, this chapter aims to provide evidence on what can be expected in terms of tourism development from the arrival of large network infrastructures to low-density areas. We intend to contribute to the policy debate on infrastructure spending and allocation decisions at both national and local levels and to better inform the perception of tourist managers and planners about the real effects of transport investments.

A panel dataset was used for those Spanish municipalities (province capitals) placed in provinces with less than 25 inhabitants per square km (and total population below 300,000) that directly benefited from HSR services (i.e., with operating stations) in the last two decades: Segovia, Cuenca, Palencia, and Zamora.[1] Guadalajara and Huesca also satisfy the definition of target municipalities, but they are unfortunately excluded due to missing information on tourism outcomes as tourist points for the necessary period to undertake the analysis.

It is examined and described how the arrival of high-speed train services affected tourism activity in these municipalities, considering the increase in the number of visitors, overnight stays, occupancy rates, and hotel bed supply. We will particularly compare the evolution of these four tourism indicators with similar municipalities— satisfying the characteristics defined above—located in three other low-density areas in Spain not benefited from HSR investments: Ávila, Teruel, and Soria.[2] The use of these controls will allow us to check whether the arrival of the new infrastructure implied a structural change with respect to what would have happened without it. Thus, the comparison group will allow us to check the changes in both groups of provinces of similar characteristics (small population, low density, located between Madrid and the coastline provinces, etc.). Our tourism analysis is based on public datasets that are available online from the National Statistical Office (www.ine.es), at the municipality level for a sufficient period of time before and after the inauguration. Information on HSR deployment has been obtained from ADIF, the public company managing railway infrastructures in Spain.

After this introduction, the structure of the rest of the chapter will be as follows. First, we will briefly review the relationship between the expected impact of high-speed rail investments on regional growth and, particularly, on tourism. Then, we

---

[1] Our analysis only refers to mainland Spain; it excludes the Canary Islands and the Balearic Islands archipelagos and the autonomous enclaves of Ceuta and Melilla, where there are no HSR services. Our definition of "high-speed" includes those services operating above 200–250 km/h when they are thus defined by the infrastructure manager (ADIF) and the service operator (RENFE) in their current portfolio.

[2] These controls have been chosen using similarity patterns. There is a high-speed rail line crossing the province of Soria, but it does not serve any station in that province. The appropriate treatment of Soria should be as a comparison province without HSR services, even if in the accounts of the railway manager or in the Ministry of Transportation there were investments and km of HSR planned in this province.

will describe the HSR deployment in Spain, its history, and why it has the unusual characteristic of connecting with this expensive mode of transportation in low-density areas. Third, we will summarize the main descriptive statistics of tourism outcomes for the municipalities considered in our analysis, as well as their comparison with other municipalities with similar low-density characteristics but that did not receive HSR investments. We devote the final sections to describe the empirical evidence about the impacts of HSR on the tourism activity for each of the municipalities, also comparing with other low-density areas. Finally, we will conclude with a discussion of the most relevant empirical findings to shed some light on what policymakers and tourist managers of low-density areas should expect from the connectivity produced by HSR. In sum, this chapter intends to offer evidence with policy implications, supporting a richer debate on the real effects of HSR versus the perceived, expected, or even wished ones.

2 HSR and Tourism: A Literature Review

The economic literature on the impact of transport investments on productivity and regional development is abundant and diverse (see Aschauer 1989; Munnell 1990; Holtz-Eakin 1994; Vickerman 2008; among other seminal papers). The real economy is characterized by high spatial unevenness, such as the disparities between densely populated manufacturing areas and thinly populated farm regions, between congested cities and peripheral rural areas. This cannot be the result of inherent differences between locations but rather the outcome of some sort of cumulative processes, necessarily involving some form of increasing returns, whereby geographic concentration can be self-reinforcing. The role of transport investments in reversing the negative consequences of these effects relies on its effective capacity to increase proximity for people and businesses.

In the case of high-speed rail, there is a growing consensus around the idea that it generally increases the accessibility of the places it serves, but the results are not evenly shared. HSR stations (and the surrounding areas) gain large communication possibilities, while the rest of the territory gains less due to a so-called "tunnel effect" and may even become less attractive than before. Bazin et al. (2006), for example, studied the impact of the French TGV new services on different economic sectors between 1990 and 1999 in rural areas of France, finding that larger impacts on productivity and higher GDP gains were obtained around the areas that were most developed before the new investments. Recent papers studying the case of China—the country with the largest HSR network—seem to challenge these results, with more positive impacts on rural areas (which, on the other hand, are also densely populated) (e.g., Jia et al. 2017; Wang and Duan 2018; Liang et al. 2020). However, they also conclude that causality links are still controversial and the effectiveness of HSR investments connecting less developed and developed regions needs to be further tested.

The works that have specifically focused on the link between new HSR stations and tourism performance at the local level have also identified different results. In principle, improvements in accessibility of a touristic destination are expected to promote the revitalization of urban and business tourism due to a reduction of the generalized cost of transport. This positive expected impact is common in the approach followed by several recent studies (Masson and Petiot 2009; Bazin et al. 2010; Delaplace et al. 2014; Duval 2020) and also appears among the most common economic positive externalities that are often claimed to be associated with HSR investment (e.g., Murakami and Cervero 2012). Undoubtedly, this expected improvement of the touristic attractiveness of destinations, if true, becomes an opportunity to renew the tourist supply for the industry (Feliu 2012) and a positive external boost for the local public revenues (Hernández and Jiménez 2014) and the labor market (Guirao et al. 2018).

The ex post evaluation of the relationship between HSR and its effects is usually much more modest. The analysis of the several lines in France shows that the availability of HSR gives value to already known and popular tourist destinations but is not sufficient by itself to promote further development. Although initial impacts on visitors' figures may be positive, the number of overnight stays may decrease (Klein and Claisse 1997) and type of visitor is now more oriented to business travel. In some cities this even produced that small hotels with limited attractions disappeared, while large national chains increased their offer, providing better quality, more appropriate to the characteristics of short-trip tourism. Also, Bazin et al. (2014) examine the effect on destinations at less than 1.5 h from Paris, finding that positive effects do exist, but they are not lasting. They also confirmed the decrease in overnights already noted by Klein and Claisse (1997). Recently, Delaplace and Bazin-Benoit (2017) concluded that HSR seems to be more profitable from its contribution to tourism in large municipalities, where stakeholders are more able to cooperate and avoid reductions in overnights. However, this is less frequent and less effective in medium and small cities characterized by limited tourism amenities.

Other recent works focused on selected tourist areas in Spain provided similar results. For example, Clavé et al. (2015) showed that the improvement in tourism indicators due to the AVE connection is irrelevant in the coastal area of Tarragona. In Alicante, Ortuño-Padilla et al. (2015) estimated an increase of just over 20,000 tourists per year in the province—that received a total of 22 million of tourists in 2013—after the link to Madrid and Valencia was opened, and Albalate (2015) showed that the number of tourists grew more over the last years in Spanish provinces not connected to the HSR network than in destinations connected to it, indicating that factors other than the availability of this service may have a higher influence on tourist attraction.[3] These results were later confirmed by Albalate and Fageda (2016), Campa et al. (2016), and Albalate et al. (2017).

A reason for this unexpected lack of significant impact at the local level should be found in how HSR availability affects destination choice. Guirao and Soler (2008) studied the case of the small city of Toledo, Pagliara et al. (2015) analyzed the impact of HSR in Madrid on tourists' destination choice, and Gutiérrez et al. (2019) focused on the Catalan coast. In general, their results indicate that the presence of HSR does not seem to be a key factor influencing the destination choice of tourists because most of them are international tourists that can only arrive by air transportation. However, the use of HSR appears to be attractive to international tourists to visit nearby locations only. A similar conclusion was reached by Chen and Haynes (2015) when investigating the impact of the Chinese high-speed rail systems on its international tourism demand.

As noted by all these studies, tourism decisions may be determined by the interaction between HSR and air transportation. Positive impacts from HSR are expected from increasing the overall number of transport users or by promoting a given type of visitor (high income, longer stays, etc.). However, HSR usually exerts a substitution or even predatory effect on air transportation. Indeed, a growing literature has emerged on the modal competition between high-speed rail and air transportation in recent years (see Givoni and Dobruszkes 2014, for a review). HSR harms air transportation above all alternative modes due to its ability to attract a relatively large market share in medium distances. For this reasons HSR becomes one of the main determinants of market power loss for traditional carriers and a strong entry barrier for new airlines. Since the relationship between air transport and tourism as two deeply interconnected activities is well established in the literature, the potential damage that HSR may exert to the airline industry will affect net tourism outcomes.

Finally, several papers have also explored the cooperation possibilities between both modes, and some have even found several specific cooperation programs between HSR and air carriers (Grimme 2006; Givoni and Banister 2006; Dobruszkes 2011; Clewlow et al. 2012). However, most HSR network designs have been oriented to replicate routes and compete with air transportation, and, thus, it is not surprising that empirical research has been unable to find systematic complementarities, although some room for them do seem available in hub airports due to the feeding strategies of airlines and the presence of HSR stations within the airport (Albalate et al. 2015a).

In sum, the literature has focused on the role of HSR on city-route tourism case studies or integrated within the national transport system, neglecting the specific features of low-density areas as a particular object of study. Thus, the literature on the effects of high-speed rail in low-population density areas is surprisingly scarce,

---

[3]Among other factors, it is well-known that air transportation has a major role in the development of tourism industry. For Spanish regions, Albalate and Fageda (2016) showed the dominant role of air traffic to feed tourist destinations at Spanish provinces when compared with high-speed rail.

so the contribution made in this chapter may constitute a first relevant approximation to fill this gap.

3   HSR Deployment in Spain and Expectations

As described in the previous section, among the countries that have adopted the HSR technology, the experiences of China and Spain stand out for their investment efforts and the length of their networks. In Europe, Spain overtook the traditionally longer networks of France (a pioneer on the continent with its first lines built in the early 1980s), Germany, and Italy in a relatively short period of time, given the intense expansion of its HSR network and the consolidation of the rest of the European networks, which have hardly increased in recent years.

Although the first line in service was inaugurated between Madrid and Seville in 1992, it was in 2000 when the government established as the main objective of its transport policy the deployment of a high-speed rail network capable of connecting all provincial capitals with Madrid in less than 4 h (see Albalate and Bel 2011). This objective was shared by successive governments, even reducing the target time to less than 3 h. To achieve this goal, Spain has devoted between 3 and 5 billion euros a year to this policy—also during the worst years of the Great Recession—which approximately represented two-thirds of the country's railway investments and one-third of the total annual investment in transport.

The resulting HSR network was consistent with this objective, and it currently emerges as a radial infrastructure with a central node in Madrid and extremes on the coastal cities in the periphery of the Iberian Peninsula. Given the urban and demographic characteristics of Spain, where the population is mainly concentrated in dense areas along the coasts as well as in the surroundings of the capital (14% of the Spanish population lived in the Madrid region in 2019), this meant that the new rail infrastructure (with a different width gauge with respect to the traditional one) had to pass through less populated and less economically dynamic regions on its way to the final nodes of the corridors, giving access to a new medium-/long-distance interurban transport mode to low-density regions that until that moment only relied on bus services and conventional trains.

Numerous cost-benefit analyses have been provided to estimate the socioeconomic contributions of HSR investments in Spain, considering the need for this evaluation given its large cost per km and the growing concerns about their supply/capacity and demand/use gaps (Albalate et al. 2015b; Beria et al. 2018). The deployment of HSR in low-density areas and the building of stations placed in low-demand cities are also a source of concern on its socioeconomic profitability, beyond the financial feasibility. Indeed, studies evaluating the cost-benefit analysis of these investments provided disappointing findings.

For example, De Rus and Inglada (1997) analyzed the first HSR line in Spain (Madrid–Seville) and, according to their results, it was socially unprofitable mainly due to low demand and, consequently, economically not justified in the moment in which the investment and corridor were selected and decided. Indeed, later research has suggested that HSR investments are difficult to justify when the expected first year demand is below 8–10 million passengers for a line of 500 km, an optimal length for HSR to compete with road and air transport (De Rus and Nombela 2007). All HSR lines in Spain failed to satisfy this minimum level of demand for comparable investments, which casts doubts about the socioeconomic contribution of the huge plan of investments in HSR at all.

More recent developments and new deployments promoted since 2000 were also evaluated from both the financial and the socioeconomic approaches in Betancor and Llobet (2015). Their results were consistent with a negative contribution to welfare of these investments. All corridors in operation at the time of the analysis (2013) showed negative financial and welfare surpluses. Particularly, the study argued that investments will never be recovered or offset with social benefits during the life cycle of the assets. This outcome should not be attributed to a relative expensive cost of investments in Spain with respect to other experiences but to very low intensity of use of the available infrastructure (Campos and De Rus 2009; Albalate and Bel 2015), also with respect to other comparable networks (Albalate et al. 2015b; or Beria et al. 2018).

However, the arrival of HSR services is often accompanied by optimistic expectations about possible positive effects in the territories receiving the investment, which are justified by increased access and connectivity to other markets. Expectations are particularly significant in the tourism industry (Delaplace and Bazin-Benoit 2017), which is sensitive to the contribution of transport infrastructure and mobility services that play a crucial role in facilitating greater flows of visitors. This is even more pronounced in Spanish low-density regions, where citizens and their elected representatives often see transport investments as a unique opportunity to boost growth, foster economic convergence, and ensure prosperity for the future. This, however, contrasts with current depopulation patterns and the lack of economic alternatives in these regions, which, unlike the more dynamic and larger nodes—such as Madrid or Barcelona—are experiencing permanent population outflows.

On the other hand, investments in the HSR should not be viewed as the only component of the transport system. The density of the airport network and the extension of existing high-capacity roads also place Spain in the first positions within the European lists of transport infrastructure provision (Albalate et al. 2015b). In fact, the HSR cannot break by itself the isolation of the low-density regions in terms of transport, but its effects also depend on its interaction with other transport modes, mainly air transport, which is the main gateway for (international) tourists, as pointed out by Albalate and Fageda (2016). Indeed, as reviewed in the previous section, there may also be a variety of negative effects or threats to these low-density regions with the arrival of HSR that may offset the benefits or damage specific aspects of their economies.

In this chapter, therefore, we provide evidence on the impact of HSR on low-density regions in Spain by empirically examining the evolution of tourism outcomes and comparing it with other low-density areas with similar characteristics that never received this investment. Our goal is to disentangle whether its

Fig. 1 HSR Spanish network and selected low-density areas (2020). Source: Adapted from http://www.adif.es

contribution meets the expectations of low-density territories or, on the contrary, implied a drainage of activity in one of the most relevant economic sectors of the Spanish economy.

4   Data and Variables

We have built a monthly database to study the effects of high-speed rail projects on local tourism in province capitals of low-density provinces in Spain. It includes relevant tourist information both for municipalities in which new AVE (acronym for Spanish high-speed rail) stations were built (treated) and for those similar municipalities (control) that did not benefit from this investment. We compared the evolution of various tourism indicators that measure the demand, occupation, and supply of seven low-density municipalities in Spain that differ in having benefited or not from the AVE. The municipalities (province capitals) in the first group are Segovia, Cuenca, Palencia, and Zamora, while the second includes Ávila, Teruel,

Table 1 Tourism in treated and control municipalities (1999–2019)

City	Population	Total number of firms	% Firms in commerce, transport, and hospitality (CTH)	Hotel beds	% Foreign tourists at hotels
Segovia	52,814 (−0.85)	3684 (−1.3)	37.6% (−1.8)	2091 (2.4)	22% (3.8)
Cuenca	55,484 (−0.60)	3670 (1.0)	38.3% (−0.9)	2071 (0.7)	14% (−2.6)
Palencia	79,586 (−0.50)	5210 (−1.2)	41.1% (−2.7)	926 (−2.0)	12% (−5.8)
Zamora	63,430 (−0.89)	4840 (−0.4)	39.4% (−1.8)	1048 (0.5)	10% (2.4)
Ávila (control)	58,387 (−0.28)	3649 (−0.1)	38.9% (−1.1)	2681 (0.2)	15% (−1.6)
Teruel (control)	35,712 (0.02)	2591 (0.8)	36.2% (−1.3)	1570 (3.3)	12% (7.1)
Soria (control)	39,393 (−0.27)	2797 (−0.8)	35.2% (−1.5)	1166 (0.6)	8% (1.1)
Total national	46,600,064 (0.04)	3,234,018 (0.7)	38.3% (−0.6)	1,462,553 (0.8)	29% (1.6)

Source: Own elaboration from INE. Average annual growth rate for all period among brackets

and Soria (Fig. 1).[4] All of them are municipalities (province capitals) in provinces with overall population less than 300,000 and less than 25 inhabitants per square km.[5] Our monthly database covers the 1999–2019 period, and the corresponding dates when the referred AVE services entered into service were December 22, 2007 (Madrid–Segovia); December 18, 2010 (Madrid–Cuenca); September 29, 2015 (Madrid–Palencia); and December 17, 2015 (Madrid–Zamora).

Descriptive information on the tourist industry characteristics of these municipalities is displayed in Table 1. Figure 1 shows the Spanish HSR network and its projected segments and the location of the cities considered in this study.

Tourism is an essential asset of the economy of some of these province capitals, as it is shown by the percentage of firms that are devoted to commerce, transport, and hospitality (Table 1) and the amount of hotel beds available for tourists in these small cities, all of them below 80,000 inhabitants. Also, they are characterized by being mainly visited by domestic tourists, which could be precisely promoted by HSR services.

Segovia, for instance, is an old city with a Roman aqueduct declared a World Heritage Site by UNESCO in 1985, which is considered the most important and well-preserved Roman civil engineering work in Spain. It is at a close distance from

---

[4]The name of the province and its capital city is the same.

[5]Most of these provinces/municipalities are located within the same region of Castile and Leon, at the center-northwest of Spain. The city of Cuenca is the Castile-La Mancha region, southeast of Madrid, whereas Teruel is in the Aragon region. They all have regular intercity services by bus and conventional train. The closest and largest international airport is Madrid–Barajas (see Fig. 1).

Madrid, which makes this city an important enclave for both short-term domestic and international visitors, attracted by the ancient roman architecture. Indeed, Segovia is the city considered with the highest percentage of international tourists. Similarly, the economy of Cuenca is mainly focused on tourism, especially since 1996, when its historical quarter was declared World Heritage Site. Its cathedral and the so-called hanging houses became its main attractions, together with its art museums. Palencia and Zamora, like most Castilian cities, has a great historical-artistic heritage. They receive few international tourists and have available lower supply of hotel beds.

Among the control group municipalities, Ávila enjoys a well-known historical, cultural, and landscape value that makes this city an enclave for short-term domestic tourists, especially from Madrid metropolitan area due to its close distance. Perhaps because of this short distance, Ávila is the second city among the considered group in terms of percentage of international tourists. Teruel and Soria are characterized by being the capitals of quite isolated low-populated provinces. The first is considered the world capital of Mudejar architecture and a World Heritage Site by UNESCO. The second is known for its medieval streets and its Romanesque architecture.

For all seven municipalities, the following variables were collected from the "Hotel Occupancy Survey" (*Encuesta de Ocupación Hotelera*), which summarizes main tourism data in the country and is available online at the Spanish Statistical Office (www.ine.es):

- VISITORS$_{imt}$, defined as the total number of overnight visitors (those spending one or more nights at a hotel of any category) at city i, during month m of year t.[6]
- AVERAGE STAY$_{imt}$: defined as the ratio between the total overnight stays and the total number of visitors. It provides the number of nights that on average each visitor spends at destination. A larger average stay is commonly correlated with a higher level of expenditure.
- OCCUPANCY RATE$_{imt}$: defined as the ratio (given as a percentage) between the total overnight stays and the tourism supply (which is measured as the number of temporary and permanent hotel beds multiplied by the days they are available).
- HOTEL BEDS$_{imt}$: defined as the number of existing hotel beds at city i, during month m of year t.

Table 2 provides the average and standard deviations (in parentheses) of these four variables separately. To compare treated municipalities (Segovia, Cuenca, Palencia, and Zamora) with the control group (Ávila, Teruel, and Soria), we decided to build a synthetic "control unit" that integrated these three municipalities. Therefore, the impacts of HSR on the first group will be compared to the changes experienced by this control unit, acting as our counterfactual, that is, what would have happened to treated municipalities without the AVE investment.

---

[6]Information about tourists that stay at apartments and less conventional accommodations (e.g., AirBnB) is less comparable and has not been included. In any case, there are no reasons to assume that these figures are quite different across the selected municipalities.

Table 2 Tourism in treated and control municipalities (1999–2019)

Average monthly data	Total number of visitors (hotels)	Average stay (nights)	Hotel beds (supply)	Occupancy rate (%)
Segovia	19088.1 (5611.2)	1.65 (0.13)	1941.5 (291.17)	50.4 (12.3)
Cuenca	16,155 (3810.7)	1.60 (0.11)	2009 (145.2)	43.1 (9.7)
Palencia	6717.2 (1568.1)	1.77 (0.17)	946.4 (47.5)	41.1 (9.5)
Zamora	9245.5 (2656.6)	1.63 (0.11)	1079.1 (81.1)	45.1 (11.3)
Control unit[a]	13186.1 (7011.9)	1.69 (0.17)	1712.2 (672.9)	41.6 (11.6)

[a]Includes the average values for Ávila, Teruel, and Soria
Source: Own elaboration. Standard deviations in parentheses

The results in the first column of Table 2 clearly show that Segovia is the most touristic city among them, leading in number of visitors and occupancy rate. It is a historical city located at northwest Madrid with close historical ties to the capital and good road connections. Its better results in terms of tourism attractiveness are probably superior to other treated cities (18% higher than Cuenca, the second) because it is the closest to Madrid (93 km by road). The equivalent distance to other cities is always at least 15% larger: 111 km (to Ávila), 168 km (to Cuenca), 228 km (to Soria), 256 km (to Zamora), 262 km (to Palencia), or 302 km (to Teruel). In addition, travelling between Madrid and Segovia by HSR just takes about 27 minutes, making same-day excursions and short trips for tourists staying in Madrid possible. The rest of treated and control municipalities require longer journeys to/from larger cities by HSR, road, or conventional train and, possibly, overnight stays.

As for the other variables in Table 2, apart from the total number of visitors, the average monthly values of all of them are very similar in all of the cities, except for the very low values of hotel beds in Palencia and Zamora (they represent about half of the hotel supply in Cuenca or Segovia) and the higher occupancy rates in Segovia than in others. Our control unit, made up of control municipalities, also shows comparable figures in these variables, which indicates that it could perform well as a reference point for the treated municipalities.

5   HSR and Tourism in Low-Density Areas in Spain

The aim of this section is to address the following research question: How did tourism indicators change after the arrival of the Spanish AVE to low-density areas? To answer this question, we have implemented a quantitative analysis based on before-and-after analysis, using both a statistical and a graphical approach drawing

Table 3 Before and after averages in treated *vs* control municipalities (I)

Visitors	Before	After	Rate of change (after *vs* before)
Segovia	14,679.7	19,900.2	26.2
Control	11,070.2	13,566.6	18.4
Rate (control *vs* Segovia)	−24.6	−31.8	**7.8**
Cuenca	17,010.9	15,682.7	−8.5
Control	11,573.62	14,066.53	17.7
Rate (control *vs* Cuenca)	−32.0	−10.3	**−26.2**
Palencia	6621.5	7251.2	8.7
Control	11,918.2	16,655.4	28.4
Rate (control *vs* Palencia)	80.0	129.7	**−19.8**
Zamora	8802.6	10,574.4	16.8
Control	11,894.2	17,042.7	30.2
Rate (control *vs* Zamora)	35.1	61.2	**−13.5**

Source: Own elaboration. In bold, difference between average rate, treated-control

Table 4 Before and after averages in treated *vs* control municipalities (II)

Average stay	Before	After	Rate of change (after *vs* before)
Segovia	1.49	1.6	6.9
Control	1.75	1.68	−4.2
Rate (control *vs* Segovia)	17.4	5.0	**11.0**
Cuenca	1.64	1.66	1.2
Control	1.73	1.68	−3.0
Rate (control *vs* Cuenca)	5.5	1.2	**4.2**
Palencia	1.74	1.95	10.8
Control	1.71	1.67	−2.4
Rate (control *vs* Palencia)	−1.7	−14.4	**13.2**
Zamora	1.63	1.62	−0.6
Control	1.71	1.66	−3.0
Rate (control *vs* Zamora)	4.9	2.5	**2.4**

Source: Own elaboration. In bold, difference between average rate, treated-control

on the secondary data presented in the previous section. Tables 3, 4, 5, and 6 summarize the averages of each covariate (VISITORS, AVERAGE STAY, OCCUPANCY RATE, and HOTEL BEDS) in the periods before and after the AVE inauguration in each municipality and the start of the connection services with Madrid. In addition, we have also calculated both the differences between control and treated municipalities and between before and after the treatment (last row and column of each sub-table).

The growth in the total number of VISITORS in each city is firstly shown in Table 3. This analysis confirms that the AVE does not seem to increase the arrival of tourists in the treated municipalities if we compare them with the results obtained in our control unit (without AVE), except for Segovia. Even though most cities

Table 5 Before and after averages in treated *vs* control municipalities (III)

Occupancy rate (%)	Before	After	Rate of change (after *vs* before)
Segovia	50.1	50.4	0.6
Control	43.4	41.3	−5.1
Rate (control *vs* Segovia)	−13.4	−18.1	**5.7**
Cuenca	48.1	40.4	−19.1
Control	41.9	41.5	−1.0
Rate (control *vs* Cuenca)	−12.9	2.7	**−18.1**
Palencia	39.2	51.2	23.4
Control	39.8	46.6	14.6
Rate (control *vs* Palencia)	1.5	−9.0	**8.8**
Zamora	43.2	50.9	15.1
Control	39.7	47.2	15.9
Rate (control *vs* Zamora)	−8.1	−7.3	**−0.8**

Source: Own elaboration. In bold, difference between average rate, treated-control

Table 6 Before and after averages in treated *vs* control municipalities (IV)

Hotel beds	Before	After	Rate of change (after *vs* before)
Segovia	1431.5	2035.4	29.7
Control	1428.5	1761.9	18.9
Rate (control *vs* Segovia)	−0.2	−13.4	**10.7**
Cuenca	1886	2077.8	9.2
Control	1554.9	1797.1	13.5
Rate (control *vs* Cuenca)	−17.6	−13.5	**−4.2**
Palencia	954	904	−5.5
Control	1652.3	1875.2	11.9
Rate (control *vs* Palencia)	73.2	107.4	**−17.4**
Zamora	1078.1	1082.1	0.4
Control	1655.1	1881.7	12.0
Rate (control *vs* Zamora)	53.5	73.9	**−11.7**

Source: Own elaboration. In bold, difference between average rate, treated-control

experienced an increase in the number of tourists after the treatment—except Cuenca, which suffered a decrease of −8.5%—their rates were lower than the growth rate experienced by the control unit. Thus, the counterfactual shows that low-density areas without AVE performed better at least in the number of visitors. This would contradict the expectation of receiving more visitors thanks to high-speed rail services. The numbers in bold in Table 3 are the difference between before-and-after rates of change in the treated city and the control cities. Note that only Segovia improved local tourism performance by 7.8 percentage points more than our control unit, while Cuenca, Palencia, and Zamora decreased by 26.2%, 19.8%, and 13.5%, respectively.

Once evaluated the effects on the main outcome (VISITORS), we are also interested in examining the effects on the remaining tourism indicators. Interestingly, the lower number of tourists received does not come together with a reduction in the AVERAGE STAY. Thus, visitors travelling to and overnight staying at province capitals of low-density areas are not staying less once the AVE arrives, but apparently more nights on average. This outcome, thus, seems to be more favorable to the AVE arrival. Indeed, we find relative increases in all treated cities above the corresponding increase experienced by our control unit (see Table 4).

We have also replicated the analysis for the OCCUPANCY RATE at hotels. Results summarized in Table 5 are mixed, and no clear conclusion can be extracted from them. According to our results, comparing treated and the control unit, we find some municipalities where the AVE seems to be associated with higher occupancy rates with respect to our counterfactual (such as Segovia, 5.7%, or Palencia, 8.8%), while the opposite result is achieved in Cuenca (-18.1%) and Zamora (-0.8%). We are not able to find a rational or a common pattern.

Finally, the change in the provision of HOTEL BEDS is also assessed in Table 6. In this case, the supply, measured as the number of beds available in the hotels, does not seem to increase after the entry of the AVE services. In fact, the control cities show a better evolution of this indicator compared to what happened in Cuenca, Palencia, and Zamora. Again, only in Segovia does the tourist industry seem to have increased its supply. This result is consistent with the first evidence examined on the number of visitors, given that supply and demand tend to change in parallel. What we found is that neither supply nor demand (number of visitors) increased after the AVE services in most treated municipalities—compared to the counterfactual—as might be expected. On the contrary, we found that it decreased in Palencia, Zamora, and Cuenca.

From a graphic point of view, Figs. 2–5 show the actual monthly evolution of the total number of visitors to each municipality over the 1999–2019 period and the corresponding linear trends (in red for the control, in green for the treated city). The vertical dotted line signals the month when high-speed rail (AVE) services started operating in each city, which can be considered as the beginning of the treatment (before and after). The control variable (defined by the sum of the three untreated municipalities) is shown for comparative reasons, since we implicitly assume that (without the investment) the evolution of the treated municipalities would have behaved in a similar way.

Figure 2 shows the total number of visitors to Segovia before and after the AVE. The red and green trends follow a clear different pattern, and this does not change excessively after the AVE entrance. In fact, the slope of Segovia trend is reduced after the treatment and the control cities seem to experience a faster growth rate. The same analysis can be considered in the case of Cuenca (Fig. 3), where the green trend line for Cuenca after AVE is almost flat, while at control cities increases considerably. In Palencia (Fig. 4) the green trend line for Palencia after the treatment is even flatter while at control cities increases again. Only in the case of Zamora (Fig. 5) we can see that the differences between the two trends are not noteworthy.

It is reasonable to consider that all these results should be only seen as a first approximation—fundamentally descriptive—to the problem of measuring the

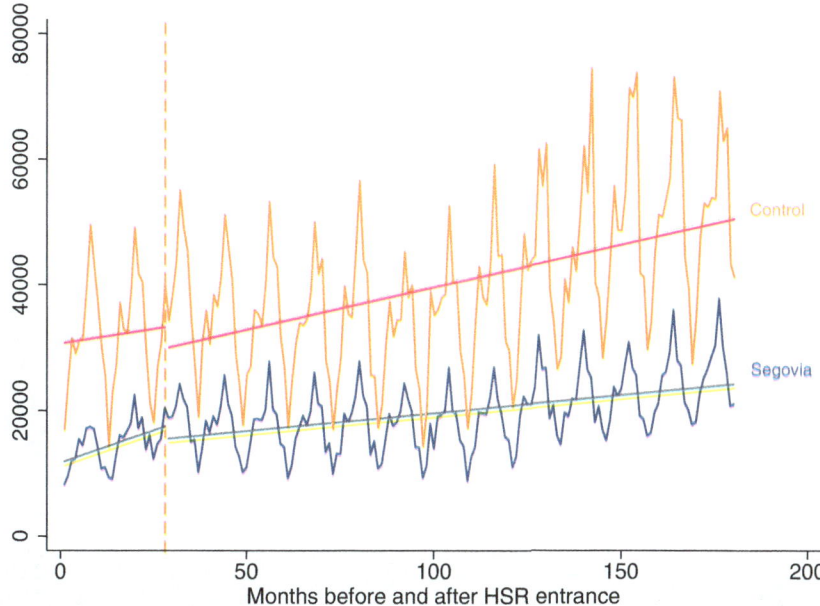

Fig. 2 Total number of visitors (before-and-after) in Segovia. Source: Own elaboration. Control is the sum of Ávila, Teruel, and Soria

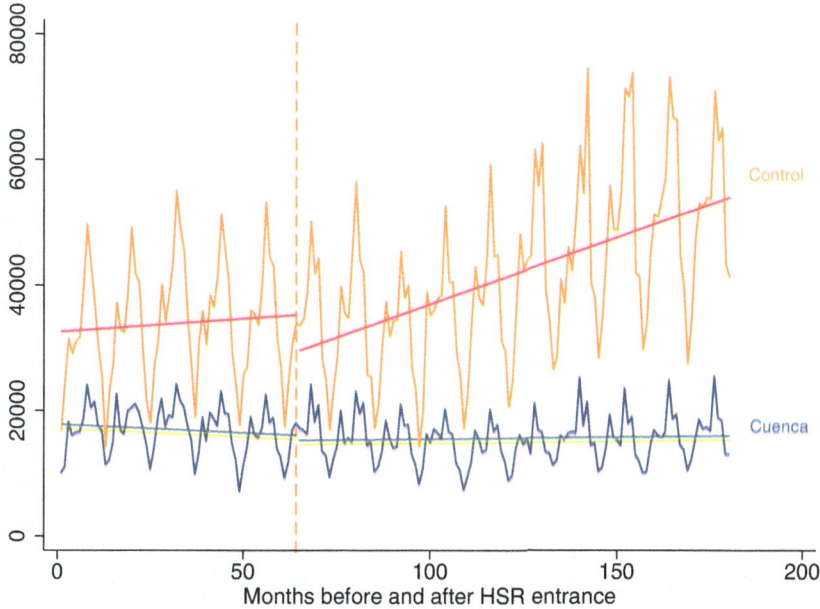

Fig. 3 Total number of visitors (before-and-after) in Cuenca. Source: Own elaboration. Control is the sum of Ávila, Teruel, and Soria

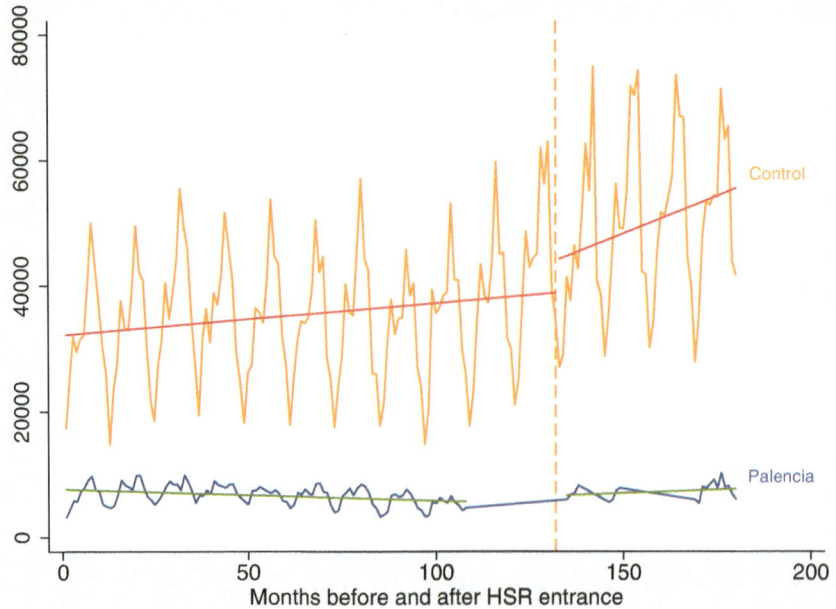

Fig. 4 Total number of visitors (before-and-after) in Palencia. Source: Own elaboration. Control is the sum of Ávila, Teruel, and Soria

impact on tourism of investments in high-speed rail. Explaining and monitoring trends before and after the treatment generally requires more sophisticated tools (e.g., diff-in-diff models) than those used in this chapter. In fact, finding deeper causes or explanatory factors requires a complete econometric assessment—with more detailed information about non-hotel stays and short trip visits—that is well beyond the scope of this chapter. However, and despite acknowledging these limitations, our evidence seems to confirm that, at least in Spain's low-density areas, the AVE has not served as a driving force in the tourism industry and many of these territories were expecting.

6   Conclusions

In this chapter we have intended to contribute to the policy debate on infrastructure spending and allocation decisions at both national and local levels and to better inform the perception of tourist managers and planners about the real effects of the arrival of HSR services in low-density areas.

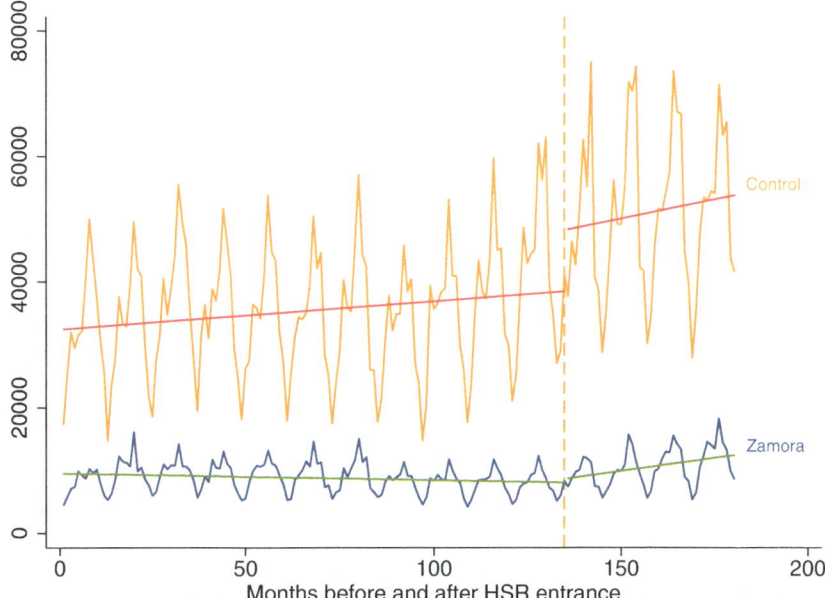

Fig. 5 Total number of visitors (before-and-after) in Zamora. Source: Own elaboration. Control is the sum of Ávila, Teruel, and Soria

Although there are obvious limitations in the data (e.g., on more detailed aspects of the tourism industry at the local level) and it would be interesting to be able to apply quasi-experimental methods to establish causal relationships, we believe that our empirical results confirm that HSR is not necessarily able to promote the tourism industry in low-density areas. In fact, it may have a negative impact if, for example, it is damaging other forms of transportation—other gateways through which tourists arrive—or if it is draining economic activity and transferring it to more dynamic and larger nodes.

In Spain, from the four treated provincial capitals of this kind of territories—receiving HSR stations—only Segovia appears to have benefited from this connection. When compared to similar municipalities of low-density areas not receiving HSR during the period considered, we find that the growth of visitors (tourism demand) and the growth of beds (tourism supply) were even larger in municipalities without HSR than in Cuenca, Palencia, and Zamora. Note that it is expected and consistent with the literature to find effects close to HSR stations, what should be identified by considering the province capitals where stations are placed. Thus, even less effects are expected in other municipalities of the same province that are obviously more disconnected to the network and may receive less impacts. Some of these municipalities, however, could be more connected to conventional regional services, that, with the arrival of HSR, were dismantled or reduced in frequencies, eroding its quality or service and relative attractiveness.

This result casts some doubts on HSR contribution to these territories and, especially, on tourism as a new source of development of this laggard areas of Spain with fewer economic opportunities. Also, this calls for caution in the formation of expectations and on future plans of HSR deployments. Also, it gives arguments against the local demand for HSR investments, usually led by local politicians and lobbies, given that—perhaps, contrary to expectations—it may harm more than benefit the territory's welfare.

One of the most striking results of our analysis is the exception of Segovia. This municipality appears to be a winner from the policy, unlike what we find in the rest of treated municipalities. The most likely explanation of this result is that HSR may produce some impacts for short trips, given that Segovia, besides its historical quarter and its own touristic interest, is only at about 27 minutes from Madrid's city center in HSR—35 minutes in 2008 when it was inaugurated. This would suggest the presence of heterogeneous impacts on tourism depending on the travel distance or travel time. All the rest of municipalities are further away from Madrid, what makes more difficult combining the visit to Madrid with this other attraction points.

No doubt, the arrival of HSR implied a large time-saving with respect to the conventional railway in Segovia, which takes more than 2 h to connect this province capital to Spain's capital. Somehow, Segovia was too far away in public transportation for tourists before the arrival of HSR to be considered as an interest point for Madrid's visitors. Even if the HSR station is outside the core of Segovia (Segovia–Guiomar) and there is need to pick a bus to get to the touristic quarter, the difference in time between the conventional and the HSR is still huge, also in terms of frequencies. Thus, the arrival of HSR to nearby cities or regions that allow for same-day trips or allow for the combination or bundling of tourism activities, including staying in Madrid and visiting other historical nearby attraction points in a few days, may have benefited Segovia as destination. This result is consistent with some evidence related to tourism outcomes in Toledo (see Guirao and Soler 2008), another comparable city with touristic attractiveness that received a HSR station and that is close to Madrid (53 km of HS railway and around 30 min of journey). Despite not being considered in this study because it does not belong to a low-density province, Toledo also seems to have benefited from this new service (inaugurated in 2005). Note that about one-third of ridership travels for tourism purposes and 70% are international tourists (Guirao and Soler 2008).

One could argue, consequently, that HSR is not bringing a significant number of new tourists to low-density areas and, therefore, does not have a positive contribution to this industry—when compared with a counterfactual—unless it facilitates an efficient and rapid transfer from big nodes concentrating many tourists to this touristic attraction points in nearby locations. Note, however, that the essence of HSR is not being a short-distance interurban mode of transportation but a medium- to long-distance mode that is planned to compete with high-capacity roads and airlines. It seems, at a minimum, a very expensive way to spread dubious tourism benefits beyond large cities.

References

Albalate D (2015) Evaluating HSR access on tourism: evidence from Spanish provinces and cities. Workshop on High Speed Rail and the City: Tourism and Dynamics around stations, January 21–23, 2015, Paris

Albalate D, Bel G (2011) Cuando la Economía no importa: Auge y esplendor de la alta velocidad en España "Cuando la Economía no importa: Auge y esplendor de la alta velocidad en España". Revista de Economía Aplicada 19(55):171–190

Albalate D, Bel G (2015) La experiencia internacional en alta velocidad ferroviaria, FEDEA WP 2015-02. FEDEA, Madrid (Spain)

Albalate D, Fageda X (2016) High-speed rail and tourism: empirical evidence from Spain. Transp Res A Policy Pract 85:174–185

Albalate D, Bel G, Fageda X (2015a) When supply travels far beyond demand: causes of oversupply in Spain's transport infrastructure. Transp Policy 41:80–89

Albalate D, Bel G, Fageda X (2015b) Competition and cooperation between high-speed rail and air transportation services in Europe. J Transp Geogr 42:166–174

Albalate D, Campos J, Jiménez JL (2017) Does the high-speed rail increase local visitors? Ann Tour Res 65:71–82

Aschauer D (1989) Is public expenditure productive? J Monet Econ 23:177–200

Bazin S, Beckerich C, Delaplace M (2006) Analyse prospective des impacts de la Ligne à Grande Vitesse Est-européenne dans l'agglomération rémoise et en region Champagne-Ardenne". Report Final de recherché pour le Conseil Régional Champagne-Ardenne, Université de Reims Champagne-Ardenne

Bazin S, Beckerich C, Delaplace M (2010) Grande vitesse, activation des ressources spécifiques et développement du tourisme urbain: le cas de l'agglomération rémoise. Belgeo 1–2:65–78

Bazin S, Beckerich C, Delaplace M (2014) Valorisation touristique du patrimoine et dessertes TGV dans les villes intermédiaires à moins d'1h30 de Paris: les cas de Reims, Metz, Le Mans et Tours. Revue d'Économie Régionale et Urbaine 5:5–23

Beria P, Albalate D, Bel G, Grimaldi R (2018) Delusions of success: costs and demand of high-speed rail in Italy and Spain. Transp Policy 68:63–79

Betancor O, Llobet G (2015) La contabilidad financiera y social de la alta velocidad en España. Estudios sobre la economía española FEDEA – 2015/08. FEDEA, Madrid (Spain)

Campa JL, López-Lambas ME, Guirao B (2016) High speed rail effects on tourism: Spanish empirical evidence derived from China's modelling experience. J Transp Geogr 57:44–54

Campos J, de Rus G (2009) Some stylized facts about high-speed rail: a review of HSR experiences around the world. Transp Policy 16(1):19–28

Chen Z, Haynes K (2015) Impact of high-speed rail on international tourism demand in China. Appl Econ Lett 22(1):57–60

Clavé S, Gutiérrez A, Saladi O (2015) High-speed rail services in a consolidated Catalan Mediterranean mass coastal destination: a causal approach. Workshop on High Speed Rail and the City: Tourism and Dynamics around stations, January 21–23, 2015, Paris

Clewlow R, Sussman J, Balakrishnan H (2012) Interaction of high-speed rail and aviation: exploring air–rail connectivity. Transp Res Rec 2266(1):1–10

De Rus G, Inglada V (1997) Cost-benefit analysis of the high-speed train in Spain. Ann Reg Sci 31 (2):175–188

De Rus G, Nombela G (2007) Is investment in high speed rail socially profitable? JTEP 41(1):3–23

Delaplace M, Bazin-Benoit S (2017) High-speed rail services and tourism expansion. The need for cooperation. In: Albalate D, Bel G (eds) Evaluating high-speed rail: interdisciplinary perspectives. Routledge, New York

Delaplace M, Pagliara F, Perrin J, Mermet S (2014) Can high-speed rail foster the choice of destination for tourism purpose?. EWGT2013 – 16th Meeting of the EURO Working Group on Transportation. Procedia Soc Behav Sci 111:166–175

Dobruszkes F (2011) High-speed rail and air transport competition in Western Europe: a supply-oriented perspective. Transp Policy 18:870–879

Duval DT (2020) Transport and tourism: a perspective article. Tour Rev 75(1):91–94

Feliu J (2012) High-speed rail in European medium-sized cities: stakeholders and urban development. J Urban Plan Dev 138:293–302

Givoni M, Banister D (2006) Airline and railway integration. Transp Policy 13:386–397

Givoni M, Dobruszkes F (2014) A review of ex-post evidence for mode substitution and induced demand following the introduction of high-speed rail. Transp Rev 33(6):720–742

Grimme W (2006) Air/rail intermodality recent experiences from Germany. Airl Magaz 34:1–4

Guirao B, Soler F (2008) Impacts of the new high-speed rail services on small tourist cities: the case of Toledo (Spain). WIT Trans Ecol Environ 117:465–473

Guirao B, Campa JL, Casado-Sanz N (2018) Labour mobility between cities and metropolitan integration: the role of high-speed rail commuting in Spain. Cities 78:140–154

Gutiérrez A, Miravet D, Saladié O, Clavé S (2019) High-speed rail, tourists' destination choice and length of stay: a survival model analysis. Tour Econ 26(4):578–597

Hernández A, Jiménez JL (2014) Does high-speed rail generate spillovers on local budgets. Transp Policy 35:211–219

Holtz-Eakin D (1994) Public sector capital and the productivity puzzle. Rev Econ Stat 76:12–21

Jia S, Zhou C, Qin C (2017) No difference in effect of high-speed rail on regional economic growth based on match effect perspective? Transp Res A 106:144–157

Klein O, Claisse G (1997) Le TGV-Atlantique: entre récession et cencurrence. Evolution de la mobilité et mise en service du TGV-Atlantique: analyse des enquêtes réalisées en septiembre 1989 et septiembre 1993. Laboratoire d'Economie des Transports. Lyon. Mimeo

Liang Y, Zhou K, Li X, Zhou Z, Sun W, Zeng J (2020) Effectiveness of high-speed railway on regional economic growth for less developed areas. J Transp Geogr 82:1–10

Masson S, Petiot R (2009) Can high-speed rail reinforce tourism attractiveness? The case of the high-speed rail between Perpignan (France) and Barcelona (Spain). Technovation 29 (9):611–617

Munnell AH (1990) Why has productivity declined? Productivity and public investment. New England economic review, Federal Reserve Bank of Boston, January–February 3–22

Murakami J, Cervero R (2012) High-speed rail and economic development: business agglomerations and policy implications. UC Berkeley, University of California Transportation Centre (UCTC). Mimeo

Ortuño-Padilla A, Bautista-Rodríguez D, Fernández-Aracil P, Fernández-Morote G, Sánchez-Galiano JC (2015) HSR passengers' profile in sun and beach tourism destinations: the case of Alicante (Spain). Workshop on High Speed Rail and the City: Tourism and Dynamics around stations, January 21–23, 2015, Paris

Pagliara F, La Pietra A, Gómez J, Vassallo JM (2015) High-speed rail and the tourism market: evidence from the Madrid case study. Transp Policy 37:187–194

Vickerman R (2008) Transit investment and economic development. Res Transp Econ 23 (1):107–115

Wang L, Duan X (2018) High-speed rail network development and winner and loser cities in megaregions: the case study of Yangtze River Delta, China. Cities 83:71–82

The Role of Residents and Their Perceptions of the Tourism Industry in Low-Density Areas: The Case of Boticas, in the Northeast of Portugal

Hélder da Silva Lopes, Paula Remoaldo, Maria Dolores Sánchez-Fernández, José Cadima Ribeiro, Sara Silva, and Vítor Ribeiro

1 Introduction

Over the last 50 years, rural areas have suffered profound socioeconomic and productive changes (McAreavey 2009; Woods 2011). In fact, the changing rural landscape has been one of Europe's principal concerns over recent decades (Kristensen et al. 2004; Van Doorn and Bakker 2007), since some rural areas have been affected by the decline of arable land (a marked trend in Mediterranean Europe), falling population, weak social and economic framework and ageing of the population (Silva et al. 2016).

H. da Silva Lopes
Lab2PT (Laboratory of Landscape, Heritage and Territory), Department of Geography, University of Minho, Braga, Portugal

IdRA (Water Research Institute), Group of Climatology, Department of Geography, University of Barcelona, Barcelona, Spain

P. Remoaldo (✉) · S. Silva · V. Ribeiro
Lab2PT (Laboratory of Landscape, Heritage and Territory), Department of Geography, University of Minho, Braga, Portugal

M. D. Sánchez-Fernández
Lab2PT (Laboratory of Landscape, Heritage and Territory), Department of Geography, University of Minho, Braga, Portugal

University of A Coruña, A Coruña, Spain

J. C. Ribeiro
NIPE (Centre for Research in Economics and Management), Department of Economy, University of Minho, Braga, Portugal
e-mail: jcadima@eeg.uminho.pt

© Springer Nature Switzerland AG 2021
R. P. Marques et al. (eds.), *The Impact of Tourist Activities on Low-Density Territories*, Tourism, Hospitality & Event Management,
https://doi.org/10.1007/978-3-030-65524-2_9

This is particularly relevant for Portugal, since several low-density areas and their respective public authorities have proven to be incapable of implementing local and regional public initiatives to reverse this trend and take advantage of their endogenous resources (e.g. landscape, natural or cultural resources). As such, acquiring a better understanding of the changes that have occurred and the residents' perceptions of the possible urgent solutions seemed to be a good starting point in the search for a viable development strategy for these territories.

The use of local resources and the enhancement of social networks are key elements in developing tourism strategies when considering location-based approaches (Barca et al. 2012). This seems to be even more relevant when dealing with low-density areas, since local policies should pursue greater economic and social sustainability (Bridger and Alter 2008; Lee et al. 2015). To attain this goal, in certain cases, tourism can make a relevant contribution to increasing the multi-functionality of these territories and the enhancement of their well-being (Obonyo and Fwaya 2012).

In some cases, tourism has even been seen as a way of achieving a development strategy that may reverse the trend towards depopulation in some low-density areas, in particular rural ones. This has occurred to a large extent due to the resource potential of certain territories and the tourism capacity of mobilising and interconnecting several local products and services (Walmsley 2003; Kastenholz et al. 2012). However, even in the case of this potential, attaining sustainable development requires actions to prevent any sort of *museification* of the local customs and practices of the rural communities.

If, as mentioned, tourism has become one of the solutions to diversify the economies of areas with low population density (Sharpley 2002; Iorio and Corsale 2010; Obonyo and Fwaya 2012), by taking advantage of their tourism attributes, this seems to make even more sense in the case of certain Portuguese rural territories due to their tangible or intangible tourism potential (Lopes et al. 2016). Nevertheless, one of the difficulties faced by local authorities in this process is the ability to work in liaison with the territory's main stakeholders (e.g. the local community, visitors, local and regional agents) (Lopes et al. 2016; Remoaldo et al. 2017). This is particularly relevant in the case of residents, due to the complex nature of this group, and the way that it may influence the authorities' intervention in the planning process. As suggested in the empirical results attained by Feng (2019), citizens' involvement in tourism decision-making and their trust in local and tourism authorities are vital in order to gain their political support for the development strategies to be implemented. The intervention of residents is as important as that of visitors, although their perception of the tourism industry is normally undervalued (Vareiro et al. 2013).

For this purpose, this paper aims to (1) assess residents' perceptions of the tourism attributes and potential of their municipality; (2) assess tourism's potential to contribute to the development of the territory under analysis, by enhancing (or recovering) its multi-functionality; (3) identify the main perceived positive and negative impacts of tourism; and (4) contribute to implementation of a more participative and sustainable tourism strategy in the municipality of Boticas and neighbouring areas.

With these objectives in mind, we will try to answer the following questions: Do the residents of Boticas perceive the tourism industry as a potential contributor to the enhancement of the multi-functionality of their municipality and consequently to local development? Do they believe that their territory has any tourism attributes? Are they able to gain a clear image of those resources which can play a major role in the establishment of a local tourism strategy? In order to answer these questions, a quantitative research project was conducted (surveys orientated to the residents of the municipality).

In addition to the Introduction, this paper is organised as follows: Sect. 1 provides a review of the literature on the need to enhance the multi-functionality of rural areas, as well as the need to guarantee community involvement in the development of the tourism industry; Sect. 2 presents the role of residents and their perspective towards the tourism industry; Sect. 3 details the analytic methods used and identifies several characteristics regarding the areas studied; Sect. 4 reports the results of the empirical research; the final section discusses the results attained and provides the concluding remarks and a few policy recommendations.

2 The Need to Transform Rural Areas into Diversified Local Economies

Today, the term "rural" should be considered to be the result of a variety of characteristics (e.g. level of development, ability to create jobs, complementarity and cooperation between institutions and organisations), which contribute to the coexistence of a plurality of rural areas (Figueiredo 2011). Even among European countries, there is "a whole geographic, economic and social fabric [comprising] (...) a variety of activities: agriculture, business, commerce, small and medium enterprises, services" (CEE 1988: 15).

Due to this situation, several rural areas have managed to stabilise or, even, record a certain level of population growth, benefiting from the beauty of their landscape, which attracts economic activities linked to tourism, or complementary agro-forestry activities with other value-added products (Figueiredo and Kastenholz 2008; Phelan and Sharpley 2011). However, there are other more fragile rural areas that are gradually vanishing.

Clearly, on the one hand, there are certain areas that have been losing human capital, contributing to the formation of areas with progressively declining economic potential (Stockdale 2006; Wellbrock et al. 2012), while, on the other hand, there are rural areas that have been able to take advantage of the few opportunities that arise from globalisation (Wellbrock et al. 2012; Obonyo and Fwaya 2012).

In this context, rural development must be viewed as a process of economic growth where the quality of life of the local populations, the involvement of local agents in establishing their development strategy and, of course, the use of endogenous resources based on the principles of sustainability should be considered a priority (Obonyo and Fwaya 2012; Boqué and Soler 2016). This does not mean that one should overlook the fact that the development process is in fact an inside-outside duality, where there is a need to balance the mobilisation of local resources and stakeholders (internal dimension) with market demands (external dimension) (Ray 2006; Bosworth et al. 2015). Public policies should be able to address this duality.

As mentioned above, as part of their willingness not only to achieve a better future and take advantage of their resources and capabilities but also being able to address the demands of the globalised market, some rural areas have been developing their own strategies in relation to tourism and leisure activities. This may be a possible answer to the decline and restructuring of the agricultural sector in rural areas, along with several other weaknesses (Sharpley 2002; Kim et al. 2006; Lane and Kastenholz 2015). Implementing good planning and tourism development strategies can open an avenue which may make it possible to improve the livelihoods of some rural communities (Obonyo and Fwaya 2012).

In this context, of course, both tourists and the rural population have to be considered (Kim et al. 2006), which means that the tourism strategies to be adopted increasingly have to strike a balance between the territory's resources and tourists' demands. This calls for adopting sustainable strategies when approaching the development of tourism in rural areas as has been claimed by several authors, in particular Bramwell (1994), Kim et al. (2006) and Kim and Jamal (2015), among many others. These authors have also underlined the need to follow endogenous perspectives, i.e. to adopt a bottom-up and grassroots approach. In scientific literature, this is usually designated as an integrated strategy (integrating tourism as well as other industries within the rural development strategy—Oliver and Jenkins 2003; Carneiro et al. 2015). As claimed by Obonyo and Fwaya (2012: 2), "rural development calls for appropriate objectives and strategies which focus on the rural communities and sustainable utilisation of the existing resources".

If the aim is to follow an integrated development strategy, policies addressing tourism development therefore have to include the perception of local residents in relation to this issue. This topic will be further addressed in the next section.

3   Residents' Perceptions of the Tourism Industry and Their Role in the Development of Tourism Activities

We can infer that the term "perception" concerns the idea held by someone about a phenomenon or a fact. The same phenomenon or fact can be viewed differently by different individuals based on their sensibilities, education or needs. One can deduce, of course, that behaviours are based on perceptions, besides sociocultural values.

In this research we will try to evaluate residents' perceptions of the tourism attributes of the territory and of the development of the tourism industry and its impacts, in general. In the study of this topic, two major approaches can be followed, although interconnected: (1) the use of tests on variables that can show or predict residents' perceptions and (2) residents' segmentation, in accordance with their level of support for tourism (Sharpley 2014; Vareiro et al. 2013; Feng 2019).

The use of this type of analysis in tourism dates back to the 1970s. Among the first authors to emphasise this issue were Pizam (1978) and Rothman (1978). Since then, residents have been viewed as an integral part of the tourism phenomenon. Several studies have also highlighted that they can play an essential role in the success or failure of a tourist destination (Ap 1992; Faulkner and Tideswell 1997; Dyer et al. 2007; Nunkoo and Gursoy 2012; Vareiro et al. 2013; Vargas-Sánchez et al. 2015; Malik et al. 2017; Martín et al. 2018; Eusébio et al. 2018). In fact, in early research conducted on this issue, the idea of integrating local communities in the process of tourism development also dates back to the 1970s, coupled with the interest for alternative tourism practices, following the guidelines issued by international institutions, such as the United Nations (Dodds et al. 2018).

As mentioned by Vareiro et al. (2013) and by Chen et al. (2018), among others, there are many studies on residents' attitudes towards tourism and its impacts. Part of these studies have focused on residents' socio-demographic characteristics (e.g. age, gender, education and income) as well as their behaviour regarding the tourism industry and host-tourist interactions (e.g. Besculides et al. 2002; Kuvan and Akan 2005; Vareiro et al. 2013; Abdollahzadeh and Sharifzadeh 2014; Wang and Xu 2015; Almeida-García et al. 2016; Rezaei 2017; Eusébio et al. 2018). This interest in residents' perceptions is closely related to the idea of a sustainable tourism strategy and the way that the former can have a decisive influence on the latter and therefore the need to take into account residents' perceptions and attitudes (Gursoy et al. 2002; Jackson 2008; Lee 2013; Renda et al. 2014; Eusébio et al. 2018; Feng 2019; Lopes et al. 2019). It is also related to the impacts of tourism felt by communities and thus the need for tourism planners and managers to adopt measures that will mitigate or minimise potential negative impacts (Vareiro et al. 2013; Feng 2019).

Since the 1990s, this issue has been the focus of multiple studies conducted abroad (e.g. Long et al. 1990; Ap 1992; Lankford 1994; Faulkner and Tideswell 1997; Chen 2000; Besculides et al. 2002; Jurowski and Gursoy 2004; Nunkoo and Gursoy 2012). However, it only attracted the attention of Portuguese researchers much later (Vareiro et al. 2013).

For decades, the implemented planning processes have followed a so-called decision-making model, i.e. top-down political approaches (Gursoy and Kendall 2006). More recently, a more democratic approach has been pursued. This approach tries to combine the planning process with technical rationality and participatory democracy (Getz 1991; Gursoy and Kendall 2006). However, pursuing a collaborative decision-making model is certainly more complex, due to the high number of stakeholders involved and the commitment towards building a consensus (Lopes 2016).

At this level, the process is managed through political implementation of tourism strategies that interconnect the macro- (e.g. central government), meso- (e.g. regional and intermunicipal commissions, municipal companies) and micro-planning dimensions, which should be sustained, in particular by the opinions of local communities, and promote their empowerment (Table 1).

Table 1 Stakeholders involved and the commitment towards building a consensus on rural tourism planning

Analysis scale	Focus	Key concepts (travel behaviours)	Planning and policy focus	Key concepts (planning and policy focus)	Stakeholders	
					Public	Private
Macro (national)	Aggregation	• Standard distribution and flows • Activity	• National state (government) • Structure • Ideology	• National and state interest • Political culture • Political provisions	• Central government • Central government organisations • Large public companies	• Large air, rail and road transport companies • Large hotel groups, travel agents and tour operators • Organisers of major events • National business and professional associations
Meso (regional and local)	• Combines aggregation and individual analysis	• Mobility, travel phase, lifestyle, travel career	• Organisation • *Decision-making*	• Individual organisations as political actors • Political partners • Policy networks	• Regional government • Coordination and regional development commissions • City councils Municipal companies	• Regional road transport and river transport companies • Organisers of sporting and religious events, etc. • Regional business associations
Micro (local)	Individual	• Personality, lifestyle • Motivation, expectation and satisfaction	• Individual • Agency	• Political psychology • Personality • Motivations • Individual political values • Individual actors	• Local population	• Local population • Hotels and restaurants Independent travel agents • Tourist entertainment companies • Local event organisers (festivals, fairs and pilgrimages)

Source: Authors' own elaboration, based on several authors

This debate has given rise to several studies on the issue (Vargas-Sánchez et al. 2011; Nunkoo and Gursoy 2012; Feng 2019). Generally speaking, we can conclude from these studies that the viewpoints of residents that are less favourable towards the tourism industry may have negative effects on the actions of other stakeholders, including governmental organisations and local businesses, and may also affect contacts between tourists and residents (Garau-Vadell et al. 2014).

As reported by Nunkoo et al. (2013) and taking into account some of the most prestigious journals in leisure and tourism (Annals of Tourism Research, Tourism Management, and Journal of Travel Research) as well as analysing the period from 1948 to 2010, most of the articles published on the issue followed a quantitative approach. Moreover, most of those articles did not invoke a theoretical framework, even if they used a variety of theories drawn from other disciplines. Relatively few studies used qualitative and mixed-method approaches.

One cannot forget that the implementation of a sustainable tourism strategy needs to take into account several impacts resulting from tourism expansion, especially with regard to the economic, sociocultural and environmental dimensions, not all of which are positive. This has been highlighted by several authors since the late 1990s (e.g. Besculides et al. 2002; Kuvan and Akan 2005; Cadima Ribeiro et al. 2012; Obonyo and Fwaya 2012; Almeida-García et al. 2016; Muresan et al. 2016; Rasoolimanesh et al. 2019).

4 Research Methods

4.1 Boticas: Short Presentation

The municipality of Boticas was chosen for the empirical research. This municipality is located in the district of Vila Real, in Alto Tâmega (NUTS III), North of Portugal (NUTS II).

The municipality covers a total area of 322 km^2 and extends from the River Tâmega to the *Alturas* Mountain and *Marcos* and *Leiranco* Mountains, contributing to a diversity of landscapes throughout its territory. The landscape contributes to the configuration of an identity associated with the municipality's lifestyle. In fact, the habits and customs are considered to be consistent with this type of natural context and biophysical conditions (Lopes 2016; Remoaldo et al. 2017; Lopes et al. 2019).

The demographic weakness this municipality has experienced over recent decades has contributed to its designation as a "remote rural area". In 2014, of the municipality's ten existing parishes, three were considered to be predominantly rural areas (P.R.A.) and seven median urban areas (M.U.A.), according to the statistical classification of the territory used in Portugal, designated as *Types of Urban Areas* (TIPAU) (INE 2014b).

In 2011, according to the last census, the municipality had 5750 inhabitants, of which 26.3% lived in the Union of Parishes of Boticas and Granja (INE 2012). As mentioned, this municipality, like many others in the Northeast of Portugal, has been

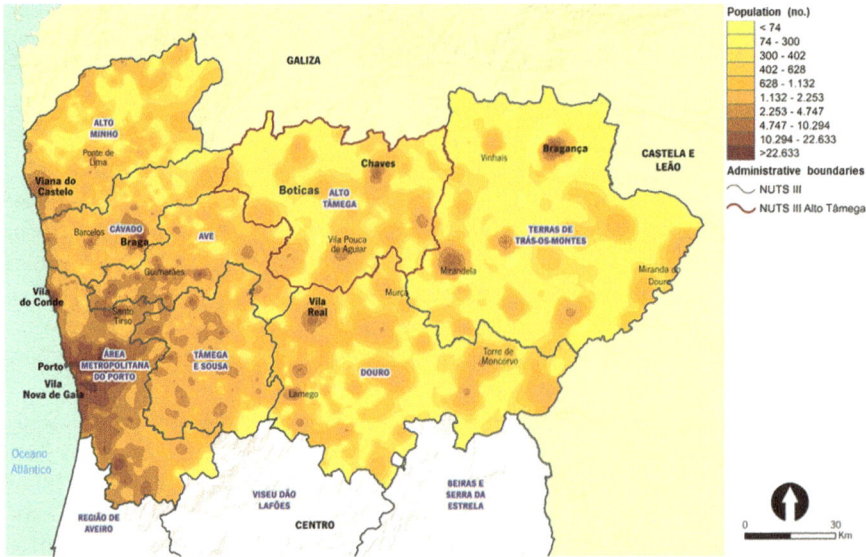

Fig. 1 Population in the Northern region of Mainland Portugal, in 2011. Source: Authors' own elaboration based on C.A.O.P. 2015 and Census 2011 (INE 2012)

experiencing a significant demographic decline. This result is shown in Fig. 1, where the lighter colours represent a lower percentage of people per square kilometre.

In this territory, the primary sector (which employs 18% of the working population), mainly constituted by agriculture, is the major contributor to local income and employment. Half of the economically active population is linked to the tertiary sector, which is relatively fragile.

Despite the importance of the tertiary sector, tourism does not play a relevant role as a source of development of this territory. This is partly because local resources are not being properly recognised and used for this purpose.

The supply of tourist accommodation in the municipality of Boticas is still limited. In 2013, the municipality of Boticas registered only 1329 guests in its hotels, with an average overnight stay of 1.4 nights (INE 2014a). In addition, the activity has a strong seasonal profile, with the majority of visits occurring in the summer (July and August). This is a generic problem in Portugal and is particularly marked in Boticas, above all due to its extreme climate (with hot summers and cold winters).

Nevertheless, Boticas is relatively close to the Portuguese coast and the country's largest cities: it is around 90 minutes from Porto's *Francisco Sá Carneiro Airport*. The time required to reach the destination is the result of substantial improvements in road infrastructures over the last two decades, in particular the construction of the A11, A7 and A24 motorways. The first two connect Boticas to the coast and to Porto airport, and the latter connects Boticas to the neighbouring city of Chaves and the Spanish border (Galicia).

4.2 Sample, Data Collection and Questionnaire

The design of the questionnaire was based on the review of the literature (Jurowski and Gursoy 2004; Látková and Vogt 2012; Kim et al. 2013; Vareiro et al. 2013; Stylidis et al. 2014), the results of the focus groups which had previously been carried out, the objectives underlined in the project and the object under study (residents). The questionnaire consisted of four sections (global image, tourist attributes, development of the tourist industry in the municipality, and the socio-demographic characteristics of the respondents), using a Likert scale (of 5 points) in the vast majority of questions asked.

A pre-test was carried out in December 2015 involving ten respondents. After the pre-test, suggested improvements were introduced into the final questionnaire. The survey was distributed by a self-administered procedure (737 questionnaires) between December 2015 and May 2016, with logistical support from the municipality. A stratified sample was obtained, with a 61.5% response rate. From the 453 questionnaires collected, 390 were valid, the rest were rejected since they had incomplete answers. The sample size obtained has an error margin of 0.05%, a confidence level of 95%, and $Z = 1.96$.

The sample obtained is considered to be appropriate in view of the municipality's total population, geographical distribution by parishes and the time and cost requirements to complete the questionnaire (Gebremedhin and Tweeten 1994). Based on our review of the literature on the question of response rates (Vareiro et al. 2013), the response to this sample was even higher than that of other studies conducted (Kuvan and Akan 2005).

4.3 Data Analysis

The data was subjected to descriptive statistics and factor analysis, using SPSS software (version 23.0). It was decided to use descriptive statistics due to the need to verify the suitability of the data according to subsequent needs, based on measurements of central tendency (mean, mode and median), dispersion (minimum, maximum and standard deviation) and distribution (kurtosis and asymmetry).

Subsequently, in order to verify whether or not the data is applicable for factor analysis, preliminary analyses were made to verify its behaviour, in particular, (1) the correlation matrix (most correlations must exceed 0.3); (2) the Kaiser-Meyer-Olkin (KMO) test, where the minimum level of KMO should be equal to 0.5; (3) the Bartlett's test of sphericity in order to test the null hypothesis, which means that the significance level should be close to 0 and always less than 5%; and

(4) Cronbach's alpha test in order to examine reliability, where the minimum value is assumed to be 0.7.

Using principal component analysis, we tried to synthesise information from individual data through a smaller number of explanatory factors. Thus, a communality of 0 indicates the inability of factors to explain the variable as a whole, whereas a value of 1 means that it can be fully explained by the factors.

After checking these assumptions, the matrix of the main components was analysed, following its explanatory rank, in order to achieve one or more factors. For this purpose, the varimax rotation method was used. After this analysis, we were able to identify the loading of the different original variables and their relationship to the different factors (principal components).

5 Results

5.1 Profile of Respondents

Table 2 summarises the socio-demographic profile of the survey's respondents, which were 45.8% males and 54.2% females. This result is close to that found in other studies (Sharma and Dyer 2009; Vareiro et al. 2013; Stylidis et al. 2014). The sample was compared with the municipality's figures to check its representativeness. In relation to the gender characteristics of Boticas, the 2011 census conducted by the National Institute of Statistics (INE) showed that 51.6% of its residents were females, a figure close to that obtained in our survey.

The majority of the residents across the study area were between the ages of 45 to 64 years (35.4%) and 25 to 44 (32.2%) years. The most representative education level in the sample was completion of fourth grade (primary school) (36.5%). In terms of income, 42.5% of the residents reported annual earnings between €501 and €1000. These results correspond to a population considered to be middle- to lower-middle class.

5.2 Descriptive Statistics

It is important to highlight some general facts for the sample as a whole, using descriptive statistics. Most residents have a favourable image of the municipality's tourism potential, with the overall average score close to 4 (3.88). Given that Boticas does not hold a tourist destination status, these results may suggest the high expectations of residents towards the economic potential of its tourism development.

In particular, residents underlined the attractive landscape, the existence of relevant historic sites and the sense of security felt in Boticas. In contrast, public transportation, road infrastructures and public services were less favourably perceived.

Table 2 Social-demographic characteristics of the respondents

Variables		N	%
Gender	Male	179	45.8
	Female	211	54.2
Age	15–24	32	8.1
	25–44	125	32.2
	45–64	138	35.4
	65 and over	95	24.3
Education	At least up to fourth grade	142	36.46
	Up to sixth grade	63	16.20
	Seventh-ninth grade	52	13.42
	Tenth-twelfth grade	75	19.24
	University	57	14.68
Occupation	Domestic	42	10.89
	Unemployed	70	17.97
	Employed	150	38.48
	Pensioner	105	26.84
	Student	23	5.82
Marital status	Married	226	57.97
	Not married	98	25.06
	Divorced	23	5.82
	Widower	43	11.14
Monthly income	< €500	130	33.42
	€501–€1000	166	42.53
	€1001–€2500	79	20.25
	€2501–€3000	10	2.53
	>€3000	5	1.27

Source: Authors' own elaboration based on self-administrated questionnaire to residents between January and May 2016

With regard to tourism attributes, residents seem to have a sense of belonging to their territory, as they assess almost all items with a mean score of 4. However, the attributes most valued by residents were gastronomy, events and festivities. Some of the items were assigned five points, especially music and popular music, gastronomy and local products. The attribute perceived to be least relevant was painting and sculpture (Table 3).

The economic impacts expected were generally classified as positive. Specifically, residents considered jobs and the generation of income from the local economy as the main economic impacts expected from tourism development. Nevertheless, tourism is seen as having a possible negative impact on the local cost of living. One of the main problems raised is related to the effect that many communities experience with tourism development, which is well documented in the literature (e.g. Johnson et al. 1994; Almeida-García et al. 2015; Lopes et al. 2019). Attraction of visitors has a negative effect on the price of products and real estate, in particular, due to higher demand and tourists' consumption habits, which tend to differ from those of residents.

Table 3 Descriptive statistics of tourism attributes

Item		X	M	x	σ	Mx	Mn	A	K
Global image of the municipality	*Global image of the municipality* **3.88**								
	Landscape	4.34	4.00	4.00	0.66	5.00	1.00	−1.24	2.89
	Architectural heritage	4.06	4.00	4.00	0.74	5.00	1.00	−1.08	2.49
	Historic sites	4.20	4.00	4.00	0.67	5.00	2.00	−0.66	0.58
	Cultural programme	3.94	4.00	4.00	0.87	5.00	1.00	−1.12	1.46
	Dissemination of cultural events	3.87	4.00	4.00	0.91	5.00	1.00	−1.15	1.52
	Quality hotel offer	4.00	4.00	4.00	0.82	5.00	1.00	−0.94	1.02
	Catering services	4.09	4.00	4.00	0.82	5.00	1.00	−1.44	3.02
	Signposting and tourist information	3.70	4.00	4.00	0.98	5.00	1.00	−0.97	0.62
	Public services (schools, health centres, etc.)	3.43	4.00	4.00	1.13	5.00	1.00	−0.87	−0.02
	Public transportation	2.95	4.00	4.00	1.24	5.00	1.00	−0.36	−1.01
	Road infrastructures	3.41	4.00	4.00	1.08	5.00	1.00	−0.93	0.17
	Safety	4.30	5.00	4.00	0.73	5.00	1.00	−1.66	4.66
	Cleaning	4.13	4.00	4.00	0.80	5.00	1.00	−1.27	2.17
Tourism attributes	*Tourism attributes* **3.95**								
	Popular music	3.61	4.00	4.00	1.03	5.00	1.00	−0.88	0.57
	Festivities and events	4.30	5.00	5.00	0.78	5.00	1.00	−1.61	3.55
	Painting and sculpture	3.60	4.00	4.00	0.99	5.00	1.00	−0.62	−0.04
	Gastronomy	4.37	5.00	5.00	0.77	5.00	1.00	−1.60	2.90
	Ancestral traditions	4.08	4.00	4.00	0.84	5.00	1.00	−1.13	1.65
	Local products	4.18	5.00	4.00	0.84	5.00	1.00	−1.17	1.39
	Natural conditions	4.05	4.00	4.00	0.84	5.00	1.00	−0.92	0.76
	Museums	3.89	4.00	4.00	0.89	5.00	1.00	−0.80	0.57
	Churches and chapels	4.02	4.00	4.00	0.85	5.00	1.00	−1.05	1.51
	Archaeology and history	3.95	4.00	4.00	0.88	5.00	1.00	−0.91	0.92
	Local crafts	3.74	4.00	4.00	0.92	5.00	1.00	−0.75	0.57
	Hunting and fishing	3.74	4.00	4.00	0.92	5.00	1.00	−0.73	0.46
	Sports	3.74	4.00	4.00	0.94	5.00	1.00	−0.69	0.32

(continued)

Table 3 (continued)

Item		X	M	x	σ	Mx	Mn	A	K
Effects of tourism	*Economic effects* **3.96**								
	Job creation	4.21	4.00	4.00	0.74	5.00	1.00	−1.25	2.58
	Revenues from local economy	4.18	4.00	4.00	0.74	5.00	1.00	−1.10	2.09
	Increase of residents' income	3.72	4.00	4.00	0.95	5.00	1.00	−1.07	1.17
	Investment in hotels, restaurants and shops	4.12	4.00	4.00	0.76	5.00	1.00	−1.26	2.92
	Higher living costs	3.55	4.00	4.00	1.01	5.00	1.00	−0.69	−0.03
	Sociocultural effects **3.70**								
	Improvement of the quality of public services	3.82	4.00	4.00	0.91	5.00	1.00	−1.06	1.40
	Increase of leisure and recreational opportunities	4.15	4.00	4.00	0.70	5.00	1.00	−1.10	3.02
	Preservation of historical and archaeological heritage	4.04	4.00	4.00	0.83	5.00	1.00	−1.56	3.71
	Local culture and crafts	4.21	4.00	4.00	0.67	5.00	1.00	−1.10	3.04
	Contact with different cultures	4.13	4.00	4.00	0.73	5.00	1.00	−0.96	1.74
	Increase of criminality	2.58	2.00	3.00	1.21	5.00	1.00	0.26	−0.91
	Difficulty in preserving values, customs and traditions	2.65	2,00	3,00	1,3	5,00	1,00	0,08	−1,2
	Increase of community self-esteem	3.93	4.00	4.00	0.81	5.00	1.00	−0.97	1.56
	Improvement of residents' quality of life	3.81	4.00	4.00	0.94	5.00	1.00	−1.03	1.04
	Environmental effects **2.94**								
	Excessive noise	3.01	3.00	3.00	1.19	5.00	1.00	−0.14	−0.90
	Amount of waste	2.88	4.00	3.00	1.25	5.00	1.00	−0.06	−1.12

Notes: *M* mode, *X* mean, σ standard deviation, *x* median, *K* Kurtosis, *Mn* minimum, *Mx* maximum, *A* asymmetry

Source: Authors' own elaboration based on self-administered questionnaire to residents between January and May 2016

The sociocultural impacts were also evaluated positively.

Residents expressed positive feelings regarding, in particular, the opportunity given to visitors to enjoy the local culture and handicrafts, taking advantage of the recreational opportunities and facilities available. Similarly, they positively assessed the potential of cultural exchange associated with the possibility of being exposed to different cultures. It is also worth mentioning that they perceived tourism as having little effect on local levels of crime and preservation of their values, customs and traditions. Less positively, residents expressed a certain level of concern with the possibility that tourism may increase the level of noise in the centre of Boticas (score 3), with differing opinions on whether or not the tourism industry may lead to more litter in the streets.

Bearing in mind the embryonic status of Boticas in the tourism market, these results and evaluations should be considered carefully. In other words, they primarily reflect the opinions of individuals (residents) on what tourists are looking for and their expected behaviour, rather than the product of practical experience or a profound reflection on the issue.

5.3   Factor Analysis

The items mentioned above in the application of the descriptive methods were subject to factor analysis, using principal components as the extraction method. The data was subjected to different tests using the statistical SPSS package (version 23.0).

First, the data was subjected to visual inspection. In all areas we found that the data was suitable for perform the factor analysis. However, despite the appropriateness of the tourism attributes in view of the assumptions, the explanatory power of two factors was only around 60%. Table 4 summarises the main results achieved in the tests conducted using the factor analysis, regarding perceived global image, local tourism resources and effects of tourism.

Table 4 Summary of the results of the tests

	Global image		Tourism attributes		Effects of tourism	
Tests	Results	Suitability	Results	Suitability	Results	Suitability
Correlation matrix	>0.3	✓	>0.3	✓	>0.3	✓
Determinant value	0.003	✓	0.001	✓	0.001	✓
KMO	0.850	✓	0.905	✓	0.829	✓
Bartlett's test of sphericity	0.000	✓	0.000	✓	0.000	✓
Cronbach's alpha	0.867	✓	0.889	✓	0.828	✓
Total explained variance	64.347	✓	61.975	✓	62.394	✓
Factors	3	✓	2	✓	3	✓

Source: Authors' own elaboration based on self-administrated questionnaire to residents between January and May 2016

Table 5 Factor analysis of the perceived global image of Boticas

Analysis	Factors	Loading	Mean
Global image of Boticas	**Factor I: tourism resources**		4.07
	Landscape	0.590	
	Architectural heritage	0.731	
	Historic sites	0.714	
	Cultural programme	0.744	
	Disclosure of cultural events	0.742	
	Quality hotel offer	0.720	
	Restaurants and catering services	0.718	
	Factor II: public services and support to tourism		3.37
	Signposting and tourist information	0.683	
	Public services (schools, health care centres, etc.)	0.782	
	Public transportation	0.799	
	Road infrastructures	0.750	
	Factor III: safety and cleaning		4.21
	Safety	0.823	
	Cleaning	0.733	
Tourism attributes of Boticas	**Factor I: religion and popular issues**		4.08
	Popular music	0.748	
	Festivities and events	0.787	
	Gastronomy	0.730	
	Ancestral traditions	0.717	
	Churches and chapels	0.641	
	Factor II: culture and sport		3.81
	Museums	0.614	
	Archaeology and history	0.696	
	Local handicrafts	0.683	
	Hunting and fishing	0.843	
	Sports	0.799	
Effects of tourism development on Boticas	**Factor I: generated opportunities**		4.15
	Leisure and recreational opportunities	0.687	
	Preservation of historic resources	0.746	
	Local culture and crafts	0.844	
	Contact with different cultures	0.777	
	Job creation	0.699	
	Revenues from local economy	0.761	
	Factor II: environmental, social and cultural conditions		2.78
	Excessive noise	0.874	
	Amount of litter	0.921	
	Criminality	0.870	

(continued)

Table 5 (continued)

Analysis	Factors	Loading	Mean
	Difficulty in preserving values, customs and traditions	0.650	
	Factor III: welfare		3.82
	Residents' income	0,747	
	Community self-esteem	0,767	
	Quality of life	0,827	

Source: Authors' own elaboration based on self-administrated questionnaire to residents between January and May 2016

Then, the test of commonalities across the different groups of items under consideration was applied (Table 5).

Based on the empirical results, we found the first answers to the identified research questions.

With regard to the first question (Do the residents of Boticas perceive the tourism industry as a potential contributor to the enhancement of the multi-functionality of their municipality and consequently to local development?), the answer was clearly affirmative. This raises the question as to whether the respondents had a pertinent image of what the tourism market is, as well as consumers' motivations, needs and behaviours.

Regarding the second question (In your opinion, does the territory have any tourism attributes?), a first glance at the empirical data (the results from residents' perceptions) enables us to infer that the resources are not scarce. However, the attributed average rates raise a doubt as to whether the territory of Boticas has, in fact, the tourism potential that residents see in it and, if so, which strategy should be applied. In any case, the most valuable attributes seem be those related to Boticas' historical and cultural heritage (tangible and intangible) and its natural landscape.

"Are residents able to get a clear image of those resources which can have a major role in the establishment of a local tourism strategy?" In a way, the answer to this question has already been given through the previous questions. The answer is clearly negative. This does not mean that residents should not be viewed as major stakeholders in the establishment of a local tourism strategy. To include or to listen to them is not the same as transforming them into planners or decision-makers. That role belongs to other agents, who should be able to implement a participative planning and decision-making process.

6   Discussion of the Results and Conclusions

Over recent decades, many outlying regions in Portugal have been taking advantage of the expansion of the tourism industry. In fact, a substantial proportion of visitors increasingly choose such destinations to achieve more authentic tourist experiences.

The empirical results enable us to infer that residents perceive tourism as an opportunity to enhance the development of the municipality of Boticas, but they harbour doubts as to whether they will personally benefit from it. Considering that the municipality is not yet a tourist destination, these results have to be considered carefully, in the sense that they may be linked to strong (unrealistic) expectations concerning the economic potential of tourism development (Brida et al. 2011; Vareiro et al. 2013).

Moreover, the multitude of attributes perceived as having tourism potential and the average rates and ranking attained, raise the question as to whether the high rates are not primarily due to residents' self-esteem and commitment to their territory rather than to the latter's intrinsic tourism potential. Similarly, we wonder whether the result attained with regard to the expected impacts of tourism on the territory and on its population is not primarily based on residents' ideas of what tourists are looking for and their expected behaviour rather than on practical experience or deep reflection on the issue.

There are, of course, certain policies that may be adopted in order to favour the development of rural territories such as Boticas. In this regard, taking advantage of strategies that have been successfully implemented in other territories with similar characteristics seems to be advisable.

In terms of the local strategy, given the results obtained from the survey, it is necessary to deal with the expressed concerns, whether in relation to the preservation of local values, practices and customs or rising prices of goods, services and properties, for example. It is important to bear in mind the relevance that the local people generally attach to religious issues and cultural and traditional events.

In terms of perceived global image, residents were clear in assigning relevance to the territory's tourism resources and public services and showed their support towards tourism development. Regarding the effects generated by tourism on social, economic and environmental dimensions, residents clearly valued the opportunities it could generate, but they were resolute in the statement that tourism should be based on environmental sustainability.

In order to follow the residents' expressed expectations with regard to the tourism development of Boticas and to respect their sensibility about several of the issues that were raised, their concerns and hopes should be included in tourism strategies to be defined by local authorities. A difficulty also raised by the empirical results lies in the unclear image harboured by residents concerning the endogenous attributes that have real tourism potential and the lack of experience in dealing with visitors, i.e. with their motivations, needs and behaviours.

The global image of Boticas held by residents is connected to its historical heritage and natural landscape, the existence of historic sites (some of which date back to the Celtic period) and the public security that it offers to residents and visitors. In addition, the results also revealed that certain tourism assets have the potential to be explored more fully, such as festivities, events and, of course, local products, including handicrafts. Regarding the gastronomy of Boticas and a few other assets, without questioning their quality and singularity, there are many issues to be resolved before considering them to be tourism products: gastronomy cannot be a product if there are no restaurants or related shops available to visitors.

Our study is in line with other studies conducted in several territories. Residents' perceptions of the image of their territories are usually favourable (e.g. Stylidis et al. 2014; Stylidis 2016), and positive economic impacts of tourism development are expected. Tourism is seen as an opportunity to increase the quality of life of the local population, by contributing to job creation and increased revenues for local businesses (e.g. Besculides et al. 2002; Gursoy et al. 2002; Kuvan and Akan 2005; Kim et al. 2013; Almeida-García et al. 2016; Muresan et al. 2016; Feng 2019). The results also confirm that residents' perceptions of the positive effects on quality of life or the economic dimension also influence their opinion on environmental sustainability (e.g. Perdue et al. 1990; Vargas-Sánchez et al. 2009; Yu et al. 2011; Boqué and Soler 2016).

Part of these results should be seen in relation to the current level of development. In fact, support towards the local tourism industry and the consideration of the positive effects achieved are sustained by several factors. Residents reveal a state of "euphoria" because they are aware of the low percentage of tourists and the contribution that tourism can contribute to local development over the medium to long term (Perdue et al. 1999; Butler 1980; Vareiro et al. 2013).

In the study published by Remoaldo et al. (2017), the willingness of stakeholders to implement a strategy towards tourism development in Boticas was identified, considering the territory's potential in natural and landscape terms. Notwithstanding the fact that a few segments of the community of Boticas maintain different levels of optimism towards tourism development, globally, the local people are willing to contribute to enhancement of tourism activity, assuming the territory's capacity to endorse a strategy based on (1) the global level of the activity, based on the integration of the various stakeholders; (2) the channelling of resources to a set of factors at the territorial level (attractiveness, accessibility and nature); and (3) developing a promotion and dissemination strategy of the available tourist supply (Lopes et al. 2019).

The results of the analysis undertaken reveal that the main tourist attractions of Boticas are related to nature, gastronomy and wine and cultural (and religious) tourism. Regarding this type of products, the Portuguese Tourism Strategy for the period 2013–2015 (PENT 2013–2015) and "Tourism 2020—Five Principles for an Ambition" lines of action have defined strategic territorial approaches bearing in mind that there is little or no consolidated development (Ministério da Economia e da Inovação 2007; Ministério da Economia e Emprego 2016) in some territories, in particular Boticas, which is a peripheral area, whose tourist activity still has very insignificant presence. Within the framework of the European Union's LEADER programme, also addressing the case of rural development, several guidelines and financial resources may be mobilised to support policy action towards the development of sites such as Boticas. In this context, the promotion of partnerships between local entities and governments is encouraged and may certainly constitute a major instrument to achieve tourist and general development of these communities. In the aim of these local development programmes, the current proposal involves a total investment of around €14 million for development of the municipalities of the Alto Tâmega region, including the municipality of Boticas.

Due to the fact that some political and strategic decisions have already been taken towards the development of tourism, it seems to us that the development of additional research, to strengthen and consolidate the strategy to be implemented, should be conducted. Three recommendations emerge from this research, in particular, (1) the need to create a supra-municipal network and develop partnerships, which should also include and commit private stakeholders; (2) the need to involve community members in the planning process and development of the future tourism strategy, taking advantage, in particular, of their creative and co-creation skills; and (3) the importance of developing a long-term tourism strategy that encourages community participation and preservation of local customs/traditions and the community's culture.

In future research, there are certain paths that can be followed in order to test the consistency and complete the results presented herein. First, gender differences by income, age group, profession or place of residence should be considered, since these can significantly influence how the results are analysed. Moreover, it would be relevant to compare the results obtained in this research with those of another territory with similar characteristics. Further analysis may be conducted based on the insights extracted from these methods, whether of a qualitative (resulting from the application of semi-structured interviews to the heads of associations and institutions) or a quantitative nature. In this regard, it is important to verify whether there are similarities between the opinions of all stakeholders. Based on the factors extracted from the analysis of the data presented herein, we intend to build a structural equation model (SEM).

As mentioned above, this research may be helpful in the design of a tourism development strategy for Boticas and other similar rural territories, for example, by identifying the most relevant tourism assets and creating a basis for establishing good relationships between residents and visitors, which are crucial for the success of any tourist destination (Dyer et al. 2007; Wang and Pfister 2008; Eusébio et al. 2018). As underlined, residents' perceptions are vitally important in the development of successful strategies and tourism plans (Vareiro et al. 2013; Stylidis et al. 2014; Feng 2019), since communities are the primary and most important stakeholders in tourism. However, that does not mean that they have the power to choose the main drivers of the strategy to be followed.

Through this exploratory empirical research, we have tried to show that tourism may be an instrument for the development of rural territories by taking into consideration the set of endogenous resources available and the way local populations can directly benefit from them. The tourism industry can surely be, at least for some of those territories, a relevant contributor to the establishment (or recovery) of their multi-functionality.

Exploring those tourism assets only makes sense, of course, if a sustainable development strategy can be put into practice; otherwise, local stakeholders and population, as a whole, will not benefit from them.

References

Abdollahzadeh G, Sharifzadeh A (2014) Rural residents' perceptions toward tourism development: a study from Iran. Int J Tour Res 16(2):126–136

Almeida-García F, Vázquez AB, Macías RC (2015) Resident's attitudes towards the impacts of tourism. Tour Manag Perspect 13:33–40

Almeida-García F, Peláez-Fernández MÁ, Balbuena-Vázquez A, Cortés-Macias R (2016) Residents' perceptions of tourism development in Benalmádena (Spain). Tour Manag 54 (3):259–274

Ap J (1992) Residents' perceptions on tourism impacts. Ann Tour Res 19:665–690

Barca F, McCann P, Rodríguez-Pose A (2012) The case for regional development intervention: place-based versus place-neutral approaches. J Reg Sci 52(1):134–152

Besculides A, Lee M, McCormick P (2002) Residents' perceptions of the cultural benefits of tourism. Ann Tour Res 29(2):303–319

Boqué JB, Soler SR (2016) Desenvolvimento rural. In: Fernandes J, Trigal L, Sposito E (eds) Dicionário de Geografia Aplicada. Terminologia da análise, do planeamento e da gestão do território. Porto Editora, Porto

Bosworth G, Annibal I, Carroll T, Price L, Sellick J, Shepherd J (2015) Empowering local action through neo-endogenous development; the case of LEADER in England. Sociol Rural 56 (3):1–23

Bramwell B (1994) Rural tourism and sustainable rural tourism. J Sustain Tour 2(1-2):1–6

Brida J, Osti L, Faccioli M (2011) Residents' perception and attitudes towards tourism impacts: a case study of the small rural community of Folgaria (Trentino-Italy). BIJ 18(3):359–385

Bridger JC, Alter TR (2008) An interactional approach to place-based rural development. Community Dev 39(1):99–111

Butler RW (1980) The concept of a tourist area cycle of evolution: implications for management of resources. Can Geogr 24(1):5–12

Cadima Ribeiro J, Vareiro L, Remoaldo PC (2012) The host-tourist interaction in a world heritage site: the case of Guimarães. China-USA Bus Rev 11(3):283–297

Carneiro MJ, Lima J, Silva AL (2015) Landscape and the rural tourism experience: identifying key elements, addressing potential, and implications for the future. J Sustain Tour 23 (8-9):1217–1235

CEE (1988) The future of rural society. Commission communication transmitted to the council and to the European Parliament on 29 July 1988. Office for Official Publications of the European Communities, Luxembourg

Chen J (2000) An investigation of urban residents' loyalty to tourism. J Hosp Tour Res 24(1):5–19

Chen N, Dwyer L, Firth T (2018) Residents' place attachment and word-of-mouth behaviours: a tale of two cities. J Hosp Tour Manag 36:1–11

Dodds R, Ali A, Galaski K (2018) Mobilizing knowledge: determining key elements for success and pitfalls in developing community-based tourism. Curr Issue Tour 21(13):1547–1568

Dyer P, Gursoy D, Sharma B, Carter J (2007) Structural modelling of resident perceptions of tourism and associated development on the sunshine coast, Australia. Tour Manag 28 (2):409–422

Eusébio C, Vieira A, Lima S (2018) Place attachment, host-tourist interactions, and residents' attitudes towards tourism development. J Sustain Tour 26(6):890–909

Faulkner B, Tideswell C (1997) A framework for monitoring community impacts of tourism. J Sustain Tour 5(1):3–28

Feng H-Y (2019) Residents' perceptions of tourism impacts in Miaoli, Taiwan. J Tour Hosp Manag 7(2):147–157

Figueiredo E (2011) Um rural cheio de futuros? 100 Luz, Castro Verde

Figueiredo E, Kastenholz E (2008) Papel do Turismo no Desenvolvimento Rural em Portugal. A importância da integração das visões dos visitantes e residentes. Actas do 14 Congressso da Associação Portuguesa para o Desenvolvimento Regional. Tomar: APDR, 1963–1992

Garau-Vadell JB, Díaz-Armas R, Gutierrez-Taño D (2014) Residents' perceptions of tourism impacts on island destinations: a comparative analysis. Int J Tour Res 16(6):578–585

Gebremedhin TG, Tweeten LG (1994) Research methods and communication in the social sciences. Praeger Publishers, Westport

Getz D (1991) Festivals, special events, and tourism. Van Mostrand Reinhold, New York

Gursoy D, Kendall KW (2006) Hosting mega events: Modelling locals' support. Ann Tour Res 33 (3):603–623

Gursoy D, Jurowski C, Uysal M (2002) Resident attitudes: a structural modeling approach. Ann Tour Res 29:79–105

INE IP (2012) Censos 2011 – XV Recenseamento Geral da População; V Recenseamento Geral da Habitação. Instituto Nacional de Estatística, Lisboa

INE IP (2014a) Anuário Estatístico da Região Norte – 2013. Instituto Nacional de Estatística, Lisboa

INE IP (2014b) Tipologia de Áreas Urbanas (T.I.P.A.U). Instituto Nacional de Estatística, Lisboa

Iorio M, Corsale A (2010) Rural tourism and livelihood strategies in Romania. J Rural Stud 26:152–162

Jackson L (2008) Residents' perceptions of the impacts of special event tourism. J Place Manag Dev 1(3):240–255

Johnson JD, Snepenger DJ, Akis S (1994) Residents' perceptions of tourism development. Ann Tour Res 21(3):629–642

Jurowski C, Gursoy D (2004) Distance effects on residents' attitudes toward tourism. Ann Tour Res 31(2):296–312

Kastenholz E, Carneiro MJ, Marques CP, Lima J (2012) Understanding and managing the rural tourism experience—the case of a historical village in Portugal. Tour Manag Perspect 4:207–214

Kim S, Jamal T (2015) The co-evolution of rural tourism and sustainable rural development in Hongdong, Korea: complexity, conflict and local response. J Sustain Tour 23(8-9):1363–1385

Kim H, Chen M, Lang S (2006) Tourism expansion and economic development: the case of Taiwan. J Tour Manag 27:925–933

Kim K, Uysal M, Sirgy MJ (2013) How does tourism in a community impact the quality of life of community residents? Tour Manag 36:527–540

Kristensen L, Thenail C, Kristensen SP (2004) Landscape changes in agrarian landscapes in the 1990s: the interaction between farmers and the farmed landscape. A case study from Jutland, Denmark. J Environ Manag 71:231–244

Kuvan Y, Akan P (2005) Residents' attitudes toward general and forest-related impacts of tourism: the case of Belek, Antalya. Tour Manag 26(5):691–706

Lane B, Kastenholz E (2015) Rural tourism: the evolution of practice and research approaches–towards a new generation concept? J Sustain Tour 23(8-9):1133–1156

Lankford S (1994) Attitudes and perceptions toward tourism and rural regional development. J Travel Res 32(3):35–43

Látková P, Vogt CA (2012) Residents' attitudes toward existing and future tourism development in rural communities. J Travel Res 51(1):50–67

Lee T (2013) Influence analysis of community resident support for sustainable tourism development. Tour Manag 34:37–46

Lee AH, Wall G, Kovacs JF (2015) Creative food clusters and rural development through place branding: culinary tourism initiatives in Stratford and Muskoka, Ontario, Canada. J Rural Stud 39:133–144

Long P, Perdue R, Allen L (1990) Rural resident tourism perceptions and attitudes by community level of tourism. J Travel Res 28(3):3–9

Lopes H (2016) O turismo como alavanca do desenvolvimento de áreas rurais: o caso de estudo do município de Boticas. Master dissertation. University of Minho, Guimarães.

Lopes H, Remoaldo PC, Ribeiro V, Cadima Ribeiro J, Silva S (2016) The creation of a new tourist destination in low density areas: the Boticas case. J Spat Organ Dynamics IV(2):118–131

Lopes H, Remoaldo P, Ribeiro V (2019) Residents' perceptions of tourism activity in a rural north-eastern Portuguese community: a cluster analysis. Bull Geograph Socio-econ Series 46:119–135

Malik M, Al Rawabi T, Kimyani N, Al Hadrami S (2017) Residents' perceptions of tourism impacts in A'Dhakhiliyah region of Sultanate of Oman. J Tour Manag Res 2(3):119–134

Martín H, de los Salmones Sánchez M, Herrero Á (2018) Residents' attitudes and behavioural support for tourism in host communities. J Travel Tour Mark 35(2):231–243

McAreavey R (2009) Rural development theory and practice. Routledge, New York

Ministério da Economia e da Inovação (2007) Plano Estratégico Nacional do Turismo para o Desenvolvimento do Turismo em Portugal. Turismo de Portugal, IP, Lisboa

Ministério da Economia e Emprego (2016) Turismo 2020 - Cinco Princípios para uma ambição - Tornar Portugal o destino turístico mais ágil e dinâmico da Europa. Ministério da Economia e Emprego, Lisboa

Muresan IC, Oroian CF, Harun R, Arion FH, Porutiu A, Chiciudean GO, Todea A, Lile R (2016) Local residents' attitude toward sustainable rural tourism development. Sustain For 8(1):14

Nunkoo R, Gursoy D (2012) Residents' support for tourism: an identity perspective. Ann Tour Res 39(1):243–268

Nunkoo R, Smith SLJ, Ramkissoon H (2013) Residents' attitudes to tourism: a longitudinal study of 140 articles from 1984 to 2010. J Sustain Tour 21(1):5–25

Obonyo G, Fwaya E (2012) Integrating tourism with rural development strategies in Western Kenya. Am J Tour Res 1(1):1–8

Oliver T, Jenkins T (2003) Sustaining rural landscapes: the role of integrated tourism. Landsc Res 28(3):293–307

Perdue RR, Long PT, Allen LR (1990) Resident support for tourism development. Ann Tour Res 17 (4):586–599

Perdue RR, Long PT, Kang YS (1999) Boomtown tourism and resident quality of life: the marketing of gaming to host community residents. J Bus Res 44:165–177

Phelan C, Sharpley R (2011) Exploring agritourism entrepreneurship in the UK. Tour Plan Dev 8 (2):121–136

Pizam A (1978) Tourism's impacts: the social costs to the destination community as perceived by its residents. J Travel Res 16(4):8–12

Rasoolimanesh SM, Taheri B, Gannon M, Vafaei-Zadeh A, Hanifah H (2019) Does living in the vicinity of heritage tourism sites influence residents' perceptions and attitudes? J Sustain Tour 27(9):1295–1317

Ray C (2006) Neo-endogenous rural development in the EU. In: Cloke PJ, Marsden T, Mooney P (eds) Handbook of rural studies. Sage, London, pp 278–291

Remoaldo P, Freitas I, Matos O, Lopes H, Silva S, Fernández MDS et al (2017) The planning of tourism on rural areas: the stakeholders' perceptions of the Boticas municipality (northeastern Portugal). European Countryside 9(3):504–525

Renda A, Mendes J, Valle P (2014) The destination is where I live! Residents' perception of tourism impacts. J Spat Organ Dynamic 2(1):72–88

Rezaei N (2017) Resident perceptions toward tourism impacts in historic center of Yazd, Iran. Tour Geogr 19(5):734–755

Rothman R (1978) Residents and transients: community reaction to seasonal visitors. J Travel Res 16:8–13

Sharma B, Dyer P (2009) An investigation of differences in residents' perceptions on the sunshine coast: tourism impacts and demographic variables. Tour Geogr 11(2):187–213

Sharpley R (2002) Rural tourism and the challenge of tourism diversification: the case of Cyprus. Tour Manag 23(3):233–244

Sharpley R (2014) Host perceptions of tourism: a review of the research. Tour Manag 42:37–49

Silva D, Figueiredo E, Eusébio C, Carneiro MJ (2016) The countryside is worth a thousand words - Portuguese representations on rural areas. J Rural Stud 44:77–88

Stockdale A (2006) Migration: pre-requisite for rural economic regeneration? J Rural Stud 22 (3):354–366

Stylidis D (2016) The role of place image dimensions in residents' support for tourism development. Int J Tour Res 18(2):129–139

Stylidis D, Biran A, Sit J, Szivas EM (2014) Residents' support for tourism development: the role of residents' place image and perceived tourism impacts. Tour Manag 45:260–274

Van Doorn AM, Bakker MM (2007) The destination of arable land in a marginal agricultural landscape in South Portugal: an exploration of land use change determinants. Landsc Ecol 22 (7):1073–1087

Vareiro L, Remoaldo PC, Cadima Ribeiro J (2013) Residents' perceptions of tourism impacts in Guimarães (Portugal): a cluster analysis. Curr Issue Tour 16(6):535–551

Vargas-Sánchez A, Plaza-Mejia MA, Porras-Bueno N (2009) Understanding residents' attitudes toward the development of industrial tourism in a former mining community. J Travel Res 47:373–387

Vargas-Sánchez A, Porras-Bueno N, de los Ángeles Plaza-Mejía M (2011) Explaining residents' attitudes to tourism: is a universal model possible? Ann Tour Res 38(2):460–480

Vargas-Sánchez A, Valle P, Mendes J, Silva J (2015) Residents' attitude and level of destination development: an international comparison. Tour Manag 48:199–210

Walmsley DJ (2003) Rural tourism: a case of lifestyle-led opportunities. Aust Geogr 34:61–72

Wang YA, Pfister RE (2008) Residents' attitudes toward tourism and perceived personal benefits in a rural community. J Travel Res 47(1):84–93

Wang S, Xu H (2015) Influence of place-based senses of distinctiveness, continuity, self-esteem and self-efficacy on residents' attitudes toward tourism. Tour Manag 47(C):241–250

Wellbrock W, Roep D, Wiskerke J (2012) An integrated perspective on rural regional learning. European Countryside 4:1–16

Woods M (2011) Rural (key ideas in geography). Routledge, New York

Yu CP, Charles Chancellor H, Tian Cole S (2011) Examining the effects of tourism impacts on resident quality of life: evidence from rural midwestern communities in USA. Int J Tour Sci 11 (2):161–186

Decision Support Indicators for Municipal Investment in Low-Density Territories: A Case Study in the Portuguese Historical Villages

Antónia Martins, Graça Azevedo, Carlos Santos, Ana I. Melo,
Augusta Ferreira, Dalila Dias, Gonçalo Gomes, Maria Manuela Natário,
Paula Rocha, Ricardo Biscaia, Rúben Duarte, and Rui Pedro Marques

1 Introduction

The lack of social, economic, and financial indicators regarding the different initiatives taken with the aim of reversing the increasing trend of human desertification in low-density territories, namely, within the network of the Portuguese Historical Villages (rAHP), has made decision-making a difficult process for potential investors in these areas, mainly the mayors of the municipalities in which the Portuguese Historical Villages (AHP) are located.

Thus, the present study, carried out within the scope of the project "PLowDeR—Framework para Análise do Impacto Económico e Social das Atividades Turísticas

A. Martins · G. Azevedo (✉) · C. Santos · A. Ferreira · P. Rocha · R. Duarte
ISCA, University of Aveiro, Aveiro, Portugal
e-mail: graca.azevedo@ua.pt

A. I. Melo · R. Biscaia
School of Technology and Management (ESTGA), University of Aveiro, Águeda, Portugal

Centre for Research in Higher Education Policies (CIPES), Matosinhos, Portugal

D. Dias
Aldeias Históricas de Portugal, Belmonte, Portugal

G. Gomes
Turismo Centro de Portugal, Aveiro, Portugal

M. M. Natário
Higher School of Technology and Management, Polytechnic of Guarda, Research Unit for
Inland Development (UDI-IPG), Guarda, Portugal

R. P. Marques
Higher Institute of Accounting and Administration (ISCA-UA), University of Aveiro, Aveiro,
Portugal

© Springer Nature Switzerland AG 2021
R. P. Marques et al. (eds.), *The Impact of Tourist Activities on Low-Density
Territories*, Tourism, Hospitality & Event Management,
https://doi.org/10.1007/978-3-030-65524-2_10

nos Territórios de Baixa Densidade: o Caso das Aldeias Históricas de Portugal"[1] (Santos et al. 2019) (PLowDeR—Framework for the Analysis of the Economic and Social Impact of Tourism Activities in Low-Density Territories: the Case of the AHP), aims to analyse investment decisions in these territories made by local mayors, providing a comparative analysis with the social, economic, and financial indicators collected using the indicator framework developed and proposed by the aforementioned research project. This analysis seeks to understand whether the decisions made were the most appropriate ones or if it was possible to make a different decision based on a set of objective indicators.

1.1 Economic/Financial Context

The development of low-density territories, namely, in the AHP network, depends on the effort made by citizens, enhancing investment in these areas with public and private money. Therefore, to allow citizens to fully enjoy such heritage, political decision-makers, through their municipalities and together with private investors, have to allocate budgets and channel appropriate funds to the development of these territories based on a well-informed intervention.

Public investment comes from the taxes paid by each of us. Thus, every citizen has the right to know what criteria were used to decide on public investment in these territories. Decisions regarding this kind of investment have to be scrutinised and transparent, and there should be accountability in these processes.

The evolution of the Portuguese tax system falls into two categories: direct and indirect taxation; the latter has significant weight in the country, exacerbating fiscal injustice for low-income populations (OCDE 2006). Thus, besides making public investment in these regions a rigorous, transparent process, specific tax measures should also be taken to encourage populations to stay in these territories, bringing new vitality and sustainable prosperity to inland regions.

1.2 Expected Contributions

This work aims to alert political decision-makers to the importance of basing their decision-making regarding investment in low-density territories not only on the intuition of local mayors but also on a set of appropriate indicators which provide a realistic picture of the social, economic, and financial situation of these territories.

---

[1]This project has the following reference: CENTRO-01-0145-FEDER-023984; supported by the budget of the Regional Operational Programme of the Centre Region, namely, the FEDER Fund.

Therefore, decision-makers are encouraged to use the framework of indicators developed and proposed by the PLowDeR research project and also contribute with data which will allow the framework to provide annual indicators.

1.3 Work Structure

Following the introduction, which provides an overview of the present study, its relevance, and expected contributions, this work is structured into three further sections, ending with the conclusions, limitations, and proposals for future research.

The second chapter is dedicated to a literature review, providing a state-of-the-art evaluation of the relevance of public and private investment in low-density territories and analysing relevant documents for this work, namely, the minutes of the last town hall meetings, held in 2017, in each of the 10 municipalities where the 12 AHP are located. In addition, in these meetings the most important decisions are usually discussed regarding the main options of the plan and budget for the following year.

The third chapter is dedicated to the empirical study and provides a presentation and interpretation of the results obtained, aiming to answer the research problem. Previously, in this chapter, the research problem is identified and defined, as well as the study objectives and the methodology used.

Finally, conclusions of the study are presented, as well as the limitations of the empirical study and proposals for future work.

2 Literature Review

This chapter is dedicated to the literature review, and several observations are made regarding the public and private investment made in the infrastructures located in low-density territories, analysing its contribution to encouraging populations to stay in these areas. It also includes the analysis of the minutes of the last town hall meetings of each of the ten municipalities, held in 2017. Usually, these town hall meetings include the discussion of the main options of the plan and budget for the following year.

2.1 The State of the Art

According to Butler (1980), the tourism destination life cycle consists of different stages of evolution: exploration, involvement, development, and stagnation. After reaching stagnation, several scenarios can be considered: immediate decline, decline, stabilisation, reduced growth, or rejuvenation. This cycle is still valid today and can be of great use in understanding the development of a tourist

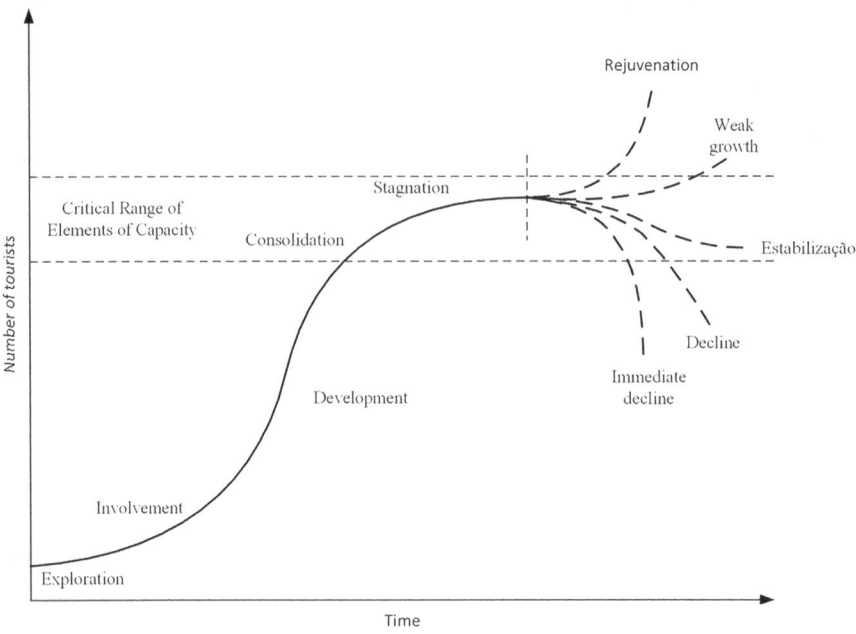

Fig. 1 Tourism area life cycle model [(Butler 1980, p. 7)]

destination, with the help of appropriate indicators, and thus in making better investment decisions (Fig. 1).

There is a real need to develop indicators which can be used to assess and validate quality of life in any context, particularly in low-density territories. According to Ribeiro (1994, p. 185), "quality of life is a global perception of personal life, and depends on the contribution of several domains and components".

The distribution of the investment allocated to low-density territories has been made according to the size of population clusters, their needs regarding basic infrastructures, and the density and preservation state of the existing historic cultural heritage (Boura 2004). These investment distribution criteria should be developed based on previously identified needs, with a visible impact at the level of economic growth and improvement of the quality of life of people living in these territories.

A number of actions can be suggested, with impact on public or private investment and with the intervention of several stakeholders: investing in computing resources and telematics; investing in the valorisation of local features; investing in tourism, valuing biodiversity; investing in restaurants, valuing the historic cultural heritage; investing in endogenous resources; and intermunicipal investment (Favareto 2005).

In order to encourage populations to stay, local authorities have long relied on several programmes which include investing in these territories, though without much success, considering the continuous flow of migration (Moreira et al. 2007). According to the same authors, these investments do not often lead to the expected results, probably because the decisions made were not based on indicators which could help identify the sectors requiring priority investment, encouraging populations to stay.

Sustainable tourism in low-density territories should favour quality rather than quantity, promoting the constant monitoring and assessment of results based on indicators and fostering proactive management strategies in order to generate benefits for the local populations (Carvalho and Correia 2007). According to Carvalho and Correia (2008), there is a belief that investment in rural areas is oriented towards the benefit of visitors, rather than the people whose daily life is in those areas.

Time has shown that the model used to allocate public investment to low-density territories has not led to sustainable development and has not prevented the phenomenon of human desertification. On the one hand, these investments have allowed the implementation of positive measures: rehabilitation of buildings and public spaces and improvement of accessibility and construction of equipment and infrastructures; on the other hand, it has also transformed those territories for the benefit of visitors rather than the local population (Pais 2008).

According to Branco et al. (2010), the fight against human desertification must include the implementation of policies which motivate people to go back to the rural world, by promoting the engagement of the population in the definition and implementation of such policies. In order to achieve this goal, there must be a set of indicators to help define those policies.

According to Ventura (2010), the development of rural areas, usually associated with low-density territories, assumes that local populations and municipalities are willing to collaborate in initiatives that increase and enhance local endogenous products, thus attracting private and public investment. The collaboration of local populations and municipalities may be enhanced if there are indicators to support a realistic strategy to attract public and/or private investment.

Low-density territories, namely, the network of Portuguese Historical Villages, have witnessed the growth of their visibility and reputation due to the investments made by both the public and private sectors. This means that the investments made have had a positive impact, and now it is necessary to introduce mechanisms that will help improve the decisions made by investors and reduce the risk of contrary results (Ferreira 2011).

In order to change the scenario presented by most of the low-density territories, several initiatives have taken place to mitigate the negative effects associated with these territories, rural exodus, and demographic aging. Therefore, several programmes and projects have been developed with the objective of revitalising these territories, motivating their populations to stay through the enhancement of public investment (Reis 2012).

Barca et al. (2012) question the future of regional development intervention and state that a development policy focussed on specific territories should consider that the knowledge needed to implement such policies is not readily available, as it must be developed through participative processes which involve all the stakeholders interested in these territories.

Reduced investment, either private or public, as a factor of creation of employment and equal opportunities, has had a huge impact on the (continuous) human desertification of low-density territories (Braga et al. 2013).

Rural development policies, in which low-density territories are included, seem to be strongly associated with the use of endogenous resources and practices based on collaborative networks which may be considered appropriate for the promotion of all its resources. This paradigm is focussed on the integration of these territories into other territories which are not affected by the evil of human desertification, and that is not an easy process. This is firstly because low-density territories are a priori in a less privileged situation as they do not possess critical mass, resources, skills, and infrastructures which allow them to be competitive (Matos 2013).

The implementation of investment, public or private, in low-density territories takes the following idea into consideration: the profile of the investment made was different from village to village according to their respective features and needs (Coutinho 2013). However, the author does not mention the identification of those features and needs, which clearly indicates the lack of a structure of indicators to help investors make their investment decision.

Public policies which reinforce investment in low-density territories are generally focussed on job creation, and recovery and implementation of new infrastructures, neglecting everything that concerns the lifestyle of the local population and the preservation of their habits and customs (Ventura 2013).

In order to allow the tourism sector to have a full, relevant role in the economic growth of low-density territories, it is necessary to recognise its importance and support the creation of appropriate policies for investing in and developing new business plans. This means that data on the role of tourism in these territories and its contribution to the local economy should be robust and convincing in order to provide some guidance and allow the tourism sector to grow, supervising its performance and adapting policies whenever required (UNWTO 2013). This process requires a set of indicators which take the surrounding environment into consideration, as well as existing pressures and the effort made to innovate and introduce endogenous products.

Until 2030, the population in low-density territories is likely to continue to present a negative growth trend, even though non-identified exceptions may occur. Therefore, these regions are likely to face a profound disarticulation and total desertification, unless public policies are developed and implemented in order to enhance the qualification and competitiveness of these territories, supported by the accuracy and transparency of public and private investment (Daniel et al. 2014).

The development of low-density territories depends on the growth of the national economy, making it necessary to allocate public funds to these regions to enhance their infrastructures, creating wealth and fostering local development (Rodrigues 2015).

The investments, with the help of several, mainly European, programmes, are made in different tourism areas (e.g. health and well-being, agritourism, hunting tourism, radical sports, wine tourism, olive oil tourism) and have enhanced the growth of exportations in the primary sector. These investments, besides the impact in the primary sector, have also contributed towards the recovery of housing stock, historic resources, and infrastructures. However, this development has not been matched with similar strategies to help improve the lifestyle of those living in these territories (Fernandes and Carolina 2015).

Protected areas, such as the network of AHP, are unexplored tourist attractions, full of resources and heritage which can be valued in order to motivate populations to stay in these territories. To make this possible, these areas must offer something which differentiates them and enhances demand; it is necessary to make investments, both public and private, which may promote the endogenous products of these regions (Ramos 2015).

Ferrão (2015) developed a framework for low-density territories which includes several ecological risks, such as fires, which mainly affect these territories (lack of forest planning, destruction of ecosystems, isolation and dependency, limited capacity to attract people and investment).

Fernandes et al. (2016) carried out a project in mountain villages, which are very low-density territories, to analyse the selection of investment considering its contribution to revitalising these territories with the aim of keeping local populations.

Considering the next community support framework, supranational decision-makers are now faced with the challenge of maintaining, strengthening, or reducing the allocation of resources focussed on territorial cohesion. The measures taken will probably be under a more intense scrutiny, and the decisions taken regarding the investment made in low-density territories will be subject to additional requirements. Also for national political decision-makers, all decisions regarding the support of low-density territories should be subject to additional requirements (Santos and Baltazar 2016).

In this context, Martins (2016) seeks to understand how populations perceive the purpose of the investment made in the areas where they live, to analyse its impact, and to assess any disparities between the different population clusters that have benefited from that investment. In general, even though there are different impacts for each cluster, there is a clear benefit for visitors, due to the existence of trails and conditions to access and visit these areas more easily, thus promoting the local economy. Seasonality is still the main obstacle to the economy and the development of these territories. In the summer, there is a higher population flow (emigrants, tourists, people who were born there), whereas in the winter these areas are subject to a lower population flow.

According to Batista (2017), investors perceive low-density territories as a source of high-potential resources to explore, but there are also factors hindering the development and implementation of enabling measures, due to the lack of initiative among local populations and also due to the prevalence of conservative and traditional behavioural attitudes. Territory managers are permanently faced with multiple challenges associated with the search for motivating factors which may attract investors, in an effort to provide the right conditions to keep local populations and improve their quality of life. According to the same author, there is little information, involvement, and dialogue among the different stakeholders and, consequently, a lack of criteria in the decisions made by investors.

In order to meet the three main needs of these territories, namely, fighting human desertification and the lack of investment, improving competitiveness, and promoting job creation, Santos et al. (2019) developed a framework of indicators for low-density territories. The authors also observed that the sustainability of these territories depends on strategies based on endogenous resources and factors, and the promotion of innovative actions, leading to greater efficiency when used.

Santos et al. (2019) believe the assessment of the economic and social impact of tourist activities in low-density territories through the creation of an appropriate set of indicators could be a good source of information to create a consistent development strategy in these territories, contributing to better decision-making by investors.

2.2 Main Options of the Plans and Budgets of the Ten Municipalities Where the Network of the Portuguese Historical Villages Are Located

We have analysed the minutes of the last town hall meetings of the ten municipalities located within the network of the AHP, from December 2017, in which the main options of the 2018 plan and budget were discussed. These are key documents, of great relevance for each municipality, and even though they are different, they are strongly linked. The budget defines the revenues and expenses within legal limits and expectations, whereas the plan options define the application of most of the expenses considered relevant within the overall expenditure. These documents reflect the will and accountability of the executive power, including the actions and work considered necessary for the maintenance and development of better living conditions for the local population.

After analysing the minutes of each town hall meeting in which the main options of the 2018 plan and budget were discussed, the most relevant parts were selected for this work in order to assess if there was a possible link with the indicators collected by the PLowDeR project team for the same year (2018).

3   Empirical Study

The present chapter aims to identify and explain the research problem and the methodology used and analyse the information found in the minutes of the last town hall meetings held in 2017, drawn up by each of the municipalities where the AHP are located. After that, the decisions regarding investment for 2018 in those municipalities are analysed in order to check if these are aligned with the indicators collected by the PLowDeR project team for the same year (2018) or if those decisions could have been different and better informed using the proposed set of indicators.

3.1 Identification of the Research Problem and Methodology

This section identifies and presents the research problem which guided our research work and also introduces the methodology used in our study.

3.2 Problem, Objectives, and Research Questions

The AHP network comprises 12 villages which share historic, heritage, and land-scape features, including their inland factor: Almeida; Belmonte; Castelo Mendo; Castelo Novo; Castelo Rodrigo; Idanha-a-Velha; Linhares da Beira; Marialva; Monsanto; Piódão; Sortelha; and Trancoso. These villages are located in three NUTS III (Beiras and Serra da Estrela, Beira Baixa, and Coimbra Region), integrated in NUTS II Centre.

The purpose of our study is to understand if the decisions shaped in the general lines of the main options of the plan and budget approved in each town hall meeting are in alignment with the indicators collected by the indicators framework application proposed by the PLowDeR project. The aim is to help reverse human desertification in these villages and share some of the competitive advantages that can make these territories attractive and able to fix and attract population (Santos and Ferreira 2010).

According to Santos et al. (2019), the main objective of the PLowDeR project was to develop and present a framework of indicators to assess the social, economic, and financial impact of tourism activities in the AHP. This study analyses some of these indicators, concerning the decisions made by the municipalities where each of the 12 villages are located. This analysis was carried out using the content from the minutes of the last town hall meetings held in each of the municipalities in 2017. The main options of the plan and budget for the following year (2018, in this case) are usually discussed and voted on in these meetings. The information collected after the interpretation of these minutes was analysed using some of the indicators collected within the PLowDeR project for the same year.

Therefore, the main purpose of our work is to ascertain whether the decisions shaped in the general lines of the main options of the plan and budget approved in the town hall meeting are aligned with the indicators collected by the indicators framework application which was proposed by the PLowDeR project.

As previously explained, our main purpose is to answer the following question:

Is the framework of indicators proposed by the plowder project a useful tool to help political decision-makers decide about public investment in low-density territories?

3.3   Research Methodology

Regarding the methodology used, the present research is document-based, supported by a bibliography research in which the keywords are "investment", "low-density territories", and "historical village". We mainly used three bibliography sources: scientific papers; professional papers; and technical reports. The objective of our bibliography research was to evaluate the state of the art of public and private investment in low-density territories and historical villages.

For the empirical study, the content analysis technique was used to analyse the minutes of the last town hall meeting held in 2017, collected from the websites of each of the analysed municipalities. The content analysis was made manually and was based on the narrative, descriptive, and interpretative analysis, mainly qualitative, since the idea was to analyse each minute from the perspective of the message conveyed to citizens.

3.4   Analysis of the Minutes

This section identifies the most relevant aspects found in the minutes of the last meetings held in 2017 in each of the ten municipalities where the AHP network is located. As previously mentioned, we selected these minutes because they reflect the discussions regarding the main options of the plan and budget for 2018 and, consequently, most of the investment decisions made in the municipality.

The main options of the plan and budget are key documents of great relevance for the municipality, and even though they are different, they are also strongly linked. The budget defines the revenues and expenses within legal limits and expectations, whereas the plan options define the application of most of the expenses considered relevant within the overall expenditure. These documents reflect the will and accountability of the executive power, including the actions and work considered necessary for the maintenance and development of better living conditions for the local population.

3.4.1   Municipality of Almeida

Analysis of the minutes of the town hall meeting held on 5 December 2017 shows the concern of the municipality of Almeida with the promotion of the potential of its Historical Villages. In this meeting, a suggestion was made to place billboards at the Vilar Formoso border to overcome the lack of information. If we establish a connection between this concern and the results obtained in the PLowDeR project (see Table 1), it is possible to observe that there is still a considerable number of visitors who are "neither satisfied nor dissatisfied", even though the vast majority feel "satisfied" with the amount of information available. Thus, we can conclude that

Table 1 Level of visitor satisfaction with the information available

Regarding satisfaction with the information available for visitors, most respondents are "satisfied" (61%) or "very satisfied" (17%) However, 21% of respondents are neither satisfied nor dissatisfied. These results show that the level of information provided can be improved so that a bigger number of visitors may declare themselves very satisfied

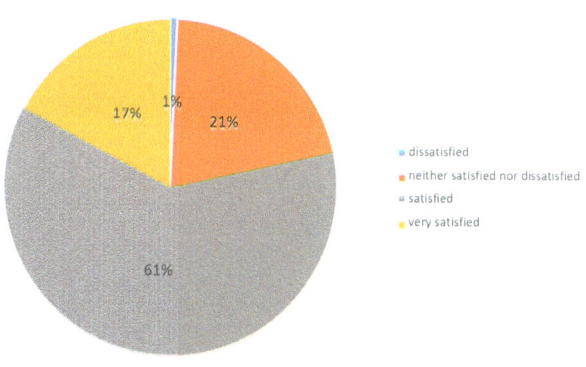

Source: Santos et al. (2019)

Table 2 Percentage of visitors per source of information regarding the tourism destination (AHP)

The number of visitors per source of information regarding the tourism destination is highly diversified However, the largest percentage of respondents reported using two main sources of information: "the Internet", with 38%, and a "suggestion made by a relative or friend", with 30%. The third most reported source was "the press (newspapers, magazines, etc.)" with 13%

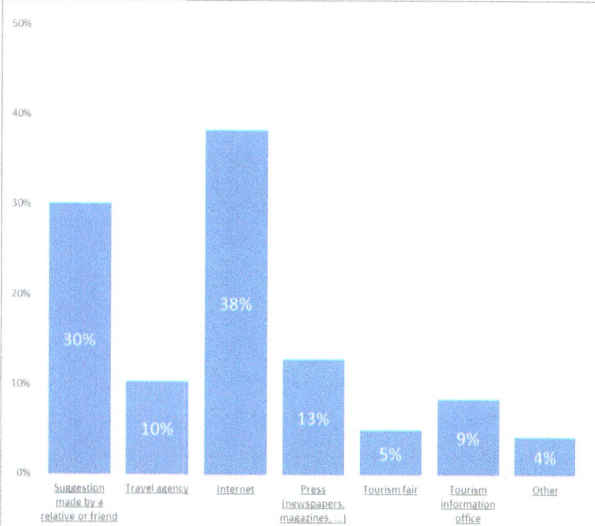

Source: Santos et al. (2019)

the decision made at the town hall meeting is aligned with the indicator "level of visitor satisfaction with the information available".

However, it is important to consider that visitors use various sources of information when planning their journeys. Among the many sources of information used by visitors, the Internet seems to be the favourite source for those visiting the AHP. This fact indicates that the means used to promote the potential of a tourism destination should be supported by online channels, namely, through the use of social networks. This concern is also aligned with the indicator "percentage of visitors per source of information regarding the tourism destination" (see Table 2).

Table 3 Level of visitor satisfaction with access roads

Regarding the level of visitor satisfaction with access roads, respondents are mainly divided between those who are "satisfied" (45%) and those who are "neither satisfied nor dissatisfied" (37%)	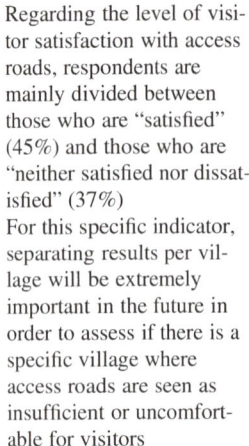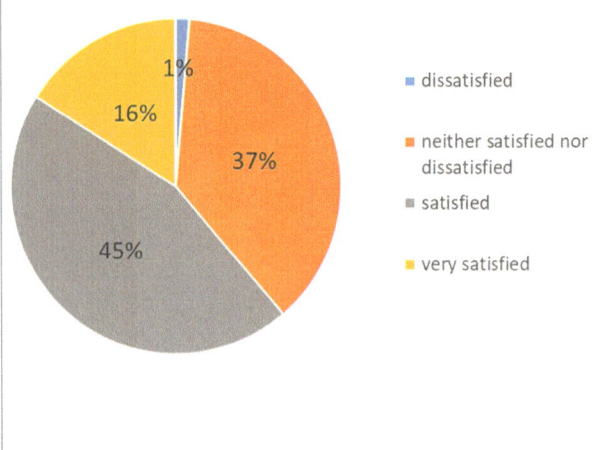
For this specific indicator, separating results per village will be extremely important in the future in order to assess if there is a specific village where access roads are seen as insufficient or uncomfortable for visitors	

Source: Santos et al. (2019)

A similar concern was also observed regarding the improvement of accessibility, a situation which was being solved through the submission of an application within the scope of the AHP. This concern is also aligned with the results for the indicator "level of visitor satisfaction with access roads" (see Table 3).

3.4.2 Municipality of Arganil

In their last town hall meeting held in 2017, the municipality of Arganil decided that the main options of the plan and budget for 2018 should include those projects considered strategic for the council. The issue of mobility was equally considered determinant and essential, through the improvement of the municipal road network.

Similarly to the results observed in the municipality of Almeida regarding the indicator "level of visitor satisfaction with access roads", the concern with the improvement of the municipal road network is aligned with this indicator, as seen in Table 3.

However, taking mobility into account, the indicator "level of visitor satisfaction with the public transport network", also collected within the PLowDeR project (see Table 4), can actually make a difference in the global level of visitor satisfaction.

The municipality of Arganil highlighted the idea that the promotion of a territory is based on the diversity of the events offered to the population. Consequently, the municipality has promoted the organisation of several events which include a variety of social, cultural, and sports initiatives.

Therefore, the development of several projects in partnership with the Intermunicipal Community of Coimbra Region (CIM RC) and the Historical Villages of Portugal—Tourism Development Association (AHP-ADT) shows the importance of collaboration between municipalities and other entities for the

Table 4 Level of visitor satisfaction with the public transport network

Concerning the level of visitor satisfaction with the public transport network, the results reflect our expectations for this item. The most common answer among respondents was "neither satisfied, nor dissatisfied" (58%), and only 25% of respondents declared themselves "satisfied". Similar to the previous item, separating results per village might reveal the origin of such dissatisfaction Knowing a priori that the transport network is weak, this indicator should serve two purposes: in the immediate term, if the existing network allows visitors to reach a place where car rental is available, and in the future, pushing the improvement of the existing network and monitoring its development	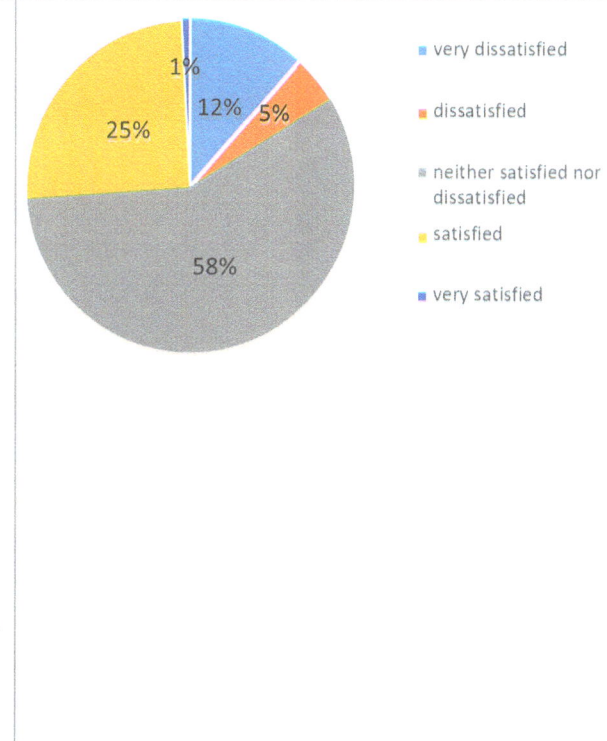

Source: Santos et al. (2019)

sustainable development of these territories, offering their visitors tourist entertainment events which have an impact in the territory. Table 5 shows that there is room for much improvement regarding the "level of visitor satisfaction with tourism animation companies".

3.4.3 Municipality of Belmonte

In the town hall meeting held in the municipality of Belmonte on 22 December 2017, the party of lights, a Jewish event, was strongly highlighted due to its high levels of participation, respect, and tolerance and the right to be different which define Belmonte. It should be noted that this municipality is investing in the promotion of Jewish tourism to attract international visitors (see Table 6).

The municipality of Belmonte hosts one of the oldest Jewish communities in the world. This fact may have an impact on the type of tourists who visit this Historical Village. The indicators "percentage of overnight stays per tourist type (age group)", which shows that the predominant age group is 46–55 (see Table 7), and the "percentage of overnight stays per accommodation type", which includes

Table 5 Level of visitor satisfaction with tourism animation companies

Regarding the level of satisfaction with tourism animation companies, answers are divided between "satisfied" (36%) and "neither satisfied nor dissatisfied" (31%), showing there is room for improvement in this tourism area within the network of the Portuguese historical villages	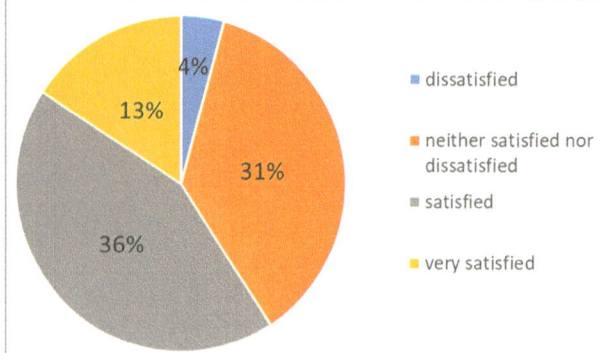

Source: Santos et al. (2019)

Table 6 Percentage of overnight stays per tourist type (nationality)

According to responding establishments, most tourists who stay overnight are Portuguese, regardless of the village However, in Marialva 40% of tourists who stay overnight are Spanish, and in Belmonte 24% are French	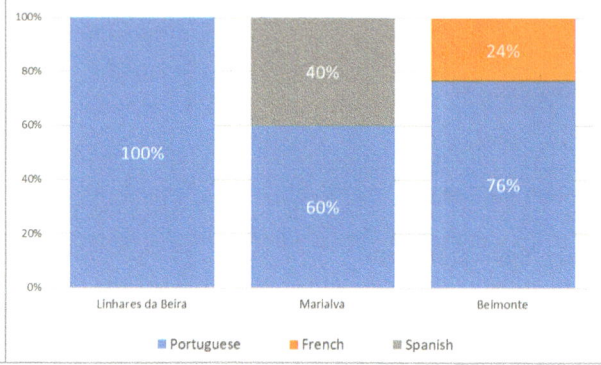

Source: Santos et al. (2019)

information about the preference of guests for furnished accommodation (see Table 8), could both indicate the existence of a specific type of tourism, such as religious tourism in this case, motivated by faith; this may help investors adapt their offer, taking this detail into consideration.

3.4.4 Municipality of Celorico da Beira

In the town hall meeting held in Celorico da Beira on 20 December 2017, the AHP *Smart Lands* application was discussed. The aim of this application is to create all the conditions needed to make WiFi networks of high quality available in historical centres and public spaces with a higher concentration of tourists. The level of visitor satisfaction with communication networks (mobile network, wireless) is not very high (see Table 9).

Table 7 Percentage of overnight stays per tourist type (age group)

According to the responding establishments, the tourists who stayed overnight in Monsanto, during the analysed period, are within the lowest age group (17–25) By contrast, in Belmonte and Marialva, the tourists who stayed overnight are over 46 years old. In Linhares da Beira, the average age of tourists staying overnight is between 26 and 45	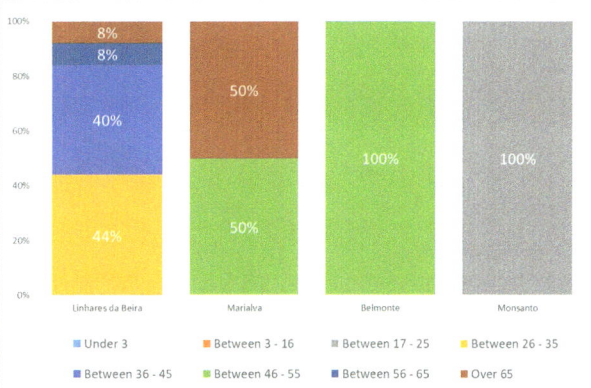

Source: Santos et al. (2019)

Table 8 Percentage of overnight stays per accommodation type

All respondents who stayed overnight in Linhares da Beira and Marialva chose rural accommodation. In Belmonte, all respondents chose to stay in furnished accommodation for tourists In Monsanto, 88% of respondents who stayed overnight chose furnished accommodation for tourists, and 12% chose short-stay accommodation Finally, in Piódão, all respondents stayed in other short-stay accommodation	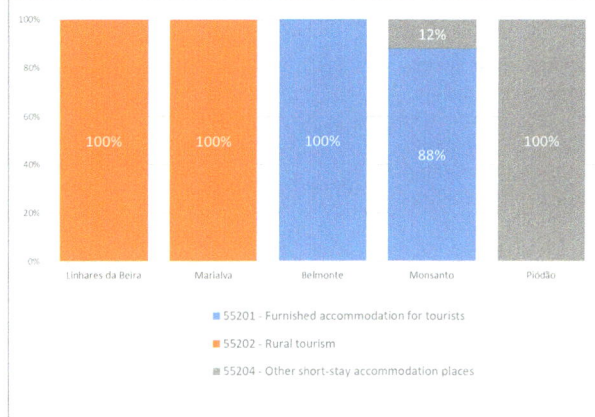

Source: Santos et al. (2019)

On the other hand, the promotion of the network of Portuguese Historical Villages shows that the Internet plays a major role when deciding on a place to visit. Therefore, the possibility of joining a network which provides access to the Internet for promotion purposes makes perfect sense. This can be observed in the indicator "percentage of visitors per source of information regarding the tourism destination (AHP)" collected within the PLowDeR project (see Table 10).

Concerning natural heritage, another application was also mentioned, contemplating the creation of infrastructures, namely, walking pathways and interpretation trails along the Mondego river. A combination of history and built heritage with contemporary features seems to stand out, thanks to the practice of paragliding.

Table 9 Level of visitor satisfaction with communication networks

Regarding satisfaction with existing communication networks, answers are varied, even though the majority falls into the "satisfied" (43%) category, followed by 31% of respondents who are "neither satisfied nor dissatisfied". From the visitor's perspective, this is clearly an issue which can make a difference in the global satisfaction with the destination, given the variety of answers when compared with global satisfaction 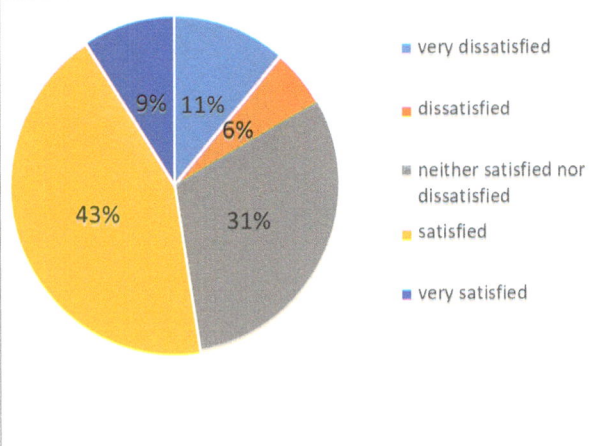

Source: Santos et al. (2019)

Table 10 Percentage of visitors per source of information regarding the tourism destination (AHP)

The number of visitors per source of information regarding the tourism destination is highly varied However, the largest percentage of respondents report using two main sources of information: "the Internet", with 38%, and "a suggestion made by a relative or friend", with 30%. The third most mentioned source of information was "the press (newspapers, magazines, etc.)" with 13% 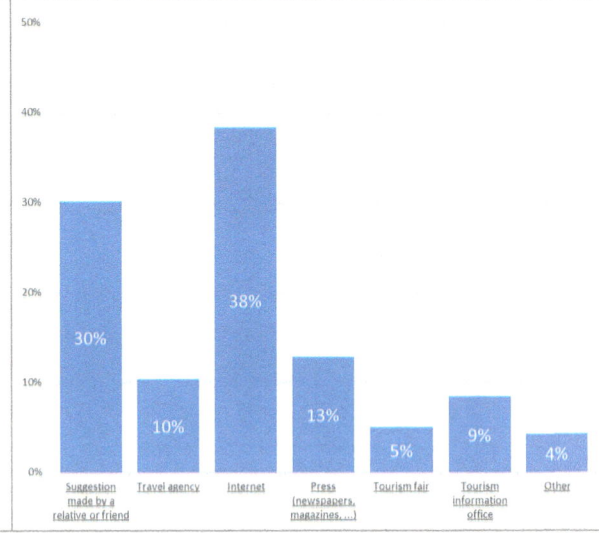

Source: Santos et al. (2019)

The indicators "level of visitor satisfaction with the quality of sports activities practised", Table 11, and "level of visitor satisfaction with cultural activities", Table 12, show a relative lack of sports facilities in some villages. The construction of walking pathways and interpretation trails, including cultural and sports infrastructures, may help reverse this situation.

Table 11 Level of visitor satisfaction with the quality of sports activities practised

Most of the responding visitors (61%) are satisfied or very satisfied with the quality of the sports activities practised, a percentage slightly lower than other items

This result may reflect the relative lack of sports facilities in some of the villages of the AHP network, as observed in the field by the research team members

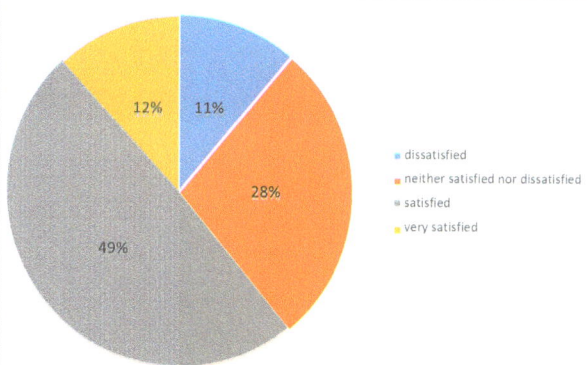

Source: Santos et al. (2019)

Table 12 Level of visitor satisfaction with the quality of cultural activities

Regarding cultural activities, most respondents (74%) said they were satisfied or very satisfied. Even so, 25% of respondents were neither satisfied nor dissatisfied. These results suggest that the AHP network should try to understand the reasons underlying these perceptions in order to improve the cultural activities offered

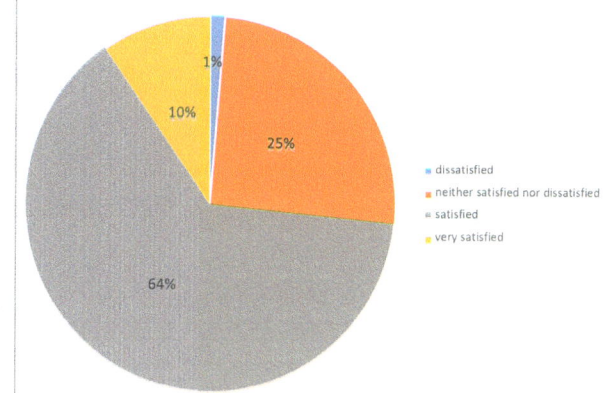

Source: Santos et al. (2019)

3.4.5 Municipality of Figueira de Castelo Rodrigo

In the town hall meeting held in the municipality of Castelo Rodrigo on 12 December 2017, the promotion of sustainable tourism was reinforced, focussing mainly on people and their quality of life and well-being. To accomplish this goal, it is necessary to implement direct support policies to help producers promote endogenous products, as shown in Table 13, which reflects the indicator "level of satisfaction of local tourism economic agents with the promotion of their business". There is still a considerable percentage of economic agents who are not satisfied with the promotion of their businesses.

The municipality of Castelo Rodrigo is aware of its invaluable richness and is keen to preserve its cultural, natural, building, religious, and gastronomic heritage through initiatives/events which enhance its promotion/value, as shown in Table 14,

Table 13 Level of satisfaction of local tourism economic agents with the promotion of their business

The level of satisfaction of the responding local tourism economic agents with the promotion of their business is highly variable The economic agents of Castelo Mendo are "very dissatisfied" with the promotion of their businesses (100%), followed by the economic agents of Monsanto, with 60%, and Trancoso with 55%. All the responding economic agents of Castelo novo are "dissatisfied" The responding economic agents of Idanha-a-Velha and Marialva are those who show higher percentages of satisfaction (50% said they were "very satisfied")	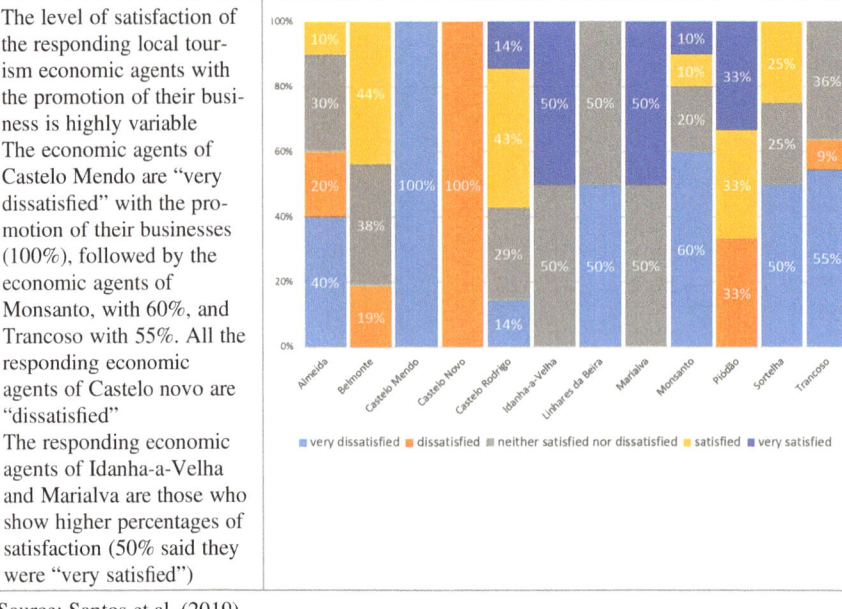

Source: Santos et al. (2019)

Table 14 Percentage of visitors attracted by the AHP network according to motivation

The motivation of the responding visitors is essentially connected with the historical and cultural heritage of the council, followed by the fact that visitors want to be close to nature and rurality It can also be seen that visitors are motivated by the local gastronomy, because of the level of participation in festivals and local parties, including the practice of sports	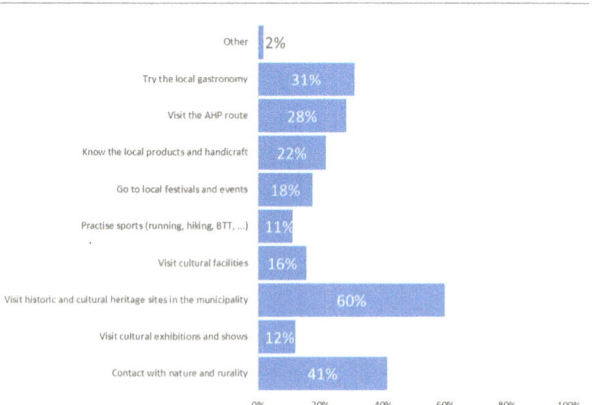

Source: Santos et al. (2019)

indicator of the "percentage of visitors attracted by the AHP network according to motivation". The vast majority of visitors have different motivations related to historical and cultural heritage, as well as nature and rurality.

In order to attract more tourists who are willing to spend more days in the council and visit different spots of interest, enjoying the variety of local products and the

Table 15 Percentage of collaborators in the tourism sector with knowledge of foreign languages in the tourism destination

According to the responding entities, all the collaborators in the tourism sector in Castelo Rodrigo have knowledge of foreign languages. However, in Castelo Mendo and Linhares da Beira, only 33% of their collaborators have language skills Besides these two tourism destinations, Trancoso also has a percentage lower than 50% regarding collaborators with language skills. The remaining villages show values around 50% and 67%	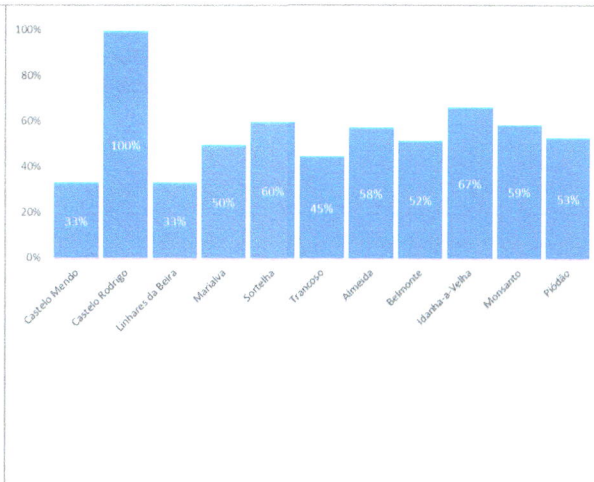

Source: Santos et al. (2019)

Table 16 Percentage of residents who participate actively in tourism activities

According to the responding residents, there is a median percentage of residents who actively participate in tourism activities The highest percentage is 52% (in Castelo Rodrigo) and the lowest is 21% (in Linhares da Beira and Marialva)	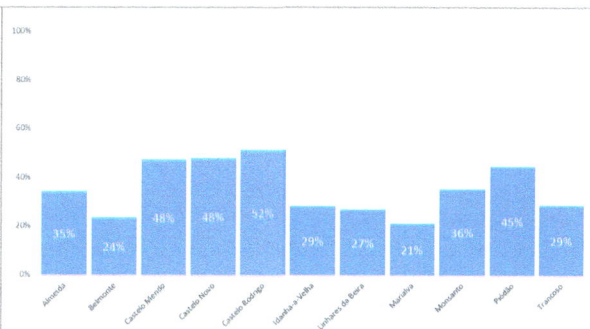

Source: Santos et al. (2019)

landscapes, the municipality decided to proceed with the restoration of some monuments. The indicator "percentage of collaborators in the tourism sector with knowledge of foreign languages in the tourism destination" (see Table 15) and the indicator "percentage of residents who participate actively in tourism activities", shown in Table 16, may be a reflection of what has been done for the municipality and what can still be done. These are good indicators to support investment decisions.

3.4.6   Municipality of Fundão

In the town hall meeting held on 14 December 2017, the municipality of Fundão highlighted the need to promote strategic sectors, such as culture and tourism, with the contribution of entities and organisations with a relevant role in the development of the region, such as Collective Efficiency Strategies (EEC PROVERE) and AHP-ATD, among others. The creation of territorial brands as a unifying element to foster the promotion of territories is a strategic investment in collective efficiency. This bet can be seen in the indicator "percentage of tourism economic agents who use the AHP brand of the tourism destination" (see Table 17). This indicator shows the percentage of economic agents per village who use the AHP brand. In Castelo Novo, it was not possible to identify the use of the AHP brand, meaning there is still a lot to do in this domain.

3.4.7   Municipality of Idanha-a-Nova

In the town hall meeting held on 29 December 2017, the municipality of Idanha-a-Nova maintained its mission to build a council centred around people, with the collaboration of local associations and institutions, parishes, businesses, and parish councils.

These partnerships allowed the municipality to submit an application, together with the AHP-ADT, to provide the AHP network with a WiFi infrastructure. This shows the importance given to the promotion of information about a specific place and the benefits it may bring to those who live there. Such relevance can be found in

Table 17 Percentage of tourism economic agents who use the brand of the tourism destination (AHP)

The number of the responding tourism economic agents who use the AHP brand varies depending on the village Piódão is the tourism destination that uses the AHP brand most (75%). Three other villages use the AHP brand similarly (50%), namely, Sortelha, Marialva, and Idanha-a-Velha. It is also possible to observe that 30% of the economic agents of Monsanto use the AHP brand, with a lower percentage (10%) for the economic agents of Almeida	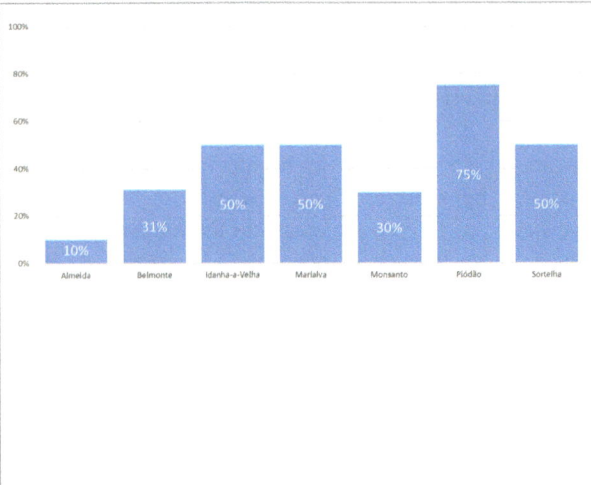

Source: Santos et al., (2019)

Table 18 Satisfaction of local tourism economic agents with the promotion of their business

The level of satisfaction of the responding local tourism economic agents with the promotion of their business is highly variable The economic agents of Castelo Mendo said they were "very dissatisfied" with the promotion of their businesses (100%), followed by the economic agents of Monsanto with 60% and Trancoso with 55%. All the economic agents of Castelo Novo feel "dissatisfied". The economic agents of Idanha-a-Velha and Marialva are those who show higher percentages of satisfaction (50% reported feeling "very satisfied")	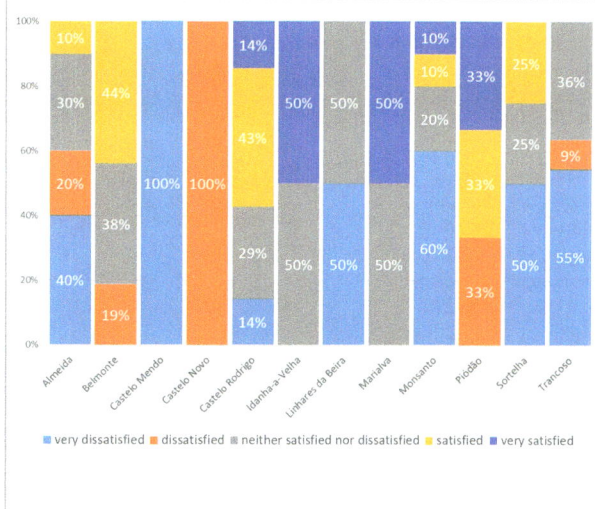

Source: Santos et al. (2019)

the indicators "level of satisfaction of tourism economic agents with the promotion of their business" (see Table 18), and "level of satisfaction of economic agents who are satisfied with the available information about the tourism destination" (see Table 19), and also the "level of visitor satisfaction with the communication networks" (see Table 9).

These indicators show the level of satisfaction of local tourism economic agents with the promotion of their business, as well as the level of satisfaction of the economic agents with the information available about the tourism destination, and the visitor satisfaction level with the communication networks (mobile network, wireless). As can be observed, regarding the first indicator, economic agents are totally dissatisfied, there is a great deal to be done; regarding the second indicator, they are completely satisfied. In the third indicator, the level of visitor satisfaction is not very high. We can thus conclude that a significant effort has been made concerning communication networks and the information available, but there is still a lot to be done regarding promotion.

The municipality of Idanha-a-Nova aims to be the capital of well-being. However, the indicator "level of satisfaction of residents in the tourism destination with the impact of tourism on the community" (see Table 20) shows that even though the percentage of residents in Idanha-a-Velha who are "satisfied" and "very satisfied" stands at 81%, in Monsanto the percentage stands at 68%. These results suggest that the municipality must maintain its strategy to improve the well-being of the local population.

Table 19 Satisfaction of the economic agents with the information available about the tourism destination

The level of satisfaction of the responding tourism economic agents with the information available about the village is highly variable Of the economic agents of Idanha-a-Velha and Marialva, 50% are "very satisfied". The other 50% are either "very dissatisfied", such as Idanha-a-Velha, or "dissatisfied", such as Marialva. The responding economic agents located in Castelo Mendo and Castelo Novo are globally satisfied with the information available about the tourism destination, followed by Belmonte, with 56%, and Piódão with 50%	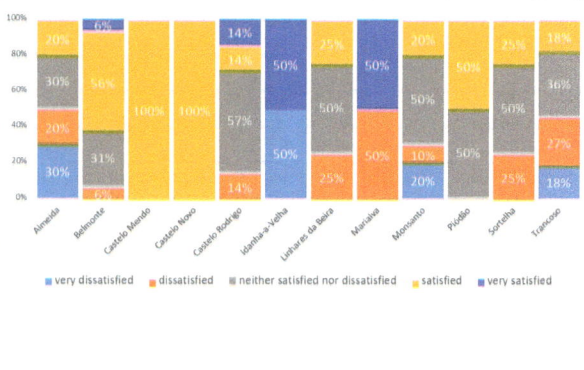

Source: Santos et al. (2019)

Table 20 Level of satisfaction of residents in the tourism destination with the impact of tourism in the community

Most of the responding residents feel satisfied or very satisfied with the impact of tourism, with the exception of Sortelha, where the responding residents feel indifferent to the impact of tourism	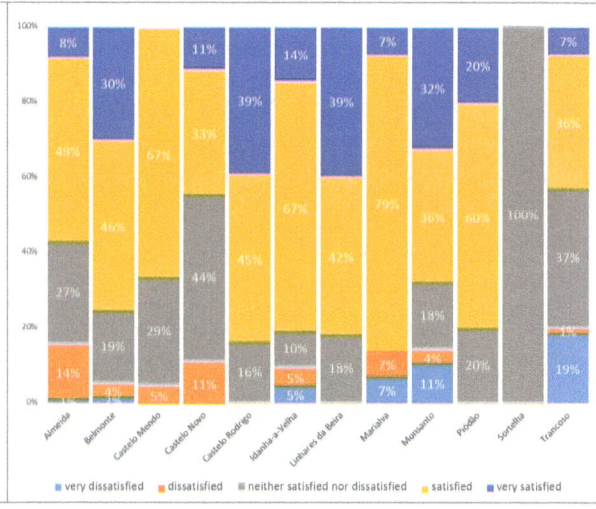

Source: Santos et al. (2019)

3.4.8 Municipality of Meda

In the town hall meeting held on 22 December 2017, besides other relevant issues, the municipality of Meda highlighted the fact that some parts of the trail "Grand Route 22" need to be cleared.

The indicator "level of visitor satisfaction with routes and pedestrian trails" (see Table 21) shows that most of the visitors (53%) do not have a positive opinion. The municipality should thus take measures regarding this domain. The existence of indicators may facilitate decision-making on the part of investors.

3.4.9 Municipality of Sabugal

In the town hall meeting held on 22 December 2017, the municipality of Sabugal identified as its main mission the promotion of the local economy through the valorisation of people and their territory and improvement of service quality, for both local residents and visitors.

Among others, the following indicators show the levels of visitor satisfaction with the AHP network: "level of visitor satisfaction with the quality of restaurant establishments"; "level of visitor satisfaction with the quality of beverage and similar establishments"; "level of visitor satisfaction with the quality of accommodation"; "level of visitor satisfaction with cultural activities"; and "level of visitor satisfaction with the global experience" (see Tables 22, 23, 24, 25, and 26). Based on objective indicators, the municipality could probably define its investment decision in a more objective manner.

Table 21 Level of visitor satisfaction with routes and pedestrian trails

Concerning visitor satisfaction with routes and pedestrian trails, respondents can be grouped into "satisfied", with 40%, and "neither satisfied nor dissatisfied", with 48% There is also room for some investment in this area on the part of political decision makers to improve information about pedestrian routes	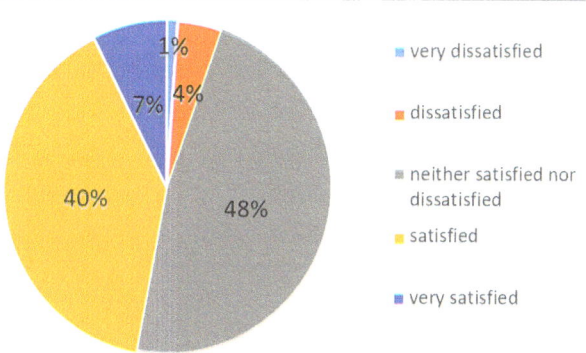

Source: Santos et al. (2019)

Table 22 Level of visitor satisfaction with the quality of restaurant establishments

Regarding satisfaction with the quality of restaurant establishments, the percentage is high, and respondents can be grouped into "very satisfied" (28%) and "satisfied" (62%)	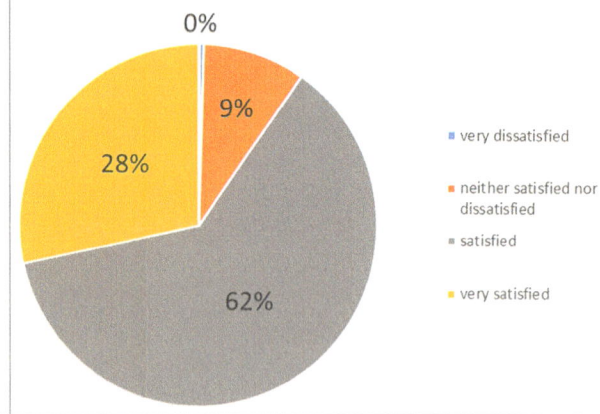

Source: Santos et al. (2019)

Table 23 Level of visitor satisfaction with the quality of beverages and similar establishments

Regarding the indicator satisfaction with beverage and similar establishments, the answers are divided into "neither satisfied nor dissatisfied" (19%), "satisfied" (35%), and "very satisfied" (23%). When contrasted with previous indicators, these results show that the experience with beverage establishments negatively influences the opinion of visitors about the tourism destination. Even though this indicator refers to the quality of establishments, it may indicate a shortage of establishments in these territories (a fact also observed in the field by the project research team)	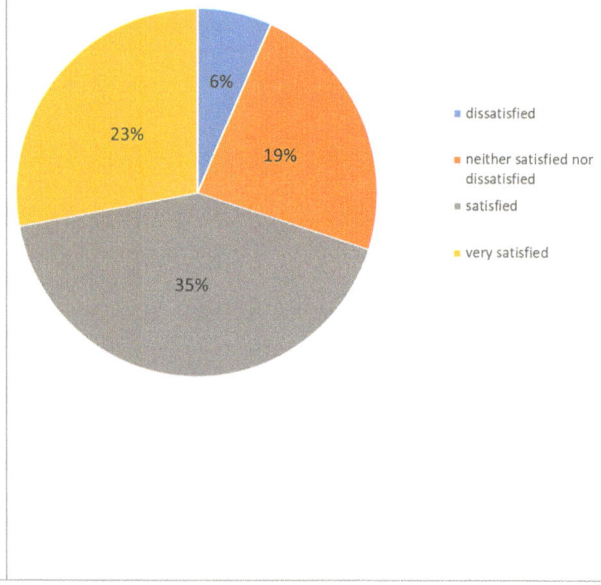

Source: Santos et al. (2019)

3.4.10 Municipality of Trancoso

In the town hall meeting held on 14 December 2017, the municipality of Trancoso highlighted the refurbishment projects for important buildings located in the historic centre of Trancoso, within the scope of tourism and heritage. Some buildings were mentioned in the meeting, such as the old National Republican Guard building, the

Table 24 Level of visitor satisfaction with the quality of accommodation

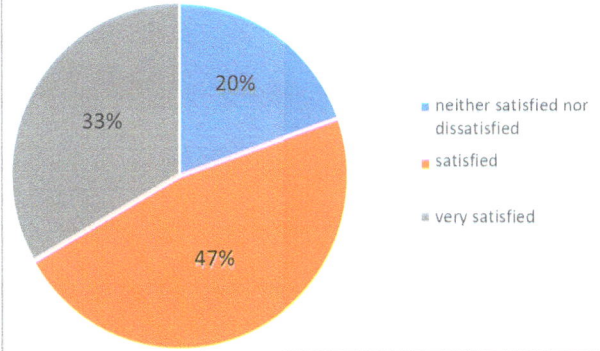

Regarding visitor satisfaction with the quality of accommodation, it can be concluded that most respondents were "satisfied", with 47%, and "very satisfied", with 33%, and there were no dissatisfied respondents. These results are aligned with the global satisfaction revealed by visitors

Source: Santos et al. (2019)

Table 25 Level of visitor satisfaction with the quality of cultural activities

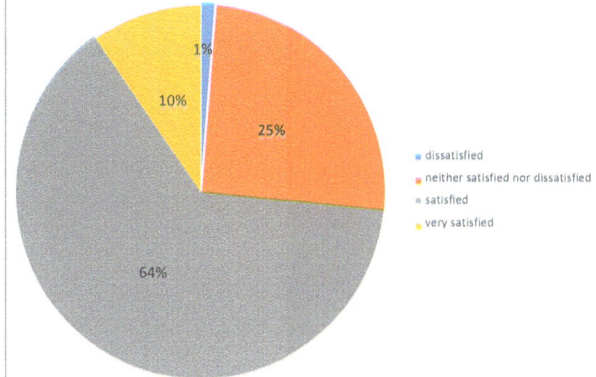

Regarding cultural activities, most respondents (74%) said they were either satisfied or very satisfied. However, 25% of respondents said they were neither satisfied nor dissatisfied. These results suggest that the AHP network should try to understand the reasons underlying these perceptions in order to improve the cultural activities offered in the territory

Source: Santos et al. (2019)

Ducal Palace, the Council Building, and the construction of the Centre for Development and Social Innovation. These investment options are supported by the indicator "percentage of visitors attracted by the network of AHP according to motivation" (see Table 27).

Attention was also given to the environment and mobility, highlighting future help and support in the prevention and fight against forest fires, including investment on the improvement of the road network. These options are also supported by the indicators "level of visitor satisfaction with communication networks" (see Table 28) and "level of visitor satisfaction with access roads" (see Table 3), since its improvement allows, generally speaking, a quicker support of the issues and concerns shared in the town hall meeting.

Table 26 Level of visitor satisfaction with the global experience

97% of respondents are either satisfied or very satisfied with the global experience of visiting the AHP	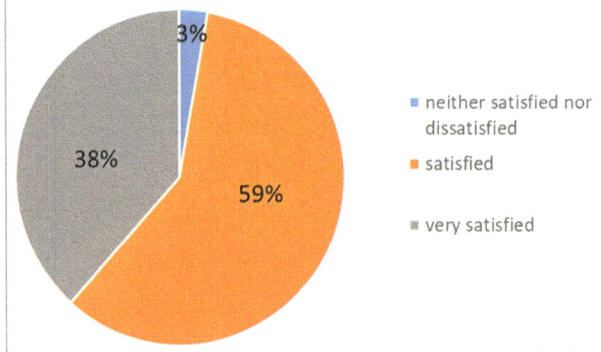

Source: Santos et al. (2019)

Table 27 Percentage of visitors attracted by the AHP network according to motivation

The motivation of the responding visitors is essentially connected with the historic and cultural heritage of the council, followed by the fact that visitors want to be close to nature and rurality. There is also great motivation to try the local gastronomy, participate in festivals and local parties, and the practice of sports	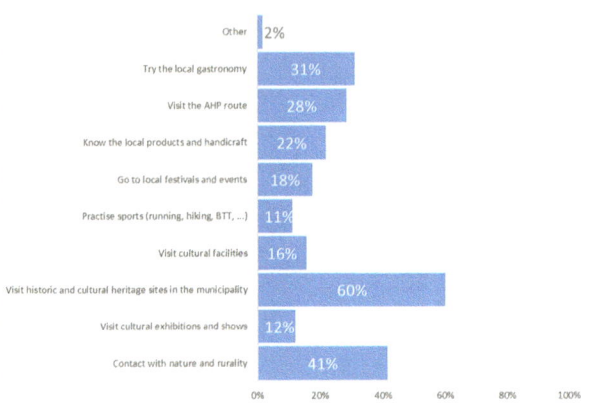

Source: Santos et al. (2019)

4   Final Considerations

Considering the analysis of the minutes of the last town hall meetings held in 2017 in the ten municipalities where the network of the AHP is located, which supported our empirical study, we can conclude that all the municipalities are willing to invest in and improve this network, according to their budgets. They believe this network is a way of increasing the number of visitors to their territories and, consequently, having an impact on the local economy and quality of life, and maintaining the population. Our empirical study provides a detailed analysis of the decisions made by each municipality concerning the main options of the plan and budget for the following year, namely, 2018.

The analysis carried out allows us to conclude that there is a connection between the indicators related to the level of satisfaction with tourism animation companies,

Table 28 Level of visitor satisfaction with the communication networks

Regarding the satisfaction level with the existing communication networks, the answers are varied, even though most are between "satisfied" (43%), followed by 31%, "neither satisfied nor dissatisfied"

From the visitor perspective, this is clearly an issue that could make a difference in the global satisfaction with the destination, given the variety of answers when compared with global satisfaction

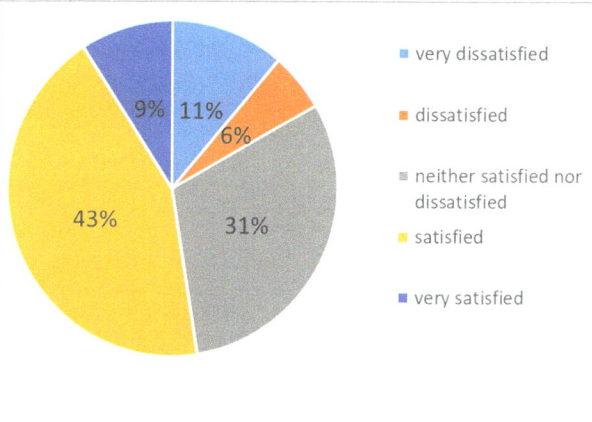

Source: Santos et al. (2019)

access roads, communication networks, transport network, and global experience. Hence, the existence of such indicators will contribute to more informed decision-making and, consequently, greater efficiency and efficacy. In the absence of a framework, the decisions made are exclusively based on the experience and intuition of the political decision-makers. Therefore, these municipalities may obtain a significant competitive advantage if they use the framework of indicators proposed by the PLowDeR project and if they actively contribute to the collection of the data needed to produce indicators on a regular basis over time. This will allow the creation of a database which may facilitate more efficient analyses and better-informed decision-making.

This work was based on the minutes of the last town hall meeting of each of the municipalities comprised by the AHP network. This could be seen as a limitation, since there was no longitudinal analysis, which may offer more detailed interpretations.

As a proposal for future work, we would like to pose a challenge: to carry out a similar analysis for a longer period of time.

The indicators framework, and consequently the analysis developed in this work, could be extended to other situations, such as schist villages, wine villages, etc., considering the fact that these villages are also mainly located in low-density territories. Therefore, this study could be extended to vast territories, allowing various other conclusions to be made about the role of public investment decided by municipalities, in order to understand the relevance of their role in the development of the inner part of the country, mainly low-density territories.

References

Barca F, Mccann P, Rodríguez-Pose A (2012) The case for regional development intervention: place-based versus place-neutral approaches. J Reg Sci 52(1):134–152. https://doi.org/10.1111/j.1467-9787.2011.00756.x

Batista A (2017) O Caso das Aldeias Serranas – Importância e limites destas unidades sociais e patrimoniais na sustentabilidade do território. Universidad de Sevilla, Seville

Boura I (2004) Património e mobilização das comunidades locais: das Aldeias Históricas de Portugal aos Contratos de Aldeia. Cadernos de Geografia 21:115–126. https://doi.org/10.14195/0871-1623_23_10

Braga A, Natário M, Daniel A, Fernandes G (2013) Tendências Demográficas da Região Centro de Portugal: Caso de Estudo dos Municípios de Baixa Densidade. In Livro de Atas das XXIII Jornadas Hispano-Lusas Gestión Científica. Málaga, Spain

Branco J, Oliveira M, Ferreira R, Póvoa O (2010) Desertificação Em Portugal: Causas , Consequências e Possíveis Soluções. Retrieved from https://comum.rcaap.pt/handle/10400.26/2049

Butler R (1980) The concept of a tourist area cycle of evolution: implications for management of resources change on a remote island over half a century view project. Can Geogr XXIV(1):5–12. https://doi.org/10.1111/j.1541-0064.1980.tb00970.x

Carvalho P, Correia J (2007) Turistificação , patrimonialização e dinâmicas territoriais em contexto rural de montanha: o exemplo do Piódão. In Actas do III Congresso de Estudos Rurais (III CER). Faro, Portugal

Carvalho P, Correia J (2008) Turismo, património(s) e desenvolvimento rural: a percepção local da mudança. VII Colóquio Ibérico de Estudos Rurais, (Vii).

Coutinho C (2013) Marialva: da Ruína à Aldeia Histórica. Universidade de Coimbra, Coimbra

Daniel A, Braga A, Fernandes G, Natário M (2014) População da Região Centro de Portugal: Que Futuro Para 2030. In Jornadas Luso-Espanholas de Gestão Científica. Leiria, Aveiro

Favareto A (2005) Empreendedorismo e dinamização dos territórios de baixa densidade empresarial – uma abordagem sociológica e econômica. Raízes 24(1–2):32–44

Fernandes J, Carolina D (2015) Entre a Harmonia e o Conflito Territorial: a Nova Ruralidade Portuguesa. Boletim Goiano de Geografia 35(1):1–20. https://doi.org/10.5216/bgg.v35i1.35481

Fernandes J, Chamusca P, Formigo N, Marques H, Silva Â (2016) Aldeias de montanha : os problemas , as perspetivas e as propostas vistos desde as serras da Aboboreira, Marão e Montemuro, no Noroeste de Portugal. Revista de Geografia e Ordenamento Do Território 9 (9):113–137

Ferrão J (2015) Relatório do Grupo de Trabalho Temático "Territórios Vulneráveis." Governação integrada: a experiência internacional e desafios para Portugal. Edição Forum para a Governação Integrada, Lisboa

Ferreira P (2011) Programa de recuperação de aldeias históricas em Portugal: um balanço. Universidade de Coimbra, Coimbra. Retrieved from http://estudogeral.sib.uc.pt/jspui/handle/10316/15822

Martins A (2016) Políticas Europeias, Desenvolvimento Local e Turismo: Balanço de uma intervenção da ARDAL (Associação Regional de Desenvolvimento do Alto Lima) em 3 aldeias do interior do Minho. Universidade do Minho, Minho

Matos M (2013) Governança e Políticas Públicas em Territórios de Baixa Densidade. Instituto Universitário de Lisboa, Lisbon

Moreira J, Simões O, Malta M (2007) A activação do património como recursos para o desenvolvimento local. O caso de uma aldeia em Terras de Basto. In III Congresso de Estudos Rurais (IIICER) (pp. 1–3)

OCDE (2006) A evolução dos impostos nos países da OCDE, no período de 1990 a 2003 : Comparação com Portugal

Pais C (2008) O Espaço Rural no âmbito das Políticas de Desenvolvimento – O Caso do Pinhal Interior. In Colóquio Ibérico de Estudos Rurais. Coimbra, Portugal

Ramos G (2015) Inovação Institucional, Turismo e Desenvolvimento em Territórios de Baixa Densidade: o caso do Geopark Naturtejo. Universidade de Coimbra, Coimbra

Reis P (2012) Desenvolvimento local em áreas rurais de baixa densidade: uma proposta de intervenção para as Aldeias Históricas de Portugal de Trancoso e Marialva. Portalegre, Aveiro

Ribeiro J (1994) A Importância da Qualidade de Vida a Psicologia da Saúde para. Análise Psicológica 2–3(XII):179–191. Retrieved from http://repositorio.ispa.pt/bitstream/10400.12/3090/1/1994_23_179.pdf

Rodrigues T (2015) Contributos para uma Estratégia de Marketing Territorial para a Região de Moimenta da Beira. Instituto Politécnico de Viseu. Retrieved from https://comum.rcaap.pt/bitstream/10400.26/4428/1/TeseFinal_Inácio.pdf?fbclid=IwAR3TyQoFw2uz3ubypv6iO23-oamCwlld7lkOwacDLw7OGKniG4E1I0MqzB4

Santos M, Baltazar M (2016) Os Territórios do Território Português: Caraterização e Perspetivas Para Territórios de Baixa Densidade no Horizonte 2030. In: IX Congresso Português de Sociologia. Faro, Aveiro, pp 1–15

Santos C, Ferreira A (2010) Governação pública em rede. In V Congresso Nacional da Administração Pública

Santos C, Melo A, Ferreira A, Augusto D, Gomes G, Azevedo G et al (2019) PLowDeR – Framework para Análise do Impacto Económico e Social das Atividades Turísticas nos Territórios de Baixa Densidade. o Caso das Aldeias Históricas de Portugal, Aveiro

UNWTO (2013) Sustainable tourism for development guidebook. Spain, Madrid

Ventura M (2010) Património e Turismo em áreas de baixas densidades : O caso das aldeias do Pessegueiro e do Esquio. Universidade de Coimbra, Coimbra

Ventura R (2013) [Re]qualificação da Paisagem do xisto – Caso de Estudo: Aldeia do Loural. Universidade do Porto, Porto

Printed by Printforce, the Netherlands